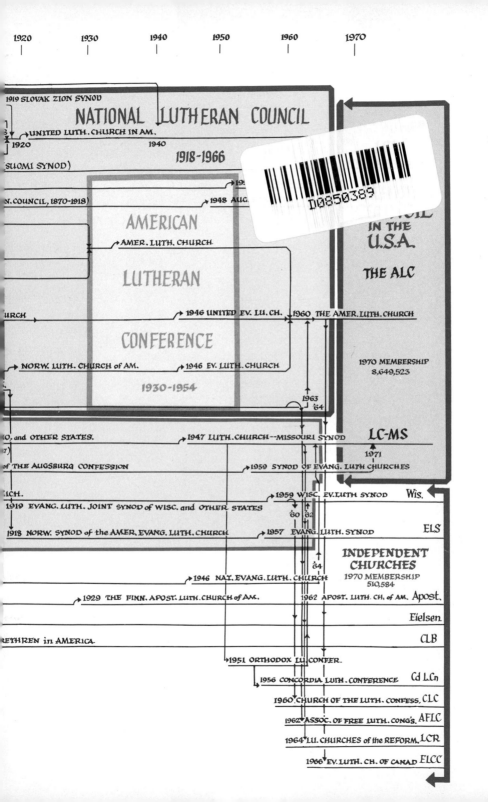

Lutheranism
IN NORTH AMERICA
1914-1970

Lutheranism
IN NORTH AMERICA
1914-1970

by

E. Clifford Nelson

Foreword by

Kent S. Knutson

AUGSBURG PUBLISHING HOUSE
Minneapolis, Minnesota

LUTHERANISM IN NORTH AMERICA, 1914-1970

Copyright © 1972 Augsburg Publishing House

Library of Congress Catalog Card No. 70-159016

International Standard Book No. 0-8066-1138-3

Page 138. Map "Lutheran Churches: 1850" from **Historical Atlas of Religion in America** by Edwin Scott Gaustad. Copyright © 1962 by Edwin Scott Gaustad. By permission of Harper & Row, Publishers, Inc.

MANUFACTURED IN THE UNITED STATES OF AMERICA

To the memory of

J. K. JENSEN, 1879-1962

Christian steward, wise churchman,
tireless advocate of Lutheran unity,
avid muskie fisherman,
generous father-in-law,
solicitous grandfather

and to

His great-grandchildren
and my grandchildren
who represent a generation that may
find it difficult to remember
the rock from which it was hewn
David Richard Melin
Kathryn Elizabeth Melin
Erik David Nelson
Nathan Paul Nelson
Baby Colburn (awaited)

CONTENTS

FOREWORD

Writing a book of history is a consummate art. Not only does it require enormous energy and technical skill but its value is almost directly proportional to the perceptive judgment used by the author. He must select, manage, and interpret complex materials and forces which resist his efforts to understand.

The historian has several choices. He may write a good gray and ostensibly objective history giving the reader only the facts he has unearthed. He may catalog his opinion of the meaning of the events under his perusal and deliver an essay of more subjective character. Or he may combine the two in varying degrees, taking documented sources and dealing with them in such a way as to present a dramatic story of the human dynamic which includes both folly and wisdom. And a writer of church history must not forget that he deals not only with institutional influence and change but with the work of God's spirit as well.

The history issuing from the first choice is usually dull and not nearly as objective as the author or the reader commonly supposes. The second attempt is probably the more fascinating and dangerous but less valuable because the reader lacks the information necessary to make his own judgment. Nelson has chosen the third way and given us careful and documented reporting combined with a loving and astute analysis. This has resulted, in my judgment, in the most helpful analysis of contemporary Lutheranism available to us.

Professor Nelson has lived through most of the events he here presents. He has known most of the personalities. He has taken sides on some of the controversial issues. He has a committed and clear concept of what the Lutheran tradition claims to be and he has his own hopes for the outcome of the story he has begun to tell. Nelson would be the first to agree that he has written from his own perspective, as careful and as expert

ix

a scholar as he undoubtedly is. And, for this reason, he can be challenged as to his understanding of the events. There is opportunity now for others to come forward with their views bringing with them documentation as persuasive as his. A debate on some of the substantive elements in this history would be most useful for the important decisions still to be made in the Lutheran community in America.

As for myself, I am immensely grateful for this gift to the task of the church. I would hope that each generation of the church would produce a scholar with a zeal and skill equal to the stature we see here. Not since Abdel Ross Wentz has American Lutheranism had such attention paid to the history of the Lutheran community in America.

I have learned much. Two basic themes stand out for me. First, these years are the period in which Lutherans in America engaged in a struggle over authority of such dimensions that the whole shape of the present community has been formed by it. This debate on the Bible has been in many ways an un-Lutheran one, since it concentrated on the form of authority rather than on its substance. It was brought about mainly by the American religious environment. Lutherans escaped many of the fundamentalist-liberal battles of the early part of the century but the fallout of those unfortunate crises affected Lutheran development to an important degree. The role, place, and effect of historical criticism of the Bible became the focus of the tensions. In some Lutheran circles the debate is not concluded but the main results of the struggle are clear—the Lutheran churches remain as committed to the authority and efficacy of the Scriptures today as in the beginning of this period. The meaning of such words as inspiration, literal, inerrancy, and infallibility have been clarified and preserved in ways in closer harmony with the original Reformation than was true when this era began. There is no doubt in my mind that the rightful place of the Lutheran confessions has been preserved and their proper evangelical interpretation strengthened. It is my hope that we can now move away from these struggles to the fundamental tasks.

Second, this is the story of the Americanization of the ethnic oriented Lutheranism of 1920. It has been the movement away from preoccupation with geographical and cultural frontiers to the more critical frontiers of mission and unity. The identity of the Lutheran tradition has been enhanced in this transition. Faced now with a very different kind of society, one permeated with a secular spirit, a deteriorating morality, the self-discov-

ery of massive problems generated by a predilection to violence, the failure
of the melting pot and the emergence of an urban society, Lutherans should
turn their attention to being the church in this place for this time rather
than concentrating on preservation of the forms of life which brought
them to this nation and served them well in their planting and early
growth. Failure to do this will imperil their future.

Nelson has paid attention not only to institutional analysis, always a
temptation for historians who find such materials more easily at hand,
but has been a leader in attempting to discover what has happened to
the Lutheran mind—that is, to the people themselves who are, after all,
the church. This may be the most important contribution of this book.
I have had to change my mind about two important judgments. First,
the Study of Generations done in conjunction with this research, has
shown that the younger generation has been shaped toward a closer relationship to the generation which made this history than I had formerly believed. This is a most positive sign for the future of the Lutheran community. The decisive shift in mood and sensitivity among the youth has
not meant a rejection of the faith, according to this study, but a reformula-
tion of its application and style of life.

And second, the unhappy news that the clear gospel teaching of the
Lutheran tradition is not as widely understood and applied as we had
once hoped is disturbing. I have often said that the real question facing
us is not "What is the gospel," but rather, "What is the church," that is,
what is the purpose, the mission and task of the church. This now has
been demonstrated to be too simplistic. I still affirm that the Lutheran understanding of the gospel is clearly taught and held. To this degree we are
still the church of the Reformation and the Apostolic faith. But I cannot
any longer assume that the faith that is taught has been appropriated in
the congregation to the degree it must if we are to remain the church of
the Reformation. Our task is cut out for us. Further delineation of the
mission of the church today remains also as a very important task.

The unity of the Lutheran community still faces us as an unfulfilled
goal despite the enormous gains of this half century. Shifts in the character of this search are occurring even as this book ends. For most of the
past five decades, leadership in bringing Lutherans together at the altar and
in their common work in common structures was almost altogether concentrated on the national level. Congregations followed reluctantly. This

leadership is shifting, almost too rapidly, to the congregation. The influence of the national church is declining and the decision making about inter-Lutheran relationships is taking place among the congregations in local communities. This varies from place to place but no one can deny that Lutheran unity is forging ahead, even structural unity, at great speed in many communities with or without national leadership. The next book of this kind will surely deal with this new fact.

Lutheran churches in America are strong—in their piety, in their communal commitment, in their theological perception and interest and in their zeal. Let us pray that the year 2000 will see this same strength in a greater community!

KENT S. KNUTSON, *President*
The American Lutheran Church

INTRODUCTION

Miguel de Cervantes once (1605) said, "He that publishes a book runs a very great hazard, since nothing can be more impossible than to compose one that may secure the approbation of every reader." This book is no exception. A few will like it; some will dislike it; others will yawn and say, "So what?" If these reactions are predictable, one might wonder, why go to the bother? It is at this point that an explanation may be helpful.

This book has grown out of a curiosity that was sparked 45 years ago. It was a lazy Sunday afternoon, and I was a teenager with nothing to do but to listen to a conversation between my uncle and his pastor. They were discussing, as I recall, the various Lutheran church bodies in America. The layman asked the clergyman, "Why can't we join the other Lutherans?" The pastor replied, "Some think *we* are not orthodox enough, while we think *others* are too liberal." I promptly forgot this exchange, but a few years later found myself puzzling over what to me was an enigmatic and unintelligible answer. During the next four decades I spent many spare moments and some carefully planned moments trying to make sense of it. This book deals in part with the results of my investigation.

I know quite well that there are immense risks in publishing reflections on movements and events with which one has been involved directly or indirectly. There are indeed serious questions whether an eye witness has any right to pose as an historian. Judgments on the immediate past can seldom be made without prejudice and without the danger of turning history into what Oscar Wilde (in *Lady Windermere's Fan*) once called "merely gossip." But when the historian is aware of his own presuppositions and acknowledges that every writing of history is an interpretation, he protects himself in a measure from the caprices of fiction. To put it in

another way, just as the meaning of a sentence is not clear until it comes
to a full stop, so also the meaning of history cannot be fully known as long
as it is still unfinished. The terminus of this book is 1970; but 1970 was not
the terminus of American Lutheran history. Interpretations, therefore, are
necessarily tentative.

It is true that some would like to have seen American Lutheran history
take a different course. They were even audacious enough to think that
God approved their views, that God would have liked to see the church
move in a certain direction. But it moved in another. As in a great cosmic
chessgame, man's move forced God to adapt his move to the new situation
created by a short supply of Christian faith, hope, and love. Although the
"game" would be God's eventually, men made some strange moves all
over the board. The purpose of this book is to trace a few of what have
been reckoned the more significant "moves."

Although some unpleasant episodes come to light, one would be wrong
to assume that the historian has seen his task as a cynical exposure of
men's foibles in the name of ruthless honesty. Rather he has seen it as a
straightforward attempt to explain why "this" happened and "that" did
not. If the reader suspects exposure for exposure's sake, he is mistaken.
He should know that a touch of sorrow was often present in the writing,
especially when a visceral interpretation seemed necessary to meet an unrelenting and irrepressible "why?" that insisted on an answer.

Furthermore, the telling of the story could not wait for "historical perspective," because the myth-creating ability of the community was already
at work. When the myths, which always have an element of truth, are
told and retold, they are only with great difficulty overcome in later years.
Time and distance ("perspective"), therefore, have some serious disad-
vantages. No one, of course, can recreate history à la von Ranke's famous
dictum, "what really happened," but some observations needed recording,
if for no other reason than the "bare-bones" nature of modern minutes and
proceedings. The historical drama, the personal and vital aspects of the
event are simply too often absent from the record. My children and grandchildren could never read between the lines of spare and impersonal minutes to visualize the tugs-of-war and the vested interests that were present
in large segments of the story.

This is what makes the task so audacious and the results so vulnerable.
This is also what makes research and writing a long and lonely business.

Each page carries the possibility of falling under the judgment of Will and Ariel Durant's observation: "Most history is guessing and the rest is prejudice."

This consciousness is one of the main reasons for the author's gratitude to those who have criticized and guided him along the way. The list of such persons has been almost beyond enumeration. A few persons, however, simply must be acknowledged:

Kent S. Knutson, president of The American Lutheran Church, not only wrote the Foreword but also spoke a word—almost exactly 11 years ago when he had read an earlier publication of mine—a word that prodded me to undertake this broader work. He said, "Now you must write the whole story."

The manuscript was read as a whole, in part, or in outline by a number of scholars and churchmen whose critical comments proved invaluable. I wish to thank especially the following: Professors T. G. Tappert, Philadelphia Lutheran Seminary; E. L. Fevold, Luther Theological Seminary, St. Paul; Fred Meuser, Ev. Lutheran Seminary, Columbus; H. George Anderson, Ev. Lutheran Southern Seminary, Columbia, S.C.; Winthrop S. Hudson, Colgate Rochester Divinity School, Rochester, N.Y.; Robert T. Handy, Union Seminary, New York; Richard C. Wolf, Vanderbilt University, Nashville; Robert H. Fischer, Lutheran School of Theology, Chicago; Harold T. Ditmanson, St. Olaf College, Northfield; President S. A. Rand, St. Olaf College; President-emeritus C. M. Granskou, St. Olaf College; Dr. Paul C. Empie, Lutheran World Federation, USA Committee, New York; Dr. Arne Søvik, Lutheran World Federation, Geneva, Switzerland; and Dr. David Scheidt, Allentown, Pa.

The libraries and the staffs of the following institutions were especially helpful: Luther Theological Seminary, St. Paul; Philadelphia (Mt. Airy) Lutheran Seminary; and St. Olaf College, Northfield. Professor Forrest Brown, librarian of the latter, deserves special mention for his unfailing courtesies.

The following archives and archivists deserve accolades: The Archives for Cooperative Lutheranism, New York (Miss Helen Knubel); the Archives of the Lutheran Church in America, Chicago (the Rev. Joel Lundeen); the Concordia Historical Institute, St. Louis (the Rev. August Suelflow); the Archives of the American Lutheran Church, Dubuque, Iowa (the Rev. Robert Wiederanders) and St. Paul (the late Rev. Ernest Sihler);

the Archives of St. Olaf College, Northfield, Minn.; The ALC Merger Papers at Augsburg Publishing House, Minneapolis, Minn.; and the Archives at Northwestern Lutheran Seminary, St. Paul, Minn.

I am especially grateful to President Fred Meuser, already acknowledged in another context, for his gracious permission to utilize his research in an unpublished manuscript on the history of North American Lutheranism, 1900-1930.

Others who helped were Miss Charlotte Jacobson who worked on the index; Miss Alma Roisum, Mrs. Arnold Petersen, and Mrs. Robert Scholz who prepared the typescript; Reidar Dittmann, Jr., who drew graphs; Robert E. A. Lee and Miss Henrietta Larsen, both of New York, who helped research the history of Lutheran film productions.

Special acknowledgment should be made to the Lutheran Brotherhood, Minneapolis, for its ready and generous response to the writer's suggestion that it subsidize a pan-Lutheran survey known as "A Study in Generations," the raw data of which is summarized in Chapter 7.

Throughout the years no one has given more candid criticisms, shown more sympathetic understanding, sustained more long-suffering, and exhibited more patience than the one who knows all my weaknesses but loves me in spite of them, my wife Lois.

E. Clifford Nelson

CHAPTER ONE

THE LUTHERAN CHURCH AT THE DAWN OF A NEW AGE: FROM 1914 TO 1930

Almost without exception interpreters of the story of religion in America give high place to the role of immigration. This has been both necessary and natural because the attitudes of immigrants towards religion, whether positive, antagonistic, or indifferent, had profound effects on the shaping and development of American religious life. Illustrative of the overall influence is what happened in the 19th century when there was a clearly discernible alteration in the profile of the religious community in America. For well over a century the Anglo-Protestant churches dominated the American ecclesiastical scene both as to numbers and as to an ethos-shaping power. This dominance, however, was steadily reduced by the Roman Catholic and Lutheran immigrations, supplemented after 1890 by the influx of Jews and Eastern Orthodox Christians. The subject of this narrative is the history of one of these immigrant groups, the Lutherans. Their role in changing the religious configuration of the nation was neither monumental nor was it insignificant, but it was noteworthy and interesting. By 1914 the Lutherans were the third largest Protestant group in America (behind the Baptists and Methodists), a position that they continued to hold in 1970.

From one point of view, the history of Lutheranism in America has paralleled the history of immigration. There were Lutherans, 40,000 of them, in the first wave of immigrants during the colonial period. Following a migratory slowdown during the early national period, the Lutherans inevitably soliloquized: "to be or not to be" Lutheran in the new world. Their inclination toward confessional particularity received the support of new movements of peoples and ideas from Lutheran portions of Europe, especially Germany and Scandinavia. This expanded transatlantic flow, beginning in the late 1830s, was partially interrupted by the Civil War, only to be followed by a third and massive migration reaching a peak in the 80s and 90s and then coming to a halt at the outbreak of World War I. Although a slight resumption of immigration took place in the early 20s, the problem of the Lutherans after World War I was no longer limited to the huge task of gathering immigrants into the fold. Now the question was how could peoples of diverse ethnic roots become *American* Lutherans. And this implied many things, such as (1) "the language question"; (2) the relation of Lutherans to new intellectual (theological) currents and social concerns; and (3) the enfleshment of their religious convictions in institutional structures, Lutheran and non-Lutheran. They were convinced that they knew "the Lord's song"; the question was how could they sing it in a land and culture strange not only to a Midwestern immigrant generation and its children, but also strange in some ways to those Lutherans who proudly traced their lineage to colonial forebears who fought *as Americans* in the War of Independence.

The events surrounding and following World War I catapulted Lutherans into the 20th century with such force and velocity that they were not permitted leisure for theological reflection, a traditional Lutheran practice customarily preceding the assumption of a new posture. World War I wrenched Lutherans from their familiar ways and propelled them into the necessities of reconciling conflicting ethnic loyalties, of facing the irrational hostilities of Americans who saw them as "foreigners" (especially as Germans), of conserving their confessional heritage, and of reacting speedily to the new demands of 20th century American society. The years between 1917 and 1920 were to become one of the most significant eras in American Lutheran history.

LUTHERAN GROUPS ca. 1914

At the outbreak of World War I American Lutherans had organized themselves largely around doctrinal and ethnic issues. The spiritual descendants of the colonial Lutherans were in three main bodies: the General Synod, the General Council, and the United Synod, South. The descendants of the German immigrants of the mid-nineteenth century were federated in the Synodical Conference, made up primarily of the Missouri Synod and the Wisconsin Synod. Other Midwest German Lutherans were the Joint Synod of Ohio, the Buffalo Synod, and the Iowa Synod. The Norwegian Lutherans found themselves in three main bodies and three smaller groups: The Hauge Synod, the Norwegian Synod, the United Norwegian Church, the Lutheran Free Church, the Church of the Lutheran Brethren, and the Eielsen Synod. The Swedes were united in the Augustana Synod. The Danes flowed in two streams: the United Danish Lutheran Church and the Danish Evangelical Lutheran Church. The Finns were divided three ways: the Suomi Synod, the Finnish National Lutheran Church, and the Finnish Apostolic Lutheran Church. The Slovaks called their group the Slovak Evangelical Lutheran Church; and finally, the Icelanders were simply organized as the Icelandic Synod. In all there were 22 church bodies with a membership of approximately 2,000,000 in the United States and Canada. (See chart, inside front cover.)

WORLD WAR I AND AMERICANIZATION

Although sociologists and historians may still debate whether or not America is "Melting Pot or Salad Bowl," [1] German and Scandinavian-Americans as well as other European-rooted Lutherans continued to be drawn into ethnic islands where they preserved their old ways of life and thought. This was most noticeable in that part of rural America stretching from Pennsylvania through Ohio to Illinois and on into the Mississippi Valley and the Upper Midwest, but it was also true of urban communities. As late as the 1940s the Bay Ridge area of Brooklyn was known as "little Oslo"; Milwaukee was romantically *gemütlich;* and the neighborhood of Kedzie and Foster Avenues in Chicago was the locale of superb Swedish *smörgaasbord* long before Italian and Greek chefs helped "Americanize" this culinary delight.

The Americanization process was most widespread among "Eastern Lutherans," [2] who had rubbed shoulders with other Americans for over a century. Naturally they had shed some traditional ways; America seemed to demand that newcomers divest themselves of inherited habits. But, as Will Herberg has pointed out, the new milieu did not force the immigrant to change his religious loyalties. [3] Thus, the Eastern Lutherans, despite a brief experiment with "American Lutheranism" (see below, p. 11) were Lutherans, a fact which the newer arrivals were reluctant to recognize. Therefore they felt conscience-bound to organize new denominations that would be more faithful to Old World patterns and to their criteria of what constituted true Lutheranism. This action was not without its blessings. Although the multifaceted Lutheranism that emerged by World War I was confusing not only to "outsiders" but to Lutherans as well, and although the ecclesiastical proliferation was hardly justifiable confessionally speaking, it contained a large measure of practical sagacity in that multilingual Lutheranism, now transferred to America, was able to conserve a large proportion of the immigrant population by the simple but necessary expedient of preaching the gospel in a familiar tongue.

World War I changed all this. Midwestern Lutherans were forced eventually to recognize Eastern Lutherans; insular linguistic communities were all but shattered; and American Lutheranism as a whole was thrust into a new situation that demanded a reexamination of its relations to other religious communities nationally and internationally and to work out tenable positions in regard to the issues that American political, social, and economic life laid upon it.

Lutheran Attitudes Toward the War

It has been said that the American people supported their government's decision to participate in the European conflict with an exuberance never before exhibited in wartime.[4] The patriotism of the general public was quickly matched by the churches and synagogues. Prior to 1917 the official neutralism of the government had been weighted toward the Allies, and America's entry into the conflict all but drowned the anti-war sentiment among religious pacifists, the British-hating Irish, and the German-Americans. Predictably the Lutherans had been sympathetic to the German cause between 1914 and 1917. Even those Lutherans of non-German background looked with suspicion on Great Britain. Among the latter the Danish-Americans were something of an exception. The Danes had bitter memories of both the British and the Germans. The bombardment of Copenhagen by the British navy in the early 19th century and the seizure of Slesvig by Bismarck's Prussians left many Danes saying "a plague on both your houses." But German-background Lutherans whether of the "Eastern" variety or of the more recent strain were largely pro-German. "This war," wrote one of the editors in the former group, "is the result of the British plan of destroying Germany's foreign commerce and relations. . . ." [5] The Missouri Synod's strong German-orientation had the strange effect of altering, temporarily at least, its idealized and absolutized "two-kingdoms" stance on social and political issues. With great vigor it denounced America's arms trade and through its president voiced the conviction that "anything that touches moral issues is within the sphere of the church." [6] That they were doing precisely what they accused "liberal" Protestants of doing when the latter exhibited concern for the church's role in public affairs hardly occurred to them.

It was to be expected that Lutherans in general and German-background Lutherans in particular would be criticized and even vilified by those who were caught up in the patriotic fervor. Lutherans in the Atlantic states suffered least; those of the central Midwest most. From the spring of 1917 through much of 1919 Midwestern Lutheranism was an object of careful scrutiny by those hoping to find evidences of disloyalty. Charges, some true and some false, were leveled against Lutheran churches and schools: they were hotbeds of treason, they harbored enemy agents, they were loyal to the Kaiser. As a consequence many parochial schools were forced to close, some were burned. German language church services were disrupted and pastors were threatened with dire consequences if they continued to speak the hated tongue. Major newspapers such as the New York *Times,* the Philadelphia *Ledger,* and the St. Louis *Globe-Democrat* urged that schools drop German from the curriculum. The governors of at least 15 states proposed legislation prohibiting the teaching of *all* foreign languages in the schools and limiting their religious use to private worship in the homes. [7] The Scandinavian-American Lutherans, heavily concentrated in the Upper Midwest, often alongside German-speaking Lutherans, shared the general American antipathy towards the latter. This was most noticeable among lay people who resented being considered just another brand of Germans and thus guilty by ethnic association. [8]

Lutherans Fall in Line

Following the government's declaration that a state of war existed between the United States and the Central Powers, the American church press and official spokesmen of the various religious communities stumbled all over themselves in their haste to pledge support of the military effort to rid the world of Teutonic evil and to make it safe for democracy.[9] Lutheran church bodies were no exceptions, although none endorsed the popular view of a "holy war." [10]

Despite their protestations of loyalty to America and its wartime objectives, Lutherans continued to be objects of scrutiny and, as a result, were forced to rely on one another in joint self-defense when unjust accusations were made. The wartime prejudice against Lutherans thus became a major reason for early experimentation in Lutheran cooperation, not least in efforts to be heard as a church in the legislative halls and the committee chambers of the secular world. In fact, a number of Lutheran cooperative enterprises found expression in the war years. One of the committees for the celebration of the 400th anniversary of the Reformation gave its publicity department permanent structure under the name "The Lutheran Bureau" (1917). This multi-Lutheran activity was shortly joined by another cooperative agency, the highly successful National Lutheran Commission for Soldiers' and Sailors' Welfare (October, 1917), in which seven Lutheran bodies worked together to raise over a million dollars and to recruit chaplains and camp pastors for the benefit of men in the military service. Alongside and partially as a consequence of these cooperative efforts, the highly significant National Lutheran Council came into existence in 1918.

All of these moves were evidences that the foreign-heritage Lutherans were increasingly aware of the need to adjust church and individual life quickly to the challenges of the new situation created by the war. There were at least three visible results. One was the movement towards church unity, a subject to which we shall return later. A second was the general conviction that Lutheranism from now on would have to be American in outlook and loyalty. And a third was like unto it: the use of German and even other languages in worship and work must give way to English. As far as the "new American outlook" was concerned, Lutherans were free, theologically speaking, to support the needs of government and society as long as the church's principle of the free proclamation of "the law and the gospel" and the administration of the sacraments "was not jeopardized." [11] Thus it was reasoned that the neutralist attitude, and especially the silence about the war in the Missouri Synod, must be overcome. Theodore Graebner, champion of this minority (in Missouri) view, wrote: "When a new situation arises, the majority can almost absolutely be counted upon to be dead in the wrong." [12]

Although some clergymen looked upon the wartime pressures as intrusions by government into the sphere of the church, most Lutherans overcame the hesitation which they had demonstrated by their timid support of the first and second Liberty Bond drives. In fact, the swing to a "pro-American" spirit was so pronounced that it produced an all-out effort by the churches to promote the third Liberty Bond drive. An instance of this eagerness to be identified as "American" occurred at a Lutheran Patriotic Rally in San Francisco in 1918. Sponsored by Danish, Finnish, Swedish, German, Norwegian, as well as Eastern Lutherans, the rally saw representatives of the government, the military, and the church vie with one another in emotional pleas that urged the audience to greater and greater dedication to the spirit of Americanism and democracy.[13]

The Language Transition

The support of the war effort was only one example of the "Americanization" of Lutherans. More far-reaching was the impetus given to the language transition. The popular prejudice against German, as noted earlier, extended to other foreign languages as well as to "foreign" ways of dress and diet. An extreme advocate of Theodore Roosevelt's "100% Americanism," asked rhetorically: "What kind of American consciousness can grow in an atmosphere of sauerkraut and Limburger cheese?" [14] Among the many who experienced some of this emotional chauvinism was a Danish-American who wrote:

> I was under no pressure to speak Danish at home but I continued to do so most of the time so my grandparents would understand what I was talking about. When I was ten, however, World War I broke out, and soon we found that Danish was a language to avoid. Most people in the Wisconsin town where we lived could not distinguish Danish from German, even if it had occurred to them to try to do so.[15]

As narrow and provincial as much pro-Americanism was, it became nevertheless sufficiently widespread to deprive a whole generation of American students of the advantages of foreign language study.

It would be a mistake, however, to give World War I sole credit for bringing about this cultural transition in the churches. Actually it was a process that had been going on for decades. Ole Edvart Rølvaag, whose novels depicted the life of Norwegian pioneers in the Upper Midwest, pointed out that much more was involved in the drama of Americanization than acquiring new habits of dressing and eating or learning to speak English without an accent. Addressing the Ibsen Festival in Oslo (1928), he asserted that most people can pick up words and phrases and some superficial habits of life in a new land. The transformation comes, he said, when "one's emotional life can express itself freely and naturally through the new idiom. . . . Not till that miracle has taken place can one feel fully at home in the new country." [16]

Rølvaag's "miracle" had been a part of immigrant church life since its inception in the new world. As a matter of fact, many Eastern Lutherans had largely experienced the phenomenon before World War I. Already in the 18th century, children of German parents in Pennsylvania and New York were clamoring for the adoption of American ways and language. In some instances, generational conflict was the result, and churches experienced bitter controversy between the "old" and the "new." [17] "Hansen's Law" was being experienced before it was formulated (the third generation tries to remember what the second generation tries to forget).[18]

The reluctance of the elders to introduce English alienated large numbers of young people. In the end, thousands left foreign-language Lutheran congregations and joined "American" denominations (Presbyterian, Methodist, Episcopalian) or lost themselves in the world of the churchless.[19] G. H. Gerberding, writing in 1914, said,

> Ours is the most polyglot Protestant church in America. We like to boast that the Gospel is preached in Lutheran pulpits in more languages than were heard on the day of Pentecost. . . . But while these many tongues are on the one hand our glory, they are on the other hand our heavy cross.[20]

Thus it was, even before World War I, that the immigrant churches faced a difficult twofold missionary task: to reach the first generation in the language that they knew best, and to retain the second generation which, in its eagerness to become "American," placed a high priority on the use of English in church, school, and home.[21]

Leaders of the more Americanized branches of Lutheranism urged those who were reluctant to introduce English not to repeat the mistakes of the past. It was not true, they argued, that "true Lutheranism" could not survive in the English tongue. This was an unfounded fear. "We Lutherans from the East," wrote Gerberding, "had a century and a half of history behind us. We had made our mistakes. . . . It is a tragic story. We did not want the [Lutherans] of the West to repeat the suicidal blunders of Germans and Swedes in the East. We wanted to help them save their children in the Lutheran Church." [22] Suspicion of the motives of those whose slogan was "The Faith of the Fathers in the Language of the Children" was eventually overcome,[23] and foreign-language church bodies soon organized an "association," "conference," "district," or "synod" whose main responsibility was to promote the use of English. By 1917 most of the churches had established English language periodicals and had published English liturgies, hymnals, and catechisms. But even the most ardent advocates of change assumed that the process of transition would extend over many years, certainly another generation at least. But in this they were wrong. World War I accelerated the change beyond all expectations. "Virtually over night," said the historian of the Augustana Synod, "the congregations . . . made the transition from Swedish to English. . . . " [24] In fact, so rapid was the changeover that the synodical president felt obligated in 1921 to urge the setting aside of "one or two congregations . . . in the large cities as exclusively Swedish churches" for those who still preferred the mother tongue.[25]

In 1917 the merger of three Norwegian Lutheran bodies had been made possible in part by the agreement to christen the new body the "Norwegian Lutheran Church of America." The next year the "pro-American" feeling was running so high that some leaders began agitation to eliminate the word "Norwegian" from the name of the church.[26] Although opposition developed and postponed formal change of name until 1946, in actuality the language transition was almost entirely completed by 1930.[27] The story was similar among the Danish Lutherans and the German Missouri Synod.[28]

Quite obviously the effect of World War I upon the churches was not limited to "Americanization," nor was "Americanization" limited to

patriotic feelings or a rapid switch to the English language. The alteration in American Lutheran church life was to reach into theological
and social attitudes as well. Furthermore, it was to force the question:
"If we all speak English and we all teach the gospel according to the
Lutheran confessions, is there any genuine reason for maintaining our
ecclesiastical separateness?" The question of Lutheran unity would ultimately lead to a search for ways in which Lutherans could participate
in the emerging ecumenical movement.

FACING NEW THEOLOGICAL AND SOCIAL THOUGHT

Despite ethnic and institutional diversity among American Lutherans
at the outbreak of World War I, there was a remarkable homogeneity
about them. This homogeneous quality was most visible in the attitude
that all the church bodies assumed over against the new intellectual
climate of the 19th century. The "evangelical liberalism" and "scientific
modernism" [29] that disturbed and polarized several Protestant denominations was stoutly resisted by Lutherans. When this "new theology" was
later wedded to what was called "the Social Gospel," Lutherans of all
varieties protested that the "new" was a dangerous distortion of the
biblical message. A look at the years between the war and 1930 will
reveal a modest alteration in the *theological* stance of at least some
Lutherans; but as far as *social* attitudes were concerned, no major change
was to appear until the depression.

In order to understand the theological travail of American Lutheranism
in the years after World War I it is necessary to make a rapid survey
of theological thought in 19th century American Lutheranism. In the
early years of that exciting era Lutherans faced a crisis compounded of
the threat of rationalism and the seduction of "Americanization" via revivalism. Religious indifference during the first years of the young
republic was judged by Protestant churches as a massive threat to spiritual
life and morals. The Second Awakening and the Great Revival in the
West were consequently welcomed as means by which to defeat the
enemy and to preserve an evangelical witness in America. When Lutherans added their strength to this effort, they tended to minimize the
distinctly Lutheran confessional principle and to embrace some of the
emphases of American "evangelicalism." [30] This attitude was to be seen
in the positions advocated by S. S. Schmucker, president of the Lutheran

seminary at Gettysburg and the most influential American Lutheran theologian of the era.[31] The movement that resulted from its leadership was given the descriptive title, "American Lutheranism," [32] and, ironically, was detected as being un-Lutheran not only by Schmucker's colleague, Charles Porterfield Krauth, but also by the staunchly Reformed theologians of Mercersburg, John Nevin and Philip Schaff. The Mercersburg men charged Schmucker with being neither Lutheran nor Calvinist in his view of Holy Communion. As a matter of fact, his was a denatured Lutheranism, hardly distinguishable from the Zwinglianism of contemporary American "evangelicalism." [33]

This "American Lutheranism" was overcome eventually by a growing interest in recently imported German neo-confessionalism that arrived in three ways: (1) by the translation of German Lutheran theological literature and its subsequent use in the General Synod just at the time the controversy over "American Lutheranism" was reaching a climax; (2) by the mass immigration of German and Scandinavian Lutherans at mid-century; and (3) by a revival of interest in the Lutheran liturgical tradition *circa* 1860-1890. The neo-confessionalism that came to America in these ways became a movement to combat religious indifference, not by the methods of American "evangelicalism," but by a repristination [34] of the scholasticism of the 17th century Lutheran dogmaticians and by a continuing emphasis on pietistic orthodoxy, the latter especially among Scandinavians.

The problem facing American Lutherans was that they could see no other options. The historically-conditioned confessionalism and the historically-oriented biblical hermeneutics of the so-called "Erlangen School" (Germany) were largely unknown, or if known, regarded with suspicion.[35] This was to be expected in the Missouri Synod whose leaders asserted that the Erlangen theology "pierced the hands and feet of Christianity," and "stabbed it through the heart," not least in its "denial of the verbal inspiration and inerrancy of Scripture." [36] Although some of the professors in seminaries of the General Synod and General Council were ready to admit, even before World War I, the necessity of moving beyond biblical literalism, they were generally skittish about theological novelty. An exception to this pattern was C. J. Sodergren of the Augustana Synod (a part of the General Council till 1918) whose views were considered dangerously liberal by some of his colleagues. He wrote in 1914 about the Bible and evolution:

> The time has arrived, it appears, for someone to say that the theory of evolution is not necessarily atheistic, and that it might be quite consistent with the Bible and with Christian belief in God as the Creator of heaven and earth.[37]

Sodergren, however, was but one of a small and untypical number of American Lutheran theologians who were open to the new insights.

On the whole, Lutheranism in America looked upon scholars who used the historical-critical approach to the Bible as subversives. Moreover, the "Social Gospel" of such Protestants as Washington Gladden and Walter Rauschenbusch was rejected outright as "another gospel" (Galatians 1:6-7). There was a genuine fear among Lutherans that to affirm it was to substitute sociology for theology and to secularize Christianity. Very few would have disagreed with reports from the General Synod and the General Council that the main task of the church was "the faithful preaching of the Gospel, and . . . [the] bringing of individual members of society to a saving knowledge of Jesus Christ . . . "; "His relation to society is through the individual soul and through the community of saints . . . but He is not . . . a reformer of its evils, or an adjuster of its economic distresses." [38]

As far as the church as a whole was concerned, the theological-social climate of American Lutheranism remained relatively unchanged until after World War I. The congregations rested in indolent satisfaction with "the received faith," a confession of the Lutheran tradition interpreted in large measure according to the canons of the 17th century. The problems of American Lutheranism, it was reasoned, were basically not theological; rather they were practical and immensely urgent. Unchurched immigrants and second or third generation Lutherans, new missions in city and country, colleges and seminaries, hospitals and orphanages, missions in Africa and Asia, and, of course, "Americanization"—these were "the real problems." In the light of the pressing tasks to establish the church in the American setting there was precious little time to reflect on the "new theology" or the role of the church in a society rapidly being urbanized and industrialized.

ON THE ROAD TO UNITY

Despite Lutheranism's common front in the matters mentioned above, it must be remembered that organizational unity was a long way from being achieved. The ever-present ethnic origins problem and the estrangement between "Eastern Lutherans" and the immigrant churches of the Midwest prevented Lutheran unity for decades to come. The Eastern Lutherans' brush with "American Lutheranism" led other Lutherans to regard them as confessionally indifferent and consequently as questionable bearers of the Reformation tradition. What the Lutherans of the Midwest did not realize was that no segment of Lutheranism in America had been won over to liberalism. Even the confessionally indifferent groups of individuals remaining in the old General Synod were not "liberals" in the sense of 19th century German theology. The Missouri Synod and other conservative bodies judged the Eastern Lutherans as guilty of "liberalism" because of their attitudes toward "unionism," freemasonry, and chiliasm. What they failed to understand was that these were not the concerns of liberal theology. Nevertheless, by the 400th anniversary of the Reformation (1917) the question of church unity was "in the air." Spokesmen for the cause were present in several quarters, and they would not be denied.

Major steps in the direction of Lutheran unity were taken in the late war years (1917-1918). The merger of three Norwegian-background bodies into the Norwegian Lutheran Church of America (1917), the reunion of Eastern Lutherans into the family named the United Lutheran Church in America (1918), and the formation of a cooperative agency, the National Lutheran Council (1918)—all these were events of far-reaching importance. Influences from these developments continued to flow into the life of American Lutheranism for the next half century.

The Formation of the Norwegian Lutheran Church of America [39]

Norwegian immigrants began arriving in the Midwest in 1839. By 1890 those who had been gathered into the church were to be found in three "synods": Hauge's Norwegian Evangelical Lutheran Synod in America (1846 and 1876), the Synod for the Norwegian Evangelical Lutheran Church in America (1853), and the United Norwegian Lutheran Church in America (1890). The latter suffered two schisms in the decade after its founding, the Lutheran Free Church (1897) and the Church of the Lutheran Brethren (1900). Despite these setbacks the United Church lost none of its enthusiasm for ultimate merger of Norwegian Lutherans in America. Year after year it extended overtures to the other churches and arranged conferences for the purpose of resolving differences. The Norwegian Synod, strongly influenced by the Missouri Synod with which it had been in fellowship from 1872 to 1883 (in the Synodical Conference), rejected the overtures for doctrinal reasons. Hauge's Synod, reflecting pietistic and low church concerns, feared that some of its emphases, such as preaching by laymen, would be jeopardized, if not lost, in a large union of churches. Then, quite unexpectedly, the Haugeans reversed themselves in 1905 and appointed a union committee and invited the United Church and the Norwegian Synod to do the same.[40] Fruitful conferences were held until 1908 when negotiations were threatened by the long-standing and troublesome question of election (predestination) in which the Norwegian Synod held the Missourian viewpoint. Despite the efforts of H. G. Stub, president of the Norwegian Synod, to make room for both the Missourian and anti-Missourian interpretations of election, the discussions reached an impasse in 1910. Nevertheless, proponents of union on both sides revived the discussions by the expedient of appointing completely new committees which, with considerable encouragement from laymen, finally reached a "settlement" (Opgjør) in 1912. Both the United Church and the Norwegian Synod (Hauge's Synod had stepped aside but supported the United Church) agreed that, although there were two interpretations of the doctrine of election, each could be accepted as orthodox.

With this theological barrier removed the three churches were able to work out practical and constitutional matters over the next few years and bring about the first major Lutheran merger of the 20th century, the Norwegian Lutheran Church of America. Its first president, H. G. Stub, had great gifts of leadership but carried with him into the new church not a little of the spirit of the Missouri Synod. The impact of his strong personality on the new half-million member church would be unmistakable during the eight years (1917-1925) of his presidency.

A small party within the former Norwegian Synod rejected the merger and formed in 1918 the Norwegian Synod of the American Evangelical Lutheran Church. Casting its lot with the Missouri and Wisconsin Synods in the Synodical Conference, it declared its purpose was to preserve orthodox Lutheranism among the Norwegians in America. In the early 50s it changed its name to the Evangelical Lutheran Synod.

The Reunion of the Muhlenberg Tradition[41]

The ecclesiastical descendants of the "patriarch" of colonial Lutheranism, H. M. Muhlenberg, had divided into three general groups in the

1860s: The General Synod, the General Council, and the United Synod, South. Following overtures made by the General Synod in the 1870s, the General Council proposed an informal conference for "all Lutherans who accept the Unaltered Augsburg Confession." Two "Free Lutheran Diets" (1877 and 1878) revealed that the three eastern general bodies, from whom attendance was primarily drawn, were of a common mind. In terms of their confessional stance the diets revealed the following: the General Synod was considered "left," the General Council "right," and the United Synod, South, "middle." But as contacts increased there was a perceptible moving towards a common confessional attitude.

While the three groups were moving together theologically, they were working towards common forms for worship. By 1888 a joint committee had produced The Common Service based on "the common consent of the pure Lutheran liturgies of the sixteenth century...." When there was no complete agreement among these liturgies, "the consent of the largest number of those of greatest weight" would be determinative.[42]

Although the new service was initially opposed in numerous congregations of the General Synod, which was less liturgical (more "Americanized") than the other two bodies, by 1917 when a common hymnal was adopted to take its place alongside the new liturgy, most of Eastern Lutheranism was using the *Common Service Book*. Its preface declared, "this book . . . witnesses to the essential strength and spiritual oneness of the Lutheran Church in America." It is noteworthy that church bodies in the Midwest—especially the Missouri Synod, the Augustana Synod, the Joint Synod of Ohio, and the Norwegian Lutheran Church of America—soon made The Common Service available to their congregations.

The new spirit of good will and cooperation, created and promoted by "Free Diets" and joint work on common worship, led to formal (the "Free Diets" had been just that, free and informal) discussions by official representatives of the churches. In response to a proposal by the General Council, the first General Conference of Lutherans in America was held in 1898. This was followed by similar conferences in 1902 and 1904. The total impact of such meetings was the growing conviction that the confessional condition for unity (Augsburg Confession, Article VII: "For the true unity of the church it is enough to agree concerning the doctrine of the Gospel and the administration of the sacraments") was present, and, therefore, should be implemented. This did not come without fear of "confessionalism" on the part of some in the General Synod.[43] The whole issue, however, was pressed by the General Council's insistence that closer relationships depended on the General Synod's unequivocal affirmation that the Bible *is* (not merely *contains*) the Word of God and that the Lutheran confessions are a correct exhibition of the faith and doctrine of the church.[44] The General Synod acquiesced to council wishes and thus prepared the way for the merger of 1918. Its action also placed all Lutherans in America for the first time on virtually the same confessional basis.[45]

Theological and liturgical advances had been supplemented by a history of cooperation between the three synods in home and foreign missionary enterprises. Moreover, laymen of the various groups had learned to know each other in a variety of organizations that crossed synodical lines. It was, in fact, the union enthusiasm of laymen that helped to spark the actual merger. The occasion was the inter-synodical preparation for the 400th anniversary of the Reformation. A joint committee had been making arrangements for the celebration since 1914. The laymen on this committee spearheaded in 1917 a move for "immediate and organic union." The entire committee responded favorably to a resolution that the three synods "together with all other bodies one with us in our Lutheran faith" merge as soon as possible into an organization "to be known as the United Lutheran Church in America." [46] The reaction was prompt and overwhelmingly favorable. The presidents appointed a joint committee that produced a constitution for submission to the synods in 1918. "Beginning on November 11, 1918, the day of the armistice in Europe," says A. R. Wentz, "each general body held an adjourned meeting in New York City, completed its business . . . and then, November 14-16, joined in . . . the first convention of the United Lutheran Church in America." [47] The new church, numbering about one million baptized members, elected Frederick H. Knubel (General Synod) as its first president.

The preamble of the constitution hoped to set the stage for further union by inviting all Lutherans, who subscribed to the confessional position stated in the constitution, to unite in one Lutheran Church in America.[48] Other Lutherans, however, did not respond favorably. The Augustana Synod, which had been a national rather than geographic unit in the General Council, did not participate in the merger, but preferred to preserve its identity without cutting off the possibility of continuing friendly relations with the new church.[49] The Norwegian Lutheran Church, having just consummated its own merger, was hardly prepared to consider the invitation seriously. The Synodical Conference under the strong leadership of the Missouri Synod maintained that there were confessional differences between it and the new body. The Joint Synod of Ohio preferred a pan-Lutheran federation to organic merger and the Iowa Synod continued to feel uneasy about the Eastern Lutherans. The invitation by the United Lutheran Church, considered by its framers as a gesture of good will towards other Lutherans, was actually regarded by not a few Midwest Lutherans as an arrogant affront.

Despite the lack of response from other Lutherans, the United Lutheran Church moved into the new era with great enthusiasm and rejoiced that, after more than 60 years of separation, the churches of the Muhlenberg tradition were reunited. The church stood ready to take its place in the postwar world and to give leadership in both American and international Lutheranism and in the emerging ecumenical movement.

Solidarity: Joint Synod of Wisconsin and Other States

There were some Germans in the Midwest whose history in the 19th century revealed a move from the left to the right on "the scale of orthodoxy." Three synods (Wisconsin, 1850; Michigan, 1860; and Minnesota, 1860) traced their roots to leaders who were not "strict constructionists" with regard to the norms of confessionalist Lutheranism. The largest of these, Wisconsin, participated in the organization of the General Council (1867) but within less than a decade (1871) had withdrawn because the council was judged to be doctrinally inadequate. The Michigan Synod, also a member of the General Council, withdrew in 1888. The Minnesota Synod, originally a part of the General Synod, moved into the General Council in 1867. The latter proved to be unsatisfactory and led to Minnesota's withdrawal in 1871.

These three synods, with common German ancestry and growing theological conservatism, found it expedient in 1892 to enter a loose federation, the Joint Synod of Wisconsin, Minnesota, Michigan and Other States which became a part of the larger federation, the Missouri Synod-dominated Synodical Conference, in the same year.[50] By 1904 a fourth synod (Nebraska) had become a part of the 1892 federation. These four bodies, three-fifths of whose membership was contributed by the Wisconsin

Synod, dissolved their loose federation in 1919 and formed an organic merger called the Evangelical Lutheran Joint Synod of Wisconsin and Other States (later shortened to the Wisconsin Evangelical Lutheran Synod). After World War I and especially after World War II, this church grew increasingly critical of its sister church in the Synodical Conference, the Missouri Synod. In the early 1960s it, together with the Evangelical Lutheran (Norwegian) Synod, found it necessary to disavow fellowship with the Missouri Synod for the latter's deviations from the standards of "true Lutheranism." [51]

Broadening Cooperation: The National Lutheran Council

One of the sad facts of Lutheran history on the North American continent has been the operation of what has been called the "calamity theory" in the movement toward cooperation and unity.[52] There had been no little discussion about the necessity for Lutherans working together in America. A few optimists predicted that closer fellowship was at hand.[53] But, as a matter of fact, it was only in the face of dire necessity, external pressures, and threatening crises that Lutherans began to close ranks. Ironically, this confessionally-oriented ecclesiastical family found itself drawn together more often by common disaster than by common confession. This was illustrated when America entered World War I. Lutheran churches were suddenly confronted with the necessity of caring for the spiritual needs of their young members in the armed services. The crisis-nature of the situation did not permit the luxury of arguing old differences. Moreover, the government was unwilling to deal with major denominations individually, preferring that churches work through the YMCA or the Federal Council of Churches. Unwilling, for both theological and practical reasons, to join other Protestants in using these agencies and certainly unwilling to leave young Lutherans in military service spiritually unshepherded, there remained no other course but to unite in common action. The result was the formation (October 19, 1917) of the National Lutheran Commission for Soldiers' and Sailors' Welfare. Called together by the United Inner Mission of the General Synod, General Council, and the United Synod, South, seven groups, later joined by six others, committed their memberships to a well-defined program of cooperation. The Missouri Synod, although originally represented, felt constrained to withdraw. Nevertheless, it and the other churches of the Synodical Conference maintained "at least an external cooperation" in order to deal with those matters that required a common approach to the government and the military.

President of the commission through its five-year life was Frederick H. Knubel, chairman of the United Inner Mission and president-to-be of the United Lutheran Church in America. Under his leadership the commission brought the churches into every area of wartime ministry, raising what was then considered the unattainable and amazing sum of $1,350,000 to underwrite the various services. The Missouri Synod in a similar effort collected $560,000.

The success of the commission and the obvious benefits of working together led to the suggestion that a "permanent national council or committee representing the entire Lutheran Church so far as possible" be organized. It was clear that the commission, successful as it was in its limited area of ministry to servicemen, could not serve all the cooperative needs of American Lutheranism. Missions in new defense communities, permanent offices for contact with government, European war relief and care of orphaned missions, publicity and fund-raising—all of these areas made it imperative that a more comprehensive agency be authorized by the churches. By mid-1918 several proposals, including one from the National Lutheran Editors' Association (established 1910), urged immediate action. Knubel suggested that the presidents of the General Council, General Synod, United Synod, South, and the Norwegian Lutheran Church take the lead in the matter.[54] Preliminary meetings of the presidents and representatives of "various Lutheran Synods"[55] were held at Harrisburg and Pittsburgh in July and August, 1918. The purposes, duties, and functions of a "Lutheran Federation Council" were spelled out. A few weeks later, September 6, 1918, the church presidents meeting in Chicago took action—without waiting for the approval of their church bodies—to establish the National Lutheran Council. Involved were the Norwegian Lutheran Church, the Augustana Synod, the Joint Synod of Ohio, the Iowa Synod, the Buffalo Synod, the Danish Lutheran Church, the United Danish Lutheran Church, the Lutheran Free Church, the Icelandic Synod, and the three synods soon to become the United Lutheran Church in America. The Missouri Synod, although represented in the preliminary meetings, declined to participate on doctrinal and practical grounds. Moreover, friction had risen between its Army and Navy Board and the National Lutheran Commission for Soldiers' and Sailors' Welfare. On top of this, the synod's unrestrained criticism of the emerging United Lutheran Church made its continued isolation inevitable.

The founders' awareness of the long-range possibilities of the National Lutheran Council was apparent in the statement of purpose [56] "to promote, as far as possible," the following:

1. To issue true and uniform statistical information of the Lutheran Church of America.
2. To speak for and publicize the position of the Lutheran Church in matters that called for "common utterance."
3. To represent the Lutheran Church in both its relations and attitudes toward organized entities outside itself, including national and state governments.
4. To handle activities dealing with, or to create agencies to deal with, problems arising out of war and other emergencies, where there was no common Lutheran agency, and to coordinate and unify the activities of the existing agencies.
5. To coordinate the activities and agencies of the Lutheran Church in America for the solution of problems arising from social, economic or intellectual conditions or changes affecting religious life and consciousness.
6. To foster true Christian loyalty, and the maintenance of "religious relation" between Church and State as separate entities with correlated yet distinctly defined functions.
7. To call to the attention of the participating bodies such matters as required common utterance or action.
8. To undertake additional functions by the express consent of the member bodies.

Headquarters of the new council were to be in New York. Representation in the council was to be one for every hundred thousand confirmed members or one-third fraction thereof. The first officers were H. G. Stub (Norwegian Lutheran Church), president; John L. Zimmermann (General Synod layman), vice-president; Lauritz Larsen (Norwegian Lutheran Church), secretary. Other significant leaders in the early years were to be F. H. Knubel (United Lutheran Church), C. H. L. Schuette (Joint Synod of Ohio), G. A. Brandelle (Augustana Synod), T. E. Schmauk, H. E. and C. M. Jacobs, John A. Morehead (United Lutheran Church), and L. W. Boe (Norwegian Lutheran Church).

It has been correctly observed that "the Council came into being because of a sense of urgency shared by many Lutherans," that it "sprang into existence" and was "born running" with a full agenda from the start.[57] But hardly had it been launched when intra-council differences began to emerge and to cause strained relationships for decades to come.

Troubles in the Twenties

In 1918 there were two main groupings of Lutherans, the Synodical Conference (1872) and the new council. The largest body in the former was the Missouri Synod; the largest body in the latter, the United Lutheran Church. These two represented opposite views regarding church unity. The latter was committed to unity on the basis of the generally received confessions of Lutheranism. The Missouri Synod went beyond this to require agreement in extra-confessional theses covering doctrine and practice.

To understand developments in the 20s and subsequent decades one must be aware that non-Missourian Midwestern Lutherans stood uneasily between these two ecclesiastical colossi. On the one hand, they cooperated with the United Lutheran Church as witnessed by the formation of the National Lutheran Council, but at the same time, they were suspicious of the doctrinal and ecumenical stance of their "big sister." Their feelings about Missouri and the Synodical Conference were likewise mixed. They were unhappy about Missourian exclusivism, but, in large measure, they judged this body to be "more Lutheran" than the United Church. Although the division in the National Lutheran Council was not articulated in 1918 and therefore did not immediately hinder the cooperative efforts of the council, it was now clear that two potentially divisive points of view regarding confessional Lutheranism lay alongside each other in the council.

The occasion that brought out the differences was the definition and implementation of the council's policy of "cooperation in externals." Fearing "unionism" (i.e., fellowship without doctrinal agreement),[58] some Midwestern Lutherans insisted that cooperation be limited to *res externae* in contrast to *res internae*. But where was the boundary between "external" and "internal"? What could be done cooperatively without complete doctrinal agreement? [59]

One of the most critical problems after World War I was that of ministering to people who had moved into wartime industrial centers.

Clearly this ought to be a cooperative enterprise because the home mission boards of individual church bodies were unable to cope with the situation. The Federal Council of Churches had proposed a joint Protestant undertaking. This, however, was unacceptable to the Lutherans who looked to the National Lutheran Council as the proper agency for this work.[60] It was deemed essential that the council work with the various Lutheran home mission boards in developing a program. Therefore, a meeting of the council's excutive committee and home mission representatives was held at Columbus, Ohio, December 18, 1918. It produced agreement that the work should be undertaken. However, at the insistence of H. G. Stub a resolution was passed requesting the presidents of member churches to constitute a "Joint Committee to confer on questions of doctrine and practice, with a view to the coordination of their home mission and other work." [61] Behind this resolution lay Stub's fear of unionism, because joint home mission work was hardly cooperation "in externals." [62]

The Joint Committee on Doctrine and Practice met March 11-13, 1919, at Chicago.[63] It had been previously agreed that four papers reflecting the viewpoints of their respective churches should be presented by H. E. Jacobs (ULCA), C. H. L. Schuette (Ohio Synod), F. Richter (Iowa Synod), and H. G. Stub (NLCA). A special National Lutheran Council resolution had requested F. H. Knubel "to prepare a statement which shall define the essentials of a catholic spirit as viewed by the Lutheran Church." [64]

After the reading of Knubel's paper on the general principles of catholicity, the particular synodical viewpoints were presented. Jacobs moved that Stub's paper be made the basis of the preliminary discussion before turning to the question of catholicity. Therewith the remaining sessions were devoted to Stub's presentation. After considerable discussion and amendment, the paper was referred by the group to the churches. The articles contained in it were subsequently known as "The Chicago Theses." [65] The other main paper, Knubel's "The Essentials of a Catholic Spirit," could not be discussed for lack of time. Therefore, a subcommittee consisting of Knubel, Stub, and T. E. Schmauk was appointed to consider the paper and report to a later meeting of the same group. Moreover, the conference voted to publish both Knubel's and Jacobs' papers, the latter titled, "Constructive Lutheranism." [66]

These papers—Knubel's, Jacobs', and Stub's—proved to be of profound significance in the shaping of American Lutheranism, setting forth two points of view: "ecumenical confessionalism" (Knubel and Jacobs) and "exclusive confessionalism" (Stub). Later developments among churches of the National Lutheran Council revolved about the positions expressed and implied in these documents. The Knubel-Jacobs statement insisted that there is an organic union among all parts of God's truth, but a necessary difference of order and importance. The central must ever be distinguished from the peripheral. When it is recognized that the gospel alone is central and constitutive of the church, there is the foundation for a true catholic spirit in the church.

The second point of view enunciated at the Chicago conference can safely be said to have represented Midwest Lutheranism, including the Missouri Synod which was not involved in the discussion.[67] Stub's presentation did not in any sense attempt to cover all the doctrines and practices of Lutheranism. Rather he included only those points that had been troublesome in the history of Midwest Lutheranism.[68] There being no general disagreement in the group on these matters, the paper was, as noted above, passed on to the churches.

Two things were now clear: (1) Although the National Lutheran Council had called the meeting, the Joint Conference action was not an action of the council. All enactments would have to be referred to the member churches. (2) The Joint Conference had not completed its task, because the council request for a statement "which shall define the essentials of a catholic spirit as viewed by the Lutheran Church" had not been discussed.

When Knubel returned home, he set down "A Personal Statement Concerning the Chicago Conference on Faith and Practice," [69] and sent a letter to Stub seeking to arrange a time for the subcommittee to consider "the essentials of a catholic spirit."

In "A Personal Statement . . ." Knubel gave a précis of the Chicago meeting, stating his own view that a policy statement on the "essentials of a catholic spirit" was urgently needed because of the pressing problems facing the church in the postwar world. The issues of Bolshevism and other anti-Christian forces in addition to the ecumenical discussion of "Faith and Order" demanded that the Lutherans think through the problem of catholicity.[70]

In November, Knubel, Stub, and Charles M. Jacobs[71] met to carry out their assignment. It was already apparent by the fall of 1919 that Stub was not eager to pursue the problem of catholicity. His own theological position (the Chicago paper) was, he felt, the proper point of departure for an approach to other Lutherans.[72] Moreover, certain elements in his own church body, notably pastors of the former Norwegian Synod, were extremely critical of the National Lutheran Council. L. W. Boe wrote confidentially to Knubel that Stub had become nervous because of the opposition. Therefore, said Boe, "he will insist strongly on the Chicago Theses. . . . As I understand it you people feel that the Lutheran Church cannot get together on a negative declaration, and *I agree with you* [italics added]. Dr. Stub, however, is liable to look at the question from the standpoint of a settlement of . . . old difficulties . . . rather than . . . making a common declaration over against the outside world." Boe went on to assure Knubel that he himself supported the United Lutheran standpoint and hoped "The Chicago Theses" would not be the cause of the National Lutheran Council's dissolution.[73]

The Joint Conference on Doctrine and Practice met a second time in Chicago, January 27-28, 1920, this time to hear the report of the subcommittee on "the essentials of a catholic spirit." C. M. Jacobs had recast Knubel's earlier paper which now bore the signature of these two men alone. Stub had requested permission to explain why he had refused to affix his signature.[74] It was this document that came to be known later as "The Washington Declaration." [75] Consisting of five parts, it defined the Lutheran attitude toward cooperative movements, church union, and "organizations, tendencies and movements" within and without the organized church. Part one, "Concerning the Catholic Spirit in the Church," pointed out the ecumenical character of the Lutheran confessions within which frame catholic relations should be fostered. The church, it said, will always be ready:

1. To declare unequivocally what it believes concerning Christ and His gospel, and to endeavor to show that it has placed the true interpretation upon the gospel . . . and to testify definitely and frankly against error.

2. To approach others without hostility, jealousy, suspicion, or

pride, in the sincere and humble desire to give and receive Christian service.

3. To grant cordial recognition to all agreements that are discovered between its own interpretation of the Gospel and that which others hold.

4. To cooperate with other Christians in works of serving love insofar as this can be done without surrender of its interpretation of the gospel, without denial of conviction, and without suppression of its testimony as to what it holds to be the truth.[76]

Part two dealt with relations to other Lutherans and said that there should be no reasons against union where there was subscription to the Lutheran confessions. Part three, "Concerning the Organic Union of Protestant Churches," held that organizational union was less important than agreement in the proclamation of the gospel and that the church catholic exists "through and under divergent forms of extended organization." Until a more complete unity of confession could be achieved, the Lutheran church was bound in conscience to maintain a separate identity; "and its members, its ministers, its pulpits, its fonts and its altars must testify only to that truth." Part four delineated eight doctrinal essentials as a "positive basis for practical cooperation among Protestant Churches." Part five warned against "Movements and Organizations Injurious to the Christian Faith." Here it was said that lodge members were to be dealt with in an evangelical rather than in a legalistic fashion.

Following Jacobs' presentation of the report, Stub gave several reasons why he could not sign the document. First, it was too voluminous; "The Chicago Theses" (Stub's own product) were short and more easily understood. Second, the Missouri Synod's official organ, *Lehre und Wehre,* had commented that "The Chicago Theses" were excellent. In other words, he implied, one should not risk alienating the Missouri Synod by going beyond a position acceptable to that church. Third, the section on "Cooperative Movements" was inadequate because it did not mention the Bible as "the inerrant Word of God" and the real presence in the sacrament. Fourth, the whole position on catholicity was contrary to Article Three of the "Articles of Union" of the Norwegian Lutheran Church of America, which article bound the church to refrain from churchly cooperation with non-Lutherans.[77]

The discussion that followed produced no definite decision regarding "the essentials of a catholic spirit." Knubel and Jacobs pleaded "very earnestly" with the opposition, but to no avail.[78] Before adjournment, however, it was agreed that further meetings would be at the call of Stub, Knubel, and Secretary Lauritz Larsen.

It was soon evident that Stub was averse to further conferences.[79] Nevertheless, he agreed to meet in Chicago, March 11-12, 1920. No minutes have been accessible to the writer, but a memorandum by Knubel provides a summary of the discussion.[80] Two things were to the fore: (1) the feeling among Midwest Lutherans that the United Lutheran Church was pressing for something contrary to their desires; and (2) the lodge question and unionism. The discussion revealed that Iowa had left the council because it feared that the principle of *res externae* was being transgressed. Similar feeling prevailed in Ohio and among the Norwegians. Knubel felt compelled to comment on the phrase, *res externae*. First, he said, the term as now used among American Lutherans had no relation to the use of the term in the Lutheran confessions. Second, the use of the term was not scriptural and, therefore, not Christian. "There are no *res externae* in the life of the Christian and the Church (1 Cor. 10:31)." Therefore, any attempt to solve the question of inter-Lutheran or other relationships by use of the term would be doomed to failure. Some other solution must be found. For this reason the United Lutheran Church insisted on the approach presented by Jacobs and him, and, said Knubel, "The Chicago Theses" would not be put before the church unless some "true foundation be laid for them, as the paper on Catholicity attempts to give."

On the lodge question and unionism Knubel insisted that these matters must not be made the tests or shibboleths of Lutheranism: "They are not the proofs that a man is a Lutheran, although they are the things to which I believe a Lutheran will come sooner or later."

Once again the conference broke up without general acceptance of "The Essentials of a Catholic Spirit." It was agreed, however, to refrain from using the phrase *res externae,* although some did not see the utter inadequacy of the term; and by common consent, the "Chicago Theses" were to be discarded for the time being. This action was not to preclude further conferences, nor was it to prevent the United Lutheran Church from continuing its study of catholicity at its October (1920) convention in Washington.

Some time between this meeting and April 15, 1920, the church presidents agreed to abandon the Joint Conference on Doctrine and Practice.[81] With this decision Lutheranism within the National Lutheran Council came to a parting of the ways. The United Lutherans moved on to the "Washington Declaration" on catholicity; the Midwest Lutherans picked up Stub's "Chicago Theses" as a banner. Instead of a single-voiced and full-orbed Lutheran testimony within the National Lutheran Council, there emerged two distinct parties, each waving its own flag. Needless to say, the initial cause—mission cooperation in industrial areas—was forgotten.

In this way, the situation came to an uneasy rest in 1920. The National Lutheran Council had been established, two theological and ecclesiastical points of view had emerged within the council, and cooperation was theoretically limited to "external affairs." [82] Meanwhile, the churches cooperated in overseas relief for European Lutheran churches. Out of this action there developed an interest for a world organization of Lutherans. This brought National Lutheran Council bodies into the Lutheran World Convention (1923). Despite overseas and domestic cooperation, however, the next few years witnessed a pulling away from the United Lutheran Church and a drawing together of the Joint Synod of Ohio, the Iowa Synod, and the Norwegian Lutheran Church. One of the contributing factors, in addition to those evident from the previous discussion, was the Modernist-Fundamentalist controversy of the 20s, in which the Lutherans actually took no part. The Midwest Lutherans, however, felt the United Lutheran Church was equivocal on the question of the inerrancy of the Bible. "The Washington Declaration" asserted "the supreme importance of the Word of God" and "the authority of the Scriptures . . . as the only rule and standard by which all doctrines and teachers are to be judged." Stub, Lenski (Joint Synod of Ohio) and others were especially insistent that a statement on the verbal inspiration and consequent inerrancy of Scripture, in the context of modernism, ought to be promulgated. In this setting, the non-Synodical Conference Lutherans of the Mississippi Valley, especially the Norwegians and the Germans, were moving closer together. By 1925 a new alignment within the National Lutheran Council was in process.

The Formation of the American Lutheran Church [83]

Two new organizations emerged from inter-Lutheran negotiations in the 20s, the American Lutheran Church (1930) and the American Lutheran Conference (1930). Both—one an organic union, the other a federation of churches—reflected what has been loosely called "the middle way" of Midwestern Lutheranism within the National Lutheran Council. As such both entities occupied a position between the United Lutheran Church and the Missouri Synod.

The American Lutheran Church was the culmination of associations that had begun in the 19th century. The Joint Synod of Ohio and the Iowa Synod had participated in the 1866 conference that led to the formation of the General Council. Neither synod gave enthusiastic support to the council that was formed the next year. In fact, the Ohio Synod broke its associations with the General Council and cast its lot with the Synodical Conference (1872). The Iowa Synod maintained ties with the council by sending fraternal delegates to its conventions. This association continued until the council became a part of the United Lutheran Church in 1918.

Meanwhile, the Ohio Synod withdrew from the Synodical Conference during the controversy over predestination during the 1880s, taking the "anti-Missourian" position that characterized the Iowa Synod and the majority of the Norwegians. Although a common German background was a strong factor in bringing Ohio and Iowa into closer association, Iowa's ties with the General Council continued to be an offense to the Ohio Synod. This ended, however, when the Iowans broke relations with the council.

Thus the way was prepared for an official declaration of fellowship in 1918 and the beginning of conversations leading to organic union. The direction of the new movement was evident in the hopes expressed by C. C. Hein of the Ohio Synod. He yearned for closer ties with Missouri because he was convinced that unity of faith already existed. The same could not be said of the new United Lutheran Church. But if "relations could be established with Iowa *and* the Norwegian Lutheran Church, a long step would be taken" toward establishment of genuine Lutheranism in America.[84]

By 1924 a joint commission representing the Ohio and Iowa Synods recommended union. The same year the Buffalo Synod joined the consultations. Rapid progress was made in the next two years. Doctrinal agreements were reached and a constitution was drafted. Union seemed an accomplished fact. Meanwhile, however, a sharp disagreement had arisen over a statement concerning the inerrancy of Scripture. The previous year (1925) a colloquy in Minneapolis between representatives of Ohio, Iowa, Buffalo, and the Norwegians affirmed that the Scriptures were "the divinely inspired, revealed, and inerrant Word of God." This part of the "Minneapolis Theses" was opposed by the theological leader of the Iowa Synod, J. Michael Reu. After two years of controversy, an official "Appendix" interpreting the constitutional article on Scripture was approved. This action placed the new church in the position of affirming inerrancy of "the original texts" and recognizing the present Bible "as substantially identical with the original texts and as the only inspired and inerrant authority. . . ." [85] With this accomplished, the Ohio, Buffalo, and Iowa Synods (the latter included a semi-independent Texas Synod that retained separate legal existence until 1930) merged as the American Lutheran Church on August 11, 1930, at Toledo, Ohio. The new church elected C. C. Hein as president, received official greetings from the Lutheran World Convention and most of the Scandinavian Lutheran churches of the Midwest. Neither the Missouri Synod nor the United Lutheran Church was represented. After voting to join the projected American Lutheran Conference, the National Lutheran Council, and the Lutheran World Convention, the church reached out to the Missouri Synod "looking toward better mutual understanding." With regard to other Lutherans (the United Lutheran Church was not mentioned by name), the new church expressed its willingness to negotiate "on the basis of the Minneapolis Theses." [86] It was patent that the American Lutheran Church had assumed a conservative stance that included a view of Scripture completely unaffected by the options to verbal inspiration and inerrancy that numerous Lutherans in Europe and a few in America were beginning to adopt.[87]

The American Lutheran Conference

From one point of view the most important organizational development within American Lutheranism during the decade of the 20s was the clustering of the non-ULCA churches in the National Lutheran Council. The formation of the American Lutheran Conference (1930), a federative association of the synods that were in process of becoming the American Lutheran Church together with the Norwegian Lutheran Church, the Lutheran Free Church (Norwegian), the United Danish Lutheran Church, and the Augustana Synod (Swedish), was to have far-reaching results. The self-styled "middle group" rejected quite consciously the theological and ecumenical stance of the United Lutheran Church—in the process almost destroying the National Lutheran Council —and sought to assure the Missouri Synod that, despite its dislike of Missourian exclusivism, it was nevertheless sympathetic to and supportive of its view on unity in doctrine and practice prior to fellowship and union. The attitude expressed in the events of 1925-1930 persisted through the 50s and into the 60s when the National Lutheran Council found its membership reduced from eight church bodies to two by the organic mergers known as The American Lutheran Church (1960) and the Lutheran Church in America (1962), the former assuming in general the posture of the American Lutheran Conference. It becomes necessary, therefore, to remember that there was a definite connection between the unsuccessful conferences held within the National Lutheran Council during 1918-1920 and the negotiations that produced the American Lutheran Conference during the last half of the decade.

In 1924 the Joint Synod of Ohio had elected a new president, C. C. Hein. As pointed out earlier, Hein was eager to assure the Synodical Conference that Midwestern Lutheranism, outside the United Lutheran Church, was one with all those holding to "orthodox" Lutheranism. From the side of the Norwegian Lutherans similar sentiments were expressed by H. G. Stub who wrote to Hein suggesting fellowship. He said he looked upon this "as a matter of conscience"; "orthodox" Lutherans ought to be united *"over against the modernists and all who have another faith* [italics added]." [88] It was quite evident that he did not consider the United Lutheran Church an ally in the struggle against "modernism." [89]

During the summer of 1925 Stub retired from office and was succeeded by J. A. Aasgaard. Hein immediately invited him and other Norwegians to discuss a doctrinal basis for fellowship between the Joint Synod of Ohio, Iowa Synod, Buffalo Synod, and the Norwegian Lutheran Church. The meeting was held in Minneapolis, November 18, 1925.[90] The chief results of the colloquy were the formulation of the previously mentioned theological propositions known as the "Minneapolis Theses" and the decision to expand by inviting other selected synods to join. After affirming Stub's "Chicago Theses" (1919), the new statements addressed themselves to specific points of "opposition to the ULCA." [91] Three main areas of concern were spelled out. On Scripture the theses affirmed verbal inspiration and inerrancy. On the confessions the whole of their doctrinal content was accepted "without exception or limitation in all articles and parts, no matter whether a doctrine is specifically cited as a confession or incidentally introduced for the purpose of elucidating or proving some other doctrine." In contrast to the United Lutheran Church's "ecumenical confessionalism," the Minneapolis document asserted that cooperation "in the strictly essential work of the Church" presupposed doctrinal agreement. In contrast to the clarity of the ULCA declaration, no definition was made of the "strictly essential work of the Church." The intent was to draw the line against cooperation with non-Lutherans and to sharpen the lineaments of inter-Lutheran relationships. A final article on secret societies was likewise directed against the United Lutheran Church, which had inherited the problem of lodge-membership among a small minority of pastors in the former General Synod. In contrast to the Missouri Synod position, the theses did not absolutely prohibit lay membership in lodges nor did it prescribe regulations for church discipline.

The major issue of the theses, however, was the question of inspiration and inerrancy of the Bible. The Norwegians, to their dismay, discovered that J. Michael Reu, one of the Iowa representatives, was in their judgment a "liberal." His "liberalism" consisted in this that he considered infallibility of the Scripture limited to its message of salvation. Reu's view did not prevail and the colloquy adopted what was essentially the position of Stub and Hein: the Scriptures "as a whole, and in all their parts, [are] the divinely inspired, revealed, and inerrant Word of God. . . . " [92]

Before the Minneapolis conference ended (it lasted but one day), there was agreement to invite the Augustana Synod, the Lutheran Free Church, and the United Danish Lutheran Church to join forces with the original signers of the "Minneapolis Theses." Although Hein questioned the "orthodoxy" of both the Augustana Synod and the Free Church, Aasgaard assured him that both bodies were "sound." By 1929 a constitution was drafted and during the next year all five bodies (the three ALC synods were one) ratified the proposals. The American Lutheran Conference was established in Minneapolis, October 29-31, 1930. Its executive committee (Otto Mees, L. W. Boe [later resigned and replaced by T. F. Gullixson] J. P. Nielsen, H. O. Sletten, and P. O. Bersell) was authorized to implement the cooperative functions stipulated in the constitution: home, inner, and foreign missions, student service, publications, and exchange of theological professors.[93]

The decade of the 20s now ended had been an exciting one for America. The revolution in manners and morals, the growing hedonism and self-indulgence in society at large, the expansion of communications especially by radio, the growth in mobility by automobile and airplane, and the pre-1929 economic boom—all these had contributed to the strange and somewhat "unreal" world of America just before the Great Depression.

In the churches it was a decade when the dynamic of faith seemed to fade. The battle between the fundamentalists and the modernists had become a public spectacle and had disrupted many of the denominations. At the same time, the decade was an era of burgeoning interest among the churches in public relations, business methods, and the mass media of communication. Economic prosperity encouraged the building of bigger and more beautiful church buildings, not a few of which thrust congregations into financial obligations that became life-threatening millstones in the years ahead.

Poised on the edge of the new decade, American Lutheranism no doubt shared some of the ingredients that made up the ethos of the 20s. Unlike some churches that exuded a kind of optimistic messianism, Lutherans did not expect America to give birth to a new Eden. But, quite like other churches and American society as a whole, it was hardly prepared for the trauma and pathos associated with the Great Depression. To this we must now turn our attention.

NOTES

1. Carl N. Degler, *Out of Our Past* (Harper Colophon Books; New York: Harper and Row, 1962), p. 290.

2. This term has more than a geographic connotation. The colonial Lutherans of the Atlantic seaboard, like other settlers, moved west and in so doing encountered their co-religionists of more recent arrival. The latter were ill at ease among their partly Americanized brethren. They were "Eastern Lutherans" even in the West.

3. *Protestant-Catholic-Jew* (New York: Doubleday and Co., 1955), p. 35.

4. Clifton E. Olmstead, *History of Religion in the United States* (Englewood Cliffs, N.J.: Prentice-Hall, Inc., 1960), p. 599.

5. T. E. Schmauk, "The Great War of Germany against Europe," *Lutheran Church Review,* XXXIII (1914), 764. Cited by Fred Meuser, "North American Lutheranism, 1900-1930" (unpublished manuscript), p. 10. The writer is grateful to Professor Meuser for permission to read and to use some of the results of his research recorded in this manuscript.

6. See Carl Meyer, ed., *Moving Frontiers* (St. Louis: Concordia Publishing House, 1964), p. 236; and *Der Lutheraner,* LXXII (1916), 63. For some latter-day evaluations of the church's war attitudes see Carl Wittke, *German-Americans and World War I* (Columbus: Ohio State Archeological and Historical Society, 1936); Frederick Nohl, "The Lutheran Church–Missouri Synod Reacts to United States Anti-Germanism during World War I," *Concordia Historical Institute Quarterly,* XXXV (1962), 49-66; and Frederick C. Luebke, "Superpatriotism in World War I: The Experience of a Lutheran Pastor," *ibid.,* XLI (1968), 3-11.

7. Governor W. L. Harding of Iowa issued such a proclamation in May, 1918. It was illustrative of the tenor of the times. See *Lutheran Standard,* LXXVI (June 22, 1918), 378. Cf. Alan N. Graebner, "The Acculturation of an Immigrant Lutheran Church: The Lutheran Church–Missouri Synod 1917-1929," (unpublished Ph.D. dissertation, Columbia University, 1965), p. 31; microfilm copy in Concordia Historical Institute, St. Louis, Mo.

8. The writer recalls his hometown community in South Dakota after America's entry into the war. There were two Lutheran congregations—one German, the other Norwegian—and no love was lost between them. When the parsonage of the German congregation was daubed one night by yellow paint, the Norwegians tended to excuse the vandalism.

9. See Ray H. Abrams, *Preachers Present Arms* (New York: Round Table Press, 1933). Abrams tends to overdraw his case when he concludes that the American clergy were victims of well-planned British and American propaganda.

10. A collection of loyalty statements from the Lutheran churches is in the Archives for Cooperative Lutheranism, 315 Park Avenue So., New York. See file "State and Society-Loyalty." Cited in Meuser, "North American Lutheranism, 1900-1930," Chapter II, p. 29. Notes 11, 12, and 13 below are also cited by Meuser.

11. Theodore Graebner, "Stop, Look, and Listen!" *Lutheran Witness,* (November 13, 1917), 406.

12. Letter: Theodore Graebner—Martin Graebner, March 4, 1919, in "Theodore Graebner Papers," Concordia Historical Institute, St. Louis, Mo.

13. See file "Liberty Loans," National Lutheran Council in the Archives for Cooperative Lutheranism, 315 Park Ave. S., New York.

14. Quoted in Carl Malmberg, *America Is Also Scandinavian* (New York: G. P. Putnam's Sons, 1970), p. 66.

15. *Ibid.,* p. 71. Malmberg has a good summary of this misguided and foolish attempt to eliminate all "un-American" influences. See pp. 119-122.

16. Cited in Theodore Jorgenson and Nora O. Solum, *Ole Edvart Rølvaag, A Biography* (New York: Harpers, 1939), pp. 396-397.

17. H. E. Jacobs, *A History of the Evangelical Lutheran Church in the United States* (American Church History Series; New York: Chas. Scribner's Sons, 6th edition, 1912), pp. 320-331.

18. See M. L. Hansen, "The Problem of the Third Generation Immigrant," *Augustana Historical Society Publications,* VIII, Part I (Rock Island, Ill.; 1938). Herberg makes use of "Hansen's Law" in his *Protestant-Catholic-Jew.*

19. A. R. Wentz, *A Basic History of Lutheranism in America* (Revised Edition; Philadelphia: Fortress Press, 1964), pp. 72-73. Cf. David L. Scheidt, "Recent Linguistic Transition in Lutheranism," *The Lutheran Quarterly,* XIII (February, 1961), 34-35.

20. *Problems and Possibilities* (Columbia, S.C.: Lutheran Board of Publication, 1914),

p. 171. The author bemoans the loss of such well-known persons of wealth and prominence as John Wanamaker, Jacob Riis, Wm. Augustus Muhlenberg, Victor Lawson (Larsen), and the Weyerhaeuser family.

21. "Second generation" parents were usually bilingual, but used the foreign tongue only when their parents ("first generation") were present or when their children ("third generation") were to be excluded from some intelligence best reserved for parents.

22. G. H. Gerberding, *Reminiscent Reflections of a Youthful Octogenarian* (Minneapolis: Augsburg Publishing House, 1928), p. 155.

23. Gerberding comments that finally the Scandinavians learned to trust him. "They were no longer afraid of my Lutheranism." *Ibid.,* p. 173. Cf. G. H. Trabert, *English Lutheranism in the Northwest* (Philadelphia: General Council Publication House, 1914), pp. 65-77, 139-157.

24. G. Everett Arden, *Augustana Heritage* (Rock Island: Augustana Press, 1963), p. 246.

25. *Ibid.,* p. 247.

26. "The Change of Name," *Lutheran Church Herald,* (May 17, 1918), 305.

27. E. Clifford Nelson, *The Lutheran Church Among Norwegian-Americans* (Minneapolis: Augsburg Publishing House, 1960), II, 250.

28. Paul C. Nyholm, *The Americanization of the Danish Lutheran Churches in America* (Copenhagen: Institute for Danish Church History, 1963), pp. 292-322; Everette Meier and Herbert T. Mayer, "The Process of Americanization," in *Moving Frontiers,* ed. by Carl S. Meyer, pp. 380-381.

29. For a brief discussion of these two distinct—but often equated—movements see Winthrop S. Hudson, *Religion in America* (New York: Chas. Scribner's Sons, 1965), pp. 269-277; especially, p. 274, n. 16.

30. For an insightful examination of "American Evangelicalism" see Leigh Jordahl, "The American Evangelical Tradition and Culture Religion," *Dialog,* IV, (Summer, 1965), 188-193.

31. See S. S. Schmucker, *The American Lutheran Church, Historically, Doctrinally, and Practically Delineated . . .* (Springfield, Ohio: D. Harbaugh, 1851); and *Fraternal Appeal to the American Churches, with a Plan for Catholic Union, on Apostolic Principles* (New York: Gould and Newman, 1838; reprinted in Seminar Editions, Philadelphia: Fortress Press, 1965). Cf. A. R. Wentz, *Pioneer in Christian Unity: Samuel Simon Schmucker* (Philadelphia: Fortress Press, 1967).

32. For a discussion see Vergilius Ferm, *The Crisis in American Lutheran Theology* (New York: The Century Co., 1927).

33. See James H. Nichols, *Romanticism in American Theology: Nevin and Schaff at Mercersburg* (Chicago: University of Chicago Press, 1961), pp. 92-93.

34. For discussions of "repristination theology" see Hjalmar Holmquist and Jens Nørregaard, *Kirkehistorie* (København: J. H. Schultz Forlag, 1940), III, 45-47; Otto W. Heick, *A History of Christian Thought* (Philadelphia: Fortress Press, 1966), II, 199-203; and J. A. Dorner, *History of Protestant Theology* (Edinburgh: T. and T. Clark, 1871), II, 120-140.

35. Fidelity to the Lutheran confessions understood historically, exposition of the Bible, not as a compendium of verbally-inspired proof texts, but as witness to God's redemptive activity in history *(Heilsgeschichte),* and the affirmation of the personal, inner experience of new-birth and justification by faith as the controlling principle of systematic theology were hallmarks of "Erlangen Theology." See Heick, II, 203-216, and "Erlangen Schule," *Religion in Geschichte und Gegenwart,* 3rd edition, II, 566-567.

36. See F. Bente, "Vorwort," *Lehre und Wehre,* L (January, 1904), 14.

37. *The Lutheran Companion,* December 26, 1914; cited in Arden, *Augustana Heritage,* p. 285. It is interesting that Sodergren in 1914 was using theological vocabulary popular in the 1960s; he wrote of the God of the "gaps"!

38. General Synod, *Minutes . . . 1913*, pp. 150 f.; and General Council, *Minutes . . . 1911*, p. 228. Cited in Meuser, "North American Lutheranism, 1900-1930," p. 49.

39. For a detailed discussion of the Norwegian Lutheran union movement see Nelson, *The Lutheran Church Among Norwegian-Americans*, II, 183-225.

40. The same invitation went out to the Eielsen Synod (earlier Haugeans who refused to participate in a synodical reorganization in 1876), the Lutheran Brethren, and the Lutheran Free Church. Only the latter responded, saying it was interested in co-operation but not merger.

41. For a detailed discussion of the formation of the United Lutheran Church in America see A. R. Wentz, *A Basic History . . .*, pp. 140-168; 221-239; and 269-285.

42. *Ibid.*, pp. 225-226.

43. See especially J. W. Richard, *The Confessional History of the Lutheran Church* (Philadelphia: Lutheran Publication Society, 1909). Richard, together with Milton Valentine, was fearful of a "repristination" theology.

44. See T. E. Schmauk's comments quoted in George S. Sandt, *Theodore Emanuel Schmauk, D.D., L.L.D., A Biographical Sketch* . . . (Philadelphia: United Lutheran Publication House, 1921), pp. 176-178; cf. pp. 133-136.

45. For an account of development in the General Synod, see A. R. Wentz, *A Basic History . . .*, pp. 230-232.

46. *Ibid.*, p. 272.

47. *Ibid.*, p. 273.

48. For further details on the formation of the church see the account in *The Lutheran World Almanac . . . 1921* (New York: National Lutheran Council, 1920), pp. 76-83; and ULCA, *Minutes . . . 1918*, pp. 37-42, 63-68, 90-92.

49. For Augustana's position see Arden, *Augustana Heritage*, pp. 157-159.

50. The Synodical Conference was begun by the Missouri and Ohio Synods because the General Council was considered too lax. For the next decade it was the largest general association of Lutherans in North America. Wentz, *Basic History . . .*, pp. 217-218.

51. This brief account of the Wisconsin Synod is based on *ibid.*, pp. 262-268. Cf. John Philipp Koehler, *The History of the Wisconsin Synod* (edited and with introduction by Leigh D. Jordahl; Mosinee, Wis.; The Protestant Conference, 1970).

52. The most recent account of the National Lutheran Council is F. K. Wentz, *Lutherans in Concert* (Minneapolis: Augsburg Publishing House, 1968); Wentz uses this expression. See p. 95.

53. In 1915 J. A. Bergh of the United Norwegian Lutheran Church addressed the Illinois Conference of the Augustana Synod and proposed a federation of all American Lutheran bodies. C. O. Solberg pointed to the relationship between the General Council and the Augustana Synod as facilitating the federation of all Lutheran groups. See *The United Lutheran*, VIII (June 18 and July 30, 1915), 393, 520-521. In addition the Joint Synod of Ohio proposed an all-Lutheran federation. R. C. Wolf, *Documents of Lutheran Unity in America* (Philadelphia: Fortress Press, 1966), pp. 285-292.

54. The presidents: T. E. Schmauk, V. G. A. Tressler, M. G. G. Scherer, and H. G. Stub.

55. Wolf, *Documents . . .*, p. 292.

56. Richard C. Wolf, *Lutherans in North America* (Philadelphia: Lutheran Church Press, 1965), pp. 118-119.

57. Wentz, *Lutherans in Concert*, p. 19.

58. "Unionism" was originally a term applied to fellowship between Lutherans and non-Lutherans. As such it was often described as "sinful unionism." Under pressures from the Missouri Synod, however, the term now went beyond its original meaning and was being applied to inter-Lutheran relations.

59. Lauritz Larsen, "Unity," *Lutheran Church Herald*, III (April 1, 1919), 194. Cf. Osborne Hauge, *Lutherans Working Together. A History of the National Lutheran Council* (New York: National Lutheran Council, n.d. [1945?]), pp. 39-40.

60. National Lutheran Council, *Annual Report . . . 1919,* pp. 13-14.

61. *Ibid.,* p. 15. Cf. Hauge, *op. cit.,* pp. 41-42.

62. Stub admits his part in this. See his "Representatives from Eight Lutheran Church Bodies . . . , " *Lutheran Church Herald,* III (March 21, 1919), 180. In a letter to Knubel, Stub reported that certain elements in the NLCA were attacking the NLC. Moreover, the Church Council of the NLCA, having endorsed the organization of the NLC, refused to approve cooperation with other Lutherans in home mission work. Stub wrote, "I hope, my dear Dr. Knubel, that you will now better understand . . . my specific reasons for having advocated strongly the meeting in Chicago on doctrine and practice. If I had not insisted so strongly on this meeting which so many regarded as entirely superfluous, I would have made myself subject to the charge of unionism." Stub-Knubel, 2-20-19, microfilm, Luther Seminary Library, St. Paul.

63. See microfilm copy of minutes in Knubel-Stub Correspondence, Luther Theological Seminary, St. Paul. NLCA representatives were, besides Stub, J. N. Kildahl and C. J. Eastvold.

64. *Ibid.,* p. 13.

65. The original paper is in *ibid.,* pp. 4-8. Cf. H. G. Stub, "Representatives from Eight Lutheran Church Bodies . . . , " *Lutheran Church Herald,* III, 180-182.

66. Joint Committee, *Minutes . . . March 11-13, 1919,* p. 18. The papers by Knubel and H. E. Jacobs were published in *The Lutheran Church Review,* XXXVIII (April, 1919), 187-197, 198-212.

67. Stub later reported Missouri enthusiasm over "The Chicago Theses." Joint Conference on Doctrine and Practice, Chicago, Ill., *Minutes . . . January 27-28, 1920* (microfilm copy, Luther Theological Seminary, St. Paul), p. 19.

68. "A Memorable Event in American Lutheranism," *Lutheran Church Herald,* III (March 25, 1919), 184.

69. This statement is in the Knubel-Stub Correspondence, microfilm copy, Luther Theological Seminary, St. Paul.

70. Knubel was far from satisfied with the Chicago conference. He felt that the Midwest Lutherans were unfair to the ULCA in questioning its Lutheranism. Writing to Stub following the conference he said, "We are not on trial as Lutherans and do not propose that we shall be on trial." Knubel-Stub, 8-26-19. Writing to Schmauk, whose illness kept him from the conference, he remarked that the Joint Synod of Ohio men especially were discourteous; Lenski's outright attack on the ULCA had provoked Knubel's quiet but firm rejoinder. Knubel-Schmauk, 3-18-19.

71. C. M. Jacobs, professor at Philadelphia (Mt. Airy) Lutheran Seminary, Philadelphia, replaced the ailing T. E. Schmauk; C. M. Jacobs, more than any other individual, was to place the ULCA in the general theological tradition of the Erlangen School of von Hoffmann, Frank, *et al.*

72. See Knubel-Stub Correspondence, letter C. M. Jacobs-Knubel, November 29, 1919. Jacobs says to heed Stub's objections would be to remove the heart from "catholicity."

73. Knubel-Stub Correspondence, letter Boe-Knubel, 10-17-19.

74. The minutes of this Joint Conference are in the Knubel-Stub Correspondence, Luther Theological Seminary, St. Paul.

75. The paper, fully recorded in the minutes, was again reworked by C. M. Jacobs for presentation to the 1920 convention of the ULCA at Washington, D.C., where it was adopted as an official policy of the church. ULCA, *Minutes . . . 1920,* pp. 85, 92-101, 449-455. The spirit and purpose of the report, said C. M. Jacobs, grew out of the problems in the history of American Lutheranism. The old General Synod had the habitual attitude of tolerance toward other churches; the General Council, together with most of the rest of American Lutheranism, kept aloof from others. Therefore, in dealing with the problem of catholicity in the church, it was necessary to disregard both of these historical traditions and "endeavor to get down to bed-rock of what is always right and true; to determine, and then to define the principles." C. M. Jacobs, "The

Washington Declaration: An Interpretation," *The Lutheran Church Review*, XL (January, 1921), 1-21.

76. ULCA, *Minutes* . . . *1920*, p. 96.

77. Joint Conference, *Minutes* . . . *January 27-28, 1920*, pp. 18-27. Stub did not mention that two-thirds of the Norwegian Lutheran Church (United Church and Hauge's Synod) had unanimously accepted an "Interpretation" of Article Three which allowed participation in the ecumenical movement. However, his former church, the Norwegian Synod, had accepted the "Interpretation" with the stipulation that it reserved the right to "witness against" cooperative practices. Obviously Stub was now speaking not as president of the NLCA but as a former member of the Norwegian Synod.

78. ULCA, *Minutes* . . . *1920*, p. 454.

79. Stub wrote Knubel in February that he saw little point in pursuing discussions. The Iowa Synod had dropped out of the NLC, Ohio was objecting to "catholicity," the Norwegians were becoming restive, and even Augustana was uncertain. Stub-Knubel, 2-19-20. Stub was being urged by some members of the NLCA to heed the call to catholicity. His own son, J. A. O. Stub, sought earnestly but unsuccessfully to get him to see the Knubel-Jacobs point of view. Letter, Luther B. Dick-Knubel, 3-31-20.

80. See "Brief Statement Concerning Meeting in Chicago, March 11 and 12, 1920," in Knubel-Stub Correspondence, Luther Theological Seminary, St. Paul.

81. ULCA, *Minutes* . . . *1920*, p. 85

82. L. W. Boe, writing to J. A. Aasgaard in 1942, said " . . . the Lord has never permitted it [the NLC] to be only an agency for cooperation in external affairs. Time and again we re-wrote the constitution and regulations . . . to safeguard this line that we arbitrarily set up, only cooperation in externals, but the Lord . . . pushed us across the line every time." Boe-Aasgaard, October 29, 1942. Boe Papers, Archives, St. Olaf College, Northfield, Minn.

83. The definitive account of the steps leading to the merger is Fred Meuser, *The Formation of the American Lutheran Church* (Columbus: The Wartburg Press, 1958).

84. *Ibid.*, pp. 158-159.

85. *Ibid.*, pp. 218-230. The texts of the constitution and the appendix are found on pp. 300-301.

86. C. V. Sheatsley, *The Story of the Formation of the American Lutheran Church* (Columbus: The Lutheran Book Concern, 1930), pp. 33-36.

87. Generally, Lutheran scholars in Germany and Scandinavia had rejected the 17th century idea of verbal inspiration and inerrancy in favor of an emphasis on Scripture as the faithful witness of the early church to the revelation (Word) of God. The first public declaration of this view, which had gradually been received in the ULCA, was made by C. M. Jacobs, "Inaugural Address," *The Lutheran Church Review*, XLVI (July, 1927), 207-225.

88. Meuser, *The Formation of the ALC*, p. 237.

89. It should be recalled the American Protestantism was being rocked by the "Modernist-Fundamentalist Controversy" about this time.

90. For an account see NLCA, *Report* . . . *1926*, pp. 76, 81-83. Cf. Meuser, *The Formation of the ALC*, pp. 238-241.

91. *Ibid.*, p. 238. The "Minneapolis Theses" may be found in G. M. Bruce ed., *The Union Documents* . . . *Evangelical Lutheran Church* (Minneapolis: Church Council of the Evangelical Lutheran Church, 1948), pp. 81-83.

92. For accounts of the colloquy see Meuser, *The Formation of the ALC*, pp. 182-186; and Nelson, *The Lutheran Church Among Norwegian-Americans*, II, 303-306.

93. For an account of the constituting convention see "The American Lutheran Conference," *Lutheran Church Herald*, XIV (November 11, 1930), 1587-1593.

CHAPTER TWO

THE CHURCH IN THE ECONOMIC DEPRESSION

Certain years, like certain uncommon men, etch themselves on the collective memory of mankind. Such a year was 1929. Unerringly that year found its place among those watersheds that almost everyone recalls: A.D. 476, 800, 1066, 1492, 1517, 1776, and 1914. To say that the four decades after 1929 were unusually significant for the church as well as for American society as a whole is scarcely trite.

The Great Depression that followed hard on the heels of the Great Crash of 1929 was, psychologically speaking, traumatic. It was traumatic because the heady optimism of economic prosperity had not prepared men to withstand the pain of economic collapse. It was traumatic, too, because it lasted so long. Surely "good times" were "just around the corner"—thus men whistled as they walked in the dark of depression, little realizing that the end would not come until the economy was energized by lend-lease and defense spending prior to America's entry into World War II.

AMERICA IN DEPRESSION

The depression shook the nation's structure to its depths. One American historian has called it "The Third American Revolution"; that is, 1929 stood alongside 1776 and 1861.[1] This third revolution had a corrosive effect on long-accepted basic institutions, such as the family, the school, and the government. All underwent changes that threatened the stability of society. Many families were demoralized by the necessity of "going on relief"; transient youth "took to the road"; boy and girl tramps added their number to the already large company of adult vagabonds. The Joad family in John Steinbeck's *Grapes of Wrath* illustrated the vicissitudes and disillusionment of dust bowl victims seeking new hope in golden California. Once comfortable and firmly established families experienced the loss of homes, the depletion and exhaustion of resources and credit, and concomitant psychological destitution that threatened the very structure of family life.

School authorities agonized not only over the ravages of malnutrition among children, but also witnessed the narrowing of the tax base upon which schools were dependent for life and growth. This resulted, not unexpectedly, in the deterioration of physical facilities and drastic reduction of academic budgets. More serious were the long-range cultural and psychological wounds that were inflicted by a lowered quality of education. In many instances communities passed the burden of economic loss on to the teachers and the students. One commentator said, "No one will ever be able to calculate the cost to American civilization that resulted from inadequate education . . . during the Great Depression." Leading the list of unemployed among the professions were teachers.[2]

Government itself was threatened. Western Europe, also in the throes of depression, exhibited chaotic political situations. In Germany the Weimar Republic gave way to Hitler's National Socialism; Italy was already in the grip of Mussolini's fascism; and Russia was experiencing the terror of Stalinism. In America some talk of violent overthrow of government was heard, but it was more common for men to express the need of social and economic revolution without incitement to riot.[3] Ten thousand unemployed men demonstrated at the national Capitol in January, 1932, and "the Bonus Army" marched on Washington the same year—the shanty encampment came to be known as "the Shame of Anacostia Flats"—but violence and bloodshed were, for the most part, prevented.[4]

Social, political, and economic change was to come, but it came when a majority of the electorate transferred its loyalty from the Republican Party of Herbert Hoover to the Democratic Party of Franklin Delano Roosevelt. Hoover, the earlier symbol of heroic humanitarianism, became the scapegoat of the depression, shanty-towns and tent cities being dubbed "Hoover Valley" or "Hooverville."

Harry Hopkins, head of the Federal Emergency Relief Administration (FERA) and later the Works Progress Administration (WPA), had voiced an aphorism—"Hunger is not debatable"—which everybody admitted was true, but about which few, if any, did anything. Bankers, business men, politicians, professional and laboring men all seemed helpless before the undebatable hunger that stalked the nation.

It has been difficult for later generations to explain what life was like in the depression. To attempt to communicate the temper of the 30s, even when one's hearers have tried to be sympathetic and attentive, has often produced a sense of bafflement among those for whom the experience is a vivid memory. Perhaps the most one can expect is that exposure to the literature of the time—the novels of the era may be better known than the tragedy out of which they grew—may recreate the mood that swept the nation. An unforgettable picture of the hopeless job hunter has emerged in James T. Farrel's *Studs Lonigan:*

> Studs stepped out of another building. Four straight turn-downs, one right after another. It was about a quarter to three, and disappointment was deep and like a worm inside him. Walking again in the rain, he was afraid, afraid that he was no good, useless, that he would never be able to get anywhere.[5]

This is what Arthur Schlesinger, Jr., meant when he wrote in 1937, "The fog of despair hung over the land." [6]

The marshalling of the total resources of the federal government by Franklin Delano Roosevelt's New Deal began slowly to bring about reform, recovery, and a new outlook. The "depression within a depression" (1937-1938) retarded the new growth, but by the end of the decade the economic gains achieved by the New Deal were outdistanced by the transformation of American industry and agriculture into the "arsenal of democracy." Domestic problems faded in the light of overwhelming international developments.

THE GREAT "KNIFE OF THE DEPRESSION" IN THE CHURCHES

It is against this background that the life of Lutheran churches in America must be seen. How did the Great Depression affect the churches? Was there a "depression of religion" too? Or did despair drive men to their knees? Was there a "revival of religion" in the midst of the economic chaos of the depression?

Regarding the overall effect of the depression on the fiscal status of the churches the oft-quoted phrase of Robert and Helen Lynd was quite as applicable to the Lutheran denominations in particular as it was to all religious groups in general. Writing about their now famous "Middletown," the Lynds said,

> Unlike most socially generated catastrophes, in this case virtually nobody in the community had been cushioned against the blow; the great knife of the depression had cut down impartially through the entire population, cleaving open the lives and hopes of rich as well as poor.[7]

The authors then moved on to analyze the influence of the depression on religious life in Middletown, and concluded that it had been negligible. Whether Middletown's apparent lack of depression-born religious renewal may appropriately be generalized to include Lutheranism is questionable. But it is incontestable that "the knife of depression" had cut deeply into the body of American Lutheranism. The drastic reduction of budgets, the curtailment of missionary and educational enterprises, the general retrenchment in the local and general work of the churches have been abundantly and statistically demonstrated in the annual reports of the various Lutheran bodies.

The painful awareness that the churches were deeply involved in the tragedies that were occurring on all sides is evident from frequent articles appearing in the official denominational periodicals. From the industrial East to the drought-stricken Great Plains the story was the same: gloom and desolation. Almost always, however, the articles and editorials included, not a Polyanna "everything-will-turn-out-all-right" attitude, but an honest appraisal of the difficulties in the situation and appeals for united action in faith and love directed to temporary and permanent relief of the suffering.

The official organ of the United Lutheran Church in America, whose main constituency lived east of the Mississippi River, reflected editorially and otherwise the mood of the most urbanized portion of American Lutheranism. For example, the president of the United Lutheran Synod of New York, Samuel G. Trexler, wrote toward the end of 1932 about the great metropolis:

> The Empire State Building greets me every morning as I enter
> my office. . . . There it stands—a graceful shaft piercing the
> heavens to the height of 1,248 feet. . . . It was conceived in the
> proudest period of the city's history, and . . . makes a story
> . . . of man's mastery over things in such a way that one felt he
> was part of a race of supermen.

After continuing in this vein, Trexler turned to the havoc wrought
by the depression, its shattering of the tower of Babel idealism:

> The two-thirds empty Empire State Building is a symbol of the
> entire city . . . the great tragedy [of which] is that one million
> of her people are out of employment. . . . What of the churches?
> It is always difficult to make themselves felt in the face of such
> great movements, whether of prosperity or depression. . . . The
> churches have gone on quietly. . . . Dealing with the mysterious
> elements of Word and Sacrament, they are doing a work which
> can never be measured in the terms with which New York
> usually speaks. . . . Our own church has been brought out of
> its insular position in recent years by the work of the Inner Mis-
> sion Society, and by the development of other movements which
> bring them closer together.[8]

The reference to the Inner Mission Society suggests the effective social
ministry in urban areas where Lutheran churches cooperated in relief
work under the leadership of men known as experts in this field. S. C.
Michelfelder, later to become identified with the Lutheran World Federation and the World Council of Churches in post-World War II reconstruction, was for many years the resourceful superintendent of the
Lutheran Inner Mission Society of Pittsburgh.[9] Another leader was
G. H. Bechtold, secretary of the Board of Inner Missions of the Lutheran
Ministerium of Pennsylvania. He was among those at the beginning
of the depression whose advice was sought by President Hoover.[10]

One of the more articulate of the men who challenged the churches
to alleviate the suffering of the poor and the unemployed was Ambrose
Hering (d. Jan. 1, 1971). Having served as executive secretary of the
Lutheran Welfare Society of Minneapolis-St. Paul and later as the superintendent of the Lutheran Inner Mission Society of New York, Hering
was in a unique position to analyze and depict some of the tasks that
the depression forced upon churchmen. He soon developed the convic-

tion that the church must move beyond welfare on an individualistic basis to a program of action based on a sense of collective social responsibility. Writing in 1932 out of his New York experiences he dramatized the summons that faced Christians.

> Let no one minimize the critical emergency this winter. . . . About 25,000,000 unemployed and their dependents need aid. Hunger marchers appeal to their bankrupt cities without avail and are clubbed down by police. In Albany, the other day, a tenyear-old child collapsed in school and actually died of starvation. . . . In Pennsylvania miners are keeping their families alive on four cents a day per person. . . . That we are facing "the darkest winter in many years, perhaps in the country's history," is now the sober statement of those who know the facts. . . . Will the Christians of the land share what they have [with] the hungry and naked . . . ? [11]

The following spring (1933) the situation was worse because, according to Hering, the depression was eroding spiritual resources as well. Men and women who came into the Lutheran relief agency were tottering on the edge of nihilism. "What's the use?" one man asked. "I'm through. Others work the racket and get by and I'm no fool." So, why be worried about religious principles? From now on, get what you can any way you can get it. Hunger takes no holiday!

Hering continued his account by relating the story of some formerly well-employed women whom the depression reduced to broken-spirited job hunters. The erosion of morale was illustrated in the following:

> As one of the younger women remarked the other week, "When I wake up, I pull the cover over me and try to sleep again. It occurred to me I might go down some morning and pull the river over me; then I wouldn't have to wake up again."

No part of the continent suffered longer nor more acutely than the Great Plains. It is sometimes forgotten that an agricultural depression antedated the general collapse by almost a decade. Bernhard Ostrolenk, writing in *The New York Times,* has pointed out that while industry boomed, the farmer "met one financial setback after another." Ironically industrial prosperity served only to worsen the plight of the farmer. He found himself forced to pay more for labor and equipment and at the same time received less and less for his products. Ole Swanson's 18-

year-old daughter, according to Ostrolenk, received an annual income of $800.00 as a typist. Her father's toil was rewarded with one-half as much! [12]

Moreover, extreme drought in the 1930s brought unforgettable dust storms, unforgettable, at least, to those who experienced them. On November 12 and 13, 1933, an enormous dust cloud covered an area stretching from Texas in the south to the Dakotas in the north, forming a triangle with its point over Milwaukee, Wisconsin. The sun was hidden and dust penetrated dwellings no matter how tightly sealed. Reports of dust at sea came from ships off the Atlantic coast. A widespread and continued deficiency of rainfall struck the mid-continent with the ferocity of war and revolution.

One of the areas hardest hit was the Upper Midwest. In some respects this was a vast "Lutheran empire," created by the great waves of German and Scandinavian immigrants of the 19th century. The consequences of the depression for many of them, including the second- and third-generation descendants, were delinquent loans, mortgage foreclosures, unpaid taxes, and in some cases, forsaking the homestead and becoming the northern counterpart to John Steinbeck's "Okies" in search of new life on the West Coast. Not all left. Most hung on tenaciously in the dogged hope that "the good earth" would eventually "come back."

The plight of the farmer who sought to remain at his place and also to serve as a loyal member of the local congregation during those desolate years was illustrated by the following "letter to the editor":

> Seven years ago I bought a farm of 240 acres. I made a small payment down and the first few years I was able to make enough so that I could pay my interest and taxes and a little on the principal; but the last two years my income has been so small that I have been unable to pay interest and taxes. . . . We have enough to eat; but could easily use more clothing. My Sunday suit and shoes were bought in 1929 and my overcoat in 1919 and my wife's and children's clothes have been mostly made-over things for many years. . . . With wheat selling at 28 cents a bushel, butterfat at 12 cents a pound, eggs at 10 cents a dozen, turkeys at 16 cents a pound, and cattle and hogs at from 1 to 4 cents a pound you can easily see where a farmer is. . . . There are thousands of farmers in just as bad shape as I am and many much worse.

I write this so that pastors and others who seem to think that there is nothing but willingness and right spirit lacking among our people may see that there are very good reasons why not so much is coming in in donations from our farmers. . . . It is not just miserliness in regard to God's work. It is plain helplessness and no one feels worse about it than the farmers themselves.[13]

The knowledge of such experiences led Hering, who knew both the agricultural Midwest and the industrial East, to urge the church to move beyond individualistic dole. To be sure, relief was desperately needed, but it was no substitute for jobs. Therefore, social and economic planning was imperative. But, he said, "The planned society which this period of business upheaval will unquestionably usher in will need the highest religious idealism. Unrestrained individualism and class privilege must be replaced by an inclusive brotherhood and . . . zest for the common welfare." [14]

A RELIGIOUS DEPRESSION TOO?

The relation of *Christ and Culture,* to use the title of H. Richard Niebuhr's well-known book (New York, 1951), has been a major interest of church historians and theologians and, in these latter days, of sociologists of religion as well. The basic question has been the interaction of church ("religion") and society ("world"). To what extent do church and society influence each other? And if there has been noticeable interaction, has the interplay of impulses and forces resulted in genuinely substantial or merely superficial changes? For generations many writers ignored or paid scant attention to the significance of the religious factor in history. The decisive forces seemed always to be political, economic, military, geographic, but not religious. The last decades have witnessed a welcome change, partly perhaps because church historians themselves have been willing to concede the role of so-called non-religious or non-theological elements in the life of the churches. At all events, the present age has seen a spate of works devoted to the "Christ and Culture" theme.

It is under this rubric that the question raised by Robert T. Handy's essay, "The American Religious Depression, 1925-1935," must be placed.[15] He concluded that there was a general religious as well as economic de-

pression. This era, said Handy, marked the end of "American Protestantism" as a "culture religion" or a "national religion." As far as
the latter was concerned, there seemed to be a striking analogy to the
earlier European experience: the dominance of *Kulturprotestantismus* which
was broken by World War I. The parallel American phenomenon of
virtually identifying Protestantism with culture was likewise shattered,
not by the war, but by the depression a decade later.[16]

As far as the main thesis (that there was a depression of religion) is
concerned, the answer given by Handy was limited to the mainline
Anglo-American Protestant denominations.[17] Since the present study is
centered on American Lutheranism, it must be asked whether the "depression of religion" described above was applicable to the Lutheran
scene. Edward Traill Horn III demonstrated that statistically "a depression of religion" began to appear in the United Lutheran Church as
early as 1925.[18] Using communing membership figures as his criterion
—by itself a questionable standard for measuring depth of spirituality—
he showed that from 1921 (three years after the formation of the United
Lutheran Church) to 1925 the percentage of confirmed members who
communed at least once during the year increased from 74.60 to 75.51.
The next six years witnessed a marked decline; by 1931 the percentage
had dropped to 69.06. Horn said he could only suggest *possible* explana-
tions. They were, first, the corrosive effect of liberalism and secularism;
second, a decline in effective catechetical instruction; and third, "the financial situation," that is, the depression.[19] Although Horn used a different
bench mark from that employed by Handy, the conclusion was remarkably
similar: 1925 marked the beginning of "the religious depression."

Further evidence that the Lutheran churches east of the Mississippi did
indeed experience a "depression of religion," if by that was meant lowered
membership, decreased attendance, and reduced income, was reported by a
historical seminar devoted to this subject and conducted at the Philadelphia Lutheran Seminary.[20] The study indicated that not a few churchmen expressed the belief that the depression would produce a spiritual
awakening. Earlier depressions (1854-1859, 1873-1879, 1893-1897) had been
accompanied by "revivals" of religion.[21] Here it should be noted paren-
thetically that "revivals" were a religious pattern confined almost exclusively to the "Anglo-American Protestant" tradition. Religious renewal
was customarily viewed in terms of the American "revival" phenomenon,

which, since the Great Awakening, had become a way of life in the "American Protestant" community. When one spoke of religious rebirth and renewal, the image that popped into one's mind was that of the revival.[22] Thus when churchmen in the early 30s expressed the hope that men would be "driven to God" by the depression, they were in reality reflecting their unconscious but mistaken assumption that the "Anglo-American Protestant" tradition was still dominant on the American religious scene.[23]

The Philadelphia seminar report had implied that not a few Lutherans likewise saw a causal relationship between irreligion and depression. A good illustration of this was the preaching often heard on the well-known radio broadcast, "The Lutheran Hour." Walter Maier's voice called the nation to repentance and assured his listeners that all would be well if America turned to Christ.[24] Maier, of course, was not the only one who spoke in this manner. When Ambrose Hering pleaded with the National Lutheran Council to deal realistically with the role of the church in public life, Ralph H. Long, the council's executive director, replied that he had no great confidence in resolutions and conferences. He was not sure that it was the business of the church to involve itself in the public issues. He wrote:

> I have before me a special letter from the Babson report in which it is stated, that "Every economic event of history has proved that the right way is Jesus' way. . . . The cause of the present depression was that the people lost the spirit of service during the years of prosperity. . . . " I am fully convinced that this hits the nail on the head and that no lasting remedy can be found until we get down to . . . fundamental truths. . . . As long as human selfishness is allowed to go unchecked and the love of Christ does not constrain the hearts of men, we are going to have difficulty.[25]

Long's favorable reference to the Babson Report[26] indicates that a theologically based social ethic was glaringly absent. Both Maier and Long, together with all those who moved within the cause-effect continuum (irreligion leads to depression, depression leads to revival, revival leads to prosperity) revealed that prominent American Lutherans did not understand the implications of their own theology for social ethics.

It was this kind of "religious" thinking that blinded many well-meaning churchmen to the massive social ethical problems with which the depression confronted the church. To this subject we will need to return later and show how the churches were gradually awakened to the nature of the questions that faced them. In any case, all simplistic judgments about the relation of religion to the depression ought to be viewed with a measure of skepticism. That there was a religious depression of sorts alongside the economic depression is, as we have seen, demonstrable. But much closer to the realities of the situation was the observation that those "church historians and sociologists of religion who have tried to draw a close parallel between the two depressions have been frustrated by such a wealth of evidence that a direct and intimate correlation simply will not hold up." [27]

We must conclude, nevertheless, that whether or not the "religious depression" in Lutheranism was a profound erosion of spiritual life, there was an undeniable statistical depression. The seminar study, mentioned above, though confined to the area east of the Mississippi, produced conclusions that were generally applicable to the whole of American Lutheranism. All church bodies experienced a loss of income. And economic loss meant a retrenchment in home and world missions and a cutback in the support of church-related educational institutions. Unemployment and reduced personal incomes meant late marriages and a falling birth rate. These circumstances, in turn, were reflected in parochial statistics on baptisms, confirmations, and church school enrollments.[28]

When one has admitted "the statistical depression," especially as it was related to the economic disabilities of the churches, one must be aware that not all statistics reflected decline. In some portions of the nation church and communion attendance rose steadily. Church sponsored charities and social welfare programs were extended. Perhaps most significant of all was the appearance during this period of numerous new "religious" activities which, though not consciously calculated to produce "revival" or even to counter a depression of religion, nevertheless did provide certain spiritual resources and a deepening of theological concern (as, for example, in the area of Christian social ethics). In many instances, no doubt, Christian commitments also were developed and strengthened and the "religious activities" that appeared were in a sense a reflection of genuine spirituality. Before considering this possibility, however, it is necessary to note the effects of the depression in certain specific areas of church work.

PARA-DEPRESSION TRENDS AND EVENTS

Periodicals and reports of the member bodies in the two Lutheran constellations—the National Lutheran Council and the Synodical Conference —exhibited the gloom that had settled on the churches by 1930. The events of 1931-1933 served only to exacerbate the general atmosphere of desperation.[29]

On the parish level many congregations were struggling with huge debts brought on by overbuilding in the late 20s. Some church councils and boards of trustees, faced with staggering interest payments and budget deficits, looked covetously at funds designated for extra-congregational benevolences and missions. The temptation to "borrow" such funds to meet local expenses loomed as a moral crisis and elicited warnings from church officials. Typical of the situation was "An Official Appeal" which was sent to the congregations of the United Lutheran Church in mid-summer, 1933:

> The serious financial conditions which have steadily grown worse in the Church since the beginning of the "depression," reached a climax with all of the Boards and Agencies when the "bank holiday" was suddenly proclaimed. . . . Yet we dare not go into a panic, nor entertain the thought of disaster. . . . Because even the individual feels these same conditions in his personal life, we are in grave danger of losing our sense of corporate responsibility and of following the primitive instinct of "every one for himself." That we have already yielded far to that instinct is apparent in the most deplorable fact that many congregations have deliberately taken money contributed and designated for the benevolences of the United Lutheran Church in America and have used it for local expenses. . . . Simply to hold funds that are desperately needed is bad enough, but that anyone in the Church would divert designated funds from the purpose for which they were given is almost unbelievable, because it is a deliberate violation of a most sacred trust.[30]

Illustrative of the kind of difficulty faced by all church bodies in the National Lutheran Council and the Synodical Conference was the chaotic condition of the home mission department of the Norwegian Lutheran Church of America (Evangelical Lutheran Church after 1946). The department had carried on an ambitious but ill-conceived program during the previous decade. Through unwise budgeting it had distributed over $300,000 more than its income during the "boom years." [31] Since other departments had similarly incurred deficits, it meant that the church body, which had almost unlimited bank credit in Minneapolis (where the church headquarters were located), was entering the 30s with fiscal shortages that would multiply its sorrows during the stern years of the depression.[32]

One of the first steps taken to remove the imbalance was the curtailment of administrative staff and the transfer of its duties to the president of the church body, J. A. Aasgaard.[33] The significance of this depression-initiated action may have been lost upon the church, struggling for life in the midst of the necessities of the moment, but in time the long-range implications became apparent. Other churches, too, were being forced by the pressure of economic circumstances to accept an increasing centralization of authority. For example, later research pointed out that the Missouri Synod, long an exponent of congregational autonomy, began, perhaps unconsciously, to alter its traditional polity during the depression era.[34] Likewise the Augustana Synod's new and energetic president, P. O. Bersell, in 1935 chose to make Minneapolis the administrative center of the synod. The second step was the appointment of department executives who were to work closely with the synodical president. In connection with this a vigorous home mission program, which became a stimulus to other churches, got under way by 1939. A third step was the creation and organization of several service departments or agencies, such as stewardship and finance, youth activities, audio-visual aids, and architecture. Finally, the move to centralization was seen in the struggle which resulted in the separation of Augustana Seminary from Augustana College, thus bringing the seminary under synodical control and support and making the college a regional institution.[35]

A positive effect of the economic squeeze was its undoubted influence in furthering cooperation among the various Lutheran home mission boards. The building of altar against altar by competing church bodies was a "Christian" luxury whose true nature was unmasked by the contemporary exigencies. Competition gave way to some unrefined comity agreements whereby Lutheran churches were expected, as a matter of courtesy, to confer with one another before beginning mission work in a given locality. This concern eventuated in the organization of an informal inter-Lutheran group known as the Lutheran Home Missions Council of

America (1931) representing all major Lutheran denominations outside the Synodical Conference.[36] This council became the forerunner of the National Lutheran Council's Commission on American Missions and the Regional Home Mission Committee during World War II.[37]

This action implied the recognition of at least two developments. One was the transcending of ethnic boundaries in doing home mission work. Hitherto most of the missionary outreach, especially in the Midwest, had been determined by national origins. Danish Lutherans sought out Danish immigrants; the Germans, Germans; the Swedes, Swedes.[38] It was now recognized that Americanization had proceeded to the point where ethnic concerns had to give way to confessional ones. That is to say, home missions meant "seeking and saving" diaspora *Lutherans*. This did not mean, however, that efforts were confined only to reaching unchurched Lutherans —the membership lists of many mission congregations of these years were evidence of this—but it did mean that when decisions were made to enter a new field, one of the main factors was the percentage of unchurched *Lutherans* living in the area which had been surveyed.[39]

The second implication of the comity arrangement, at least for churches of the National Lutheran Council, was the tacit acceptance of the Lutheranism of other Lutheran bodies. If one church body could entrust a mission field to another, it was clear, despite occasional rumblings and huffings and puffings, that the churches recognized one another as one in the faith. Although formal pulpit and altar fellowship was slow to arrive—more than 30 years were to elapse before this was achieved—the building of competitive Lutheran churches was to some extent eliminated. The exception to this was, of course, the Missouri Synod and other members of the Synodical Conference. Shunning cooperation because they believed "God-pleasing unity in doctrine and practice" was not present among the churches of the National Lutheran Council, the Missouri Synod felt under no obligation to abide by decisions reached by other bodies. Despite the financial rigors of the 1930s, the Missouri Synod continued an active home mission program. An oversupply of candidates for ordination [40] gave the synod an army of available, if inexperienced, missionaries. President Behnken, writing in his autobiography, said, "The Districts were urged to find ways and means to keep the candidates active in church work. Many accepted work at a mere subsistence pay, some as low as $25 a month." [41]

The depression forced the churches to examine their educational program on all levels: parochial schools, residence high schools or academies, junior colleges, senior colleges, and seminaries. One of the recurring denominational phenomena during the 19th century had been the establishment of church schools on all levels to undergird the faith of the youth and to provide a training ground for pastors and teachers. The Lutheran churches were no exception to the rule.

It is a well-known fact that the largest system of parochial schools outside Roman Catholicism has been maintained by the Lutheran Church–Missouri Synod and other members of the Synodical Conference. In some bodies where there were few Christian day schools in the parishes, it was not uncommon to find church operated boarding schools or academies.[42] The academy movement was especially popular at about the turn of the century, one of the reasons being that the villages and towns of the time often lacked well-equipped and adequately staffed public high schools. In all of the churches junior colleges, senior colleges, and seminaries had sprung up across the continent in those regions where there was a relatively high Lutheran population. In the course of the years, schools were founded in Pennsylvania, New York, Virginia, the Carolinas, Ohio, Indiana, Illinois, Missouri, Wisconsin, Iowa, Minnesota, the Dakotas, Kansas, Nebraska, Alabama, Texas, Oregon, Washington, and California in the United States; and Ontario, Saskatchewan, and Alberta in Canada.[43]

This far-flung educational program was drastically shaken by the depression. Although the Missouri Synod parochial school system survived the storm, one after another of the remaining Lutheran academies (many had been casualties of earlier years) were forced to close their doors.[44] In like manner junior colleges began to fall. Only a few strategically located and well-supported institutions continued through and beyond the depression. The annual reports of denominational boards of higher education from 1932 to 1936 showed that all the major Lutheran bodies were staggering under the burden of supporting their colleges. Each church authorized a program of consolidation or discontinuance of its schools.[45] Some colleges which previously had admitted only male students became coeducational in order to survive the depression, for example, Luther, Decorah, Iowa; Roanoke, Salem, Virginia; Wagner, Staten Island, New York; and Gettysburg, Gettysburg, Pennsylvania. Within the Missouri Synod one of the most significant moves was the opening of junior colleges to other than pre-seminarians, including coeds.[46]

On the seminary level, those churches with numerous theological schools faced major problems of consolidation and/or discontinuance of institutions, and this included the United Lutheran Church and the American Lutheran Church. Although the Missouri Synod, which had two seminaries, considered the closing of its "practical" seminary at Springfield, Illinois, it survived the fiscal wars and remained to flourish in the post-World War II era.[47]

The United Lutheran Church, made up of approximately 30 district synods, was operating an excessive number of seminaries, some very small and poorly supported. As early as 1932 the church sought to face the "seminary problem" that had been bequeathed to it by the merger of 1918. By consolidation it was hoped to reduce the number from thirteen to seven: one in the East, one in the Midwest, one on the Western Plains, one in the South, one on the Pacific coast and two in Canada.[48] The objectives of the 1932 program were still unrealized in 1940. Nevertheless, budgetary realities overcame local loyalties in three instances, leaving the church with 10 rather than 13 theological schools.[49]

The American Lutheran Church, born at the outset of the depression, found itself in financial straits at the very beginning. This was especially reflected in its educational program. In 1932 the church authorized its Board of Trustees to inaugurate a "Pay-As-You-Receive" plan to avoid deficits. At the same time it announced an educational policy that regarded its schools primarily as institutions for training ministers, teachers, missionaries, and other church workers. Only as funds permitted would the program be expanded to embrace training for leadership in "other walks of life." Meanwhile junior and senior colleges were closed or merged with other institutions. The two seminaries, however, continued as before at Dubuque, Iowa (Wartburg) and Columbus, Ohio (Capital).[50]

One of the most significant seminary developments during the depression was the expansion of the theological curriculum to include a year of "internship" or practical training between the second and final years, thus producing a four-year program. The Missouri Synod, the Augustana Synod, and the Norwegian Lutheran Church of America were the pioneers in this successful venture. Within the Missouri Synod the internship or "vicarage" was not originally conceived as a part of the theological training of ministers, but as an emergency measure to delay the graduation of students and allow for the absorption of a ministerial oversupply.[51] In the

Augustana Synod and the Norwegian Church seminaries (Rock Island and St. Paul), the decision to add the internship as a year of practical parish work was a calculated curricular addition. At Augustana Seminary the change took place in 1933; at Luther Theological Seminary, in 1935 (authorized in 1934).[52] It is noteworthy that 20 or 25 years later other denominational and interdenominational seminaries saw the value of the Lutheran innovation and adopted it with alterations to fit their circumstances. Today the American Association of Theological Schools recognizes that some form of internship or clinical education is an invaluable part of ministerial training.

SIGNS OF NEW LIFE

We have already dealt with the question of a religious depression alongside the economic depression. Although it is virtually impossible to establish any causal connection between the two, it was quite clear during this era that American Lutheranism witnessed the emergence of numerous phenomena that, from one point of view, could be called "signs of new life."

There was, in the first place, an unmistakable theological renaissance and a new ecumenical awareness. We shall return to these topics in the next chapter, but they should be mentioned here as having surfaced in American Lutheranism during the depression years. Many historians in the church would be willing to call them signs of new life.

In the second place, despite a generally acknowledged "statistical depression," the Lutherans in some ways were the exception proving the rule. Kinchloe's *Memorandum,* referred to above, mentions the probability that conservative churches, such as the Lutheran, fared better than the liberal British-American denominations. He says, "If it were certain that no factors other than the type of theology were relevant, these data would tend to bear out the theory stated." [53] The following membership graph (reproduced by Kincheloe) tended to support this assertion, especially in American Protestantism.

The graph shows that growth of Lutheran churches was proportionately greater than that recorded in British-American Protestantism and Roman Catholicism, but less dramatic than that among those labeled "Fundamentalist Groups." Among the Lutherans it was the more conservative Missouri Synod, according to Kincheloe, which fared best in membership

CHURCH MEMBERSHIP FOR SELECTED DENOMINATIONS: UNITED STATES
1920-1935

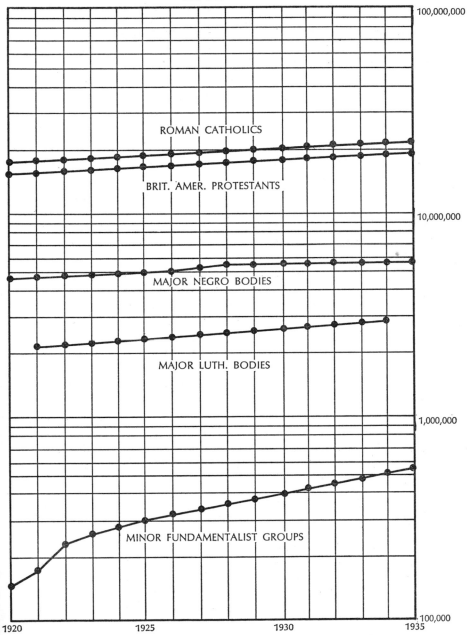

ROMAN CATHOLICS

BRIT. AMER. PROTESTANTS

MAJOR NEGRO BODIES

MAJOR LUTH. BODIES

MINOR FUNDAMENTALIST GROUPS

100,000,000

10,000,000

1,000,000

100,000

1920   1925   1930   1935

From S. C. Kincheloe, **Research Memorandum on Religion in the Depression.** (New York: Social Science Research Council, 1937), p. 7.

growth and financial support.[54] This last observation, however, was hardly borne out by parochial and denominational reports. The statistical summaries in the *Lutheran World Almanac* (1929-1937) and the denominational yearbooks from 1929 to 1941 showed virtually no differences as far as the major Lutheran bodies were concerned. There was a steady but not phenomenal growth in the United Lutheran, Augustana, Norwegian Lutheran, American Lutheran, and Missouri churches. All groups exhibited almost exactly the same level of financial support.[55] The significant thing to be observed was the fact that Lutheran people gave *proportionately* more money in the straitened circumstances of 1931-1935 than in the relatively affluent years of 1929 and the 40s and 50s.[56]

A third area of "religious" activity was the ministry to youth and students. Although this ministry was in the doldrums during the 1960s, it is no exaggeration to say it was flourishing in the 30s. The depression-burdened churches found encouragement in the vitality of the youth movement as represented in the Luther Leagues of the National Lutheran Council bodies and the Walther League of the Missouri Synod.[57] The Luther Leagues of the Augustana Synod and the Norwegian Lutheran Church, to use two examples, sponsored "international" conventions (delegates from Canada gave the leagues at least a bi-national character) that attracted thousands of youth. The continent-wide youth conventions, begun in the decade after World War I, mushroomed in the depression era and continued with annual growth to contribute to the "revival of the 50s."

Closely associated with the Luther League conventions was the Choral Union which drew youth choirs from congregations, schools, and colleges. Choirs with international reputation, such as the St. Olaf College Choir of Northfield, Minnesota, contributed their musical artistry to such assemblies. In 1931, for example, the Young People's Luther League convention, held in Chicago, drew a total of 7,000 delegates. The concluding concert, presented in the Chicago Stadium, drew 15,000 listeners. In 1935 a similar convention at Sioux Falls, South Dakota, drew an estimated attendance of 60,000.[58]

Closely allied with the Luther League was the so-called "Bible Camp Movement." Begun in 1927 in California, it was not until the next decade that the movement acquired support in large numbers.[59] By 1934 these summer church camps in the Norwegian Lutheran Church alone had grown to 40 with an annual attendance of about 10,000 young people between the ages of 15 and 19.

The program of the youth movement was directed largely to the cultivation and deepening of spiritual life through Bible study, music, service, counselling, and recreation.[60] Criticisms were sometimes levelled against the movement, but on the whole its influence seemed to be salutary.[61]

The churches also saw their campus ministries develop and prosper during the depression. Though there was a pre-history, including the inter-denominational Student Christian Movement, the YMCA and YWCA, and the Student Volunteer Movement, the specifically Lutheran work on college and university campuses got under way in the 20s through the initiative of the United Lutheran Church. In 1920 this body listed 21 clergymen as "student pastors" and stated that "The religious life of the student should be centered in the Christian congregation." [62] Campus student centers for study and social life were set up but they were not to be substitute congregations. The students were to take their place in nearby Lutheran churches. As A. Henry Hetland comments, "Perhaps it was a declaration of independence vis-a-vis Y type student movements and those denominations which sought to channel that momentum into student centers." Full time student pastors, without responsibilities for a parish or developing one, arrived on the campuses in 1937. The American Lutheran Conference, formed in 1930, added its strength to that of the United Lutheran Church in 1938 by calling F. A. Schiotz to direct its student ministry.[63] Cooperative student service had already been achieved in 1935-1936 and joint planning meetings of the two staffs were held from 1939 until the two bodies transferred their student work to the National Lutheran Council which created a Commission on Student Service in 1945.[64]

Although voices were raised for student work in the Missouri Synod as early as 1926, it was not until 1938 that approval was given and money appropriated. R. W. Hahn was called as the first full time executive secretary for "Student Welfare Work" in 1940. By the late 40s it was not uncommon for Missouri student pastors to cooperate unofficially with their counterparts of the National Lutheran Council campus ministry.[65] The synod as such, however, was extremely sensitive to the implied "unionism" of such cooperation. In fact, even when the Lutheran Church—Missouri Synod joined the Lutheran Council in the United

States of America (1966), one of the areas in which cooperation could not yet be condoned was student service. The Lutheran Church in America and The American Lutheran Church found it necessary to continue the old joint campus ministry of the National Lutheran Council under an organization apart from the new Lutheran Council. This was known as the National Lutheran Campus Ministry. On July 1, 1969, the administration of the latter was transferred to the Lutheran Council. The Missouri Synod continued its separate campus ministry through its Board of Mission,[66] but coordinated its work with that of other bodies through the Division of Educational Services of the council. The complete consolidation of campus ministry among Lutherans is awaiting the establishment of pulpit and altar fellowship between the Missouri Synod and the Lutheran Church in America and the resolution of structural differences in the agencies responsible for student service.

Closely allied with the official campus ministry of the churches was the Lutheran student movement that, like the campus ministry, had its beginnings in the 20s but began to prosper during the depression years. Organized in May, 1922, at Toledo, Ohio, the Lutheran Student Association of America became in time the local campus fellowship through which the student ministry of the National Lutheran Council churches was carried out.[67] The first president, C. Walter Young, a student at Northwestern University, was unable to complete his term because of an assignment in Japan. At the first national convention, held at Augustana College, Rock Island, Illinois, in April, 1923, Young was succeeded by the second vice-president, F. A. Schiotz, a student at St. Olaf College. The convention authorized two "official visitors" to attend the Lutheran World Convention which was organized that same year in Eisenach, Germany. It is of some interest that the "voice of youth" sought expression at a world assembly of churchmen in 1923 and that one of the two voices belonged to Frank N. D. Buchman, who ten years later had become world famous as the founder of the Oxford Group Movement.[68]

The student movement in American Lutheranism, as in broader ecumenical circles, was the seedbed for numerous future leaders of the church. F. A. Schiotz, the second president of LSAA, became in 1954 the president of The Evangelical Lutheran Church, in 1960 the president of The American Lutheran Church, and in 1963 the president of the Lutheran

World Federation. The late Carl E. Lund-Quist (d. 1965), the only LSAA president to hold office for two terms, became the well-known and highly respected General Secretary of the Lutheran World Federation during that organization's years of immense growth and influence, the decade of the 50s. Other prominent "alumni" of the LSAA include Donald Heiges, president of Gettysburg Lutheran Seminary; Kent Knutson, president (1970) of The American Lutheran Church; and Albert E. Anderson, manager of Augsburg Publishing House.

Two national student conferences were held in the 20s but the depression prevented similar assemblies until 1936 when the first national "Ashram" was held.[69] This continued to be a feature of the Lutheran Student Association of America until the 1960s.

Although not a few Missouri Synod students found their way into the LSAA, the synod itself felt it desirable to organize its own student "social" association, the Gamma Delta, in 1934.[70] Numerous attempts to unite the two student organizations were finally realized in the summer of 1969 when the Lutheran Student Movement was born.[71]

The search for spiritual resources took many additional forms in the decade of the depression. All major church bodies were engaged in extensive efforts to nurture and cultivate piety, to deepen the motives for the stewardship of money, and to foster a sense of mission and evangelism.

The Oxford Group Movement or Buchmanism, referred to above, had a short but striking appeal to many individuals because its stated goal was "a Christian revolution, whose concern is vital Christianity. Its aim is a new social order under the dictatorship of the Holy Spirit." [72] In the context of the depression, this sounded a note of hope and promised the kind of renewal that many were looking for. However, the movement soon received severe criticism as being theologically syncretistic and chameleon-like.[73] It took on the religious and theological hues of the region it visited. In Lutheran Scandinavia, where it was popular in the 30s, it received a Lutheran coloration. In pluralistic America with its multicolored religious mosaic the chameleon either suffered a nervous breakdown or lost any cross-centered theology it may have picked up in Europe. Its famous "Four Absolutes" soon were seen as being primarily ethical, the moral categorical imperative of Kant. In time the Oxford Group changed its name to "Moral Rearmament" and no longer sought "to make Christians out of Episcopalians and Lutherans." [74] Nevertheless, its short-lived acceptance in some Lutheran circles indicated at least that there was a search for spiritual resources at this time.

More acceptable and consequently farther-reaching were programs to cultivate family piety by publishing aids to home devotions, and to reach via radio not only those already won for the gospel but vast numbers unrelated to the church. Outstanding leadership in the former sphere was the pioneer work done by the Synod of the Northwest of the United Lutheran Church. Its booklet, *The Word in Season,* originated in 1933; by the end of the depression it had a circulation of about three-quarters of a million. Its success was directly and indirectly responsible for similar ventures in other church bodies, Lutheran and non-Lutheran.[75]

Most noteworthy were the successful attempts to use nation-wide radio broadcasting for evangelistic purposes.[76] Walter A. Maier, professor of Old testament at Concordia Seminary, St. Louis, was the originator and for a long time the well-known preacher of "The Lutheran Hour." Maier felt that the National Broadcasting Company's "National Radio Pulpit," donated by the network for religious services, was an inadequate witness to evangelical and authentic Christianity.[77] Maier's argument that the NBC should donate time to the Missouri Synod because it was not a member of the Federal Council naturally fell on deaf ears. Since NBC policy did not permit sale of time for religious purposes, Maier turned to the Columbia Broadcasting System, which at the moment was planning to launch its "Church of the Air." Maier, finding CBS willing to sell time, asked the Missouri Synod's "Lutheran Laymen's League" to underwrite his venture.[78] Assurances were received and "The Lutheran Hour" went on the air October 2, 1930. CBS officials were overwhelmed by the immediacy of the favorable response. An estimated five million listeners supplied more "fan mail" than the top-rated entertainment shows during the first weeks of Maier's experiment. At the end of nine months the CBS was receiving more response to "The Lutheran Hour" than to any other program. Despite this huge success, the deepening economic depression forced the temporary discontinuance of the program.

Meanwhile, the NBC had broadened its "National Radio Pulpit" to include Lutherans. Hitherto it had featured such men as S. Parkes Cadman, Harry Emerson Fosdick, and Ralph W. Sockman, all of whom represented the "liberal" wing of Anglo-American Protestantism. NBC officials agreed that the voice of Lutheranism ought not be excluded and invited the president of the United Lutheran Church to conduct what was first known as "The Knubel Hour." [79] Joined later by Paul E. Scherer, pastor of Holy Trinity Church, New York City, Knubel in time relinquished his place in the "National Radio Pulpit" to his colleague.[80] Scherer's sermons, though never so popular as those heard on "The Lutheran Hour," received a wide and sympathetic hearing.

When, as we have seen, "The Lutheran Hour" found it necessary for financial reasons to suspend its ties with CBS, the broadcasting company picked up its original plan to produce its own "Columbia Church of the Air." [81] Turning to the National Lutheran Council for assistance in selecting Lutheran speakers, CBS began a cordial relationship that was to last for many years. This came about largely through the efforts of Ralph H. Long, the council's executive director. Puzzled by CBS's failure to use the expertise and experience of Walter Maier, Long arranged that the Missouri Synod should at least be represented among those appearing on the "Church of the Air," and he proposed Maier's name. CBS demurred because it felt that "someone less aggressive and pugnacious should take over this hour." When Maier learned of this he refused Long's insistent invitation and began a new and vigorous campaign to resume "The Lutheran Hour" broadcasts on another network.[82] With the help of his personal friend, William S. Knudsen, president of General Motors, Maier succeeded in getting "The Lutheran Hour" back on the air in February, 1935. In a short time it was being carried nationally by the Mutual Broadcasting System. Although Maier died in 1950, the broadcasts that he made world-wide carried on into the 70s.

The liturgical movement of the 30s was, from one point of view, another depression-born spiritual resource. Although thousands of people inside and outside the churches were helped spiritually by the religious activities mentioned above, not a few were unhappy with the pietistic and individualistic trends that were to the fore. In some circles, therefore, men sought spiritual authority and certainty by emphasizing the liturgical and sacramental tradition that Lutheranism shared in part, at least, with the pre-Reformation church. This had been revived in the 17th century, eroded in the 18th, and romanticized in the 19th. Faced with 20th century secularism and the threat to traditional Lutheranism posed by post-World War I liberalism, ecumenism, and depression-born religious pragmatism, numerous pastors and laymen in *all* of American Lutheranism looked to the liturgical revival for spiritual renewal and corporate expression of devotional life.[83] The Lutheran interest was soon focused in two liturgical associations—the Society of St. James (chiefly in the Missouri Synod) and the Society of St. Ambrose (chiefly in the United Lutheran Church). These "high churchmen" emphasized a liturgical use of the church year, the observance of church festivals, the role of sacramental life (baptism as incorporation into the body of Christ and communion as nurturing life in the body), the revival of canonical prayer hours, the practice of private confession and absolution, the use of proper vestments (cassock, surplice, stole, and eucharistic garments), and the fostering of liturgical or Gregorian music. Both societies reached their peaks in the 1930s and then gradually declined during the next decade. Their influence, however, was far-reaching even among those who criticized their enthusiasms as being thinly-veiled leanings towards Anglo-Catholicism or even Roman Catholicism.[84]

Illustrative of this influence was the fact that most Lutheran bodies saw a rather wide use of cassock, surplice, and stole already in the 30s. Likewise, the desire for a common liturgy had many and prominent proponents in all branches of the church.[85] The movement of liturgical renewal which evidenced such vigor in the decade of the depression was to continue with varying degrees of strength and a variety of emphases for the next 30 years.

In conclusion, one can say that North American Lutheranism, like all other denominations, had been subjected to a profound shock and severe trial by the depression. Certain weaknesses, especially theological, ethical, and ecumenical, were laid bare. What these weaknesses were and how the churches moved to meet them will form a part of subsequent chapters. But there was strength as well. If Anglo-American Protestantism lost "its sense of being the national religion" (Handy), Lutheranism, like Roman Catholicism, became more self-conscious and aggressive. It probed and publicized its own theological and religious heritage with an eye to relating it to the American scene. Already a new interpretation of the Lutheran tradition was in the making. The reorientation that resulted and slowly became visible was to have abiding effects on the church's stance vis-à-vis the ecumenical movement and American society as a whole in the future.

NOTES

1. Carl N. Degler, *Out of Our Past. The Forces that Shaped Modern America* (New York: Harper Colophon Books, 1962), p. 379.

2. David A. Shannon, ed., *The Great Depression* (Englewood Cliffs, N.J.: Prentice-Hall, Inc., 1960), pp. 92-93. Shannon tells the story of the depression in terms of the people who experienced it by assembling contemporary accounts: news articles, case histories, transcription of Senate hearings, etc. Numerous other helpful books on the depression are available. Some of those consulted: Stanley Coben and Forest G. Hill, eds., *American Economic History. Essays in Interpretation* (Philadelphia: J. B. Lippincott Co., 1966); John Kenneth Galbraith, *The Great Crash* (Boston: Houghton Mifflin Co., 1961); the two works by Robert S. Lynd and Helen Merrel Lynd, *Middletown. A Study in American Culture* (New York: Harcourt Brace and Co., 1929) and *Middletown in Transition. A Study in Cultural Conflicts* (New York: Harcourt Brace and Co., 1937), hereinafter referred to as *Middletown in Transition;* Broadus Mitchell, *Depression Decade* (New York: Rinehart and Co., Inc., 1947); and Arthur M. Schlesinger Jr., *The Age of Roosevelt: The Politics of Upheaval* (Boston: Houghton Mifflin Co., 1960), hereinafter referred to as *Age of Roosevelt.* Volume I is entitled *The Crisis of the Old Order* (1957).

3. Schlesinger, *Age of Roosevelt*, pp. 96-207.

4. Mitchell, *Depression Decade*, pp. 108-110. Bricks were thrown at the police, and two veterans were killed.

5. Cited in Harvey Swados, ed., *The American Writer and the Great Depression*, The American Heritage Series (Indianapolis: The Bobbs-Merrill Co., 1966), p. 260. Hereinafter referred to as *American Writer*.

6. *The Crisis of the Old Order*, (*The Age of Roosevelt*, Vol. 1), (Boston: Houghton Mifflin Co., 1957), p. 3. Cited in Swados, ed., *American Writer*, p. xii.

7. Lynd and Lynd, *Middletown in Transition*, p. 295.

8. Samuel G. Trexler, "The Church Looks at New York City," *The Lutheran*, (December 15, 1932), 3.

9. O. M. Norlie and G. L. Kieffer, eds., *The Lutheran World Almanac and Encyclopedia 1931-1933* (New York: The National Lutheran Council, 1932), p. 89.

10. *Ibid.*

11. Ambrose Hering, "Again God Is to Be Found in a Stable," *The Lutheran*, December 15, 1932, pp. 8-9.

12. Bernard Ostrolenk, "The Farmer's Plight," *The New York Times*, September 25, 1932. Cited in Shannon, ed., *The Great Depression*, p. 17.

13. Letter by Arthur Quanbeck, "From the Mail Bag," *The Lutheran Messenger*, (March 1, 1933), 11. Cited by E. L. Fevold, *The Lutheran Free Church* (Minneapolis: Augsburg Publishing House, 1969), pp. 185-186.

14. Hering, "An Ambrose Hering Story," *ibid.*, (April 13, 1933), 10-11.

15. *Church History*, XXIX (March, 1960), 3-16. The significance of this article has been recognized by the fact of its re-publication (1968) by the Fortress Press in the Historical Series of its Facet Books. References hereinafter will be to the latter.

16. *Ibid.*, p. 22.

17. A letter from Handy to the writer July 28, 1969: " . . . the spiritual decline I have suggested was especially evident in the 'Anglo-American' bodies, as their 'dominance' on the American religious scene faded." Other studies of religion in the depression are similarly limited. Cf. Samuel C. Kincheloe, *Research Memorandum on Religion in the Depression* (New York: Social Science Research Council, 1937). The author admits that most of his data refer "to Protestant churches" (p. vii). A closer look at the *Memorandum* reveals that by "Protestant" he means Methodists, Baptists, Congregationalists, Presbyterians; once again, the British-American tradition. The volume is hereinafter referred to as *Memorandum*.

18. "A Serious Trend Downward: A Statistical Analysis," *The Lutheran*, (December 7, 1933), 8-9, 22-23.

19. *Ibid.*, p. 23.

20. T. G. Tappert, *et al.*, "Lutherans in the Great Depression," *The Lutheran Quarterly*, VII (May, 1955), 145-154.

21. *Ibid.*, p. 145.

22. The same kind of mentality is expressed today by sociologists of religion and others in the use of the cliché "the Protestant ethic." The theory that is described bears little resemblance to the "ethic" which Lutheran Protestants know.

23. Kincheloe, *Memorandum*, pp. 1-4. Cf. Martin E. Marty, *Righteous Empire: The Protestant Experience in America* (New York: Dial Press, 1971).

24. This theme occurs repeatedly in Maier's collected radio sermons. See, for example, Walter A. Maier, *Christ for the Nation* (St. Louis: Concordia Publishing House, 1936), pp. 28-37.

25. Letter, Ralph H. Long to Ambrose Hering, November 12, 1931, Archives of Lutheran Cooperation, 315 Park Avenue South, New York, R. H. Long Papers, Box 1.

26. Some years after this letter was written, Babson, as chairman of the Commission on Church Attendance of the Congregational-Christian Church, published his conclusion that lack of religion is a main cause of depressions. Roger W. Babson, *How to Increase Church Attendance* (New York: Fleming H. Revell Co., 1936); cited in Kincheloe, *Memorandum*, p. 2, n. 4.

27. Wolf, "Introduction" in Handy, *The American Religious Depression, 1925-1935*, p. vi.

28. Tappert, "Lutherans in the Great Depression," pp. 146-152.

29. The minutes and proceedings of the major Lutheran churches for the first few years of the depression carry the same story. The reports of church presidents and executive boards are virtually identical: drastically cut budgets and emergency appeals for funds.

30. *The Lutheran*, (July 13, 1933), 2. The editor comments, "Most of the denominations began issuing demands for extra giving a year or more ago. . . . It took three years of adverse economic conditions to bring our work to the stage that called for prompt [action]. . . . No impatience with the appeal, reluctance to publish and announce it or unwillingness to respond to it is justifiable." *Ibid.*, p. 16.

31. See treasurer's summary in NLCA, *Annual Report . . . 1925*, p. 96.

32. NLCA, *Annual Report . . . 1940*, p. 93.

33. NLCA, *Annual Report . . . 1934*, p. 68. In addition to his regular duties as president and these newly added responsibilities, Aasgaard was asked by the church to assume the direction of the Department of Charities.

34. August R. Suelflow, "Spontaneous, Optional, or Luxury? A Survey of Welfare in the Lutheran Church–Missouri Synod" (unpublished manuscript, Concordia Historical Institute, St. Louis, 1963), pp. 2-6. Cf. Carl S. Meyer, ed., *Moving Frontiers* (St. Louis: Concordia Publishing House, 1964), pp. 398-404.

35. See G. Everett Arden, *Augustana Heritage. A History of the Augustana Lutheran Church* (Rock Island: Augustana Press, 1963), pp. 328-349.

36. NLCA, *Annual Report . . . 1932*, p. 262.

37. Frederick K. Wentz, *Lutherans in Concert. The Story of the National Lutheran Council 1918-1966* (Minneapolis: Augsburg Publishing House, 1968), pp. 102-105.

38. The large and notable exception to this was the program of American missions conducted by the ULCA and its antecedent bodies. The Synod of the Northwest of the General Council, for example, sought to stop the flow of the second generation away from the Lutheran church by emphasizing "English Lutheranism." Its motto was "The Faith of the Fathers in the Language of the Children." See G. H. Trabert, *English Lutheranism in the Northwest* (Philadelphia: General Council Publication House, 1914).

39. The actual allocation of a particular field to a particular Lutheran body did not

take place until the 1940s. But the idea was born in the depression. See Wentz, *Lutherans in Concert,* p. 105.

40. W. A. Baepler, *A Century of Grace* (St. Louis: Concordia Publishing House, 1947), p. 277. Cf. Gladys Gertrude Leech, "The Lutheran Church–Missouri Synod in the Great Depression, 1929-1941" (unpublished M.A. thesis, Washington University, St. Louis, Mo., 1956), pp. 11-12, 32.

41. John W. Behnken, *This I Recall* (St. Louis: Concordia Publishing House, 1964), p. 81.

42. For a survey of the academy movement in one branch of Lutheranism, see B. H. Narveson, "The Norwegian Lutheran Academies," *Norwegian-American Studies and Records,* XIV (Northfield, Minn.: Norwegian-American Historical Association, 1944), 184-226. See also E. Clifford Nelson, *The Lutheran Church Among Norwegian-Americans. A History of the Evangelical Lutheran Church* (Minneapolis: Augsburg Publishing House, 1960), II, 112-121. For a personal and somewhat nostalgic account of the Missouri Synod educational system, see Behnken, *This I Recall,* pp. 58-75.

43. See *The Lutheran World Almanac 1934-1937,* pp. 344-355.

44. Enrollments at academies began to decline before World War I, largely due to the improvement of public high schools. The depression administered the *coup de grace* to the academy movement. See Nelson, *The Lutheran Church Among Norwegian-Americans,* II, 118-119.

45. *Lutheran Companion,* August 11, 1934, pp. 996-997.

46. Missouri Synod, *Proceedings . . . 1935,* p. 84; cited in Leech, "The Lutheran Church–Missouri Synod in the Great Depression, 1929-1941," pp. 11-12. The Missouri "system," quite different from the higher educational program of other bodies, included 14 schools: a two-year upper level (senior) pre-seminary college for men; three schools were four-year colleges which at the upper level included teacher education (for the system of parochial schools); and ten were junior colleges. Ninety percent of the pastors were educated in "the system."

47. The Springfield seminary was actually closed for one night! The 1935 synod decided by a single vote to close the school. The next day it reconsidered the decision and Springfield remained open. Behnken, *This I Recall,* p. 68.

48. ULCA, *Minutes . . . 1932,* pp. 453-454; *The Lutheran,* (June 1, 1933), 14.

49. ULCA, *Minutes . . . 1940,* pp. 484, 496. Cf. *The Lutheran,* (December 14, 1933), 7-8. For an account of "the seminary problem" which the ULCA faced in the East, see Theodore G. Tappert, *History of the Lutheran Theological Seminary at Philadelphia 1864-1964* (Philadelphia: The Lutheran Theological Seminary, 1964), pp. 86-89; and A. R. Wentz, *Gettysburg Lutheran Theological Seminary* (Harrisburg, Pa.: The Evangelical Press, 1965), I, 361-366.

50. *The Lutheran World Almanac, 1934-1937,* p. 49. Cf. "Some Iowa Lutheran Centennials," *The Palimpsest,* XXXV (June, 1954), 17-24; *Thank God for the Church. American Lutheran Church 25th Anniversary* (Columbus: The Wartburg Press, 1955), pp. 7-8, 14, 58-69. The seminary at St. Paul was merged with Wartburg at Dubuque.

51. Missouri Synod, *Proceedings . . . 1932,* pp. 30-32, 66-68. Cf. Missouri Synod, *Proceedings . . . 1935,* "Seminaries and Colleges," pp. 1, 4, 49; also Baepler, *A Century of Grace,* p. 277; and Carl S. Meyer, *Log Cabin to Luther Tower* (St. Louis: Concordia Publishing House, 1965), p. 157.

52. Gustav Andreen, "The Story of Augustana College and Seminary" in *After Seventy-five Years, 1860-1935* (Rock Island: Augustana Book Concern, 1935), p. 43; Nelson, *The Lutheran Church Among Norwegian-Americans,* II, 271, n. 77.

53. Kinchloe, *Memorandum,* p. 20. See *supra* of this chapter, p. 46, n. 17.

54. *Ibid.,* pp. 7-8, 20.

55. Using the United Lutheran Church as an example, communing membership increased numerically from 680,836 (1929) to 824,559 (1941). The financial statistics in 1929 reveal a total of over $22,000,000. The depression low (1933) was $13,000,000.

It was not until 1943 that income climbed back to the 1929 level. A similar pattern applied to the other Lutheran bodies.

56. Using the Missouri Synod as an example and basing computations on the USA annual per capita income, church giving reached a high of 3½ percent at the bottom of the Depression (1933). In 1943, when church income first moved up beyond 1929 levels, giving dropped to its lowest point (2-2/5 percent)! Other Lutheran bodies showed similar trends. Data supplied by Dept. of Stewardship, Lutheran Church–Missouri Synod, and W. A. Jensen, formerly associate director, Section on Stewardship and Benevolence, National Council of Churches of Christ/USA.

57. A careful study of the Lutheran youth movement has been made by Clarence Peters, "Developments of the Youth Programs of the Lutheran Churches in America" (unpublished Th.D. thesis, Concordia Seminary Graduate School, St. Louis, Mo., 1951).

58. The Lutheran World Almanac, 1931-1933, p. 92; ibid., 1934-1937, p. 75.

59. Peters, "Developments of the Youth Programs . . . , " p. 183.

60. The Lutheran World Almanac, 1934-1937, p. 74. The peak attendance was reached in 1945 with 15,200 in 92 camps. Peters, "Developments of the Youth Programs . . . , " pp. 191, 193. The interdenominational Pocket Testament League was introduced to Luther Leagues at this time. By 1949 it numbered 60,000. This movement may not have been as popular in the youth organizations of the other Lutheran churches.

61. Paul Nyholm, "The Lutheran Bible Camp Movement," "Journal of the American Lutheran Conference, IV (February, 1939), 23-38.

62. A. Henry Hetland, Ferment (Chicago: National Lutheran Council, Division of College and University Work, 1966), p. 6.

63. "American Lutheran Conference Student Service Secretary," Journal of the American Lutheran Conference, III (November, 1938), 72. F. A. Schiotz, "We Introduce Ourselves," ibid., IV (February, 1939), 11-22.

64. Frederick K. Wentz, Lutherans in Concert, pp. 118-119. Schiotz took the lead in convincing a reluctant American Lutheran Conference to unite its work with that of the ULCA under the aegis of the NLC. Cf. Mary E. Markley, The Lutheran Church and Its Students (Philadelphia: The Muhlenberg Press, 1948), pp. 118-121.

65. Missouri Synod, Proceedings . . . 1938, p. 131; ibid., 1939, p. 168. Cf. Markley, The Lutheran Church and Its Students, pp. 117-118.

66. Interchange, III (June, 1969). See also news release, News Bureau, LC/USA, June 15, 1969, p. 6.

67. Markley, The Lutheran Church and Its Students, pp. 129-141. Cf. Letters: Oswald C. Michelmann-L. W. Boe, 1-16-1923 and 2-1-1923; in L. W. Boe Papers, St. Olaf College Archives, Northfield, Minn.

68. Ibid., p. 140. "The Oxford Group Movement" was also called "Buchmanism." Buchman remained a Lutheran minister till the end of his life.

69. The decision to resume national student conferences was made at the National LSAA Council in Chicago, August, 1935. This documentation is not based on the official minutes but is a recollection of the writer, who presided at the council meeting. The word "Ashram," borrowed from India, denoted "a corporate spiritual quest." Ibid., p. 136.

70. Gould Wickey, The Lutheran Venture in Higher Education (Philadelphia: Board of Publication, ULCA, 1962), p. 99.

71. The Lutheran Standard, (September 16, 1969), 30.

72. G. T. Lee, "The Oxford Movement," Theological Forum, VII (October, 1935), 200. Not a few youth leaders and pastors who were deeply committed to furthering personal Christianity, social concern, and missionary outreach were attracted to "the evangelists in dress suits," as the Buchmanites were called, because of their interest in reaching the upper strata of society. A book by F. A. Schiotz, Release (Minneapolis: Augsburg Publishing House, 1935) possessed evidence of Buchmanite influence.

73. Oscar N. Olson, "The Oxford Group Movement," The Lutheran Companion, (December 15, 1934), 1576-1578. Cf. editorial in the same periodical, "New Move-

ment Analyzed." Cf. G. T. Lee cited above, footnote 72. Cf. "The Oxford Group in Canada," *The Lutheran*, (January 16, 1933), 2, 25; and "Two Books on Buchmanism," *ibid.*, pp. 20-21.

74. This phrase was used by a group leader at a Buchmanite "house party" in the Nicollet Hotel, Minneapolis, Minn., attended by the writer in the spring of 1936.

75. Dorris A. Flesner, ed., *70th Anniversary Review . . . Synod of the Northwest*, 1891-1961 (n. p. [Minneapolis ?], n. d., [1961?]), pp. 21-22. Cf. Synod of the Northwest, *Minutes . . . 1935*, p. 51; *ibid., . . . 1936*, p. 61; *ibid., . . . 1938*, p. 58; *ibid., . . . 1941*, p. 66.

76. Regional religious broadcasts were begun by WCAL, St. Olaf College, Northfield, Minn., in 1922; and by KFUO, Concordia Seminary, St. Louis, 1924. Cf. W. C. Benson, *High on Manitou. A History of St. Olaf College* (Northfield, Minn.: The St. Olaf College Press, 1949), p. 282; and Paul L. Maier, *A Man Spoke, A World Listened. The Story of Walter A. Maier* (New York: McGraw-Hill Book Co., 1963), p. 72.

77. *Ibid.*, p. 111. Maier gives an interesting account of his father's interest in radio and his struggle to get nation-wide *Lutheran* broadcasts on the networks. See especially pp. 110-126, 164-240.

78. The Laymen's League had built radio station KFUO at Concordia Seminary and shared Maier's interest in broadcasting religious services. *Ibid.*, p. 113.

79. *The Lutheran*, (July 2, 1931), 14.

80. *Ibid.*, August 27, 1931, p. 2; May 19, 1932, p. 2; November 10, 1932, p. 17; July 27, 1933, p. 2. Cf. W. S. Gertner, "Paul E. Scherer: Preacher and Homiletician" (unpublished Ph.D. dissertation, Wayne University, Detroit, Mich., 1967).

81. *The Lutheran*, September 10, 1931, p. 23. Cf. Osborne Hauge, *Lutherans Working Together* (New York: National Lutheran Council, 1945), pp. 65-66.

82. See correspondence between Long and O. H. Pannkoke, Long and Maier from August 4, 1931 to December 5, 1931. Archives of Cooperative Lutheranism, 315 Park Avenue South, New York. R. H. Long Papers, Box 1. It is clear from the exchange of letters that Long was reluctant to inform Maier about the CBS criticisms of his delivery. Maier's radio voice brought numerous negative criticisms. "He sounds as if he is pronouncing the benediction with boxing gloves," said one friendly critic. Another, not so friendly, wrote on a postcard, "4 [*sic*] Christ's sake, change your voice. It sounds like hell." Mrs. Maier refused her husband's desire to frame this one! When radio engineers succeeded in toning him down, according to *Time* magazine, listeners wondered if Maier were sick; fan mail dropped off 1000 letters a day. The next week Maier resumed his radio voice. See Maier, *A Man Spoke . . .* , pp. 186, 207.

83. A liturgical renewal in other denominations occurred at about the same time. Cf. E. B. Koenker, *The Liturgical Renaissance in the Roman Catholic Church* (Chicago: University of Chicago Press, 1954) and Massey H. Shepperd Jr., ed., *The Liturgical Renewal of the Church* (New York: Oxford University Press, 1960).

84. For an objective account of the liturgical revival, see David L. Scheidt, "The 'High Church Movement' in American Lutheranism," *The Lutheran Quarterly*, IX (November, 1957), 343-349.

85. See articles in *Pro Ecclesia Lutherana*, Volumes I (1933) and II (1934); *Sursum Corda*, Volumes I (1939) and II (1940). *Una Sancta* became the movement's organ in the 40s and continued precariously into the late 60s. Several articles in *Journal of the American Lutheran Conference* bore titles such as "Liturgical Uniformity," "The Place of Liturgy in the Lutheran Church," "Worship and the Inner Life of the Church," etc. See *ibid.*, II (April, 1937) and (September, 1937). See also H. A. Preus, "Recent Developments and Trends within the Church," *Theological Forum*, VI (January, 1934), 80-85; and Franklin Clark Fry, "Sursum Corda: On Adoring God through the Liturgy," an abridgement of an address before the Synod of Ohio, ULCA, May 20-23, 1935.

CHAPTER THREE

THEOLOGICAL AND ECUMENICAL
CONCERNS IN THE THIRTIES

During the depression one of the chief preoccupations of the churches, as well as of other institutions, was balancing budgets and meeting bills. To be sure, there was a latent interest in theology, but time for vigorous and sustained reflection was often absorbed by programs seeking to ameliorate the economic and social plight of the people.

It may not be an over-simplification to say that American Protestantism showed several faces in the early 30s. There was, first of all, the strong, but already cresting, theological liberalism that had all but completely separated itself from the theology of the Reformation. H. Richard Niebuhr judged humanistic liberalism and scientific modernism as follows: "A God without wrath brought men without sin into a kingdom without judgment through the ministration of a Christ without a cross." [1] Sydney Ahlstrom added to the criticism by saying that much of liberal theology "came increasingly to center its interests on man, not God; on social theory, not the Gospel. It grounded its message on little more than certain ethical passages from the Sermon on the Mount, and fastened its hope on the evolutionary process and American politics." [2]

World War I, the severe and satirical social criticism of the 20s, together with the moral revolt spawned by such literary figures as Theodore Dreiser, H. L. Mencken, F. Scott Fitzgerald, and others, contributed to a growing climate of opinion that questioned the adequacy of the theologically liberal spirit to meet the advancing secularism. It remained for the depression, however, to administer the knockout punch to the underlying optimism that characterized so much of liberalism.[3]

Another face presented by Protestantism in this era was "the lingering impact of the fundamentalist controversy." [4] Although the fundamentalists came out of the controversy theologically tattered and embittered, it should be noted that it was they and the non-fundamentalist conservatives, rather than the liberals, who experienced the sharpest numerical growth. Denominational leaders, fearing the potential divisiveness implicit in continued exchange of theological vitriol, were more or less successful in switching theological concerns to institutional ones. That they were not completely successful is witnessed by the Machen controversy in the Presbyterian Church in the USA. J. Gresham Machen and his followers charged their church with liberalism and consequently established Westminster Seminary (Philadelphia) in opposition to Princeton. A new but small church, the Presbyterian Church of America, was also formed together with an Independent Board for Presbyterian Foreign Missions.[5] Not unrelated to this dispute was that which grew out of the Laymen's Foreign Missions Inquiry (1930). This was followed by the famous Hocking report (1932), *Re-Thinking Missions,* which criticized traditional missionary policy and urged a tolerance toward non-Christian religions. Such toleration was interpreted by conservatives as an undercutting of the finality of Jesus Christ. When mission boards were asked "to give largely without preaching; to cooperate with non-Christian agencies for social improvement; and to foster the initiative of the Orient in defining the ways in which we shall be invited to help," this was understood as an abdication of the missionary responsibility to proclaim the gospel to all peoples.[6] Lutherans, as will be noted later in another context, shared this reaction.

Meanwhile the influence of Karl Barth, Emil Brunner, and other European representatives of post-World War I "crisis theology" began to be felt in American Protestantism.[7] Some of the themes emanating from this theological revival were echoed in America by the writings and students of the famous Niebuhr brothers, Reinhold and H. Richard. Practically every major premise of liberalism was called into question and a "new orthodoxy" was in process of formation. Attacking fundamentalism on the right and liberalism and modernism [8] on the left, the new theology of the Christian realists gave expression to such familiar Reformation concepts as the sovereignty of a gracious God, the demonic power of sin, the centrality of the biblical revelation, and the primacy of Christ as God's Word in the justification of the sinner. But religious individualism, which so often characterized liberalism's ecclesiological and ethical views, was replaced by an ecumenical fulness and a social ethical thrust. Conservative Christians, including many American Lutherans, found themselves in an ambivalent position regarding this "new orthodoxy." They responded gratefully to the general Reformation emphases, but they were nervous about the use of historical criticism of the Scriptures, the emphasis on ecumenism, and the social and public role of Christianity as taught especially by Reinhold Niebuhr. In fact, it was only when similar ideas appeared as fruits of the "Luther Renaissance" occuring in Germany's "neo-Lutheranism" and Sweden's "Lundensianism" that American Lutherans began to take a positive attitude toward the new theology. Before observing the details of the Lutheran theological reconstruction which began to take form in the 20s and the 30s, a look at the stance of the major Lutheran bodies in 1930 is necessary.

THEOLOGICAL ATTITUDES OF THE CHURCHES

As the 1930s opened it was evident that Lutheran church bodies presented a picture of theological diversity within a confessional community. The "community," however, was not sufficiently communal to permit intercommunion and fellowship among its members. The earlier and continuing movement toward the union of Lutheran churches in America had been hindered in large measure by strong sociological and cultural factors, notably ethnic backgrounds. By the opening of the new decade "non-theological factors" had receded somewhat. But whereas one set of factors began to lessen, another set—the parallel theological problems— began to assume prominence. The disturbing questions centered around the varying definitions of confessional unity. All groups identified themselves as Lutheran by their subscription to the confessional writings of Lutheranism. That is, they were united in their official confession of the doctrine of the gospel; it was this that made them a confessional community. The question that remained unanswered was whether a confessional community required theological uniformity. Some answered the question in the language of the confessions themselves: for the unity of the church it is enough to agree concerning the doctrine of

DOCUMENTS OF LUTHERAN UNITY — 1919-1940

Name and Date	Author(s)	Purpose and/or Status
Chicago Theses (1919)	H. G. Stub, pres. of NLCA & NLC.	To provide "orthodox" basis for NLC churches to cooperate in home missions. No church adopted Theses, but they represented "exclusivist" confessionalism of Midwest German Lutherans. Later a part of "Minneapolis Theses."
The Essentials of the Catholic Spirit in the Church (1919)	Authors, F. H. Knubel - C. M. Jacobs, (ULCA).	Counterpoise to Chicago Theses; stressed ecumenical character of confessional Lutheranism.
The Washington Declaration (1920)	Adopted as an official position document by ULCA.	Based on The Essentials of the Catholic Spirit.
Minneapolis Theses (1925)	Prepared by representatives of so-called "Middle Churches": Ohio, Iowa, Buffalo, Norwegian. Leaders: Hein, Reu, Aasgaard, Stub. Became basis for American Lutheran Conference (1930).	Self-styled "middle way" between ULCA and Missouri, but essentially orthodoxist and fundamentalist confessionalism.
Intersynodical [Chicago] Theses (1925-1928)	Prepared by representatives of Ohio, Buffalo, Iowa, Missouri, and Wisconsin.	Unsuccessful attempt to provide basis for fellowship among strictly conservative confessionalists (Midwest German Lutheran bodies).
A Brief Statement (1932)	Adopted by Missouri Synod; chief author F. Pieper.	Missouri authoritative statement for unity discussions. Special emphases on election, conversion, church, and inerrancy of Scripture.
The Savannah Declaration (1934)	Adopted by ULCA; chief author, C. M. Jacobs.	Confessions, interpreted in historical context, are sole "standards or tests of Lutheranism."
The Baltimore Declaration (1938)	Adopted by ULCA; chief author, C. M. Jacobs.	Defined "Word of God" in relation to Gospel, to divine revelation completed in Christ, and to Scriptures.
The Sandusky Declaration (1938)	Adopted by ALC; chief author, J. M. Reu.	Directed toward Missouri Synod. Stressed similarities between Chicago Theses, Minneapolis Theses, Brief Statement.
Pittsburgh Agreement (1940)	Outgrowth of ULCA-ALC negotiations (1936-39); chief authors, Reu and Knubel.	Adopted with qualifications by both ALC and ULCA; failed of purpose: fellowship and organic merger, because it did not reflect ULCA position (Washington, Savannah, Baltimore Declarations).

the gospel and the administration of the sacraments in conformity to the gospel (Augsburg Confession, Article VII). Others insisted that confessional unity meant theological uniformity, that there could be no church fellowship until it could be demonstrated that the churches agreed theologically. As these differing points of view continued to separate the churches organizationally during the next decades, the two positions received sharper delineation in a few carefully worded statements (see accompanying chart). From these documents it became apparent that the major issues within the American branch of the Lutheran confessional family were threefold: First, how was the authority of the Bible to be assured? Second, what constituted "unionism" (the question of pulpit and altar fellowship)? And third, what was the proper attitude of the church towards secret societies (the lodge membership question)?

The United Lutheran Church in America

By 1920 the United Lutheran Church had assumed an evangelical posture toward the emerging ecumenical movement with its two-fold bearing on inner- and extra-Lutheran relations. As noted earlier, its attitude was enunciated in "The Washington Declaration" adopted by the church in 1920 and based upon a position paper, "The Essentials of the Catholic Spirit in the Church," prepared by F. H. Knubel for presentation to the National Lutheran Council in 1919.[9] The view expressed has been called a "catholic" or "ecumenical" confessionalism as contrasted with the exclusivist confessionalism of most other American Lutherans.

Although the church did not publish an official document on the relationship between the Word of God and the Scriptures until 1938,[10] already in 1920 "The Washington Declaration" refused to speak of verbal inspiration and inerrancy of the Scriptures (". . . we believe that in the Holy Scriptures we have a permanent and authoritative record of apostolic truth which is the ground of Christian faith.") [11] By 1927-1930 individual professors of theology were taking positions incompatible with an orthodoxist view of scriptural inerrancy. They used the method of historical criticism and carefully distinguished between the Scriptures and the Word of God without separating one from the other.[12]

In 1918 the church found it unnecessary to define the role of the Lutheran confessions beyond a constitutional statement regarding the Augsburg Confession "as a correct exhibition of the faith and doctrine of the Evangelical Lutheran Church . . . ," and the recognition of the other Lutheran confessional documents "as in the harmony of one and the same pure Scriptural faith." It was not until 1934 that a more explicit statement was published in the "Savannah Declaration," which stated that the confessions "are to be interpreted in their historical context, not as a law or as a system of theology, but as 'a witness and declaration of faith. . . .' " [13]

The Norwegian Lutheran Church of America

Next to the United Lutheran Church the Norwegian Lutheran Church was the ranking member of the National Lutheran Council. As a product of a merger of three Norwegian Lutheran church bodies in 1917, it represented a combination of the tendencies present in the uniting groups: Norwegian Lutheran pietism, Norwegian Lutheran confessionalism and Missouri Lutheran orthodoxism, and incipient ecumenism.[14] Pietism and orthodoxism were the dominant features of the church during the first two or three decades of its existence. A cautious ecumenism was visible after World War I when it demonstrated a certain openness to other Lutherans by joining and providing vigorous leadership to the National Lutheran Council.[15] Its "ecumenical spirit" was limited to Lutheranism until 1956 when it joined the World Council of Churches.

In 1930, therefore, this church still represented a confluence of conservative theological streams which in some respects refused homogenization. A common *Norwegian* and *Lutheran* heritage, however, helped to transcend the implicit theological tensions that were present. The question of theological and religious authority was dominated by a view of Scripture that held the Bible to be verbally inspired and hence inerrant; a view of the confessions as authoritative "because" *(quia)*, not "in so far as" *(quatenus)*, they agreed with the Bible; and a view of fellowship governed by a strict interpretation of an incomplete version of the Galesburg Rule ("Lutheran pulpits for Lutheran pastors only, and Lutheran altars for Lutheran communicants only."). The view of Scripture represented a retrogression, especially from the relatively advanced view on inspiration held by some leaders who opposed the rigid views of the Norwegian Missourians as early as 1892.[16] This change is best understood as a reaction to the "Modernist-Fundamentalist Con-

troversy" of the 20s. Conservative Norwegian Lutherans accepted uncritically the presuppositions of fundamentalism because their heritage
had equipped them with neither the knowledge nor the tools by which
to combat liberalism as evangelical Lutherans. Therefore, they found
theological security, along with the recently formed American Lutheran
Church, in the orthodoxist-fundamentalist "Minneapolis Theses" (1925)
which had become the basis for the establishment of the American Lutheran Conference (1930).

American Lutheran Church

Fred W. Meuser's detailed picture of the forces at work in the merger
of four (including Texas) German background Midwest Lutheran synods
in 1930 indicated that much the same pattern was present as that found
in the Norwegian Lutheran Church.[17] The notable exception was the absence of pietistic attitudes that characterized most Lutherans of Scandinavian origin. The inerrancy of Scripture, the binding quality of the
confessions, and the fear of "unionism" with non-Lutherans dominated
the outlook of the church from its founding. As will be noted later, this
body liked to regard itself as a bridge between Eastern ("liberal") German
Lutheranism and Missouri ("orthodox") German Lutheranism. This somewhat baffling role as the bridgebuilder within Lutheranism was bequeathed
to the second American Lutheran Church in the 1960 merger.

The Evangelical Lutheran Augustana Synod

When the Augustana Lutheran Church celebrated its centennial (1960),
it published a series of essays that depicted the ethos of the church body.
One writer called the period from 1870-1930 a time of "Preservation and
Growth of a Tradition." [18] Like other Scandinavian Lutherans, Augustana
possessed a religious heritage that was an amalgam of pietism and orthodoxism. The most powerful forces in shaping this pattern were the first
president of the seminary, T. N. Hasselquist, and a professor of dogmatics,
C. E. Lindberg, whose career covered 40 years (1890-1930). For almost
50 years (1870-1918) the Augustana Synod was associated with the confessionally conservative General Council. When the latter became a part of
the United Lutheran Church in 1918, Augustana, largely for cultural reasons, chose to maintain its synodical identity. Cordial relations were maintained with the United Lutherans, but in 1930 Augustana joined the new

federation of Midwest Lutherans known as the American Lutheran Conference. This action reflected the essential conservatism of Augustana, but, as its historian noted, it was doubtful that the leaders or the people had any clear understanding of the "theological issues involved in this alliance."[19] But even as it associated itself with the American Lutheran Conference, it resolutely affirmed its determination to maintain contacts with the United Lutheran Church, thus casting itself in a role similar to that of the American Lutheran Church. Whereas the latter sought to build a bridge between the United Lutheran Church and Missouri, Augustana sought to be the bridgebuilder of the National Lutheran Council churches, seeking closer fellowship between the United Lutheran Church and the American Lutheran Conference. The role of bridgebuilders in history has seldom been successful and the well-intentioned efforts of both Augustana and the American Lutheran Church were relatively unfruitful. But, it should be noted, in 1930 Augustana stood on the threshold of a new theological era. The next year the seminary experienced what has been called "an upheaval" with the resignation of four professors and the advent of a new corps of theologians who were to change the course of the Augustana Synod.[20]

The Evangelical Lutheran Synod of Missouri, Ohio and Other States

The Missouri Synod in 1930 continued to be the most influential partner in the Synodical Conference. Its very size assured it the place of prominence. The Wisconsin Synod, one-third as large, numbered about 300,000 members. The stance of the Missouri Synod and the other churches in the Synodical Conference in 1930 was easily the most conservative in the American Lutheran family.

The chief architect of Missouri's theological position was Franz Pieper, professor at Concordia Seminary and author of the synod's guide to dogmatic rectitude.[21] A theological pike among lesser fry, Pieper reacted primarily to German liberalism of the 19th century and secondarily to its impact on American churches. He found it necessary to advance what he liked to call a "strictly confessional" theology. As a matter of fact, the phrase was hardly correct because Pieper viewed the Lutheran confessions through the eyes of the 17th century dogmaticians who were "repristinated" by an anti-Schleiermacherian group of German Lutherans about mid-century. The advocates of "repristination theology" felt that true Lutheranism could only be secured by asserting the inerrancy of a verbally inspired Bible and a dogmatic use of the confessions. Pieper rose to defend this position by saying,

> The claim is made that by identifying Scripture and the Word of God our theology will lead to intellectualism. . . . I considered it necessary to refute the unwarranted charge and to remove any misgivings concerning "repristination theology," and have therefore set forth . . . the religious life of a church body which is definitely committed to the "repristination theology." [22]

Pieper effectively shaped Missouri's attitude toward biblical criticism, evolution, ecumenism, social action, and numerous other questions until well after World War II. The synod remained sharply divided into the 1960s on the matter of allegiance to "repristination theology" as epitomized in the so-called Brief Statement (1932) whose main author also was Pieper.[23]

The Smaller Church Bodies in 1930

In addition to the "major" Lutheran churches, one must take note of several smaller bodies such as the United Danish and the Danish Evangelical Lutheran Churches, the Suomi Synod and the National Evangelical Lutheran Church (both Finnish), the Slovak Evangelical Lutheran Church and Zion (Slovak) Synod, and the Lutheran Free Church (Norwegian). In general these bodies found themselves so preoccupied with the financial exigencies of the depression years that very little time or thought was given to theological issues. Perhaps it can be said that each of these groups shared the theological outlook of those larger bodies with whom they were in fellowship. For example, the Danish pietism of the United Danish Church found itself more comfortable with the other Scandinavians than with United Lutheran or Missouri German Lutheranism. The same can be said of the Lutheran Free Church. The Finns and the Slovaks, on the other hand, were each divided by their individual emphases. The pietistic churchliness of the Suomi Synod drew these Finns ultimately in the direction of the United Lutheran Church. The National Evangelical Lutheran Church found Missouri's emphasis on "pure doctrine" attractive. The two Slovak groups aligned themselves similarly. On the whole, "they went along" with the decisions of the larger groups with whom they had ties.[24]

LUTHERAN GROUPS
1930-1960

I. NATIONAL LUTHERAN COUNCIL (1918) GROUP

United Lutheran Church in America (ULCA, 1918)
Danish Ev. Lutheran Church in America (1872; name changed 1953, Am. Ev. Luth. Church)
Finnish Ev. Lutheran Church in America (1890, Suomi Synod).
Icelandic Ev. Lutheran Synod of America (1885; joined ULCA, 1940)

American Lutheran Conference 1930 {
Ev. Lutheran Augustana Synod in North America (1860; name changed, 1948, Augustana Ev. Lutheran Church)
Norwegian Lutheran Church of America (NLCA, 1917; name changed, 1946, Ev. Lutheran Church)
American Lutheran Church (ALC, 1930)
United Danish Ev. Lutheran Church (1896; name changed, 1946, United Ev. Lutheran Church)
Lutheran Free Church (LFC, 1897)

II. EV. LUTHERAN SYNODICAL CONFERENCE (1872) GROUP

Ev. Lutheran Synod of Missouri, Ohio, and Other States (1847; name changed, 1947, Lutheran Church—Missouri Synod)
Ev. Lutheran Joint Synod of Wisconsin, Minnesota, Michigan and Other States (1892; name changed, 1959, Wisconsin Ev. Lutheran Synod)
Norwegian Synod of the American Lutheran Church (1918; name changed, 1955, Ev. Lutheran Synod)
Slovak Ev. Lutheran Church (1902; name changed, 1959, Synod of Ev. Lutheran Churches; merged in 1971 with Missouri Synod)

III. INDEPENDENT GROUP

Church of the Lutheran Brethren (1900)
Church of the Lutheran Confession (1960)
Ev. Lutheran Church of America (Eielsen Synod, 1846)
Finnish Apostolic Lutheran Church in America (1872; name changed, 1962, Apostolic Lutheran Church of America)
Finnish Ev. Lutheran National Church of America (1898; name changed, 1946, National Ev. Lutheran Church; merged in 1964 with Missouri Synod)

THE ROLE OF THE AMERICAN LUTHERAN CONFERENCE

By 1930 about 98 percent of American Lutheranism could be found in one of two umbrella-like organizations, the National Lutheran Council (1918) and the Synodical Conference (1872). American Lutheranism, however, existed not only in two *organizational* constellations but also in two *theological* camps that unfortunately—for ease of understanding—were not coterminous with the two organizations. One view, historically advocated by the United Lutheran Church since its Washington Declaration, held that

> In the case of those Church Bodies calling themselves Evangelical Lutheran, and subscribing to the Confessions which have always been regarded as the standard of Evangelical Lutheran doctrine, the United Lutheran Church in America recognizes no doctrinal reasons against complete cooperation and organic union with such bodies.[25]

The other view, traditionally held by the Missouri Synod and its affiliates in the Synodical Conference, insisted that in spite of the fact that some churches called themselves Lutherans, they were in actuality heterodox; therefore, no fellowship could be practiced with them. This view held that the unity of the church is best reflected in intellectually refined doctrinal propositions. The greater the agreement in these theological statements, the greater the unity. Moreover, there must also be agreement in actual proclamation, teaching, and "practice;" that is to say, pastors and people whose teaching was false or who engaged in a "practice" deemed inconsistent with "pure doctrine"—for example, membership in the Masonic lodge—were to be disciplined by excommunication.

Complicating the ecclesio-theological picture was the fact that this "Missourian way to unity" [26] had influenced large segments of Lutheranism outside the Synodical Conference. For example, some church bodies associated with the United Lutheran Church in the National Lutheran Council were, at least in their attitude toward fellowship and unity, sympathetic to the Missourian viewpoint and distrustful of the Lutheran "latitudinarianism" expressed in The Washington Declaration. This attitude prevailed especially in the American Lutheran and Norwegian Lutheran churches, both of which had Missourian elements in their constituencies. Consequently, as noted in the first chapter, it was evident that tension would be inevitable within the National Council, harboring as it did both points of view. Nevertheless, it should be pointed out that both viewpoints were "confessional," one saying that the confessions are adequate safeguards for the church's proclamation, the other that extra-confessional statements are needed to assure the genuineness of one's Lutheranism. These two attitudes have been variously labelled: "catholic (ecumenical) confessionalism" over against "exclusivist confessionalism"; or "historically-conditioned confessionalism" versus "repristination confessionalism." Missourians were inclined to speak of "nominal or lax confessionalism" versus "real or strict confessionalism."

In any case, by 1930 the cleft within the council, detected as early as 1919, took on institutional form in the establishment of the American Lutheran Conference by five Midwest Lutheran groups. Though *practically* related to the ULCA in the work of the National Lutheran Council, they were *ideologically* and *sociologically* akin to the Missouri Synod.

As pointed out earlier, the doctrinal propositions that became the theological basis for the American Lutheran Conference, The Minneapolis Theses,[27] emphasized three points that were deemed necessary over against the United Lutheran Church. These were (1) the inerrancy of the verbally-inspired Scriptures (Article I), (2) "exclusivist confessionalism" on the question of church unity (Article III), and (3) proscription of lodge membership, especially by ministers.

When one seeks to assess the significance of the American Lutheran Conference, he is torn between two evaluations. One was that of the idealists who wanted to see the conference as a step along the road to ultimate Lutheran union. The other was that of the church politicians who saw the new federation as a means of withstanding the strength of the United Lutheran Church and, at the same time, of persuading the Missouri Synod that "true Lutheranism" was still alive outside of the Synodical Conference. L. W. Boe, one of the leaders in the council and a member of the Norwegian Lutheran Church, expressed both evaluations. At the constituting convention he said:

> The United Lutheran Church and the American Lutheran Conference are affiliated in common interests and activities of such a character that they inevitably will approach each other, *unless events are permitted to generate a hostile feeling entirely at variance with the history of the past* [italics added].[28]

Three years later he wrote again. Still expecting the American Lutheran Conference to be a positive influence toward Lutheran unity, his earlier idealism was now noticeably tempered:

> It is, perhaps, the one movement that has started in the Lutheran Church of America pretty much from the top and has worked down. Not many knew about the movement before it was presented all ready for organization. I have the impression that from the standpoint of the administrative officers of the different synods concerned *it was the intention to form a kind of protective league over against other Lutherans* [italics added].[29]

That the American Lutheran Conference possessed the character of a defensive alliance particularly over against the United Lutheran Church can hardly be denied. When the latter published The Washington Declaration, the Norwegians and the Ohio and Iowa Germans were convinced that the United Lutherans lacked theological orthodoxy. Says Meuser, " . . . it was one of the reasons for the determination of the midwestern synods to remain apart from the ULCA." [30] When Presidents H. G. Stub and C. C. Hein prepared theses in anticipation of the 1925 Minneapolis meeting, which in turn prepared the way for the American Lutheran Conference, they did so with "specific points of their opposition to the ULCA" in mind.[31] The Minneapolis Theses declared to Lutheranism that the "middle synods" would continue "to protest against the ULCA position." [32] Moreover, President Hein "repeated his hopes for a body bearing testimony against the ULCA" so often that Professor M. Reu, the chief theologian of the Iowa Synod, warned that the American Lutheran Conference would hardly prosper if its purpose was simply "to do battle" against other Lutherans.[33]

In relation to the Missouri Synod the new conference saw no need to be defensive. The reasons for this was that according to influential elements in the American Lutheran Conference, the doctrinal position of the Missouri Synod was aggressively and pleasingly Lutheran. There was no point in raising defenses against Missouri; the task was rather to convince Missouri of the doctrinal orthodoxy of the arbitrarily designated "middle group." Exhibit A, as supporting evidence, was The Minneapolis Theses.

The reaction to the new federation among the leaders of the United Lutheran Church was one of profound regret and no little frustration. A member of the church's newly-appointed commission on relations with other Lutherans wrote to President Knubel in 1930 wondering why the United Lutheran Church had been excluded. In his reply, Knubel reviewed the history of The Chicago Theses (and later The Minneapolis Theses), showing that at one time (1919) they and the "Essentials of a Catholic Spirit" were intended as two parts of a common effort, around which conferences were held. "Any who were present can tell you that I begged literally with tears that the conferences should not cease." Knubel continued by saying that to follow the line of The Minneapolis Theses would turn American Lutheranism into a mere sect and would cast gloom for a long time over the future.

> That is exactly what the Minneapolis Theses standing alone would accomplish. They cannot live ultimately in the life of American Lutheranism for they do not represent pure Lutheranism. Some day before a great while, although not while you and I are alive, American Lutheranism will cast those things aside.[34]

Although the church withheld official comment on the American Lutheran Conference, its president's article, "What Does the United Lutheran Church in America Stand For?" included a staunch apology for the orthodoxy of his own church. Veiled in this was the fact that he and his church had taken umbrage at the obvious exclusion of the United Church from the American Lutheran Conference.[35]

Later it was reported that the creation of the American Lutheran Conference all but shipwrecked the National Lutheran Council.[36] An extensive correspondence between the recently elected executive director of the council, Ralph H. Long, and several leaders of the churches, indicated that Long had become doubtful about accepting the position because of the ill-will that existed between the United Lutheran Church and the leaders of the new conference. Although Long was assured that the conference was not organized with any hostility toward the United Lutherans, the acting director, F. H. Meyer, admitted to President Poppen of the American Lutheran Church, that the secrecy of the preliminary negotiations had aroused ULCA suspicions. "If . . . the leaders of the American Lutheran Conference," he wrote, "had told the brethren of the ULCA what had been done, the hurt to these brethren would not have been felt so deeply." Poppen replied that the action of ULCA pastors had "served to make some of our men and others suspicious of the quality of ULCA Lutheranism." Long's close friend, S. C. Michelfelder, wrote that he too knew that "some very nasty things" were being said; but, he continued encouragingly, "I believe you are the best fitted to pull this thing out of the fire." [37]

Long's decision to accept the position perhaps saved the National Lutheran Council, for with a weaker man at the helm the council might very well have sunk into oblivion. Though it never admitted a mistake, the American Lutheran Conference did seek to repair the damage by inviting President Knubel to address its 1932 convention in Milwaukee. Knubel expressed his wishes for God's blessings upon the conference and then said,

> Let me speak in utter frankness. It is true that at the time when the American Lutheran Conference was organized we were deeply grieved. . . . This is not the time nor the place for me to specify the elements in that grief.[38]

Attitudes were not measurably altered, however. In fact, one cynical commentator said that at some meetings of the National Lutheran Council "about the only complete unanimity of purpose discoverable was that exhibited at the luncheon table. Everyone present had a good appetite." Since the formation of the American Lutheran Conference, he continued, the council was split and there were serious questions whether the council could justify its continuance.[39]

Despite the historical circumstances out of which the American Lutheran Conference emerged, once under way it served good purposes. The bringing together of Lutherans of diverse national origins was significant. The vigorous student service program at tax-supported universities and colleges, and the far-sighted all-Lutheran seminars were particularly praiseworthy. However, it should be observed that these were the activities that were customarily identified in the ex post facto rationalization of those who found it necessary to justify the existence of the conference. At times the fact that these very purposes have been or could have been accomplished quite as effectively through the National Lutheran Council was overlooked.[40]

As the decade moved on it became apparent that the American Lutheran Conference, quite as the National Lutheran Council, was of two minds on theological issues and church relations. A theologian of the Missouri Synod described the situation by saying that the two largest churches in the conference (the NLCA and the ALC) were drawn more to the Missouri Synod than to the United Lutheran Church. On the other hand, the Augustana Synod's direction was "overwhelmingly toward the United Lutheran Church." [41] This observation was given substance by the public statement of P. O. Bersell, the president of the Augustana Synod. Addressing the 1940 convention of the American Lutheran Conference, he pointed out that a major weakness of the organization was its approach to Lutheran unity. "The . . . weakness," he said, "is that our fellowship has been more exclusive than inclusive." [42] Although the editor of the conference *Journal,* G. M. Bruce of Luther Seminary, St. Paul, dismissed Bersell as "the voice of a rather officious and superior-minded church official, who rolls out his words with ponderous accents on every syllable even when uttering the most puerile thoughts," [43] Bersell's critique nevertheless pointed to the realities of the situation. Meanwhile Augustana became aware of "a new theological climate . . . which was essentially incompatible with the 'exclusive confessionalism' espoused by the American Lutheran Conference." [44] In order to understand subsequent developments in American Lutheranism, especially as they impinged on the question of church unity, it is necessary to describe briefly the advent of a new theological outlook in some Lutheran quarters.

THE BEGINNINGS OF THEOLOGICAL RECONSTRUCTION

Our brief survey of the theological stance of the churches at the beginning of the 30s showed that American Lutheranism found difficulty in meeting the problems posed by liberalism and fundamentalism. All Lutherans by the beginning of the 20th century were committed to a confessionalist viewpoint. The debates that took place were largely limited to problems within this tradition. As pointed out above the first intimation of theological change appeared in the United Lutheran Church. For the first time on American soil a major church body, definitely committed to the Lutheran confessions, sought to take an evangelical position in relation to contemporary questions. The Modernist-Fundamentalist controversy of the mid-twenties forced the issue of biblical criticism. Was the choice that lay before Lutherans, who wished to be loyal to the gospel, limited to two alternatives, either to repristinate an orthodoxist view of Scripture (as did traditional Roman Catholicism and Protestant fundamentalism) or to abandon the Lutheran confessions? Some concluded these were the only options, and as far as Scripture was concerned, they found it impossible to disassociate themselves from a fundamentalist viewpoint: the verbally-inspired inerrancy of the Bible.[45] The Synodical Conference, the American Lutheran Conference, and not a few people and pastors in the United Lutheran Church rested in this kind of attitude. But, as pointed out earlier, several professors in ULCA seminaries had found that Martin Luther himself had liberated them from orthodoxism and had led them to a Christ-centered view of Scripture. Scripture was God's Word because it bore faithful witness to the Christ who is the gospel of God. With this Christocentric view of the Bible they were no longer threatened by either textual or "higher" criticism of the Bible. The Bible's authority lay not in its inerrancy but in its religious message, the Word of God concerning God's self-disclosure in history, in the people of Israel, and ultimately in Jesus Christ. It was a message of sin and grace, judgment and mercy, law and gospel, bondage and freedom. The purpose of the Bible was not to be a textbook in science, history, ethics, or philosophy. According to the Scriptures themselves they were "written that you may believe that Jesus is the Christ, the Son of God, and that believing you may have life in his name" (John 20:31). When this instrumental nature of the Scriptures became clear, the authority of the Bible no longer depended on its being verbally-inspired and inerrant in historical and scientific matters. Some of the professors who took this new attitude were C. M. Jacobs and Henry Offermann in the Lutheran Theological Seminary at Philadelphia, H. C. Alleman and A. R. Wentz of Gettysburg, John Evjen and E. E. Flack of Hamma Divinity School, Springfield, Ohio. Insofar as these men, especially Jacobs and Offermann, can be classified they were most deeply influenced by the *Heilsgeschichtliche* or Erlangen School of theology as represented by such men as J. C. K. von Hofmann, Ludwig Ihmels, and the more contemporary Werner Elert.

Meanwhile, the Augustana Synod was being prepared for a new theological climate by "such independent and unconventional thinkers as Claus A. Wendell and C. J. Sodergren." The former was pastor to students at the University of Minnesota, and the latter was a teacher at the Lutheran Bible Institute in Minneapolis. Both of these men sought to keep their church out of the clutches of fundamentalism and protested the viewpoint that undergirded the American Lutheran Conference.[46]

What was adumbrated by such gadflies as Wendell and Sodergren received a sharply delineated expression in 1930-1931 at Augustana Seminary. Professor C. F. Lindberg, who had trained hundreds of Augustana pastors in the orthodoxist dogmatics of the 17th century, died in 1930. His death and the resignation of four other professors opened the door to the selection of faculty members who represented a new orientation in Lutheran theology. Quite naturally for a seminary with roots in Sweden, the new outlook was consciously shaped by the new Swedish theology, especially that of the Lundensian variety. Two of the five new professors were the chief exponents of the Swedish theology, namely Conrad E. Bergendoff and Eric H. Wahlstrom. The other three—A. D. Mattson, C. A. Anderson, and H. W. Johnson—brought their own gifts and American graduate studies to the task of theological reconstruction. Historian Everett Arden has summarized the change at the synod's seminary as follows:

> It should be noted that the new theological outlook was not "repristination theology," in the sense that it did not seek simply to reproduce a seventeenth-century interpretation of sixteenth-century doctrine. And yet the new outlook was conservatively confessional in the sense that it made the Word of God normative for faith and practice, and accepted the historic symbols of the Lutheran Church as correct and faithful expositions of God's Word. Its conception, however, of what makes Scripture the Word of God differed markedly from the viewpoint implicit in the "Minneapolis Theses." While affirming the doctrine of the divine inspiration of Scripture, Augustana's new outlook repudiated the theory of verbal inspiration, and refused to acknowledge that either this formulation or any other theological formulae were necessarily synonymous with biblical revelation. The new outlook also repudiated the Missourian insistence that Lutheran unity must be achieved on the basis of a common acceptance of certain theological refinements added to the historic confessions, and on strict uniformity in church practice. There remained, however, in the new outlook a certain Rosenian piety which insisted that Christian faith is more than intellectual assent to doctrinal formulation, that it is above all else the experience of the redeeming grace of God in Christ. Indeed, like the Swedish heritage which deeply undergirded it, there was about the new Augustana outlook a breadth and amplitude which sought to discover larger dimensions of God's truth both in the witness of other Christians as well as in the critical disciplines of scholarship. These various characteristics are clearly articulated in the writings of the new theological mentors of the Augustana Church.[47]

It was no secret that the other major bodies were suspicious of the "new theology." In the American Lutheran Church the one theologian who had maintained some openness to the historical orientation of the Erlangen School was J. Michael Reu (1869-1943), professor at Wartburg Seminary, Dubuque, Iowa. In the 20s and early 30s his views were deemed mildly "liberal" because he taught the infallibility of Scripture only in terms of its soteriological message.[48] Before 1934, however, Reu had undergone a change that led him increasingly to sympathize with the viewpoint of the Missouri Synod. When, for example, Ralph H. Long tried to obtain a faculty appointment for Professor Otto Piper, a refugee from Nazi Germany, Reu warned against recommending him because he was not sufficiently Lutheran.[49] Reu's metamorphosis was complete by 1943. His book, *Luther and the Scriptures,* in which he alleged that the Reformer was an advocate of "inerrancy," was the end-point of his theological back-tracking. No significant changes were to appear in the ALC until after World War II, but even then they were not sufficient to remove suspicions of "ULCA theology."

Within the Norwegian Lutheran Church a similar attitude prevailed, despite the fact that a few professors before World War I gave some evidence of uneasiness about scholastic Lutheranism. M. O. Bøckman and E. Kristian Johnsen, for example, represented an historical and exegetical, rather than scholastic, approach to theology, but their contribution to a new outlook was cautious and minimal. In 1930 T. F. Gullixson succeeded Bøckman as president of the church's seminary and brought to his task a wide range of gifts. He was a remarkable preacher, a socially-conscious parish pastor and churchman, a Lincolnesque personality; all of these attributes were controlled by an overriding theological conservatism and churchly pietism. With this kind of leadership it was patent that neither German "neo-Lutheranism" nor Swedish Lundensianism would find a welcome in the second largest Lutheran seminary in America.

Strangely enough, one of Gullixson's close personal friends, L. W. Boe became, alongside John A. Morehead, F. H. Knubel, and Ralph H. Long, a foremost spokesman for Lutheran unity in America and abroad. Restive with Missourianism in his own church and even in his friend Gullixson, Boe urged a declaration of fellowship by the leaders of American Lutheranism in 1934. He insisted that a "kairos" (he did not use the term) was upon the churches and therefore mutual and immediate recognition of one another's ministry of Word and sacrament was essential to the future of

American Lutheranism. "The decks should be cleared," he wrote, "so that Lutherans may move freely from one end of the Lutheran Church to the other." [50]

Boe's plea went unheeded. Finally, on his deathbed in 1942 he wrote his closest friend, President J. A. Aasgaard, urging him to state "that we are in pulpit and altar fellowship with every Lutheran body in this country." [51] Once again Boe's prophetic cry fell on deaf ears. After his death the church moved more and more toward what some justified as a necessary "middle ground" between the United Lutheran Church and the Missouri Synod, a view that was formalized in the merger called The American Lutheran Church (1960). Thirty-five years after Boe's initial call the new American Lutheran Church found it possible to declare fellowship with other Lutherans.

Virtually no signs of theological reconstruction were apparent in the smaller bodies of the National Lutheran Council and certainly none in the Synodical Conference.[52] As far as the Missouri Synod was concerned, The Brief Statement became more and more the touchstone of orthodoxy and the symbol of authority. Theologically secure, the synod carried on a broad missionary and educational program during the decade before the second World War despite the ravages of the depression. Vitality of faith and vigor in action made it possible for the church to transcend the sterility implicit in its doctrinal *status quo*. Even the rather quantitative homiletical application of the law-gospel dialectic as exhibited in Maier's radio sermons did not impede the remarkable growth of "The Lutheran Hour." [53] The best known theological non-conformists in the Missouri Synod during these years were a missionary, A. A. Brux, who was charged with heresy for praying with other Christians in India, and a maverick churchman, O. H. Pannkoke, who counted scores of friends in National Lutheran Council churches and, like Boe, expressed himself as being in favor of immediate steps to church unity.[54]

THEOLOGICAL AND ECUMENICAL RESULTS

Although no spectacular theological and ecumenical awakening took place in the 30s, certain tentative beginnings were made. It should be noted, however, that despite the fact of a minor breakthrough, Lutheran reconstructionists remained solidly confessional and exhibited a skittishness about "modernism." A case in point was the attitude of the Board of Foreign Missions of the United Lutheran Church toward the famous "Hocking Report" (1932). It had brought the entire concept of "mission" under attack. Although missionaries were commended for educational and philanthropic ventures, they were rebuked for engaging in conscious and direct evangelization. To this the ULCA Board made a careful reply, thus adding its voice to that of other denominations that sharply criticized the document. Approving "constructive criticism," the board seriously opposed evidences of liberalism. It concluded its evaluation with these words:

> Our board replies that we know as the foundation of our faith no other religion than that which finds its forgiveness, joy and life in the person of Jesus Christ, the Son of God, who died that we might live and who lives that men may never die.[55]

Other evidences of this anti-liberal attitude were often seen. Harry Emerson Fosdick's radio sermons, for example, were attacked, not only by the Missouri Synod, but also by the "liberal" United Lutheran Church.[56] Nathan Söderblom, who had been enthusiastically welcomed to America by the Augustana Synod in 1923, was charged by other Lutherans with a lack of concern for confessional Lutheranism. Six years later Augustana president Brandelle gave assurances that the synod's reception of Söderblom did not imply an endorsement of his theology.[57] Furthermore, when the United Lutheran Church rejected a fundamentalist view of Scripture, this did not mean an approval of "modernism." As a matter of fact, " . . . Modernism is rationalistic, and corrects the emaciated Bible which it uses, by modern scientific hypotheses and modern philosophic speculations. In part, it revamps old rationalism." [58] Despite the obvious overall conservative climate in American Lutheranism, the acceptance of biblical criticism as a scholarly method and the rejection of orthodoxy's theory of verbal inspiration by some Lutherans was to lead to theological polarization and a regrettable hostility.

Meanwhile, however, the new climate carried with it at least four additional features: (1) a revived interest in the theology of Luther and the thought of Søren Kierkegaard; (2) a deepened understanding of the Lutheran confessions, not as legally binding documents, but as historically-conditioned writings which were needed to safeguard the church's proclamation; (3) a growing recognition that Lutheran theology provided a foundation not only for personal, individual ethics, but social ethics as well; and (4) an openness to the new ecumenical movement. The last two items require further elaboration.

It must be admitted that American Lutheran theology prior to the depression had very little room for social ethics.[59] The "Social Gospel" era made Lutherans generally suspicious of all attempts to "Christianize the social order." The task of the church was to proclaim the gospel which would save individual men from sin, death, and the power of the devil. Christ was primarily interested in individuals. Therefore, the way "for the church to reform the world was to reform people rather than programs, to change the individual rather than his environment."[60] The "Social Gospel," with all its recognized shortcomings, was not yet seen as one of the ways by which the church was being awakened to *social* action. This was to come, but it took the depression and World War II to usher it in. Meanwhile, Christian welfare was directed largely "to rescuing individuals, the lost, the homeless, the straying . . . the least of Christ's brethren."[61]

One of the first steps in the direction of social concern was taken by the National Lutheran Council in the depression year 1933 when, in response to Ralph Long's recommendation, it established a Committee on Social Trends. Rather modest in its challenges, the committee received council approval for statements on liquor, films, the causes of war, and national loyalty in the face of the outbreak of World War II. In 1940 the committee was made a part of the council's new Department of Welfare. Henceforth social welfare was decidedly more prominent than social action. In fact, the latter concern lay dormant until several years after World War II.

Two churches within the National Lutheran Council, namely, the United Lutheran Church and the Augustana Synod, moved considerably ahead of the council in social action, while the American Lutheran and the Norwegian Lutheran churches lagged behind. Likewise when the American Lutheran Conference, pressured by the Augustana Synod, established a Commission on Social Relations (1934), the ALC and the NLCA largely ignored the new group, while Augustana pushed ahead of the conference. Lloyd Svendsbye's analysis of these four major churches from the early 30s to the early 40s reveals an interesting progression regarding the church's role in social action. A short summary follows.[62]

The Norwegian Lutheran Church of America

The minutes of this body are virtually devoid of any reference to social issues. The exceptions were the biennial resolutions on temperance and the considerable support voted for welfare and charitable institutions.[63] During the depression a few lonely prophets expressed a deep sensitivity for the plight of people caught in social and economic distress through no fault of their own. N. Astrup Larsen, a district president and former missionary in China, published an "occasional paper" in which he urged Lutherans to reappraise their stance and to move beyond abstract concern for justice and equity to positive and concrete action in social areas.[64] Another voice was that of G. M. Bruce, professor at Luther Seminary, who charged Lutherans with misinterpreting Luther on social ethics.[65] C. A. Mellby, professor at St. Olaf College, writing in the same series, maintained the church will always have a special role in social work because it has a divine mandate.[66] None of these stands were given serious attention in the church.

American Lutheran Church

Not unlike the NLCA in social attitudes, this church under the prodding of editor Edward Schramm of the *Lutheran Standard* began to recognize the necessity of a Lutheran social ethic to undergird social action. By 1940 its conscience had been stirred to the point that a Board of Christian Social Action was established.[67]

The Evangelical Lutheran Augustana Synod

Scores of writers in the two periodicals of the church, the *Augustana Quarterly* and the *Lutheran Companion,* urged participation by the church in the problems of society. The question of war and peace was often addressed along with related subjects such as conscientious objection and pacifism. Among the new theological professors, A. D. Mattson was prominently associated with the developing social concern. Most Augustana clergymen were to study Christian ethics under him during his 30-year tenure. Great as this influence was, it was complemented by Mattson's extensive writings and membership on social action committees. His theological position revolved about the biblical theme "the kingdom of God." While reflecting "Social Gospel" insights, Mattson sought to retain traditional Lutheran doctrines on man's sin and the need for redemption through Christ. Although the kingdom of God will not be consummated in history, said Mattson, God's rule on earth must increase, for "history has something to do with the Kingdom of God and the Kingdom has something to do with history." [68]

The United Lutheran Church in America

The social direction of the United Lutheran Church during the depression was shaped by a number of influences. One of the three merging synods in 1918, the General Synod, brought a distinct social concern into the new church. Books by W. H. Greever, secretary of the body, and E. P. Pfatteicher, president of the Pennsylvania Ministerium, helped to lead the church into taking specific steps to engage the church in social problems. By 1938 the national convention merged two standing committees to form the Board of Social Missions. This action placed the church on the front line of social concern. Key theological professors, alert journalists, participation in the ecumenical movement, plus the labors of effective executive secretaries through the Board of Social Missions, served to create in the ULCA a highly developed sense of social responsibility.[69]

The second aspect of the new climate in the 30s that needs brief comment was openness to the ecumenical movement. Once again the United Lutheran Church and the Augustana Synod led the way. The former, because of the cooperation of the General Synod in the Federal Council of Churches, quickly found it necessary to formulate its attitude towards other Christian churches (The Washington Declaration) and consequently maintained a "consultative membership" in the Federal Council to whose quadrennial meetings it sent "visitors." [70]

Both of these churches (ULCA and Augustana) were represented officially at the second World Conference on Faith and Order at Edinburgh in 1937, but only Augustana sent delegates to the Second World Conference on Life and Work at Oxford the previous month.[71] The World Council of Churches was to emerge from these two conferences. The question of Lutheran membership in the proposed council was considered during the next decade, and the principle of "confessional representation" was put forth in 1945 and 1946. The roots of this principle can be traced back to The Washington Declaration and to the Lutheran World Convention's 1936 statement called "Lutherans and the Ecumenical Movement." [72] This document, drafted by A. R. Wentz at the request of President Knubel and Bishop August Marahrens of Hannover, Germany, and re-worked by the author with the help of the newly-elected executive secretary of the Lutheran World Convention, Dr. Hanns Lilje, became the "Lutheran platform" for ecumenical relationships. Substantial portions of The Washington Declaration were incorporated into the 1936 Lutheran World Convention document. Of special note was the fact that the celebrated "confessional principle" which later guided some American Lutherans into the World Council of Churches was a reflection of ULCA insistence that ecumenical organizations must be constituted only of official representatives of church bodies, not of co-opted individuals.[73]

Thus by the mid-thirties American Lutherans had adopted the positive attitude of their European brethren toward the emerging ecumenical movement, asserting the essentially ecumenical character of Lutheranism and urging participation in the unity movement as a part of the church's stewardship of the gospel. Meanwhile, however, the "confessional principle" was being tested on the very doorstep of the churches by attempts to bring about a greater degree of unity within American Lutheranism itself.

THE CONFESSIONAL PRINCIPLE AND
LUTHERAN UNITY EFFORTS
1934-1940

Two positions concerning what was necessary for Lutheran unity faced each other in a series of dramatic confrontations during the last half of the decade. The United Lutheran Church rested on its Washington Declaration ("In the case of those Church Bodies calling themselves Evangelical Lutheran, and subscribing the Confessions . . . [the ULCA] recognizes no doctrinal reasons against complete cooperation and organic union with such bodies."). The Missouri Synod posited the necessity of theological and practical uniformity, as expressed in agreed upon theses, in order that it might be assured of the genuineness of confessional subscription. Despite the enormous amount of theological discussion, the demonstrations of dialectical and syntactical skills, and the unquestioned good intentions of theologians, one must ask why the production of theological theses did not assure the evangelical character of the church. Ironically most of the theses proved, in the end, to be divisive rather than unitive.

Until the 1940s the United Lutheran Church used its principle as *a description of an orientation* rather than as a new legalism that might cut the church off from those bodies who continued to insist on agreement in extra-confessional theses. Charitably interpreted, exclusion of the ULCA from the discussion that produced The Minneapolis Theses (1925) might be construed simply as a logical inference to be drawn by other Lutherans from The Washington Declaration: that is, the ULCA excluded itself from discussions with others by this declaration. To assure fellow Lutherans that this was not a proper inference, the ULCA appointed in 1928 a Commission on Lutheran Church Unity for "the promotion of Lutheran unification in America." [74]

Despite this gesture there was no response, except for brief flutterings from the Augustana Synod, which later joined those who had drafted The Minneapolis Theses as a basis for the American Lutheran Conference (1930). Rebuffed but undaunted, the United Lutheran Church felt compelled to reassert its two-pronged approach by adopting The Savannah Declaration (1934). This statement reiterated its conviction that for unity it was unnecessary to set up "other standards or tests of Lutheranism apart from (the Confessions) or alongside of them." [75] Then, in order to assure other Lutherans that it would not sit in splendid isolation grasping this evangelical principle to its breast, the church declared its willingness to enter doctrinal conversations by inviting any and all other Lutheran bodies to unity negotiations. Only two of the dozen or more bodies responded affirmatively: the Missouri Synod and the American Lutheran Church, the latter being newly formed (1930). [76]

The experiences that the ULCA encountered with Missouri and the old ALC between 1936 and 1940 brought on a sense of futility over the possibility of furthering the cause of unity by the method of extra-confessional agreements. [77] From the time of the debacle surrounding The Pittsburgh Agreement (1940) to the present, the United Lutheran Church (and after 1962, the Lutheran Church in America) has returned to the position of The Washington and Savannah Declarations and has announced that it considers itself to be in fellowship with all who subscribe to the historic Lutheran confessions.

Because the attitudes made clear in the decade of the 30s persisted into the 60s and were the cause of some exacerbation in inter-Lutheran relations, [78] an examination of the doctrinal discussions leading to 1940 may prove to be illuminating.

ULCA-Missouri Conversations, 1936-1938 [79]

Two meetings of the commissioners representing the United Lutheran Church in America and the Missouri Synod were held: the first, November 23, 1936, at Detroit; the second, February 25, 1938, at Pittsburgh.[80]

Although the conversations began amicably, the lines of separation were unmistakable from the start. F. H. Knubel led off the discussion with a paper on "The Need for Lutheran Solidarity." [81] The immediate Missouri response to Knubel's address was almost emotional, as witnessed by the following:

> Arndt: "I almost tremble when I think of what might be the result of this meeting."
> Kretzmann: "There is no doubt of the need of Lutheran solidarity and it is much closer than seventy-five years ago."
> Engelder: "We are in conscience bound to bring about Lutheran union. Dr. Knubel has spoken out of the heart of us all."

But then upon reflection some of the warmth began to disappear:

> Engelder: "We cannot call you brothers."
> Brunn: "Union of hearts and faith must precede external union. We have the truth."

The second and third papers dealt with (1) the inspiration of the Scriptures, and (2) the relation of the Word of God to the Scriptures. Professor William Arndt's essay led the Missourians to point out that their position had already been set forth in The Brief Statement (1932), especially the first section entitled "Of the Holy Scriptures." [82] The doctrine of verbal inspiration and its corollary, biblical inerrancy in all matters, scientific and historical as well as theological, was boldly affirmed.

The ULCA position paper was prepared and presented by Professor C. M. Jacobs, president of the Evangelical Lutheran Seminary in Philadelphia (Mt. Airy).[83] Its very title, "The Word of God and the Scriptures," implied a quite different approach to the problem, an approach that saw the Scriptures as the human instrument whereby God communicated his Word, the gospel. Moreover, Christ was seen as the Word because he is God's gospel or message to men.

It was a foregone conclusion, even before the second of the two conversations, that there would be no meeting of minds. After the Missouri representatives returned to St. Louis, an editorial appeared in the official organ of the synod charging the ULCA with denying that the Bible is the Word of God.[84] Professor Jacobs was offended by this and, at the suggestion of President Knubel, wrote to Professor Arndt protesting the blatant misrepresentation of the ULCA position. He urged that the Missouri commissioners take steps to make the real situation clear to their church body. Unless the false accusation by the editor of the *Witness* was repudiated, further conferences would become very difficult. "We do not venture to say," said Jacobs, "that it is the editor's purpose to prevent helpful results from our conference, but if that were his purpose he could not serve it better than by writing as he has done." [85]

A second conference was held but neither side was able to accept the other's view of Scripture. This led the Missouri Synod to take the following action in 1938:

> *Resolved,* That Synod should take steps . . . to help avoid any premature and unwarranted conclusions regarding the status of our relation with the ULCA. These negotiations must not be interpreted as implying that Synod has changed its position in any of the doctrines discussed. . . .[86]

Although the minutes of the second session of the conversations (February 25-26, 1938, Pittsburgh, Pa.) recorded the decision to leave "further joint meetings to the Presidents of the two bodies," it was hardly expected that discussion would be resumed. During the spring of 1939, there occurred a fruitless exchange of letters between Knubel and Behnken. In the midst of this correspondence, the editor of *The Lutheran Witness* wrote a second blast against the ULCA. In this chilly atmosphere, the conversations were dropped.[87]

ULCA-ALC Conversations, 1936-1939 [88]

In 1934 the four-year-old American Lutheran Church requested its president, C. C. Hein, to convey personally its greetings to the Savannah convention of the United Lutheran Church in America.[89] It was reported that Hein was both friendly and frank—friendly in his hopes for closer ties and frank in his statement of the issues that separated the two churches.[90]

The ULCA's reply was in the form of a resolution, the so-called Savannah Declaration, which (1) re-asserted the view that acceptance of the historic confessions was an adequate basis for Lutheran unity and (2) asked its president, F. H. Knubel, to invite other Lutherans to unity conferences and to appoint a commission to represent the ULCA in such conferences.

Following the ALC's acceptance of the invitation, a series of joint meetings was held by the commissioners of the two bodies between 1936 and 1939.[91] These meetings concluded with the adoption in 1940 of the Pittsburgh Articles of Agreement." They asserted that the negotiating committees had arrived at a consensus on three decisive issues: secret societies, unionism, and inspiration. Both ALC and ULCA conventions of 1940 adopted the "Agreement," but in each instance there was something less than enthusiasm for the action. The minutes show why a cordial acceptance of the "Agreement" could hardly be expected, and incidentally provide at least a partial explanation of the later unwillingness of the Lutheran Church in America to get involved in the doctrinal discussion between the new ALC and the Missouri Synod in the 60s.[92]

The Discussions on Lodges and Unionism

The first conference (February 6-7, 1936) began with some sparring regarding the topics to be discussed. This led President Hein to propose The Minneapolis Theses as a basis for the negotiations.[93] To this President Knubel replied, "I do not believe that the Minneapolis Theses are profitable for our work." [94] Knubel had deep feelings about The Minneapolis Theses because of their original church-political purpose and their theological content. It was clear to all, even to Hein, that if The Minneapolis Theses as such were to be the basis for discussion, a successful outcome was foreclosed from the beginning. Consequently, the ALC commissioners agreed that certain "topics" rather than The Minneapolis Theses, could be designated for the agenda.[95]

With the preliminary skirmishing completed, the remainder of the conference was confined to a discussion of four topics: the lodge question, fellowship with non-Lutherans, the inspiration of the Bible, and ecclesiastical discipline.

The lodge issue revolved chiefly about the appropriateness of *clerical* membership, for the ALC as well as the ULCA numbered lodge members among its laity. The ALC felt that the ULCA was lax toward those pastors who were Freemasons. Knubel replied that the lodge issue was already dead and that, given time, it would resolve itself. Meanwhile, he as president was following a "quiet persuasive method" in dealing with the question. Jacobs said that a sure way to strengthen the antagonism of the lodge members was to make membership a matter of public discipline.[96]

The discussion of "unionism" (indiscriminate fellowship with non-Lutherans) and discipline served to clarify the views of both churches, and gave promise of mutual understanding.

The discussion of biblical inspiration revealed that a sharp difference of viewpoint prevailed and that of the topics under debate this one would only with difficulty yield to resolution.

Before the conference closed two sub-committees were appointed to prepare statements for presentation at the second meeting scheduled for April 2 and 3, 1936, at Columbus. Poppen and Bagger were to draft two proposals, one on the lodge question, the other on "pulpit and altar fellowship" with non-Lutherans. Reu and Jacobs were requested to draft a joint statement on "The Scriptures and the Word of God."

After a frank and sometimes sharp exchange at the second conversation, it seemed as if the conference would adjourn without having reached any agreement. Such an outcome, however, was resolutely resisted by both sides. A new ALC statement on lodges and unionism was submitted. This was discussed and amended by the ULCA without incurring the displeasure of the authors. At this point the group voted unanimously to approve what became Articles I and II of The Pittsburgh Agreement.[97]

The Discussions on Scripture

Lengthy and detailed discussion concerning the inspiration of the Scriptures took place at each of the conferences between 1936 and 1939. At the first meeting (February 6-7, 1936, Pittsburgh) President Hein, as noted above, had sought to make The Minneapolis Theses the basis of discussion. The Minneapolis statement said: "The synods . . . accept without exception all the canonical books of the Old and New Testaments as a whole, and in all their parts, as the divinely inspired, revealed, and inerrant Word of God, and submit to this as the only infallible authority in all matters of faith and life." [98]

When Hein reminded the group that the ALC committee had "definite instruction to confer on the basis of The Minneapolis Theses," Knubel replied that the "history behind them prevents their being profitable." [99] Hein countered with the words " . . . these Minneapolis Theses do not

. . . present more about the Scriptures . . . than what we have taken from the Scriptures. . . . A sincere acceptance of the Holy Scriptures implies an acceptance of the principles laid down in the Minneapolis Theses." This statement was immediately interpreted as bringing into question the "sincerity" of the ULCA because it had not accepted The Minneapolis Theses and because, in the opinion of the ALC, it was lax in the exercise of discipline. It was apparent to all that the debate had now been led into an area of ecclesiastical quicksand from which it would be difficult to extricate both sides. At this point, therefore, Knubel said, "Very kindly, but very definitely I should say this . . . : We see no reason why we should not enter into closer fellowship, even union, with the ALC. If we enter into this discussion, it is all one-sided for your sake. We can suggest items in your life which we do not like, but they do not interfere with our willingness. It is because you find certain things in our life with which you find fault that you desire this discussion." [100]

Smarting a bit from this rebuke, Hein reluctantly backed away from the issue of "sincerity," but as he did so he insisted that there was one matter that had to be brought out in the open, namely, the ULCA's publication of Professor H. C. Alleman's studies on the Old and New Testaments.[101] Hein asked Professor Reu to state the ALC's criticism:

> Reu: "I was painfully surprised by the publication of the Alleman books. I found nothing dangerous in the book on the New Testament, but in the book on the Old Testament the author takes the position that in a large section of the Old Testament we do not have the Word of God. Many statements indicate the author's attitude that the doctrine of verbal inspiration of Holy Writ must be given up. If in a book brought out as a part of a series of textbooks officially recognized in the Church it is said that large sections of Holy Scripture are traditions or records . . . then divine inspiration must be given up.[102]

The burden of the ULCA reply was carried by Professors C. M. Jacobs and H. Offermann, and President Knubel. The latter, sensitive to the dynamics of ecclesiastical politics, was inclined to admit that Alleman was not beyond reproach, but was, at the same time, "not altogether bad." Knubel feared, however, that there was too much fundamentalism among Lutherans, and this was revealed by the negative attitude towards the Alleman books. Jacobs and Offermann, as theologians, were much more concerned about theological truth than ecclesiastical sensitivities. They insisted that Alleman must not be faulted as a biblical scholar. He wrote as one who assumed the doctrine of revelation; moreover, he did not deny the inspiration of the written record of that revelation. It must be remembered, said Jacobs, that Alleman had prepared a study in Old Testament literature, not a book in dogmatics.[103]

Offermann maintained that Lutherans should be neither fundamentalists nor liberals in their understanding of Scripture.

> The main thing is that we realize today that there is upon us the very important task to set forth before the world the Lutheran attitude toward the Scriptures. Though on the surface conservative Protestants seem in agreement as to the Scriptures, there is a distinctive Lutheran attitude. We agree neither with the liberal attitude nor with the fundamentalist. . . . Our attitude toward the Scriptures is Christocentric. This puts upon us the important task: 1. To emphasize the fact that for all of us with our whole heart there is no other authority and rule in faith and life than the Holy Scriptures. 2. We must state anew our Lutheran attitude toward the Scriptures from the Christocentric point of view. The Scriptures are more than the historical record of God's revelation in Christ. The Word of God has a center, Christ Himself.[104]

The last point was a restatement of what Knubel had said earlier: "I do not believe in Christ as my Saviour because I believe in the Scriptures. I believe in the Scriptures because I believe in Christ as my Saviour." This apparently was what was meant by a "Lutheran" attitude toward Scripture: justification by faith in Christ became both a hermeneutical principle and an authority principle.

Hein's reply was that this question could not be settled overnight. He implied that he himself might see the truth of the ULCA position, but entire groups in the ALC were "suspicious of the ULCA attitudes towards the Scriptures." [105]

The discussion had revealed that the two groups were proceeding from different premises, but Knubel, wishing to conclude that the two committees were generally of one mind and that the real problem lay not among them but among the fundamentalists in their constituencies, proposed that a sub-committee "draw up a statement of the disinctive Lutheran conception of the Scriptures to be presented to both sides." This would be "for the good of men in both groups" who had a fundamentalist view of Scripture.[106]

Following up this suggestion, W. E. Schuette (ALC) made a motion that Jacobs and Reu prepare a joint statement on the Scriptures and the Word of God for consideration at a subsequent meeting of the commission. Although Reu asked to be excused because he felt himself to be unacceptable in some ALC circles, he was eventually prevailed upon to serve with Jacobs in preparing such a statement.

At the next meeting of the Joint Commission (April 2-3, 1936, Columbus), it was explained that, due to illness (Jacobs') and the brevity of time, Reu and Jacobs had worked independently. Consequently, the members of the commission were faced, not with a joint production on "The Scriptures and the Word of God" (as requested by the February meeting), but with two statements. The one by Reu placed the emphasis on "The Scriptures"; the one by Jacobs stressed "The Word of God." Reu explained that he felt that the difficulty between the churches centered about "the origin and therefore the character of Scripture." [107] Consequently, Reu's statement focused the attention of the commission on the nature of the Bible and its inspiration, citing the familiar proof passages, 2 Tim. 3:16 and 2 Peter 1:21. Reu's original draft, interestingly enough, spoke of the Bible as being without error. This was dropped in later versions, but the final version ("The Pittsburgh Agreement") spoke of the Bible as "a complete, *errorless* [italics added], unbreakable whole. . . . " The course of the debate will reveal why Reu felt it necessary to include this word.

The statement by Jacobs dealt primarily with "The Word of God" as it is related to the Bible. In introducing his statement to the commission, Jacobs said

> I believe . . . that we would not get a satisfactory solution of our problem if we began and ended our statement with the Bible. We are all agreed that the Bible is the Word of God. . . . The problem, therefore, is not the Bible. . . . The term means something very definite and concrete. . . . When we speak of the Word of God we are coming to something that needs to be further defined. While we all agree the Bible is the Word of God, we may not all agree on exactly what we mean when we say the Bible is the Word of God. Therefore, it seemed to me to be really important that in any prepared and adequate statement . . . we must begin with the concept of the Word of God.[108]

Commencing with a quotation from the *Epitome* (Formula of Concord), Jacobs pointed out that the authority of Scriptures rests in their being the Word of God. Since, however, the term "Word of God" is used in more than one sense, it is important to understand these different senses. First, the Word of God means the gospel; second, the Word of God is the historical self-revelation of God completed in Jesus Christ and interpreted by men chosen and inspired by God; third, because God continues to make himself known in the Holy Scriptures of which Christ is the center, the Bible is properly called the Word of God. The Scriptures have their more important and less important parts, the measure of their importance being the closeness of their relation to the gospel, which is the Word of God in the primary sense. Inspiration is accepted as a fact of which "our faith in God, through Christ, assures us." The mode or manner of inspiration, however, is beyond human definition.

ALC objection to Jacobs' paper was most frequently voiced by President Hein. Jacobs, he said, did not answer to his satisfaction the question of inspiration. What does inspiration really mean? What is inspired in the Scriptures, the whole Scripture or only a part.[109] From the context of Hein's comments it was evident that he equated inspiration and inerrancy. That is, to admit errors was to deny inspiration, to affirm inspiration was to deny errors. With considerable emotion Hein asserted:

> I want to tell you frankly, Brethren, if we would come before the American Lutheran Church with Dr. Jacobs' statement, at once we would be asked the question, "Now what did your commission really mean by inspiration and how much in their estimation is inspired?" This statement . . . does not solve our difficulty.[110]

President Hein's massive fears had not been allayed by Jacobs' careful and lucid explication of his position. Because of its contemporary significance it is herewith reproduced so that the reader may make his own judgment:

> *Dr. Jacobs:* . . . Dr. Hein has felt that he has found in this statement a primary and secondary Word of God. . . . There is no such thing as a primary and secondary Word of God. . . . When we use the Word of God we use it in a primary and secondary meaning, hence when we say the Word of God we do not always mean the same thing. . . . The Word of God is the

Gospel. . . . The Augsburg Confession says the means of Grace
is the Gospel. . . . When we talk about the Word of God, then,
we mean Christ, we mean the Gospel. Take Luther's Introduction to the Epistle to the Romans, what is the Word of God
here? The Gospel. . . . But now I am going to speak very
frankly. The place where we get into difficulty is when we say
the Scriptures are the Word of God because they are inspired.
Our belief, our conviction that the Scriptures are inspired de-
pends upon our conviction that the Scriptures are the Word of
God. After, not before, but after we see that the Scriptures are
the Word of God, we are then able to say the Scriptures are inspired. Now, when we say the Scriptures are the Word of God
because they are inspired, if that statement stands by itself without
this further explanation of what we mean by the Word of God,
we fall into the danger of . . . an atomistic conception of the Word
of God. We fall into the danger of arguing this way, the Scriptures are the Word of God because they are a collection of Words
of God, and so unconsciously in our own mind we have transferred in our thought from "the Word of God" to "Words of
God." That is an altogether different conception of the Word of
God from that which I have tried to set forth here.[111]

The subsequent debate included a discussion of Reu's paper which, as
Hein pointed out, dealt with "the real problem," by which he meant
verbal inspiration and inerrancy. Both Knubel and Jacobs urged that Reu's
phrases on inerrancy ("by which He supplied the Holy Writers content
and fitting word" and "without contradiction and error") should be
either amplified or omitted. To do this, replied Hein, would be to strike
a blow at the very heart and center of the matter.[112] Knubel, seeking a way
out of the impasse, turned to Jacobs and asked him if he could take
Reu's document "and, instead of omitting, amplify those statements in
some perfectly unambiguous manner . . . ?" Jacobs was certain that he
could do so, but he was equally certain that the result would be unacceptable to the ALC. Hein agreed.

As the conference drew to a close, there was reluctance on both sides to
admit failure in the attempt to resolve the difficulty. Consequently, when
a proposal was made that Jacobs and Reu seek once more to hammer
out a joint statement, the two theologians agreed to have another go at
it before the next meeting.[113]

In summary, it can be said that the joint meetings of 1936 had revealed the following:

1) The American Lutheran Church took the position that verbal inspiration guaranteed the inerrancy of Scripture, and therefore its authority as the Word of God.

2) The United Lutheran Church began, not with the inspiration of Scriptures, but with the concept of the Word of God, coming only at the conclusion to the question of inspiration.

3) President Hein was the chief spokesman for the ALC; Professor Jacobs for the ULCA.

4) Professor Reu, though less oral than Hein, was theologically more sophisticated in his support of the ALC view.

5) President Knubel, though committed to the ULCA position, was a Bismarckian ecclesiastical politician ("politics is the art of the possible"). Hence, he was prepared to yield if by so doing closer relationships might be achieved.[114]

6) Professor Jacobs, despite his theologically careful and lucid statement on the *nature* of the Word of God and the Scriptures, would have preferred to have limited the discussion to the *function* of the Bible, which had already been addressed in the Formula of Concord. He felt that extra-confessional statements were unnecessary for Lutheran unity.[115]

The third joint meeting of the ULCA-ALC commissioners had been tentatively scheduled for July, 1936.[116] Meanwhile, however, President Hein became ill and died (April 1937). Although it was his wish that the meetings be continued, it was not until March 1938 that the two committees could be brought together. The chief item on the agenda was to be the report of the Jacobs-Reu sub-committee on the Scriptures and the Word of God. Unfortunately Professor Jacobs had also become seriously ill—he died in March 1938—and Reu submitted a revised version of his own earlier document which, he said, had been sent to Jacobs for criticism. Henceforth, therefore, Reu's statement—not Jacobs'—was the basis for discussion. Alterations, submitted by Jacobs prior to his death, were intended to keep Reu's statement from being too fundamentalistic, but the old problem of inerrancy reappeared when Reu asked that his original phrase "without contradiction and error" be reinserted into the document.[117] Reu explained that before he had read Alleman's new commentary on the New Testament, he had expressed his willingness to drop the phrase. Meanwhile, however, he had read the book and was forced to change his mind.[118]

When pressed by the ULCA men, Reu said that inerrancy applied, of course, only to the original biblical manuscripts. Knubel and Offermann retorted that this made the whole question academic because the originals are lost. Reu had the grace to say, "I know that is a weak point"; but he felt he must insist on the phrase. By way of explanation he recounted a metamorphosis which had occurred in him. In the years leading up to the 1930 ALC merger he had fought the Ohio Synod doctrine of inspiration. Since that time he had come to accept the inerrancy of the original writings, but had not deemed it an essential point. But over against recent tendencies in the Lutheran church he believed it necessary to insist on such a doctrine.[119]

Although Knubel and Offermann argued against this point, Reu remained adamant throughout the remainder of the discussion. The problem of Scripture, therefore, remained unresolved. It was agreed, nevertheless, to meet again after the 1938 church conventions. Each committee meanwhile would make a report to its church body giving the exact situation in the discussions, revealing the point where agreement could not be reached.[120]

The reports were duly made, but it is significant that each convention thereupon took action to articulate its views by adopting its own official "declaration." In the case of the ULCA, this meant the Jacobs statement, revised in a few details came to become known as The Baltimore Declaration.[121]

In like manner the ALC adopted a statement that came to be known as The Sandusky Declaration. Primarily oriented toward the Missouri Synod, this "declaration" was a public affirmation of Reu's posture on Scripture. In fact, a comparison of Reu's statement presented to the ULCA commissioners with The Sandusky Declaration shows the two to be virtually identical, even including the controversial phrase "without contradiction and error." [122]

The Missourian direction of The Sandusky Declaration drew a sharp and somewhat humorous comment from L. W. Boe. Writing to his ALC friend, Ralph H. Long, he expressed fear that the progress already achieved would now be undone:

. . . this proposition looks to me as if it may unravel every bit of advance we have made these twenty years since the NLC was formed. You will remember the story that I told you once about a man and his wife who had come home after seeing a show. When he undressed he said to his wife that he could not understand what had happened to him. He said he had his underwear on when he started out, and now he could not find it. Then his wife said, "That explains it. I saw a thread sticking out from your collar, and so I pulled it." Missouri found this little thread sticking out, and if we permit them to start unraveling they can proceed until they have finished with the National Lutheran Council and the Lutheran World Convention. . . . I do not intend quietly to sit on the sidelines and see the "underwear" of the Lutherans of America taken off without their knowing it.[123]

Although the National Lutheran Council was not "unravelled" until the 60s, it was no secret at the end of 1938 that two NLC church bodies (ULC and ALC) had assumed positions untenable and unacceptable to the other. Nevertheless, a fourth meeting of the joint commission was held in Pittsburgh, February 13, 1939. Once again Reu's statement, with the now deceased Jacobs' changes incorporated, was before the group. As before, the ALC upheld the old question of the inerrancy of the original manuscripts. Said Reu, referring to I Sam. 13.1, "This contradicts other statements of the Old Testament. We claim that in the original Hebrew Scriptures there was no such contradiction." [124] Knubel replied that such matters do not affect our salvation: "We do not wish to be asked or to be bound to make a confession on these matters." However, Knubel continued, if the ALC would understand that the ULCA would never accept a fundamentalist interpretation of inerrancy, he personally would be willing to introduce the word "errorless," although, he added, "I know that we would not understand the word in the same way." [125] Knubel had said in a previous meeting (April 1936) that his church held to the *doctrinal* perfection of the Scriptures centering in Christ.[126] The Word of God is perfect, without error. But the Word of God is primarily the gospel of our salvation in Christ. With this understanding, said Knubel, he would propose in place of Reu's "without contradiction and error" the following: the books of the Bible, taken together, "constitute a complete, errorless, unbreakable whole of which Christ is the center." [127]

Reu was reluctant to accede to the rewording. He asked Knubel if this new phrase went "farther than your [Baltimore] Declaration?" To this Knubel replied, "It does." Thereupon Reu voted for the admission of the change.

At this juncture the joint commission adopted the whole article on Scripture and the previously approved articles on lodge membership and unionism. Thus was born "The Pittsburgh Agreement," soon to be labeled "The Pittsburgh Disagreement." [128]

Aftermath

The goal of "The Pittsburgh Agreement" was noble and praiseworthy, namely, better inter-Lutheran relations. For the United Lutheran Church the hope had been organic union; for the American Lutheran Church, pulpit and altar fellowship. When the two church conventions adopted the Pittsburgh articles in 1940, the action in neither case led to the hoped-for goals. The ALC regarded the articles as the acceptance of its views on verbal inspiration. Reu had written in the ALC theological journal that now the ULCA acknowledged the complete errorlessness of the Scriptures. In fact, said he, The Pittsburgh Agreement "goes beyond the Baltimore Declaration of 1938 in two points. First, it expressly states the rightly understood (not the mechanical) verbal inspiration of Scripture; and second, the errorlessness of Scripture is no longer restricted to the portions that have reference to salvation." [129] It can be safely concluded that this was the interpretation received by the ALC as a whole. Despite this, the church failed to declare pulpit and altar fellowship because there was a general feeling that one ought to wait and see if the ULCA "lived up to" its agreement.

The Pittsburgh Agreement had a strange reception at the 1940 convention of the ULCA. The articles were accompanied by a lengthy preamble that sought to assure the convention that there was nothing in the agreement that stood in contradiction to The Washington Declaration of 1920, The Savannah Resolution of 1934, and The Baltimore Declaration of 1938: ". . . where these Articles might seem to be in conflict with the aforesaid instruments, it is to be understood that these Articles are to be interpreted in the light of those instruments and not vice versa." [130]

Although the majority "swallowed hard" and voted to adopt the articles, a significant minority led by a young pastor named Franklin Clark Fry spoke against approval. In addition, three members of the ULCA commission (Bagger, Krauss, Miller) withdrew their support of the report in the following statement:

> Though recognizing the fact that the President's statement is in complete harmony with the report submitted by the Commission, which indeed bears our own signatures and has been adopted, we ask the privilege of recording our present dissent from the report because of its implications. Though fearing it from the beginning, we are now more than ever convinced that neither truth nor the cause of unity can be served by the ambiguity of the report in question, particularly as regards the third Article of the Agreement on the Scriptures.[131]

The year 1940 was in some respects a watershed. The American Lutheran Church turned more and more to the Norwegian Lutheran Church (ELC after 1946) and the Missouri Synod. With the latter it worked out a Common Confession, Part I, in 1949, which was adopted by both churches in 1950. Part II, issued in 1952 and adopted by the ALC in 1953, was not accepted by the Missouri Synod until 1956 and then *not* as a doctrinally operative statement but as "a significant historical statement." Meanwhile, the ALC was moving towards a merger of some of the churches in the American Lutheran Conference, especially the ELC and the UELC, who shared the ALC's uncertainties about the ULCA and found the statements on Scripture in The Minneapolis Theses and The Pittsburgh Agreement preferable to The Baltimore Declaration. This eventuated in the formation of the new American Lutheran Church in 1960.

Meanwhile the United Lutheran Church, smarting under the experiences culminating in the 1940 conventions, replied to subsequent overtures regarding Lutheran fellowship and union that no further definitions of doctrine were necessary. Echoing its Savannah Resolution (1934) it would advance no tests of Lutheranism beyond the Lutheran confessions.

The question that had disturbed American Lutheranism since the 20s and 30s—does confessional unity require theological uniformity?—was to remain unresolved for at least two more decades. The United Lutheran Church and, after 1962 the Lutheran Church in America, answered the question with a clear no; the American Lutheran Church, the majority of the other members of the American Lutheran Conference, and the Missouri Synod replied in the affirmative, though their "yes" was spoken with varying degrees of resoluteness. There the problem posed by Lutheranism's confessional principle resided until the late 60s and extended itself even into the 70s.

NOTES

1. *The Kingdom of God in America* (New York: Harper and Brothers, 1937, Harper Torch Books, 1959), p. 193.
2. "Theology in America: A Historical Survey," *The Shaping of American Religion,* Vol. 1: *Religion in American Life,* eds., J. W. Smith and A. L. Jamison (Princeton: Princeton University Press, 1961), pp. 297-298.
3. To carry out the figure of speech it should be noted that most boxers suffering a knockout revive to enter other rings. Liberalism was no exception.
4. Winthrop S. Hudson, *Religion in America* (New York: Charles Scribner's Sons, 1965), p. 379.
5. For details see Lefferts A. Loetscher, *The Broadening Church: A Study of Theological Issues in the Presbyterian Church Since 1869* (Philadelphia: University of Pennsylvania Press, 1954).
6. Clifton E. Olmstead, *History of Religion in the United States* (Englewood Cliffs, N.J.: Prentice-Hall, Inc., 1960), pp. 555-556.
7. See Sydney E. Ahlstrom, "Continental Influence on American Christian Thought since World War I," *Church History,* XXXVII (September, 1958), 256-273. Ahlstrom concludes his survey by characterizing the European impact as "Kierkegaardian" (p. 270). This term transcends Kierkegaard himself and describes the widespread reappraisal of Christianity which occurred in America. However, a notable cadre of Kierkegaard specialists began to appear in the 30s and 40s on the American horizon: David Swenson, Walter Lowrie, Howard Hong, Paul Holmer, Martin Heinecken, *et al.*
8. Most historians of American theological thought distinguish between liberalism and modernism. The former took as its point of departure the Christian tradition and sought to re-think it in light of historical criticism and the scientific method. The modernists, however, were unimpressed by the liberals' attempt to maintain the Christian faith and struck out boldly to create a scientifically verifiable religious position. The "scientific modernists" (Sidney Mead's phrase) were often associated with the so-called "Chicago School." See Hudson, *Religion in America,* pp. 273-277, and H. S. Smith, R. T. Handy, and L. A. Loetscher, *American Christianity,* II (New York: Charles Scribner's Sons, 1963), 238-265.
9. A useful collection of documents has been assembled in Richard C. Wolf, *Documents of Lutheran Unity* (Philadelphia: Fortress Press, 1966). For the 1919 and 1920 statements, see pp. 292-293, 301-312, 345-355. Cf. E. Clifford Nelson, *The Lutheran Church Among Norwegian Americans,* II, 287-302, and C. M. Jacobs, "The Washington Declaration: An Interpretation," *The Lutheran Church Review,* XL (January, 1921), 1-21.
10. "The Baltimore Declaration," largely the work of C. M. Jacobs. The statement is to be found in Wolf, *Documents,* pp. 357-359.
11. *Ibid.,* p. 348.
12. C. M. Jacobs, "Inaugural Address," *The Lutheran Church Review,* XLVI (July, 1927), 216-221; John O. Evjen, Henry F. Offermann, and A. R. Wentz writing in a symposium *What Is Lutheranism?* ed. by Vergilius Ferm (New York: The Macmillan

Co., 1930) describe the authority of the Bible by such phrases as *"was Christum treibet"* (p. 25); "they [the Scriptures] are the records of that divine revelation which culminates in the historical person and work of Jesus Christ. . . . The true understanding of the gospel is always the key to the true understanding of the Word of God in its relation to the Christ . . . and to the Scriptures that testify of Him." (p. 57); "That Word is Christ, and because the Holy Scriptures are the record of God's revelation . . . they are our sole and supreme authority in matters of religion. . . . " (p. 88).

13. Wolf, *Documents,* pp. 273, 355-357.

14. For a discussion of these, see Nelson, *The Lutheran Church Among Norwegian-Americans,* II, 229-240.

15. The first president of the National Lutheran Council was H. G. Stub, president of the NLCA, and the first executive secretary was Lauritz Larsen. Others prominent in council affairs were L. W. Boe and J. A. O. Stub, the son of H. G. Stub.

16. Nelson, *The Lutheran Church Among Norwegian-Americans,* II, 132-136.

17. *The Formation of the American Lutheran Church* (Columbus: The Wartburg Press, 1958), pp. 177-253, 272-278.

18. Karl E. Mattson, "The Theology of the Augustana Lutheran Church," *Centennial Essays,* eds. Emmet Engberg, *et al.* (Rock Island: Augustana Press, 1960), p. 42.

19. G. Everett Arden, *Augustana Heritage* (Rock Island: Augustana Press, 1963), p. 279.

20. *Ibid.,* p. 284.

21. Franz Pieper, *Christian Dogmatics* (St. Louis: Concordia Publishing House, 1950-1953), 3 vols. Translated by Theo. Engelder from the original *Christliche Dogmatik* (St. Louis: 1917-1920). For an assessment of Pieper see Leigh D. Jordahl, "The Theology of Franz Pieper: A Resource for Fundamentalistic Thought Modes Among American Lutherans," *The Lutheran Quarterly,* XXIII (May, 1971), 118-137.

22. Pieper, *Christian Dogmatics,* I, Preface, ix. Pieper includes the Wisconsin Synod and the German theologian, Franz Delitzsch, as supporters of this view. See his discussion, pp. 160-186. The "repristinationists" in both Europe and America sought to preserve the evangelical witness of the church, but failed to meet the challenge of the historical method. Consequently, "repristinationism" and "historicism" were like ships passing in the night, the former wafted on the winds of 17th century syllogisms, the latter blown by the gales of the critical method. Lutheran confessionalism finally found a "modern" expression in the so-called "Erlangen School" that successfully faced the intellectualism of orthodoxists, the relativism of historicists, and the idealism of speculative theologians. For a careful study of the 19th century problem see Gerhard Forde, *The Law-Gospel Debate* (Minneapolis: Augsburg Publishing House, 1969).

23. For a detailed account, see Carl E. Meyer, "The Historical Background of 'A Brief Statement,'" *Concordia Theological Monthly,* XXXII (July, August, and September, 1961), 403-428, 466-482, 526-542. The statement is reprinted in Wolf, *Documents,* pp. 381-392. Although Pieper was "more conservative" than his older colleague, C. F. W. Walther from whom he received the mantle of leadership, Pieper actually echoed Walther's "orthodox" position on Scripture. Walther had written: "Beware, beware, I say of this 'divine-human Scripture.' It is the devil's mask. For eventually it constructs such a Bible after which I would not wish to call myself a Bible Christian. . . . For if I believed that the Bible contains errors, then it is no longer a touchstone for me, but needs a touchstone itself. In short, it is unspeakable what the devil tries with the 'divine-human Scripture.'" Cited by Robert Preus, "Walther and the Scriptures," *Concordia Theological Monthly,* XXXII (November, 1961), 674.

24. For articles on each of the groups see *The Encyclopedia of the Lutheran Church.* Careful book-length histories have been published on some of these groups. See Eugene L. Fevold, *The Lutheran Free Church* (Minneapolis: Augsburg Publishing House, 1969); J. M. Jensen, *The United Ev. Lutheran Church* (Minneapolis: Augsburg Publishing House, 1964); and Enok Mortensen, *The Danish Lutheran Church in America* (Philadelphia: The Board of Publication, LCA, 1967). Paul C. Nyholm, *The Americani-*

zation of the Danish Lutheran Churches (Minneapolis: Augsburg Publishing House, 1963); and George Dolak, *A History of the Slovak Ev. Lutheran Church . . . 1902-1927* (St. Louis: Concordia Publishing House, 1955).

25. Wolf, *Documents*, p. 350.

26. For a critique see Georg Sverdrup, "The Struggle for Unity," in *The Heritage of Faith. Selections from the Writings of Georg Sverdrup,* trans. by M. A. Helland (Minneapolis: Augsburg Publishing House, 1969), pp. 65-80.

27. Wolf, *Documents*, pp. 340-342.

28. "The American Lutheran Conference," *Lutheran Church Herald,* November 11, 1930, p. 1587.

29. L. W. Boe, "The Church and Its Work," *Lutheran Herald,* XVII (June 27, 1933), 592. Boe wrote to one of the ULCA synodical presidents, "I cannot help but tell you that I wish that [your synod] was with us in our work [in the American Lutheran Conference] and as far as that is concerned, the United Lutheran Church." Boe-R. H. Gerberding, March 9, 1932. Writing to a ULCA layman, interested in Lutheran unity, he said, "Just now we are in a rather difficult situation both because of the depression and . . . the organization of the American Lutheran Conference. It has left us without definite lines when it comes to larger relationships." Boe-J. K. Jensen, April 4, 1932. Boe Papers, St. Olaf College Archives, Northfield, Minn.

30. *The Formation of the ALC,* p. 232.

31. *Ibid.,* p. 238.

32. *Ibid.,* p. 240.

33. *Ibid.,* p. 245. Meuser suggests that President Fandrey of the Iowa Synod was not "telling the full truth" when he said that the American Lutheran Conference was not conceived in a spirit of antagonism towards any other Lutheran church body.

34. J. K. Jensen Papers; letters, Jensen-Knubel, 9-11-30; Knubel-Jensen, 9-16-30. Copies may be found in the Library, Northwestern Lutheran Seminary, St. Paul, Minn.

35. *The Lutheran,* (October 9, 1930), 5-7.

36. Wentz, *Lutherans in Concert,* pp. 77-81.

37. Archives for Cooperative Lutheranism, 315 Park Avenue South, New York, R. H. Long Papers, Box 1. The exchange includes such names as L. W. Boe, Emmanuel Poppen, F. H. Meyer, J. A. Aasgaard, H. L. Fritschel, S. C. Michelfelder, and O. H. Pannkoke.

38. "American Lutheran Conference . . . Convention," *The Lutheran,* (December 15, 1932), 2.

39. "Cordial Earnestness Prevailed," *ibid.,* (February 9, 1933), 6.

40. Among those who sought to justify the American Lutheran Conference was its secretary, L. M. Stavig. Writing on "The Genius of the American Lutheran Conference," he admitted that some churchmen conceived of it as a defensive alliance over against the United Lutheran Church and the Synodical Conference. But, he continued, "However much such a motive may have prompted the new organization at the beginning, the results of our association have included the discovery . . . that there were agreements in the fundamental concepts of the faith . . . when the Minneapolis Theses were written and adopted as the confessional basis of the conference." Emerging from this doctrinal agreement and years of working together in common enterprises, he argued that the conference represented a spirit or tendency that differed from that of the ULCA and the Synodical Conference and, as such, occupied "the middle ground of Lutheranism." See *The Lutheran Outlook,* (January, 1945), 9-15.

41. A. C. Piepkorn, "Where Leaders Stand on Lutheran Union," *The American Lutheran,* XXIII (October, 1940), 7-9.

42. "Ten Years of Fellowship in the American Conference," *Journal of Theology of the American Lutheran Conference,* VI (January, 1941), 109.

43. "The Conference Convention," *ibid.,* V (December, 1940), 896.

44. Arden, *Augustana Heritage,* p. 283.

45. It has been correctly pointed out that even the most conservative Lutherans are

not to be classified as fundamentalists. There are many theological issues to which orthodoxist Lutherans give a different answer from the fundamentalists, for example, the doctrine of the church and sacraments. But on the inerrancy of Scripture they are identical. For a discussion see Milton L. Rudnick, *Fundamentalism and the Missouri Synod* (St. Louis: Concordia Publishing House, 1966).

46. For an evaluation of these men see Arden, *Augustana Heritage*, pp. 285-288. Cf. Karl E. Mattson, "The Theology of the Augustana Lutheran Church," in *Centennial Essays*, pp. 47-49.

47. Arden, *Augustana Heritage*, pp. 288-289.

48. See Meuser, *The Formation of the ALC*, p. 229. Reu's soteriological approach to Scripture was spelled out in his 1930 contribution to the Ferm symposium *What Is Lutheranism?*, pp. 102-115.

49. Archives of Cooperative Lutheranism, 315 Park Avenue South, New York, R. H. Long Papers, Box III. Piper subsequently became the distinguished biblical theologian at Princeton and the mentor of numerous younger American Lutheran doctoral candidates. Reu was also suspicious of Dr. Hanns Lilje's orthodoxy and told Long he wished Lilje would not accept the position as executive secretary of the Lutheran World Convention. See W. E. Allbeck, "A Study of American Participation in Inter-Lutheran Cooperation Prior to the Formation of the Lutheran World Federation," (unpublished ms., 1962), p. 111. Copy in LC/USA Library, New York.

50. L. W. Boe, "God's Moment and the Next Step in American Lutheranism," *The Lutheran Church, A Series of Occasional Papers of General Interest to the Entire Lutheran Church* (Minneapolis: Augsburg Publishing House, 1934), p. 5. The writer was present at one of Gullixson's classroom lectures in which he attacked the position expressed in "God's Moment. . . . " In his lecture Gullixson clearly aligned himself with those who insisted on the solidarity of the army (the church), asserting that when the army advanced, it must do so as a unit. Boe had said ("God's Moment," p. 3), "Even an army must have its advance guards. The mistake very often made by us Lutherans is, that we have our eyes so centered on the solidarity of the army that we spend most of our time shooting our own advance guards, insisting that all move together, even to the smallest detail. . . . " Other reactions to Boe's article: (1) Letter: R. H. Long-L. W. Boe, March 13, 1934: "I like the argument which you present very much except that I do not think you go far enough. . . . I cannot see how if recognition were declared and full fellowship established it would be possible to justify independent effort and activity, at least in certain fields. . . . I do hope the matter is kept alive and not allowed to die a-borning." Archives of Cooperative Lutheranism, 325 Park Avenue South, New York, R. H. Long Papers, Box III. (2) For a sharp Missourian attack on Boe see Theodore Graebner, *The Problem of Lutheran Union and Other Essays* (St. Louis: Concordia Publishing House, 1936), pp. 14-15.

51. Letter, Boe-Aasgaard, October 29, 1942. Copy in St. Olaf College Archives, Northfield, Minn.

52. An exception may be noted in the Wisconsin Synod where the so-called "Protestant Conference" sought to perpetuate in the 20s the historical-exegetical and non-scholastic theology of J. P. Koehler. See Leigh Jordahl, "The Protestant Conference," *The Encyclopedia of the Lutheran Church*, III.

53. See Paul A. Maier, *A Man Spoke . . .* , p. 205. Cf. Gerhard O. Forde, *The Law-Gospel Debate*, pp. 175-179. Forde argues that Lutheran Orthodoxy (and thus the Missouri Synod) misunderstood Luther's concept of law, turning it into an eternal, objective order and described the ideal to which man must aspire. Rather, law is not a fixed ideal, or a collection of propositions, but an existential category. Law and gospel must be related eschatologically rather than in terms of a timeless scheme.

54. On the Brux affair see F. Dean Lueking, *Mission in the Making* (St. Louis: Concordia Publishing House, 1964), pp. 270-276. Pannkoke's memoirs were published under the title, *A Great Church Finds Itself* (Quitman, Georgia: Published by the author, 1966).

55. "A Statement of the Board of Foreign Missions of the United Lutheran Church in America," *The Lutheran*, (February 23, 1933), 2.

56. "Across the Desk," *The Lutheran*, (January 15, 1931), 15.

57. Arden, *Augustana Heritage*, pp. 274-277. Cf. Meuser, *The Formation of the ALC*, p. 243.

58. John A. W. Haas, "Where Does the Lutheran Church Stand?" *The Lutheran*, (October 27, 1932), 14; cf. Haas, "The Word and the Bible," *ibid.*, (December 8, 1932), 7.

59. The best historical study of the development of a social ethics in American Lutheranism is Lloyd Svendsbye, "The History of a Developing Social Responsibility Among Lutherans in America from 1930 to 1960, with Reference to the American Lutheran Church, the Augustana Lutheran Church, the Evangelical Lutheran Church, and the United Lutheran Church," (unpublished Th.D. dissertation, Union Theological Seminary, New York, 1966). I am indebted to this study for much of what follows.

60. *Ibid.*, p. 18.

61. Nelson, *The Lutheran Church among Norwegian-Americans*, II, 112.

62. Svendsbye, "Developing Social Responsibility," pp. 56-65.

63. *Ibid.*, p. 66.

64. *The Church and the Economic Debacle* (Minneapolis: Augsburg Publishing House, 1933).

65. *The Lutheran Church in the New Social Order* (Minneapolis: Augsburg Publishing House, 1935).

66. *The Contribution of the Church to Social Work* (Minneapolis: Augsburg Publishing House, 1939).

67. Svendsbye, "Developing Social Responsibility," Précis, pp. 5-6.

68. A. D. Mattson, "The Kingdom of God," *The Lutheran Companion*, (November 24, 1934), 1478-1481. Cf. "American Lutheran Conference . . . ," *ibid.*, (December 1, 1934), 1515, and Svendsbye, "Developing Social Responsibility," pp. 289-297.

69. *Ibid.*, Précis, p. 15.

70. "Across the Desk," *The Lutheran*, (April 9, 1931), 4, 14-15. Cf. "United Lutheran Consultative Relationships . . . ," *ibid.*, (March 2, 1933), 2 and 23.

71. A. R. Wentz, *A Basic History of Lutheranism in America* (Philadelphia: Fortress Press, 1964), pp. 364-365 (*The Lutheran*, February 4, 1937, carried an explanation why the ULCA was not at Oxford); and Arden, *Augustana Heritage*, p. 305. Augustana carried on a brief dialog with the Protestant Episcopal Church in 1935. Agreement on Scripture, the sacraments, and the creed was reached. The ministry (the historic episcopate) proved to be the main stumbling block. See "Lutherans Meet Episcopalians," *The Lutheran Companion*, (January 11, 1936), 38-39. Cf. E. E. Ryden, "A Beginning of Dialogue: Lutherans and Anglicans," *Lutheran Forum*, (May, 1967), 8-10.

72. The most thorough study of Lutherans and the WCC has been made by Dorris A. Flesner, "The Role of the Lutheran Churches of America in the Formation of the World Council of Churches," (unpublished Ph.D. dissertation, the Hartford Seminary Foundation, Hartford, Conn., 1956). The 1936 document is to be found in *The Lutheran World Almanac*, 1934-1937, pp. 35-38.

73. Flesner, "The Role of the Lutheran Churches . . . , " pp. 72-77.

74. Wentz, *A Basic History*, (1964 revised edition), p. 340.

75. Wolf, *Documents*, p. 356

76. Wentz, *A Basic History*, p. 345.

77. The former Evangelical Lutheran Church, now a part of the new ALC (1960), had reached the same conclusion, though it had not participated in the doctrinal discussions of 1936-38: "We believe no additional theses, statements or agreements are necessary for fellowship among American Lutherans." See the *Annual Report* of the Norwegian Lutheran Church of America for 1944, pp. 404-405. In deference to the strong Missouri-oriented elements within the ELC, the church never fully implemented this

conclusion by an open declaration of fellowship. Rather it adopted a cautious principle known as "selective fellowship."

78. The new American Lutheran Church (1960) and the Missouri Synod concluded doctrinal discussions directed towards pulpit and altar fellowship in 1967. The Lutheran Church in America declined repeated invitations to participate, basing its decision on its confessional principle.

79. Copies of the mimeographed minutes of the two meetings plus correspondence and other papers are in the J. K. Jensen Papers, Northwestern Lutheran Seminary Library, St. Paul, Minn.

80. The ULCA representatives (six clergymen and two laymen) were President F. H. Knubel, H. H. Bagger, E. F. Eilert, C. M. Jacobs, P. H. Krauss, H. Offermann, and laymen J. K. Jensen and E. Rinderknecht. The seven Missouri Synod representatives—all clergymen—were President J. W. Behnken, W. Arndt, T. Engelder, W. Brunner, C. Brommer, F. H. Brunn, and K. Kretzmann.

81. The text of the address is not included in the minutes, but the copy used by this writer has a rather complete pencilled outline of Knubel's presentation.

82. Wolf, *Documents,* pp. 381-382. The document was largely the work of F. Pieper, who felt called upon to defend "Repristination Theology" from its detractors. See especially Volume I, *Christian Dogmatics* (St. Louis: Concordia Publishing House, 1950).

83. Although Jacobs' paper is not attached to the minutes, his position may be readily discerned from three documents: C. M. Jacobs, "Inaugural Address," *The Lutheran Church Review,* XLVI (July, 1927); the paper which he prepared for the concurrent ULCA-ALC conversations (in J. K. Jensen Papers, Northwestern Lutheran Seminary Library, St. Paul, Minn.); and The Baltimore Declaration (1938), of which he was the chief author. See Wolf, *Documents,* pp. 357-359.

84. *Lutheran Witness,* LVI (February 23, 1937), 55.

85. Letter, Jacobs-Arndt, March 29, 1937. Copy in J. K. Jensen Papers, Northwestern Lutheran Seminary Library, St. Paul, Minn.

86. Wolf, *Documents,* pp. 377-378.

87. Letters: Behnken-Knubel, April 12, 1939; Knubel-Behnken, May 3, 1939. Copies are in J. K. Jensen Papers, Northwestern Lutheran Seminary Library, St. Paul, Minn. In 1966 Behnken wrote about Missouri's discussion with the old ALC in the thirties, but made no reference to the negotiations with the ULCA. See J. W. Behnken, "The Way We Have Come," *Concordia Historical Institute Quarterly,* XXXIX (July, 1966), 51-63. An additional Missourian commentary on the situation is to be found in Graebner, *The Problem of Lutheran Union,* pp. 1-106.

88. The mimeographed minutes of four meetings (February 6-7, 1936; April 2-3, 1936; March 11, 1938; February 13, 1939) are an unusually rich source. Copies are in the J. K. Jensen Papers, Northwestern Lutheran Seminary Library, St. Paul, Minn. Ordinarily minutes record only the results of discussion such as resolutions, expressions of consensus, and motions. These, however, include a full transcript of the discussion. This amplitude enables the reader to trace the lines of debate and specific statements, which appear in subsequent official declarations, to their origins in the theological stance of particular individuals. By way of anticipation, one should note with care the role of church presidents Knubel (ULCA) and Hein (ALC) on the one hand, and theologians Jacobs (ULCA) and Reu (ALC) on the other.

89. Transcript of meeting . . . March 11, 1938, p. 36.

90. There is no indication in the minutes that Hein identified the issues; however, named or unnamed, the questions put to the ULCA usually centered around (1) lodge membership, (2) unionism, and (3) inspiration of Scriptures.

91. ULCA Commissioners: F. H. Knubel, C. M. Jacobs, H. H. Bagger, H. Offermann, P. H. Krauss, E. Rinderknecht, J. K. Jensen, E. Clarence Miller, E. F. Eilert. ALC Commissioners: C. C. Hein, E. Poppen, M. Reu, J. N. Grabau, W. E. Schuette, E. A. Welke, O. J. Wilke, W. Altman, G. Leibold.

92. Instigated by the Joint Union Committee of the ALC in 1959, the conferences

concluded on January 23, 1967. *Lutheran Standard,* VII (March 21, 1967), p. 14. Cf. Wolf, *Documents,* pp. 622-623.

93. Minutes . . . February 6-7, 1936, p. 4. For a better understanding of the 1936 discussion it must be remembered that the ULCA had been purposely excluded from the American Lutheran Conference.

94. *Ibid.*

95. Minutes . . . February 6-7, 1936, p. 5.

96. *Ibid.,* pp. 11-13.

97. Minutes . . . April 2-3, 1936, p. 61.

98. Wolf, *Documents,* p. 340. This statement of 1925 was made an unalterable part of the constitution of the new ALC (1960). Its fundamentalistic language has since embarrassed many in the new ALC and has led its leadership to make "interpretations" that do not square with the historical circumstances and intentions out of which the statement grew in 1925 and in the years before the 1960 ALC merger.

99. Minutes . . . February 6-7, 1936, p. 4.

100. *Ibid.,* p. 6.

101. H. C. Alleman, *The Old Testament—A Study* (Philadelphia: The Muhlenberg Press, 1935) and H. C. Alleman, *The New Testament—A Study* (Philadelphia: The Muhlenberg Press, 1935). Professor Alleman, a member of the faculty at the Lutheran Theological Seminary, Gettysburg, was one of the first American Lutheran biblical scholars to employ the historical critical method in the study of the Scriptures. Most American Lutheran biblical scholars today, including some in the Missouri Synod, would hardly find the two books disturbing or revolutionary. In the late 30s, however, the ULCA found it expedient to withhold temporarily the manuscript of a larger Old Testament commentary, edited by H. C. Alleman and E. E. Flack. Knubel feared that the offending book might upset inter-Lutheran relations.

102. *Ibid.,* pp. 6-7.

103. *Ibid.,* p. 7.

104. *Ibid.,* p. 9.

105. *Ibid.,* p. 10.

106. *Ibid.*

107. Minutes . . . April 2-3, 1936, p. 29. Neither statement is incorporated in the minutes. However, copies of both are in the J. K. Jensen Papers, Northwestern Lutheran Seminary Library, St. Paul, Minn. Reu's statement eventually became the substance of "The Pittsburgh Agreement" and Jacobs' work became "The Baltimore Declaration." For the former see Wolf, *Documents,* pp. 378-379; for the latter, *ibid.,* pp. 357-359.

108. Minutes . . . April 2-3, 1936, p. 29.

109. *Ibid.,* p. 30.

110. *Ibid.,* p. 37.

111. *Ibid.,* pp. 32-34.

112. *Ibid.,* pp. 47, 48.

113. *Ibid.,* pp. 52-53.

114. In a typed "Personal Opinion" which Knubel submitted to his own committee following the Columbus (April) conference, he pointed out the sharp differences between the ULCA and the ALC in their views of Scripture. He raised the question whether discussion on the Scripture ought not be abandoned for the present. Although the suggestion was not picked up, it does show a tendency to avoid the controversial.

115. Minutes . . . April 2-3, 1936, pp. 45-46. Jacobs said: "If you will look at the first sentence of my statement, you will find a quotation from the Formula of Concord which is the . . . only confessional statement of the Lutheran Church concerning Scripture. . . . There is no man around this table who does not agree to that, and we of the United Lutheran Church believe that is sufficient basis for agreement. . . . We know there are differences between us. The discussion was brought about because you brethren insisted that we must go beyond the Confessions of the Church to find a basis of even such a matter as pulpit and altar fellowship. . . . We would agree to . . . union

with you now and not ask you to change one jot or tittle of the things you have said here this morning."

116. Minutes . . . March 11, 1938, Columbus, Ohio, p. 37. There was no meeting between April, 1936 and March, 1938.

117. *Ibid.,* pp. 2-16. It should be noted that Jacobs' statement, no longer under discussion, became The Baltimore Declaration (1938).

118. In explanation of this rather strange comment, it should be noted that here Reu referred to the *new* work by H. C. Alleman, ed., *New Testament Commentary* (Philadelphia: Board of Publication of the ULCA, 1936), and not the earlier New Testament "study" by Alleman which in 1936 Reu had not found injurious. It was *this* new book which Reu felt undermined further the "inerrancy" of the Bible. Cf. M. Reu, "A New English Testament Commentary," *Journal of the American Lutheran Conference,* III (February, 1938), 7-29.

119. Minutes . . . March 11, 1938, pp. 23-24. Reu called his short speech before the commissioners "an open confession." He added, " . . . if you want to make use of it you can do so."

120. *Ibid.,* pp. 36-38. Cf. ULCA, *Minutes . . . 1938,* pp. 468-469.

121. *Ibid.,* pp. 469-475. The motivation for the "Declaration" seems to have been twofold: (1) to make public the view of the ULCA for all other American Lutherans to see, and (2) to set forth in America a view of Scripture which was neither "liberal" nor "fundamentalistic," but in keeping with the whole Lutheran conception of the gospel. This was deemed essential in the emerging ecumenical scene. Knubel had reminded the ALC commissioners at the Columbus meeting (April 2-3, 1936) of the upcoming Faith and Order meeting (Edinburgh, 1937) where the Lutherans must speak about the Scriptures out of their *own* theological tradition. Therefore, it was necessary to draw up a statement of the distinctive Lutheran conception of the Scriptures. See Minutes . . . , April 2-3, 1936, pp. 48-49.

122. The document is printed in Wolf, *Documents.* For the section on "Scripture and Inspiration," see pp. 394-395.

123. Letter: Boe-Long, August 6, 1938. Archives for Cooperative Lutheranism, 315 Park Avenue South, New York, R. H. Long Papers, Box VI.

124. Minutes . . . February 13, 1939, p. 4.

125. *Ibid.,* p. 7.

126. Minutes . . . April 2-3, 1936, p. 17.

127. Minutes . . . February 13, 1939, p. 9.

128. H. C. Alleman, "The Pittsburgh Agreement and Lutheran Unity," *The Lutheran Church Quarterly,* XIII (October, 1940), 356.

129. *Kirchliche Zeitschrift,* LXIII (April, 1939), 239-249. Cited in Alleman, "The Pittsburgh Agreement," *Lutheran Church Quarterly,* XIII (October, 1940), 348.

130. ULCA, *Minutes . . . 1940,* p. 263.

131. *Ibid.,* p. 566.

CHAPTER FOUR

THE IMPACT OF WORLD WAR II

When Hitler came to power in 1933, the first impulse of many Americans was to prevent the United States from becoming involved in the problems of Europe. Isolationism, as this policy was popularly called, was hardly an unfamiliar American political posture. Every school boy had been told that George Washington had warned against entangling alliances. The decade after World War I witnessed a revival of the mood. Immigration was largely shut off and tariffs were raised to protect domestic industry. The failure of the Allies to pay their war debts was interpreted as ingratitude if not down right dishonesty. Therefore, why get involved in Europe's troubles? Joining the League of Nations, for example, would eventually plunge America into the vortex of Europe's volatile politics.[1]

The depression and the subsequent victory of the Democratic party did not immediately reverse the American attitude. One-time internationalist Franklin Delano Roosevelt could conscientiously support a "go-it-alone" policy. Sensational exposés of war profiteers and munitions makers as "merchants of death" (the Nye Committee hearings) were major factors in the enactment of the Neutrality Acts of 1935 and 1937 that proscribed trade with belligerents and gave substance to the desire to avoid American involvement in European affairs. Though large segments of the population, perhaps the vast majority, were opposed to the political "isms" of Hitler, Stalin, and Mussolini, there was no compulsion to stick American fingers into European pies.

116

By 1937 American opinion began to alter noticeably. Roosevelt's famous "Quarantine Speech" asked Americans actively to engage "in the search of peace," which, being interpreted, meant a break with isolationism. By 1939 only small pockets of Americans were unsympathetic to the Allies. Any earlier "wait-and-see" hesitation about Hitler's objectives was dissipated by the invasion of Poland, the crushing of France, the Battle of Britain, and the take-over of Denmark and Norway. These events effectively brought the United States into common cause with the Allies. Although actual declaration of war did not occur until the Japanese attack on Pearl Harbor, the Selective Service Act of 1940 and the Lend-Lease Bill of 1941 indicated the American temper.

The attitude of American churches underwent a similar metamorphosis. In the 20s it was popular for ministers to say they would never bless another war.[2] Prominent liberal preachers such as Harry Emerson Fosdick, Ernest Fremont Tittle, and others influenced many Protestants to repudiate all armed conflicts. Denominations other than the traditionally pacifist Mennonites, Church of the Brethren, and Quakers passed resolutions denouncing participation in war. The peace movement, sanctified by religious vocabulary, was part and parcel of the isolationism of the two decades after World War I.

A reaction, however, set in. Ray H. Abrams, who had sharply criticized pro-war clergymen in World War I, set out to describe what happened to American ministerial attitudes from the mid-30s to the early 40s.[3] The anti-war sentiment of many groups, expressed in 1939 peace rallies and articles in pacifist-inclined religious press, gradually gave in to what Abrams called "preparedness propaganda." Although the enactment of the Selective Service Act was vigorously opposed by some churches, the Lend-Lease legislation evoked only minor opposition from churchmen. Ironically, the liberal *Christian Century* and the politically conservative *Chicago Tribune* found themselves on the same side, for different reasons of course, in seeking to keep America out of the war. Meanwhile, a distinguished group of "theologians of crisis" headed by Reinhold Niebuhr began to point out the fundamental error of pacifism: one cannot "sanctify the social order and conceive it as an absolute good pitted against an absolute evil." All social and political power structures are without the possibility of being absolutely good. To wage war or not to wage war became a choice between relative evils. Niebuhr's new periodical *Christianity and Crisis* admitted that English and American motives were hardly pure as the driven snow but a Nazi victory would mean an intolerable totalitarian oppression. The defeat of Hitler was, therefore, a righteous cause despite the fact that no war is holy: warfare was always the expression of the sin of men. Roman Catholics and Jews—the latter remembering the sick humor of sadistic signs on closed Jewish shops in Germany, *"Urlaub in Dachau"* ("vacation in Dachau") —joined the Protestants in supporting American arms. But, on the whole, the churches did not "bless the war" in the manner of many exuberant clerical patriots of World War I. American participation in World War II was approached with sober restraint. Although the defeat of Hitlerism and Japanese militarism was deemed a necessity, churchmen realized that securing the peace required careful planning long before victory was achieved. As early as 1942 the Federal Council's Commission to Study the Bases of a Just and Durable Peace, presided over by John Foster Dulles, published the widely disseminated and favorably received Six Pillars of Peace. Catholics and Jews likewise issued proposals that emphasized the churches' responsibilities to work for peace and international law and order.[4]

PRE-WAR ATTITUDES AMONG LUTHERANS

On the whole the Lutherans in America reacted to international political events quite as did other Americans. First, there was profound concern; second, there was the mood "let's not get involved in Europe's problems"; third, there was growing fear of German Nazism and Japanese militarism; and fourth, there was a general commitment to the Allied cause, especially when Jews, Catholics, and fellow Lutherans were persecuted. The invasion of Lutheran Scandinavia in 1940, and the bombing of Pearl Harbor were both "days of infamy" that removed any vestiges of hesitation regarding the righteousness of the Allied cause.

Although Lutherans generally followed the response-pattern of other religious groups in America, there were a few things that set them apart from most other Protestants. There was the basic fact that Germany was the home of the Lutheran Reformation. The strong confessional loyalties within Lutheranism had long demonstrated the fact that its interpretation and proclamation of the gospel transcended geographic and ethnic limits. The formation of the Lutheran World Convention in 1923, for example, was but one evidence of this elemental but potentially complicating fact. Moreover, the European origin of American Lutheranism was another complexity to be reckoned with. Hundreds of thousands of American Lutherans were of German descent. Many families had relatives and friends in the "fatherland." At the same time hundreds of thousands of Scandinavian Americans, who historically had ambivalent feelings about Germany, and numerous other hyphenated Americans from countries where Lutheranism was a minority confession (Poland, Czechoslovakia, Hungary, Holland), had similar personal and familial ties to the lands and churches of their ancestors. Naturally German-American Lutherans were confused and upset by the rise of Hitler; and the others, though never predominantly Germanophiles, recognizing the religious and cultural debt that many of them owed to the land of Martin Luther, were willing for a time "to wait-and-see." This questioning hesitation in America among Scandinavian Lutherans and central European Lutheran minorities quickly turned to righteous wrath in 1939-1940.

It should be clear that the 30s posed a particular confessional and ecclesio-political problem for American Lutherans. While college and seminary professors were trying to understand the "theology of crisis," a new crisis—namely, an ecclesiastical one—was developing right under their professorial noses. Articles in church papers, addresses by leading churchmen, and official as well as private correspondence by well-known Lutheran personalities reflected the confusion in the minds of many.[5]

By the spring of 1933 *The Lutheran* was carrying articles and editorials on the rise of Hitlerism and the emergence of the Nazi-supported movement known as the "German Christians" *(Deutsche Christen)*. It felt that the latter, though committed to Nazi purposes, desired "to remain definitely Christian."[6] When word came from Bishop Ludwig Ihmels, a colaborer of John A. Morehead, F. H. Knubel, C. M. Jacobs, R. H. Long, and L. W. Boe in the Lutheran World Convention, it was naturally received with respect and confidence. Ihmels, no supporter of "the German Christians," urged his American friends not to paint all Germans with the same brush and requested them "to refrain from biased partisanships."[7]

Ralph Long meanwhile had written to some highly placed German churchmen including Professor Werner Elert of Erlangen and Baron Arndt von Kirchbach of Dresden. In his letters he asked his German friends to respond to the American charge *(The Christian Century,* February 15, 1933) that the church would end up in Hitler's arms. He asked four specific questions:

1) Did the edicts of the new government put attacks upon religion in a class of "verboten" activities?
2) Did the government regard the church as having a conservative political influence?
3) Had this phase of the political situation influenced the churches to any extent?
4) Did church leaders have any apprehensions concerning the dangers of an unhappy relationship between the Protestant church and the government?

The reply of Baron von Kirchbach was especially illuminating. In answer to the first question, he said yes. Many destructive attacks on religion [by Communists and Socialists], including parodies of hymns and even the "Our Father" together with mockery of church attendance and even reprisals carried out on Christian business men, made the edicts of the new government [Hitler] most welcome. Although Kirchbach admitted that faith is not built up by edicts, the attitude of the government was of real importance in the public life of the church. In answer to the second question, he said that the government had numerous reasons for supporting the church; it could be that one such was the church's political conservatism. In any case, "there is no reason to doubt that Hitler is very serious in propagating Christian faith." The third question elicited this response: There were, to be sure, reactionary forces in the government, but what Germany now expected was "a new building of our whole national life on the basis of the strengths supplied to our people by God. . . . Many people who left the church in the last 14 years are returning in large numbers." The fourth answer: There no doubt was a danger in a close relationship of church and state, a danger which Bishop Ihmels, some younger pastors, and especially the followers of Karl Barth had pointed out. But even as Americans customarily placed their national flag in the Lord's house as a sign of fidelity to their country so German Lutherans saw the connection between the church and the fate of the German people as significant, especially when the government promised "to renew our people on a Christian basis."

Von Kirchbach concluded: "And then the main thing: pray for Germany, for Field Marshal von Hindenburg and for Hitler. When God's work is beginning Satan is not far away." [8]

A later letter to von Kirchbach inquired about the influence of the *Deutsche Christen* and the prospects of a united evangelical church in Germany with an archbishop at Wittenberg and ten bishoprics throughout the nation. Von Kirchbach's reply was somewhat less euphoric than his earlier letter. The "German Christians," fortunately, were not sponsored by the church. But he himself, as a Saxon, had had little knowledge of the movement. In fact, the Saxon leader of the pastors who belonged to the Nazi party had refused the "German Christians" permission to organize in Saxony. Yes, everyone was of the opinion that there should be *one* evangelical church in Germany, not 29 *Landeskirchen* as now existed. The head of the church should be a Lutheran and would have the title of *Reichsbischof*. He should be one of the ten bishops, but not archbishop of Wittenberg as had been proposed. Generally, circumstances seemed to provide many opportunities for the church, but at the same time the situation was fraught with great danger. "We trust . . . that God will guide the Church through all difficulties." Christians greet each other again and again with the words *oremus pro ecclesia*.[9]

Having gathered information from many sources, Long prepared, in the autumn of 1933 and early 1934, lengthy articles on the state of the church in Germany. In these he assessed the role of the "German Christians" as tools of Hitler; he analyzed the movement towards one national church, recognizing the tensions existing between the Union churches, the Lutheran churches, and the Reformed churches. A new constitution, based on something called "parallel confessionalism" and eschewing interference by the state had been drafted. This, however, met the opposition of the Lutheran churches who felt that the confessional integrity of Lutheranism was being jeopardized and that a new church under Lutheran leadership, granting rights to evangelicals of other churches, could and should be organized. A committee representing the interests of the three confessions met at Loccum near Hannover with Hitler's representative, Pastor Ludwig Mueller, to draft a new constitution. It was agreed that the *Reichsbischof* should be a Lutheran and that his election should take place after the new constitution was adopted. Meanwhile, a movement to forestall appointment of a candidate unfavorable to the church — the "German Christians" supported Mueller—and to promote the candidacy of the immensely popular Lutheran, Friedrich von Bodelschwingh, director of the world famous Bethel Institute,[10] got under way. Through some incredible political blundering, the anti-Mueller group pushed for election *before* the adoption of the constitution and von Bodelschwingh was chosen for the position of *Reichsbischof* over the opposition of the "German Christians." The latter, however, retaliated by charging that the election was illegal, which indeed it was. Von Bodelschwingh had no choice but to return his commission. Out of the resulting confusion, Mueller and thus Hitler, emerged victorious. Mueller became *Reichsbischof* and the church seemed destined to fall under the complete domination of the "German Christians" whose Nazi anti-semitism led them to advocate the elimination of the Old Testament from the canon.[11] This was intolerable to Lutherans and other evangelical Christians. Moreover, the "German Christians" were perverting the doctrine of the atonement, the Pauline principle of salvation, and the New Testament concept of Christ. Was Jesus a universal savior, or a German savior? Was Luther a catholic Christian theologian or simply a Germanic hero? [12]

Long's conclusion that the church had not sold out and was not an obedient servant of the state was to be borne out by the Barmen Synod of 1934, but meanwhile, despite his efforts to explain the situation, American Lutherans were confused and dismayed by what they read.

Some of this uncertainty and confusion appeared in the correspondence between Long and L. W. Boe and in the writings of J. Michael Reu. Long wrote Boe (March 1934) that once Mueller was esconced in his position he began using dictatorial methods that were contrary to the new church constitution. Long felt there was more resistance to Mueller than was reported in the press. "You recall," he wrote to Boe, "that we had a certain picture in mind when we went over last November [1933] but came back with an entirely different picture of this situation." Boe replied that a Danish friend had reported to him that Martin Niemoeller was using politics to circumvent the Nazis but Hermann Goering had outwitted him by tapping his telephone conversations. Another disappointment was the lack of positive leadership in Bishop Marahrens of Hannover, whom Boe described as utterly incompetent to deal with the Nazis in this sensitive situation. But he still believed (writing in

July) that "Hitler has wanted to do the right thing. . . ." By early autumn, only two bishops had not been deposed by the Nazis (Marahrens and Hans Meiser of Munich). Should these two be ousted or arrested, there would be a Lutheran secession from the German National Church, a move favored by 90 percent of the clergy in the two dioceses of Hannover and Bavaria. In the event of secession, the Lutheran World Convention would be related to the dissenters. This, said Long, "would be a good thing." [13] Although the schism did not occur, the Lutheran World Convention maintained its contact with the German church through this Lutheran wing. In fact, the first executive secretary (1936) of the Lutheran World Convention, Hanns Lilje, was both a staunch Lutheran and a vigorous opponent of Hitler.

The attitude of Prof. Michael Reu of Wartburg Seminary, Dubuque, Iowa, has been variously assessed. Frederick K. Wentz has written that German-born Reu was enthusiastic about Hitler's program for the rebirth of Germany and that he believed that Nazi attacks on the Jews were not without justification.[14] In reply, Richard Reu Salzmann quoted from articles in the journal *Kirchliche Zeitschrift* to the effect that Reu, who was its editor, represented "the clearest American Lutheran opposition to the events in Germany. . . ." At the same time, Salzmann admitted Reu's admiration for Hitler about whom he had said, "I cannot believe that Hitler is aware of all this. . . ." By 1939, however, Reu was finally disillusioned with Nazism.[15]

The Missouri Synod's official organ, the *Lutheran Witness,* withheld criticism of Hitler and the Nazis for several years. Between 1934 and 1939 the *Witness* carried articles that reflected "starry-eyed approval of the Nazi regime" and silence regarding the persecution of the Jews. It was not until 1945 that the *Witness* opened its columns, and then only to a non-Lutheran, to a denunciation of the paganism and inhumanity of Nazism. After a lapse of 20 years, these facts caused a Missouri Synod scholar to raise the question "whether the church can remain silent in the presence of monstrous evil and still preserve its integrity. Can the church . . . abandon its role as a light and as conscience to the world and still remain the church?" [16]

Among the National Lutheran Council churches, the Augustana Synod reacted to totalitarianism by opposing all forms of militarism, American as well as European. During the 30s *The Lutheran Companion* frequently printed editorials and articles in support of the peace movement, and even after World War II broke out in 1939, the *Companion* continued to urge a policy of neutrality and peace. This attitude prevailed until Pearl Harbor. A random selection of topics in 1939-1940 indicate the stance of Augustana: "Another Lesson in European Perfidy" (Sept. 7, 1939); "President Makes Neutrality Plea" (Sept. 28, 1939); "Prayers for Peace in War Torn World" and "Let's Be Honest About Embargo" (Oct. 19, 1939); "Jesus in Uniform?" (Nov. 2, 1939); "Christian Crusade Against War" (Jan. 18, 1940); "Ask Synod to Back War Objectors" (April 4, 1940); "Can War Ever Be Justified?" (May 9, 1940).

On the eve of the war, the synod endorsed the Life and Work (Oxford 1937) statement:

> War is a particular demonstration of the power of sin in the world, and a defiance of the righteousness of God as revealed in Jesus Christ and Him crucified. No justification of war must be allowed to minimize or conceal this fact.[17]

Two years later shortly before Pearl Harbor, the synod went on record in support of conscientious objectors: "We ask exemption from all forms of combatant military service for all conscientious objectors who may be members of the Augustana Synod." [18]

When America officially entered the war, Augustana's resolution of loyalty to the nation was followed by the caveat: "The Synod urges its members to remain loyal to Christ, to be on guard lest the sanction of the Church be given to anything which is contrary to the spirit of Christ." [19]

The attitude of Augustana's Nordic cousins, the Norwegian Lutheran Church of America, was marked by a sharp contrast. In 1938, for example, there was no mention of the struggle going on in Europe or the problem of war and peace. Two years later, however, the presidential message began with these words:

> Today, the land of our fathers . . . is not a free land. . . . Our feelings and emotions are moved at the thought that a country that has desired to live in peace and amity with its neighbors down through the decades should reap such a harvest.[20]

The reference, of course, was to the Nazi invasion of Denmark and Norway, April, 1940, which generated among the ordinarily peace-loving Danish- and Norwegian-Americans a spirit of deep hostility to the invader. It was quite to be expected that the church would adopt the following strong resolution after America became involved:

> We recognize that in the present titanic struggle there are principles involved that are essential to human welfare and closely allied with the freedom of conscience and of worship that we value so highly. Therefore, we urge our members to manifest their loyalty by giving full support to the war efforts of their country with their substance and, if necessary, with their lives.[21]

The Churches in War and Peace, 1941-1955

One cannot think of the wartime activity of the churches apart from the National Lutheran Council. It has been noted that this agency all but collapsed in the early 30s when the American Lutheran Conference was organized by five council churches. This act, which drew a sharp line between the United Lutheran Church and the Midwest churches that constituted the conference, threatened to split the council. As a result, one historian observed, the council stood at a crossroad in 1937. Should it quietly recede into the background or should it assert itself in seizing opportunities for service on behalf of the churches before the occasions were lost? That the council chose the latter path and did not disintegrate was due in large measure to the wise and effective leadership of its executive director, Ralph H. Long, who almost single-handedly shaped an aggressive and forward-looking program.[22] This was accomplished despite the strained relationships between the United Lutheran Church and the American Lutheran Conference, and the inhibiting regulations that the churches had imposed on the council. There were four such working "rules": (1) the council was merely an "agency" for participating bodies. It was not a church nor a federation of churches, but an "agency" through which "participating" bodies could do *specific* tasks; (2) the council could act for the participating churches in emergencies that demanded a common front; (3) the council could not assume responsibility for initiating or furthering Lutheran unity or union; only "churches" could negotiate with each other; and (4) council activities were carefully circumscribed by the principle of "cooperation in externals." The distinction between *res externae* and *res internae* was always difficult to maintain. Where was the boundary between "external" and "internal"? What could be done cooperatively without prior doctrinal

agreement? [23] Actually, the distinction proved artificial and therefore untenable, but it was strategically retained as a protection against what Mis-
sourian-influenced Lutherans called "sinful unionism." It was soon admitted
openly that the cliché had become an obstacle to faith and action; it was
simply impossible to engage in any evangelical Christian program without
transgressing the rule. Therefore, Long concluded, if cooperative work was
to be carried out, the principles had to be disregarded, or, as Wentz described it, the council had to "transcend the rules." [24] L. W. Boe summarized the history of the National Lutheran Council in two sentences:

> . . . the Lord has never permitted it [the NLC] to be only an
> agency for cooperation in external affairs. Time and again we re-
> wrote the constitution and regulations . . . to safeguard this line
> that we arbitrarily set up . . . but the Lord . . . pushed us across the
> line every time.[25]

When World War II broke out, the council, thanks to Long and
other far-sighted churchmen, was "tooled up" for action. In fact, even
before 1939, at least two areas of war-time service had been entered. At
the request of the Federal Council's General Committee on Army and Navy
Chaplains, the United Lutheran Church had assumed the responsibility
for recruiting Lutheran chaplains and of serving as liaison between the
chaplains and their respective churches. By 1934 its executive board moved
to place this ministry into the hands of the National Lutheran Council.[26]
This was done and the council developed its program in cooperation
with the Federal Council's General Committee until 1939 when the
National Lutheran Council began direct negotiations with the chief of
chaplains. Meanwhile the Missouri Synod, unable to cooperate with the
council churches, inaugurated its own program in the mid-thirties, and
through its Army and Navy Commission built up a corps of highly
qualified chaplains.[27] Thus when the National Defense Program was
effectuated in 1940, the number of Lutheran chaplains in the armed services
approached the assigned quota.

A second area that the council had already entered was the support
of what was soon to be called "orphaned missions." American Lutherans
had been aiding European mission societies ever since the first World
War, but the situation became critical in 1936-1937 when the Nazi
government imposed currency regulations which tended to cut off Ger-

man mission support.[28] By June, 1939, the German fields were completely orphaned. If they were to survive, American Lutherans would have to assume responsibility for them. Representatives of the churches met (October 2, 1939) to coordinate and direct efforts to maintain the orphaned missions of Germany and Finland, the latter having been invaded by Russia. In this manner, the National Lutheran Council and the American Section of the Lutheran World Convention (which for all practical purposes was coextensive with the NLC) undertook a Lutheran Emergency Appeal. Under the direction of O. C. Mees the campaign raised $238,000 by the spring of 1940.[29]

Although America was not at war, the members of council churches in Canada were, of course, immediately involved. This prompted Long to call a conference of Canadian Lutherans at Winnipeg, April 2, 1940. At this meeting the Canadian Lutheran Commission was organized to supervise the war-time service of the dominion churches. Approved by all groups except the Missouri Synod, the commission undertook a broad-gauged ministry including services for German prisoners of war in Canadian camps. Initially the project received financial subsidies from the National Lutheran Council but by 1942 was self-supporting.[30]

The service to men in the armed forces and the support of war-orphaned missions soon became parts of a massive overall project. The Lutheran Emergency Appeal of 1940 had been undertaken primarily for the benefit of orphaned missions. Consequently there were no funds at hand to engage in a ministry to men and women in the armed services. In 1941 the annual meeting of the National Lutheran Council heard a report of a survey trip made by N. M. Ylvisaker and C. E. Krumbholz among 42 military camps and 48 communities adjacent to the camps. On the basis of the report the council voted to initiate a comprehensive program and named Ylvisaker as director. In order that the work might get under way immediately President J. A. Aasgaard arranged for the Norwegian Lutheran Church of America to make a direct appropriation of $100,000, and the Lutheran Brotherhood Insurance Company donated office space at its headquarters in Minneapolis.[31] Thus almost overnight the council was embarked on what was soon to be a vast program of wartime services masterfully supervised by its energetic director. The responsibilities of the Service Commission included maintaining close touch with the chaplains, establishing centers for service men and women (in 1944 there were 44 full-time pastors at these centers), and encouraging local parishes to keep in touch with their members in the armed services.[32]

The decision of the council in 1941 to raise $500,000, one half of which was to be used for the newly formed Service Commission, the remainder to support orphaned-missions and the program of aid to war-refugees, was named Lutheran World Action (LWA). The supervision and direction of LWA fell chiefly upon the shoulders of two of the ablest men in American Lutheranism, Ralph Long and his newly-appointed assistant, Paul C. Empie. The latter had served on a part-time basis until he was elected assistant director of the council in 1944. Thereafter LWA was Empie's full responsibility, one which he discharged with imagination, efficiency, and dedication. When Long died unexpectedly in 1948, it was only natural that Empie be asked to succeed him as executive director. Under Empie LWA became a household word in the congregations, the vast majority of whom gladly cooperated in the program. Symbolized by a strong arm thrusting the cross forward ("Love's Working Arm"), the Lutheran World Action appeal became an annual event for the next quarter of a century. By 1965 almost 80 million dollars had been raised and distributed as Christian aid to thousands of people in 75 countries around the world.[33] This became the Lutheran churches' "Marshall Plan" during the post-war reconstruction. Together with Lutheran World Relief (not an incorporated part of the NLC), which was the material aid program of the council and the Missouri Synod's Board of World Relief (after 1953), Lutheran World Action elicited the admiration of both ecclesiastical and governmental leaders. In fact, the manner in which American Lutheranism mobilized its resources for overseas aid both during and after the war did as much as anything else to enhance its stature in ecumenical circles. Voices in Asia, Africa, the Near East, and Western Europe were raised in unstinted praise. A few were critical of what they termed American Lutheranism's "confessional imperialism." The well-known Martin Niemoeller, for example, was credited with the snide remark, "Cuius dollar eius religio" (religion is controlled by those who supply the money)! Most people, however, recognized Lutheran World Action as an outpouring of Christian compassion.

As has been observed, common calamity had opened the door to bet-

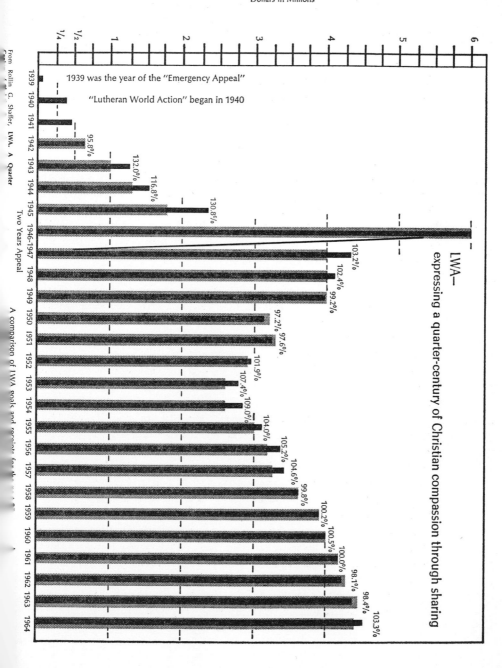

Dollars in Millions

LWA—
expressing a quarter-century of Christian compassion through sharing

1939 was the year of the "Emergency Appeal"

"Lutheran World Action" began in 1940

1939
1940
1941
1942 95.8%
1943 132.0%
1944 116.8%
1945 130.8%
1946–1947
1948 103.2%
1949 102.4%
1950 99.2%
1951 97.2%
1952 97.6%
1953 101.9%
1954 107.4%
1955 109.0%
1956 104.0%
1957 105.2%
1958 104.6%
1959 99.8%
1960 100.2%
1961 100.5%
1962 100.0%
1963 98.1%
1964 98.4% 103.3%

From Rollin G. Shaffer, LWA, A Quarter

Two Years Appeal

A comparison of LWA goals and receipts for the first 2.5

ter relationships with the Missouri Synod. The initiative displayed by
the National Lutheran Council in embarking on such an ambitious program back in 1941 had received solid encouragement from an all-Lutheran conference held two days prior to the council meeting in Columbus,
Ohio. Called at the instigation of the American Lutheran Conference,
which was eager to include the Missouri Synod,[34] the so-called First
Columbus Conference produced a policy statement by President J. W.
Behnken for the Missouri Synod. He said that he had genuine misgivings
about affixing his signature to the call for this meeting and that his
church could not cooperate "in any form in the dissemination of the
gospel." Before this could be done, he said, there must be agreement
in such doctrines as the verbal inspiration of Scripture, the doctrine of
conversion, and the concept of the church. Therefore, cooperation must
be confined to such "externals" as physical relief to orphaned missionaries
and work among soldiers and sailors.[35]

Despite Behnken's backing into contact with fellow Lutherans, the
Columbus Conference accomplished a minor breach in the wall of the
Missouri Synod. This was seen in three ways: (1) the meeting marked
the first time in history that the Missouri Synod had joined in prayer
with council Lutherans; (2) it revealed that the Missouri Synod was
open to coordinating efforts in the support of orphaned-missions, and (3)
it prepared the way for dove-tailing council and Missouri work among
Lutherans in the armed forces, especially in locating service centers. But
at the same time it revealed Missouri's traditional caution: "spiritual welfare work in the interest of members of the Missouri Synod" would be
done by Missouri pastors. As Wentz says, formal agreements with Missouri
were little changed from the World War I pattern, but a more cooperative spirit was in evidence.[36] Before the war was over the Missouri Synod
did make contributions to Lutheran World Action and signed a formal
agreement with the National Lutheran Council to establish a common
Lutheran Commission for Prisoners of War.[37]

One cannot fully assess the role of the council during the war years
by looking only at those areas that were directly associated with its
war-shaped ministries. Several domestic programs should be noted, among
them social welfare and American missions.

The social welfare department of the council, under the leadership
of Clarence E. Krumbholz, was primarily engaged in the problems of

welfare rather than in direct social action. In fact, the latter, somewhat cautiously undertaken in the 30s by the council's Social Trends Committee, was not pursued with vigor until the 50s.[38] This is not to denigrate the work of the department. As a matter of fact, it was engaged in a huge humanitarian enterprise expressing the Christian concern of the churches. Serving as the Lutheran World Convention's contact for war refugees, the department was also in close contact with Lutheran welfare or inner mission societies across America; furthermore, it kept the churches informed of social legislation, and provided invaluable assistance to Lutheran welfare institutions. Wentz summarizes: "To indicate the size of the field within which the department operated, the following statistics . . . are instructive: including the Missouri Synod, there were 461 benevolent organizations (in 1945), contacting more than a million people with services, spending 16½ million dollars, involving more than 18,000 people as employees, board members, and volunteers." [39]

Another aspect of the council's domestic program fell under the general rubric of American Missions. As pointed out in an earlier chapter, World War I had focused attention on the necessity of missionary work in the new defense industry communities. Home mission conferences during the 1920s were the occasion for the National Lutheran Council to recommend that a Lutheran Home Missions Council of North America be established. Since the various American mission boards were not yet ready to entrust this work to the NLC, some agency was needed to coordinate their activities. With this in mind, the Home Missions Council came into being in 1931 and functioned with some effectiveness until 1942. In that year at the prodding of the National Lutheran Editors' Association, meeting jointly with the National Lutheran Council, consideration was given to closer domestic cooperation. This was the background of the council's action in the fall of 1942 to organize a Commission on American Missions. Although it came on the scene under wartime conditions, it soon transcended its "emerging" nature and became a permanent Division of American Missions in the council's new constitutional structure (1945).[40]

The major work of the division, beyond the "temporary ministries" in defense industry areas, was to foster comity among council Lutherans in establishing new congregations. The Missouri Synod and other Synodical Conference churches did not participate in the comity arrangements nor in the division's Regional Home Mission Councils. Nevertheless, as years went on some Missouri Synod pastors cooperated with the council "in local urban self-study workshops." [41] Of no little interest in this connection was the fact that through the work of this division the National Lutheran Council was unmistakably involved in a "churchly" ministry. In no sense could its activity be interpreted as mere cooperation "in externals." The executive secretary of the division, H. Conrad Hoyer, recalling the war-time services, wrote ". . . in these ministries we often had pastors . . . of different Church Bodies. . . . In fact, the Synodical affiliation of the pastors in relation to the area was rarely taken into account, and it was never decisive. . . . [Pastors] were elected by our Division, paid by us, supervised by us, and the services which they conducted were considered chaplaincy services in the area." [42] Granting the Missouri Synod's theological premise, it was not strange that this church excluded itself from participation in the "churchly" work of the council.

THE CHURCH: ACIDS AND ASSETS IN WARTIME

America's somewhat equivocal position at the outbreak of World War II had been abruptly changed on December 7, 1941. The shock of Pearl Harbor thrust deep into the American body ecclesiastic, both in its local and national manifestations.

There was no reason why Lutheranism should be spared; and it was not! On the local level the life of the church was traditionally rooted in the worshiping community. All "activities," theoretically at least, were adjuncts to and fruits of the life of worship. Sunday schools, adult education, community outreach, visitations, buildings and grounds, auxiliary organizations, fund raising, church boards—all of these and more were the accoutrements of the congregation. When the war came, there was no material change in the general contour of the local church. Rather there was a deepening of mood in the life of worship, a perceptible drawing together around Word and sacrament, a growing sense of interdependence and community. When sons and daughters of the congregation were drawn inevitably into the armed forces, star-bedecked "service flags" were hung in the churches. As the war lengthened, increasing numbers of blue stars were changed to gold.

New problems, social acids that began to ulcerate spiritual vitality, soon appeared. America's vast industrial-military complex demanded more and more workers, women as well as men. Over night "Rosie the Riveter" became a familiar sight in the assembly line in defense industries across the nation. The disruption of homes, not only by the military draft and enlistments, but also by the unprecedented movement of wives and mothers into factories, offices, and schools, placed unaccustomed stresses on family life. With fathers working one shift and mothers another, children soon became the victims of familial instability. Social workers and pastors added a new phrase to their vocabularies: juvenile delinquency. To be sure, young people had gotten into trouble before, but the war years saw an unhappy enlargement of the problem. But this was not all: increased pay checks and wives with independent incomes produced a new freedom, and the new freedom often led to excesses. In many cases moral patterns broke down, divorce increased, and alcoholism surfaced with an alarming frequency. Pastoral responsibilities, already extended by the decreased number of clergymen available for civilian ministries (the Lutheran church supplied hundreds of chaplains and service-center pastors) multiplied parochial duties almost beyond human endurance. Moreover, the educational institutions (colleges and seminaries) of the church were graduating fewer and fewer men (numerous campuses were used by the government for V-12 and other programs). Accelerated education, especially on the seminary level, occupied faculties virtually on a year-round basis, resulting in exhausted teachers and inadequately prepared and immature graduates.

Meanwhile, the "war boom" economy was reflected in higher church income. Many congregations whose pre-war plans for new churches and educational units were interrupted by government-ordered stoppages used the building hiatus to husband funds for post-war construction opportunities. Other congregations, carrying indebtedness from the depression era, were able to burn mortgages and bring their financial houses into order.

The income of the church at large also mounted. In addition to the large sums raised for Lutheran World Action, the contributions to home and foreign missions, charities and welfare, and education showed substantial increment. The funds for American (home) missions were expended on programs of expansion that burgeoned in all the major bodies during the 40s. The fact that missions in Japan, China, and Southeast Asia were cut off from American churches for several years made it necessary for boards of world missions to invest a portion of wartime receipts until such a time as reactivation of some Asian missions and the opening of new fields could be undertaken. American Lutherans, like all other citizens, awaited eagerly the cessation of hostilities in order that the ways of peace might be resumed and reconstruction for a new day might enlist the energies of all loyal churchmen.

POST-WAR CHURCH LIFE

The Surge of Piety in America

Thousands of words have been written in an attempt to describe and evaluate the post-war "religious boom" in America. Although no definitive interpretation has appeared, it is now a commonplace in American religious historiography to refer to "The Revival of the Fifties." That something occurred in that era which rightly or wrongly was called "revival" cannot be denied. Visiting European churchmen were fascinated by "religious America": the full churches, the multiple services, Billy Graham crusades, Fulton Sheen on TV, Norman Vincent Peales' "positive thinking," printed table prayers in restaurants (choose your own: Protestant, Catholic, Jewish), "piety on the Potomac," bill-board advertising "Go-to-church-Sunday," and dozens of other marks of religiosity. Association with institutional religion had become socially acceptable. To be American, said Will Herberg, was to be Protestant, Catholic, or Jew. Though Herberg's phrase over-simplified the situation, there was a sense in which Americans had domesticated religion and created ministers in their own democratic image. The pastor was a "regular guy" who played baseball with the kids and went fishing with the members of the men's club. Religion could be fun. A. Roy Eckardt wrote a book about it and quoted the Dutch theologian Hendrik Kraemer's reply to the question whether there was a revival in Europe: "Why, perhaps there is. Church attendance seems to be decreasing." [43]

It is difficult to judge the American "revival." Was "true religion" absent from the popular acclaim? Was biblical faith necessarily and always confined to "the remnant"? Was not "the remnant" quite as vulnerable to demonic perversion as "mass Christendom"? Was the self-righteousness of the "little flock" less a denial of God than the superficiality of bourgeois religion? Whatever the answer, Lutherans participated in the "boom."

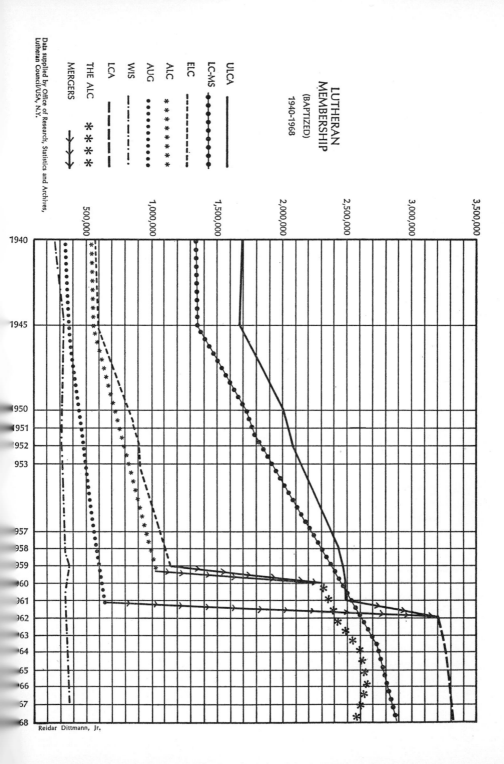

LUTHERAN
MEMBERSHIP
(BAPTIZED)
1940-1968

ULCA

LC-MS ●●●●●

ELC

ALC ✱✱✱✱✱✱✱✱

AUG ●●●●●●●●

WIS

LCA

THE ALC

MERGERS ✱ ✱ ✱ ↓

Data supplied by Office of Research, Statistics and Archives,
Lutheran Council/USA, N.Y.

Reidar Dittmann, Jr.

Lutheranism and the "Revival"

Theodore Roosevelt once said " . . . the Lutheran Church is destined to become one of the two or three greatest and most important churches in the United States. . . . " [44] Others spoke of Lutheranism in America as a sleeping giant that began to wake up between the two World Wars. Whatever the validity of these observations and whatever may be the future of American Lutheranism, there was no doubt that it experienced a vast expansion in the post-war period. In the first place, each of the major church bodies reported advances in membership and church attendance. Of the major churches the conservative Missouri Synod showed the greatest gains. That there was no correlation between Lutheran "orthodoxy" and rapid growth—a conclusion sometimes drawn—could be seen right within the Synodical Conference where the Missouri Synod's even more conservative partner, the Wisconsin Synod, experienced the smallest increase. The preceding graph gives visual indication of what happened over a period of two and a half decades.[45]

An essential part of this pattern of growth was the missionary program of the churches. Lutherans had been engaged in "home missions" ever since their arrival on these shores, but it was an activity characterized by salvaging the immigrant for the church. Roughly speaking, the missionary program progressed through three stages: (1) ethnic (e.g. Swedish-background Augustana sought out Swedish immigrants); (2) confessional or denominational (entering a new field to win unchurched *Lutherans* regardless of national origin); and (3) "American missions." Eastern Lutherans, more urbanized than others, moved quickly into stage three, but midwestern Lutheranism and linguistic synods within the United Lutheran Church made the giant leap forward in the post-war era. The Missouri Synod, the Augustana Lutheran Church, and the Evangelical Lutheran Church [46] developed strong and imaginative mission strategies. The Missouri Synod's program made it possible for its director, H. A. Mayer, to say, "Our church has had a proportionately larger growth in Home Missions than most other church bodies in America." That this was not pious braggadocio and ecclesiastical chest-thumping was evidenced by the sober comment: "Each year there are more Christians, but each year there are still more heathen. We face the strange paradox: The Church grows, and yet it becomes relatively smaller." [47] Both the Augustana Church and the Evangelical Lutheran Church possessed unusually competent home mission leadership in the persons of S. E. Engstrom and Philip S. Dybvig respectively. Engstrom carried out P. O. Bersell's "New Plan" for centralizing the administration of home missions. At Engstrom's untimely death (1955) he left behind him a model of missionary efficiency.[48] Dybvig, also carrying out the dream of a church president (J. A. Aasgaard) startled the church with an innovation that attracted the attention of most Lutheran bodies [49] and received wide acclaim among major Protestant groups. The innovation, adopted as policy on October 17, 1945, challenged the methods prevalent in most church bodies at the time. Dybvig shifted the emphasis from long drawn-out salary subsidies to complete financing of a new project by loans to new congregations from funds placed at the disposal of the Home Missions department. Dybvig called his plan "Operation New Church" and, after successfully introducing it, was asked to explain its workings to the Lutheran mission executives meeting in Chicago, December 6-8, 1948.[50] "Operation New Church" had the following main steps:

1. *Assignment of Field.* This was done on the basis of standard operating procedure of the Lutheran regional committee.
2. *Survey.* This was judged relatively unimportant. If it was an average American community, underchurched, and without evidence of being predominantly Jewish and Roman Catholic, the field was ready for entry.
3. *Calling the Pastor.* He had to be an experienced man with no congregational failures in his background. The salary paid was comparable with that received in the better established parishes. Moving expenses of household goods (but no travel expense) were paid.
4. *The Parsonage.* The practice was to build or buy a good home, not to rent. The idea was, "We are here to stay."
5. *Minimum Equipment.* Each new church was to have a parish record book, 30 hymnals, Sunday school texts and teacher's manuals, duplex envelopes, Sunday bulletins, communion set, offering plates, mimeograph, and typewriter.
6. *Preparation for the First Service.* The pastor and a parish visitor spent about a month in visitation before the first service. Much depended on a successful (numerically speaking) first service.
7. *Preliminary Committee.* Within a few weeks, the pastor or the worshiping group selected a preliminary committee to

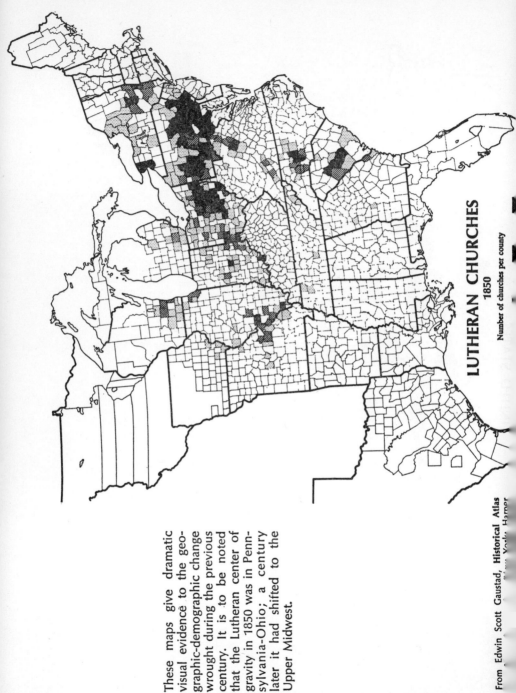

These maps give dramatic visual evidence to the geographic-demographic change wrought during the previous century. It is to be noted that the Lutheran center of gravity in 1850 was in Pennsylvania-Ohio; a century later it had shifted to the Upper Midwest.

LUTHERAN CHURCHES

1850

Number of churches per county

From Edwin Scott Gaustad, Historical Atlas
New York, Harper

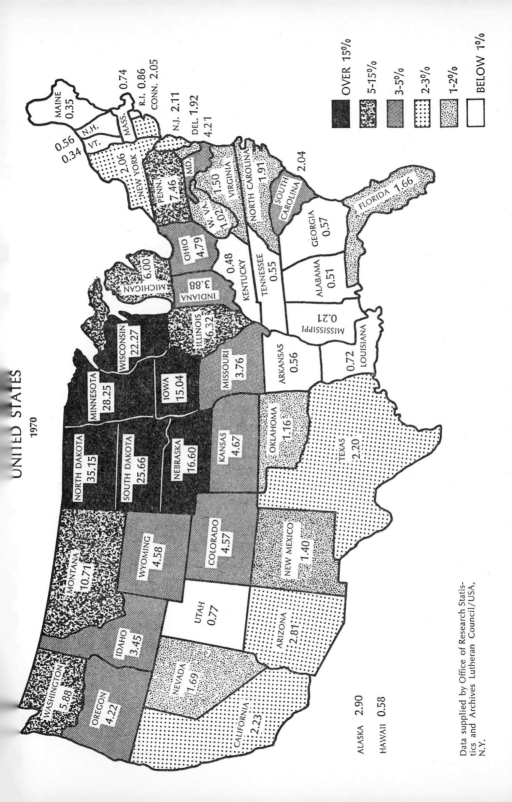

UNITED STATES
1970

OVER 15%
5-15%
3-5%
2-3%
1-2%
BELOW 1%

MAINE 0.35
N.H. 0.74
VT. 0.56
0.34
MASS. 2.06
R.I. 0.86
CONN. 2.05
NEW YORK 2.06
PENN. 7.46
N.J. 2.11
DEL. 1.92
MD. 4.21
W. VA. 1.02
VIRGINIA 1.50
OHIO 4.79
INDIANA 3.88
KENTUCKY 0.48
TENNESSEE 0.55
NORTH CAROLINA 1.91
SOUTH CAROLINA 2.04
GEORGIA 0.57
ALABAMA 0.51
FLORIDA 1.66
MICHIGAN 6.00
WISCONSIN 22.27
ILLINOIS 6.32
MINNESOTA 28.25
IOWA 15.04
MISSOURI 3.76
ARKANSAS 0.56
MISSISSIPPI 0.21
LOUISIANA 0.72
NORTH DAKOTA 35.15
SOUTH DAKOTA 25.66
NEBRASKA 16.60
KANSAS 4.67
OKLAHOMA 1.16
TEXAS 2.20
MONTANA 10.71
WYOMING 4.58
COLORADO 4.57
NEW MEXICO 1.40
IDAHO 3.45
UTAH 0.77
ARIZONA 2.81
WASHINGTON 5.88
OREGON 4.22
NEVADA 1.69
CALIFORNIA 2.23

ALASKA 2.90

HAWAII 0.58

Data supplied by Office of Research Statistics and Archives Lutheran Council/USA, N.Y.

work with the pastor arranging for a constitution and formal organization.

8. *Relation to Home Mission Department.* About three months after the arrival of the pastor, there was the first visit by a representative of the Home Mission department and the District President. Orientation to the general congregational program, financial support (assuming obligations in a specified order from miscellaneous expenses through loan payments to pastor's salary), proposed loan and amortization of same, everymember canvass, and ultimate self-support were discussed.

Under this plan almost phenomenal results occurred. Twenty new churches were organized in 1945; 22 (one every seventeen days) in 1946; 19 in 1947; 12 in 1948; 18 in 1949; 10 in 1950; 23 in 1951; 9 in 1952; 25 in 1953; and at least 40 in 1954.

The plan presupposed a large church extension fund. This was arranged by transferring a $300,000 Home Mission Emergency Fund to the Church Extension Fund, to be turned back in the event of dire necessity. Home mission endowment funds were placed into the loan program. With this accomplished, the department implemented the resolution in 1944 to permit borrowing from the church's endowment funds for church extension. Finally, the Home Mission Department received over $800,000 from a church-wide joint appeal for home and foreign missions. Thus, even in periods of economic recession the church had a workable and potentially fruitful plan for home mission expansion.

It can hardly be denied that, measured by secular "success" criteria alone, Lutheranism's missionary expansion in North America was remarkable. When President Oliver Harms of the Missouri Synod was asked in 1968 what developments in the Missouri Synod merited preservation in the collective memory of American Lutheranism, he unhesitatingly placed "missionary outreach" high on his list.[51] Other church leaders could have said the same. At its peak the mission program produced one new congregation every 54 hours!

Although this rapid expansion no doubt shared and reflected some of the undesirable aspects of the "Revival of the Fifties," in its major thrust it was without the frothy superficiality of the much-heralded "return to religion" via "positive thinking" or "revival crusades." Billy Graham's influence upon American Lutheranism would be difficult to assess. Individuals and groups were attracted by his widely-acclaimed "crusades."

Moreover, churchmen expressed gratitude for Graham's evangelical emphasis. On the whole, however, Lutherans found his techniques questionable and his message truncated. The absence of a sacramental and social dimension prevented many from giving him their wholehearted approbation. In most instances Lutheran evangelism was the missionary projection of a solidly-based doctrinal and catechetical emphasis rooted in congregations. An example of the churches' interest in parish-centered evangelism was a proposal in 1947 by President E. Poppen of the American Lutheran Church for inter-Lutheran cooperation in evangelism.[52] The Lutheran Evangelism Council, composed of representatives of the National Lutheran Council churches, sponsored evangelistic missions nicknamed "PTRs" (Preaching-Teaching-Reaching) after the successful program begun in 1952 by the Evangelical Lutheran Church.[53] The Missouri Synod also adopted this type of mission saying that it "represents one of the most effective and fruitful evangelism programs ever undertaken in the Lutheran Church." [54] The evangelistic thrust generated a new interest in the apostolate of the laity. "The United Lutheran Church," it was reported, "has never been so stirred to its depths by any previous undertaking as by the Lutheran Evangelism Mission." [55] Lutherans were concerned that evangelism center in and proceed from the congregations rather than from "revival crusades."

The Changing Face of the Churches

While the churches were experiencing the post-war "boom," some noteworthy changes occurred in the visage of the church. At the parish level in urban centers, for example, the so-called flight to the suburbs took on huge proportions.[56] Congregations in the "inner city" and on the edge of the city's central area often suffered large losses of members. Some congregations felt forced to relocate and to follow the exodus to the suburbs. Those congregations that remained were either weakened to the point of ineffectiveness or were led to reorient both their mission and priorities. For most Protestant denominations these years marked the beginning of a new understanding of the church's role in the inner-city, something which Roman Catholics had engaged in for several years with varying degrees of success. The most urban of the Lutheran groups, the United Lutheran Church, quickly asked its Board of Social Missions to make a study of Christian social responsibility and to address itself to metropolitan problems. It was soon discovered that racial and cultural relations were intertwined with other problems and, as a result, tentative beginnings were made in the integration of non-whites into congregational worship and life.[57]

Another phase of post-war religious interest was to be seen in the revitalization of church colleges. The depression and the war had all but closed the doors of many colleges. But the G.I. Bill of Rights brought a flood of veterans to Lutheran colleges as it did to all American campuses. The general religious climate served also to strengthen the church ties of most denominational schools. Hand in hand with this came a noticeable improvement in the financial status of colleges. New buildings rose; endowments were augmented; and faculty salaries increased. Typical of the interest developed was the "Christian Higher Education Year" (CHEY) financial appeal in the United Lutheran Church and similar campaigns in other bodies. Despite these successful efforts, however, the colleges soon found it necessary to utilize the newly authorized government loans for financing construction of buildings.[58]

The Campus Ministry

During the 1940s ministries to students were conducted by three groups, the United Lutheran Church, the American Lutheran Conference, and the Missouri Synod. Between 1942-1944 F. A. Schiotz, director of the Student Service Commission of the conference, urged that the campus ministries of the United Lutheran Church and the conference be transferred to the National Lutheran Council. When this was done, the council created a Commission on Student Service in 1945 and called Morris Wee to be its first executive (1946). In this way, the church had prepared itself to meet the heavy increase of post-war college enrollments. About one half of the students in 1946 were war veterans, a circumstance that allowed the council to appropriate emergency funds from Lutheran World Action to provide facilities for campus ministries at crowded state universities and Lutheran colleges. By 1949 the council granted "division status" to the campus ministry and in 1956 altered its name to the Division of College and University Work (DCUW). A noticeable change in program occurred shortly. The earlier ministry was geared primarily to "preserve Lutheran students in the faith." This was enlarged to a "mission to the university," an attempt by the church to relate the Christian faith to the academic world. Moreover, a reorientation in the life of worship took place after 1950. Initially the students had been encouraged to worship in established congregations near the campus. In the 50s the trend was to hold services on the campus led by the campus pastor, or to organize campus congregations. In addition, under the new executive secretary (Donald R. Heiges succeeded Wee in 1950), the division conducted annual staff conferences, aided the Lutheran Student Association of America in its national assemblies, and embarked on a program of aid to foreign students and arranged study-work projects in Europe. Heiges reported in 1952 that the ministry of the division "touched 600 of the 1800 colleges and universities in the United States. . . . " [59]

Service to War Refugees

One of the most dramatic stories in recent church history was the action of the churches to aid war refugees. Programs developed by Jews, Catholics, and Lutherans were rooted in the fact that the vast majority of the refugees were co-religionists of these groups. Parallel but less extensive relief work was done on an interdenominational basis by Church World Service, with which the Lutheran program was coordinated. American Lutherans, as noted earlier, had begun raising funds in 1940. Lutheran World Action money together with material aid gathered by Lutheran World Relief after 1945 amounted to over $250,000,000.[60] It was a severe, and perhaps necessary, blow to Lutheran pride in this considerable achievement when American Jews, only about half as numerous as Lutherans, raised $100,000,000 in a single year! Nevertheless, the funds and material aid provided by Lutherans made it possible to bring hope and new life to thousands of families and individuals dislocated by the tragedies of war.

There were three categories of refugees: (1) expellees (Germans pushed out of eastern territories), (2) ethnic Germans *(Volksdeutsche)* driven from non-German countries to the east (Poland, Czechoslovakia, the Baltic states) and (3) displaced persons or "DPs" (non-German political prisoners, forced laborers, and refugees from Russian-occupied countries). Altogether there were in 1945 over 25,000,000 such people in Europe. Seven and a half million DPs were repatriated by the United Nations Relief and Rehabilitation Administration (UNRRA was established in 1943) between 1945 and 1946. About 1,500,000 DPs could not or would not be repatriated for political or religious reasons. The United Nations acknowledged this and continued to assist them under the UN successor to UNRRA, the International Refugee Organization (1946). But the hordes of "expellees" and "ethnic Germans," victims of the Potsdam Agreement, were somehow supposed to be absorbed by the prostrate German economy.

It was into this situation that the Lutheran churches came with "Love's Working Arm." Before the war was over, early in 1945, Ralph Long and P. O. Bersell, representing the National Lutheran Council, and Lawrence Meyer, representing the Missouri Synod, visited Europe to lay plans for relief and reconstruction and to reactivate the war-disrupted Lutheran World Convention. The latter effort met with little enthusiasm from the Scandinavians (there was yet no contact with Germans); the Missouri Synod, having no official connection with the convention, exhibited no interest in its rebirth. But when the team (exclusive of Meyer) visited the Geneva staff of the World Council (in process of formation), it received good news from General Secretary W. A. Visser 't Hooft: the World Council would be happy to work out an agreement to coordinate Lutheran relief efforts with the newly established WCC Department of Church Reconstruction. To facilitate this a Lutheran representative, S. C. Michelfelder, was sent by the American Section of the Lutheran World Convention to Geneva to establish an office on the World Council precinct. On the same ship that carried Michelfelder to Europe in July, 1945, was Stewart Herman, another American Lutheran, who was to join the WCC staff as its officer in charge of establishing contact with the German churches. A third American Lutheran, who was to be a pioneer in the refugee program, was Howard V. Hong, St. Olaf College professor of philosophy and budding Kierkegaard specialist. He arrived in Europe in December, 1945, under the auspices of the YMCA's program for prisoners of war.

Meanwhile, the American Section of the Lutheran World Convention sent Ralph Long, Franklin Clark Fry, and J. A. Aasgaard to Europe in the fall of 1945. Their specific task was to assess the conditions among the churches and to reassemble the executive committee of the Lutheran World Convention at Copenhagen in December. This group received the resignation of Bishop Marahrens, president of the Lutheran World Convention, and appointed the Swedish archbishop, Erling Eidem, as acting president and Michelfelder as secretary. An officially called meeting of the executive committee was then arranged for Uppsala in July, 1946.

National Lutheran Commission for Soldiers' and Sailors' Welfare, 1917
(front) Lauritz Larsen, Oscar Mees, F. H. Knubel, J. A. O. Stub, Wm. Freas.
(rear) E. F. Eilert, J. J. Kildsig, H. E. Eilert, Chas. M. Jacobs, Emil H. Rausch, G. L. Kieffer.

EARLY NLC LEADERS

Lauritz Larsen
1st gen. sec., NLC, 1918-23
Pres., NLC, 1920-23

John A. Morehead
Exec. director, NLC, 1923-30
Pres., Luth. World Conv. 1929-35

H. G. Stub
Pres., NLCA, 1917-25
Pres., NLC, 1918-20

Frederick H. Knubel
Pres., ULCA, 1918-44

L. W. Boe
Leader in NLC; Luth. World Conv.
Pres., St. Olaf College, 1918-42

Chas. M. Jacobs
Prof., Phila. Sem. 1913-38

LWA Symbol
(post World War II)

**Lutheran World Convention
Executive Committee, 1923**

Pehrsson (Sweden), Morehead (USA), Boe (USA), Ihmels (Germany), Jørgensen (Denmark), von Pechmann (Germany).

Abdel Ross Wentz
Prof., Gettysburg Sem., 1916-58

J. A. Aasgaard
Pres., NLCA, 1925-54

G. A. Brandelle
Pres., Aug. Synod, 1918-35

C. C. Hein
Pres., ALC, 1930-37

Em. Poppen
Pres., ALC, 1937-50

John W. Behnken
Pres., LC-MS, 1935-62

Franz Pieper
Prof., Concordia Sem., 1878-1931

H. C. Alleman
Prof., Gettysburg Sem., 1911-40

J. Michael Reu
Prof., Wartburg Sem., 1899-1943

Ralph H. Long
Exec. director, NLC, 1930-48

Paul C. Empie
Exec. director, NLC, 1948-66

S. C. Michelfelder
Gen. sec., LWF, 1947-51

Carl E. Lund-Quist
Gen. sec., LWF, 1951-60

Kurt Schmidt-Clausen
Gen. sec., LWF, 1961-65

P. O. Bersell
Pres., Aug. Synod, 1935-51

Otto Mees
Pres., Capital U., 1912-46
1st Pres., Am. Luth. Conf.

T. F. Gullixson
Pres., Luther Theol. Sem.,
St. Paul, 1930-54
Leader in ALC merger negotiations

Theodore Graebner
Prof., Concordia Sem., 1913-50;
Editor, "The Lutheran Witness,"
1913-49

J. P. Koehler
Prof., Wis. Synod Sem., 1900-30

Walter A. Maier
Founder, "Lutheran Hour"

Paul E. Scherer
Preacher, National Radio Pulpit
(NBC)

Oswald C. J. Hoffman
"Lutheran Hour" preacher
Pres., Luth. Council, USA, 1970-

E. E. Ryden
Aug. Synod Hymnologist
and Editor

Luther D. Reed
Liturgiologist (ULCA)

F. Melius Christiansen
Conductor and composer
Founder, St. Olaf Choir

N. C. Carlsen
Pres., UELC, 1925-50

Nils Willison
Canadian Luth. leader

Earl J. Treusch
Exec. director, Luth. Council
in Canada

Franklin Clark Fry
Pres., ULCA, 1944-62;
LCA, 1963-68; LWF, 1957-63

F. A. Schiotz
Pres., ELC, 1954-60;
The ALC 1960-70; LWF, 1963-70

Henry F. Schuh
Pres., ALC, 1950-60

Oliver Harms
Pres., LC-MS, 1962-69

Conrad Bergendoff
Aug. Synod theologian
and educator

Malvin H. Lundeen
Pres., Aug. Synod, 1959-62
Pres., Luth. Council, USA, 1966-70

Julius Bodensieck
Prof., Wartburg Sem.
Editor, "The Encyclopedia of the
Lutheran Church," 1965

Theo. G. Tappert
Prof., Phila. Sem., 1931-
Historian, theologian, editor,
author

Jaroslav J. Pelikan
Luth. theologian, Yale U.

Martin E. Marty
Historian, U. of Chicago
Ed. staff, "The Christian Century"

C. Thomas Spitz
Exec. director, Luth. Council,
USA, 1966-

NLC Church Body Presidents, 1957
(back) Schuh (ALC), Schiotz (ELC), Benson (Aug), Fry (ULC),
(front) Wargelin (Suomi), Burntvedt (LFC), Larsen (UELC), Jensen (AELC)

LWF Minneapolis Assembly, 1957
Assembly Officials at Governor's Reception

Constituting Convention, The ALC, Minneapolis, 1960

Constituting Convention, LCA, Detroit, 1962

Lutheran Church Presidents
Knutson (ALC),
Marshall (LCA)
Preus (LC-MS)

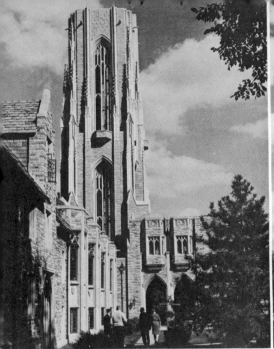

Concordia Theological Seminary
Largest Lutheran Seminary in America

Gettysburg Theological Seminary
First officially established
Lutheran Seminary, 1826

First Lutheran-Roman Catholic Dialog, Baltimore, 1965
(l. to r.) Sittler (L), Burghardt (RC), Murray (RC), Empie (L), Murphy (RC), Quanbeck (L)

Constituting Convention, Luth. Council, USA 1966

President Fry also participated in the simultaneous study commission appointed by the Federal Council of Churches. Other members were Bishop G. Bromley Oxnam and Bishop Henry Knox Sherrill. This commission, given a "guided tour" by American officials—who were inclined to say "the Germans are getting what they deserve"—returned with a report that gave little hope that American Protestants could be of much assistance because there was a ban on private relief shipments to Germany. To this Fry was utterly and furiously opposed and found it necessary publicly to denounce the American use of "starvation as an instrument of foreign policy." President Truman finally lifted the ban and thus opened the way to CRALOG (Council of Relief Agencies Licensed to Operate in Germany) of which Lutheran World Relief (established 1945) was a chief member.

In this manner, the way was prepared for additional American Lutherans to join those already in Germany. Clifford Ansgar Nelson, St. Paul, Minn., arrived to serve as short-term assistant to Michelfelder. Carl Schaffnit, Detroit, Mich., became the Lutheran representative for CRALOG. Julius Bodensieck, president of Wartburg Seminary, Dubuque, Iowa, served as commissioner to Germany for the LWC, American Section; and his remarkable wife was soon engaged in service to displaced peoples.

It was the so-called "spiritual ministry" to DPs which engaged the attention of Michelfelder and his associates at the outset. In April, 1946, he and Hong made contact with the UNRRA headquarters. Nelson surveyed the needs of the DPs and "the Lutheran churches in exile." Schaffnit, completing his assignment with CRALOG, moved directly into DP work. Mrs. Bodensieck, now attached to the WCC staff, was similarly engaged. Hong had returned to St. Olaf College to resume his teaching duties in September, 1946. The following January the annual meeting of the American Section of the Lutheran World Convention (the NLC) in Detroit approved a recommendation from Michelfelder that a permanent service to refugees be established and that Hong be appointed director to take up his duties in June, 1947.[61] The intervening months afforded Hong time to project some plans, one of which was to gather a cadre of volunteers to serve in Germany as a sort of Lutheran early-day "Peace Corps." Hong, who had a reputation for stretching dollars, determined that relief funds must be made to go as far as possible. One month after his appointment the LWC/American Section approved his proposal to

use college and seminary student volunteers to staff the program. In April
the first of these had been signed up, Kenneth Senft, Gettysburg Seminary, and James Anderson, St. Olaf College. During Hong's imaginative
administration no less than 16 other workers joined the refugee service.[62]

Before the service to refugees was to get under way, the long-delayed
meeting of the executive committee of the Lutheran World Convention
(Uppsala, July, 1946) had determined to reactivate and actually reorganize
the world body. To this end a constitution was drafted, a new name was
chosen ("Lutheran World Federation," proposed 27 years earlier by John
A. Morehead), and a place and date for a world assembly was selected
(Lund, 1947). When the Lund Assembly made the refugee program an
official responsibility of the LWF, the next step was to secure recognition
and cooperation from the Allied occupation forces. Through Michelfelder's
initiative—he had been elected the first executive secretary—the LWF
received a written agreement from the Preparatory Commission of the
International Refugee Organization to open the door for Lutheran work
among the refugees. In Richard Solberg's words, the LWF thus "began
a long and mutually fruitful relationship with the IRO. . . . " [63]

With most of the essential preliminaries out of the way, Hong and his
assistants plunged into the inchoate mass of forlorn refugees. The first
thing was to revive hope and to secure the religious moorings of the new
"churches-in-exile," as the DP Lutherans were called. Refugee pastors
were sought out and enabled to minister to their own people. Bicycles and
motorcycles provided transportation to and from scattered congregations.
Teachers and supplies for newly organized Sunday schools were brought
in. Supplementary food for DPs caught in the international chess game
was provided. But basic to the whole "spiritual ministry," as it was
called, was the LWF/Service to Refugees objective to aid the DPs to
minister to their own people. One of the boldest and most fruitful of
Hong's projects was the establishment of two LWF study centers, one at
Imbshausen near Goettingen, the other at Berchtesgaden in the Bavarian
Alps, to provide "retreat" facilities, conference opportunities, and year-
round courses for pastors, Sunday school and Bible teachers, and student
workers.[64]

One of the resolutions passed at the 1947 Assembly in Lund urged that
plans be devised for resettlement of the refugees. Hong was not slow to
carry out this resolution. Once the spiritual program among the 227,750

Lutheran and non-German DPs in Germany and Austria was under way, he presented (December, 1947) the USA Committee of the Lutheran World Federation with a proposal that the federation begin resettlement work in earnest. No action was taken, so in February, 1948, he submitted a carefully worked out resettlement plan that asked the LWF to establish in Geneva under an executive officer a Resettlement and Emigration Division for non-German DPs and the ethnic Germans and German expellees. Area offices and reception centers were to be coordinated by Geneva. A revolving fund of $500,000 would be needed for overseas passage loans to emigrants.[65] In May, Hong and Michelfelder were asked to come to New York to discuss the details of the plan and in June the USA Committee approved it, appointing Stewart Herman to be the first executive officer. The same month the U.S. Congress passed its DP Act and a year later legislation made it possible to include ethnic Germans for resettlement. Thus when Hong had to return to his professional duties in 1949, he had the satisfaction of knowing that immense steps had been taken to cope with an even more immense problem.

By this time, LWF/Service to Refugees had become a global undertaking directed by Stewart Herman with vitality and efficiency. His vision and energies were dedicated not only to the immediate problem of the refugees but also to strengthening the Lutheran churches in every continent by the lines established in the resettlement program. The American end of the program, the enlisting of sponsors, settling legal problems, and developing cooperation at national and congregational levels, was chiefly the result of the genius and energy of Miss Cordelia Cox on the staff of the National Lutheran Council. Hardly an American congregation was without some lively involvement in this action, many of them "adopting" refugee families and individuals in order that they might begin life anew. Even the Missouri Synod expressed its desire to cooperate with the NLC after Congress passed the Refugee Relief Act of 1953. The Lutheran Refugee Service, organized in 1954, thus became a joint NLC-Missouri Synod program.[66] Although statistics are a poor illustration of the human drama in which American Lutherans had engaged themselves, they nevertheless provide some indication of the magnitude of the enterprise. In 1952 it had been estimated that LWF/Service to Refugees had assisted almost 90,000 Lutheran emigrants, 37,000 of whom had been fully sponsored. By the 60s it was reported that 70,000 had been settled in the United States alone;

Canada had received over 22,000 and Australia another 20,000. The program had involved 265 full-time workers plus innumerable others both in Europe and the receiving countries. Beyond the resettlement program, the not inconsiderable refugee work in Hongkong and the Middle East together with the continuing support of orphaned missions had elicited the generous support of the churches. The direct overall cost to the LWF was above $4,000,000.[67]

In some ways, this vast missionary and refugee work, spearheaded by American Lutherans, was the high point of post-war church life. Although this was coterminous with the "religious boom," most, if not all, churchmen looked upon it as being something much more profound than a mass demonstration of religiosity.

Reorientation in World Missions

The 19th century pattern of "doing foreign missions" persisted well into the present century. The church building, the school, and the hospital were the ordinary fruits as well as loci of missionary work. Preaching (church), teaching (school), and healing (hospital), accompanied in many instances by "agricultural" and "industrial" missions, reflected the main concerns of the American churches as they sought to obey the Great Commission in Asia and Africa.

At the end of World War II missiologists and church boards were placing the missionary enterprise under close scrutiny. Some of the concerns of the earlier Laymen's Foreign Mission Inquiry and the Hocking report, Re-Thinking Missions (1932), were surfacing in Lutheran circles without the accompaniment of responses conditioned by theological liberalism. Without cutting the evangelical nerve of missions, men were nevertheless asking substantive questions which, though present before, were being raised with a new intensity. Mid-twentieth century saw a revitalizing of the great non-Christian religions of the Orient and a ferment in the Islamic and Arab world. What was the relation of Christianity to other religions? Was the classical concept of revelation in need of reinterpretation? How should the church establish contact with the non-Christian religions? What were the best ways of proclaiming the gospel to them? Moreover, as far as the "mission" and "younger churches" were concerned, the turbulence of the post-war era was pushing new problems to the fore. How could indigenization be speeded? What kind of ecclesiastical constitutions were proper to non-Western churches unacquainted with the democratic tradition? In the face of new nationalisms, how could "younger churches" escape the stigma of being outposts of Western "imperialism" and rise above the charge of being little more than "ecclesiastical Western colonies"? What was the relation of the "western" missionary to the younger churches? Was he really needed any longer? Furthermore, was it necessary or good for a Lutheran mission-church to adopt the Lutheran confessions of the 16th century, when these confessions were hardly an existential part of their tradition? Would it not be more honest to prepare new confessions, such as a *Confessio Africana* rather than a *Confessio Augustana*? Was it not the evangelical witness to the truth, embodied *in* the original confessions, that ought now be "confessed" in words and ways appropriate to the "younger churches"? In addition to all these problems, the churches in the 60s confronted the question: in the face of the violent social and political changes in Africa, Asia, and Latin America, what was the role of the church in nation-building and economic development? Clearly the issues were of immense significance.

The questions that appeared with such sharpness during and after World War II persisted with an unyielding tenacity to the present. All the answers were not in because all the questions had not been asked. One thing, however, emerged with clarity: the Lutheran churches in America were facing a reorientation in world missions. Future historians will have the task of describing and interpreting the change; for the present, it is necessary only to report on work that was being carried on by the major church bodies (ca. 1965) and their efforts at cooperation as the world moved into the last third of the 20th century.

THE AMERICAN LUTHERAN CHURCH (1960)

The old ALC (1930-1960) brought three thriving mission fields into the merger of 1960: The India mission, the Lutheran Mission of New Guinea, and the Ethiopia mission. *The ELC* (1917-1960) with strong mission work reaching back into the 80s of the 19th century, was operating in eight fields: Nationalist China and Hongkong (the residuum of a large work on the mainland up to the Communist take-over in 1949); Madagascar; Zululand and the Cameroun in Africa; Colombia and Brazil in South America; Japan; and Mexico (administered by the Board of American

Missions). *The LFC* (1897-1963) work was in three areas: Madagascar, Taiwan and Hongkong, and Japan. *The UELC* supported missionaries in Japan and India (Santal).

THE LUTHERAN CHURCH IN AMERICA (1962)

The ULCA (1918-1962) did mission work in eight countries: Argentina, British Guiana, Hongkong, India, Japan, Liberia, Malaya, and Uruguay. *Augustana* (1860-1962) operated in India, Taiwan and Hongkong, Tanganyika, North Borneo, Japan, and Uruguay. *The AELC* (1872-1962) and the *Suomi Synod* (1890-1962) operated in India (Santal) and Japan respectively. By 1970 Chile and Trinidad (1966) and Indonesia (1970) had been added to the LCA mission areas.

THE LUTHERAN CHURCH — MISSOURI SYNOD (1847)

Beginning world missions in 1893, the Missouri Synod's outreach included India, Hongkong and Taiwan, the Philippines, Japan, New Guinea, Korea, Brazil, Argentina, Chile, Central America, the Middle East, and Nigeria (a Synodical Conference undertaking).

THE WISCONSIN EVANGELICAL LUTHERAN SYNOD (1892)

A relatively small overseas work was carried on by the Wisconsin Synod in Nigeria (Synodical Conference), Northern Rhodesia, and Japan.

THE NATIONAL LUTHERAN COUNCIL

The Council was administering a program in Tanganyika (Tanzania) for The American Lutheran Church and the Lutheran Church in America. This was a continuation of support begun under "orphaned missions" during and after World War II. Although administration of personnel was under the jurisdiction of the LCA, both churches subsidized the program.

INDEPENDENT ORGANIZATIONS

A half-dozen groups, each drawing support from "interested friends" rather than a church body, were at work in various parts of the world: Latin American Lutheran Mission (Mexico); Lutheran Orient Mission (Kurdistan in northern Iran and Iraq); Santal Board (India); World Mission Prayer League (Bolivia, Ecuador, Mexico, India, Nepal, and

West Pakistan); and World Brotherhood Exchange. This last organization, later to become a part of the Lutheran Council in the USA, was essentially a recruiting agency seeking skilled men and women (craftsmen, physicians, nurses, dentists, farmers, etc.) to donate their time and talents to mission fields and underdeveloped areas.

World War II marked a turning point for world missions as well as for other church activities. For example, some churches cut off from their pre-war China fields began work in Japan, Hongkong and Taiwan. New interests were developed in Latin America and Africa. All of the churches, as observed earlier, became involved in the support of German, Finnish, Norwegian, and Danish missions orphaned by the war. Between 1939 and 1947 "orphaned missions" received over $2,500,000 from American Lutherans. To administer these and subsequent funds, the National Lutheran Council organized the Commission on Younger Churches and Orphaned Missions (CYCOM) in 1948. During the next five years another three and a half million dollars were provided for this work, the scope of which exceeded both in activity and budget the work of the International Missionary Council with other Protestant orphaned missions. Not only was the work immense, it was also dramatic. For example, at the time of the division of Palestine CYCOM's representative, ULCA pastor Edwin Moll, with great courage and devotion ministered to the fleeing Arab refugees and began a program of service that attracted international interest. Meanwhile, another CYCOM representative, F. A. Schiotz, with the assistance of Paul Empie and Frederick Nolde, arranged a partial compensation for Lutheran church properties taken over by Israel. In another part of the world, exciting rescues and hair-breadth escapes were negotiated by ELC missionary Daniel Nelson using a reconditioned airplane ("The St. Paul") to evacuate church workers from areas being overrrun by advancing Chinese Communists.

By 1955 the major portion of CYCOM's work was transferred to the Lutheran World Federation Department of World Mission in recognition of the fact that an international agency with headquarters in Switzerland was in a more favorable position to deal with international issues than an American office in New York City. CYCOM's contribution has been described in glowing terms by Frederick Wentz: "[CYCOM produced] a network of mutually valuable associations that bound together in Christian service the people of many nations on many continents, helping

Lutheranism to be truly worldwide." [68] The guiding hand and animating spirit of CYCOM from 1948 to 1954 belonged to Fredrik A. Schiotz. Two years after Schiotz left CYCOM (1954) to become president of the ELC, the National Lutheran Council restructured itself (1956) and created a Division of Lutheran World Federation Affairs that included a Department of World Missions Cooperation, the successor to CYCOM.

The impact of World War II on American Lutheranism was unquestionably deeper and farther reaching than any chronicle can possibly convey. The rise of European totalitarianism in the 30s and the emergence of controlled capitalism or "mixed economy" associated with the New Deal in America were the non-musical overture to the cacaphony of the 20 years following 1939. The explosion of World War II, the trauma-producing agonies of the era, the nuclear sudden-death at Hiroshima, the alternating heating up and cooling off of the Cold War, and the launching of the space race by Russia's Sputnik (1957)—all of these apocalyptic events gave to the age the character of a classical drama moving with predestinarian relentlessness to its tragic end. Was the post-war religious boom, in which American Lutherans shared, really only some *deus ex machina* introduced to take men's minds off unveiled horrors still to be revealed? Or was the restless ferment, the widespread seriousness more than a momentary exhilarating religiosity? Was it indeed a "voice from the other side" calling for judgment beginning in the household of faith and for renewed proclamation by Word and deed that death shall not prevail against the body of Christ?

NOTES

1. See Richard Hofstadter, William Miller, and Daniel Aaron, *The American Republic* (Englewood Cliffs, N.J.: Prentice-Hall, Inc., 1959), I, 546-547.
2. Ray H. Abrams, *Preachers Present Arms* (New York: Round Table Press, 1933).
3. Ray H. Abrams, "The Churches and the Clergy in World War II, *Annals of the American Academy of Political and Social Science,* No. 256 (March, 1948), 110-119.
4. Clifton E. Olmstead, *History of Religion in the U.S.* (Englewood Cliffs, N.J.: Prentice-Hall, Inc., 1960), p. 570.
5. In what follows, I am indebted in no small measure to Miss Helen Knubel, former archivist for the Lutheran Council/USA, who led me to the valuable Ralph H. Long Papers, especially to his correspondence with Germans and fellow-Americans involved in both the National Lutheran Council and the Lutheran World Convention. Here his correspondence with L. W. Boe, St. Olaf College, is highly important. In addition, I have relied on Frederick K. Wentz, "The Reaction of the Religious Press in America to the Emergence of Naziism," (unpublished Ph.D. dissertation, Yale University, 1954) and John G. Mager, "Nazis, Jews, and the War. What the *Lutheran Witness* Said,

1934-1945," *American Lutheran,* (November, 1964), 10-13. Helpful in understanding the German church situation is Stewart W. Herman, *It's Your Souls We Want* (New York: Harpers, 1943).

6. *The Lutheran,* (April 20, 1933), 4.

7. *Ibid.,* p. 13.

8. Archives of Cooperative Lutheranism, 315 Park Ave. S., New York; Ralph H. Long Papers, Box III. Letters: Long-Elert, Long-von Kirchbach, 3/8/33; von Kirchbach-Long, 3/29/33.

9. *Ibid.;* Letters: Long-von Kirchbach, 5/12/33; von Kirchbach-Long, 5/22/33.

10. The Bethel Institute was a healing-teaching-missionary community founded near Bielefeld (Westphalia) by "Father" Friedrich von Bodelschwingh (1831-1910). The size and outreach of the institution was unparalleled among Protestant and Roman Catholic institutions of similar nature. See *The Encyclopedia of the Lutheran Church* (Minneapolis: Augsburg Publishing House, 1965), I, 314-315.

11. The famous scholar Emanuel Hirsch was Mueller's theological adviser. Though he remained sympathetic to Nazism, Hirsch established a solid reputation as a Luther and Kierkegaard scholar. His five volume history of modern theology has been unsurpassed.

12. *Ibid.,* "The Lutherans in Germany Today," Address to Long Island Conference, Sept. 27, 1933. Cf. R. H. Long, "Development in the German Church Situation," *The Lutheran,* (June 29, 1933).

13. *Ibid.,* Letters: Boe-Long, 3/28/34; 7/20/34; Long-Boe, 9/24/34. It should be noted that both Marahrens and Meiser remained in office until after the war was over. Meiser held on despite his anti-Hitler position. He and the Roman Catholic archbishop of Munich, Michael Cardinal Faulhaber, joined in courageous resistance to the Nazis. Marahrens, however, was not outspoken. After the war, the latter was told by American Lutherans that he must resign. He was replaced by Johannes (Hanns) Lilje, who had been imprisoned by the Nazis for his role in the resistance movement.

14. "Theological Fault—Political Failure," *National Lutheran,* (February, 1965), 5-7. Cf. *The Lutheran,* (Sept. 1, 1937).

15. Richard R. Salzmann, "Lutheran Theology and Political Action," *National Lutheran,* (November, 1965), 9-11, 18.

16. John G. Mager, "Nazis, Jews, and the War. What the *Lutheran Witness* Said, 1934-1945," *American Lutheran,* XLVII (November, 1964), 10-13.

17. Augustana Synod, *Minutes,* 1939, p. 266.

18. *Ibid.,* 1941, p. 234.

19. *Ibid.,* 1942, p. 233.

20. NLCA, *Annual Report,* 1940, p. 9.

21. *Ibid.,* 1942, p. 29.

22. Osborne Hauge, *Lutherans Working Together. A History of the National Lutheran Council 1918-1943* (New York: National Lutheran Council, 1945), p. 72. Cf. F. K. Wentz, *Lutherans in Concert* (Minneapolis: Augsburg Publishing House, 1968), pp. 77-80.

23. Lauritz Larsen, "Unity," *Lutheran Church Herald,* III (April 1, 1919), 194. Cf. Hauge, *Lutherans Working Together,* pp. 39-40.

24. Wentz, *Lutherans in Concert,* pp. 84 and 90.

25. L. W. Boe Papers, Letter: L. W. Boe-J. A. Aasgaard, October 29, 1942; St. Olaf College Archives, Northfield, Minn.

26. ULCA, *Minutes,* 1928, p. 615; *ibid.,* 1932, p. 446; *ibid.,* 1934, p. 56. Cf. Hauge, *Lutherans Working Together,* pp. 64-65.

27. F. C. Proehl, *Marching Side by Side* (St. Louis: Concordia Publishing House, 1945), pp. 1-11.

28. It has been estimated that over $200,000 had been given by the NLC to the Gossner (India) Mission alone after World War I and in the 30s.

29. Wentz, *Lutherans in Concert,* pp. 106-107; cf. Hauge, *Lutherans Working Together,* p. 73.

30. *Ibid.,* p. 75.

31. *Ibid.,* p. 76. The Norwegian Lutheran Church funds were a balance carried over from the Soldiers' and Sailors' appeal in World War I. It is interesting to note that the NLCA made no demand in 1941, as it had done in 1919, for doctrinal agreement before it could engage in "churchly cooperation." This was a clear example of what Boe meant when he said the Lord had not permitted the NLC to stay within the rule marking a distinction between *res externae* and *res internae.* Moreover, it must not be forgotten *Norway* had been invaded! Cf. NLCA, Report, 1941, pp. 8-9; *ibid.,* 1942, p. 21; *ibid.,* 1943, p. 9.

32. Wentz, *Lutherans in Concert,* pp. 100-101.

33. *Ibid.,* p. 128. For a brief history of Lutheran World Action see Rollin G. Shaffer, *LWA. A Quarter Century of Christian Compassion* (New York: Lutheran World Action, 1966). It should be noted that interpretation of the accompanying chart should bear in mind the factor of inflation.

34. "Convention Proceedings," *Journal of Theology . . . Am. Lutheran Conference,* VI (January, 1941), 85-86. The meeting, including Missouri, was held at Columbus, January 20, 1941. The NLC met there January 22-23, 1941.

35. "Report of Representatives to an Intersynodical Lutheran Conference," January 20, 1941, Columbus, Ohio. J. K. Jensen Papers, Northwestern Lutheran Seminary Library, St. Paul, Minn. Cf. ULCA, *Minutes,* 1942, pp. 117-119.

36. "The Twenty-Third Annual Meeting of the NLC," *The Journal of Theology of the ALCf,* VI (April, 1941), 387. Cf. E. E. Ryden, "The Birth and Youth of the Council," *The National Lutheran,* XXXIV (December, 1966), 6. Ryden informed Behnken that the ULCA would attend on one condition, that the conference be opened with prayer. Behnken offered no objection. Cf. Geo. V. Schick, "The Columbus Conference and Its Repercussions," *The Lutheran Witness,* (May 13, 1941); "Coordination with National Lutheran Council," *ibid.,* 172. Cf. Wentz, *Lutherans in Concert,* p. 102.

37. *Ibid.,* p. 108. Cf. Augustana Synod, *Report,* 1944, "The National Lutheran Council," p. 299.

38. Lloyd Svendsbye, "The History of Developing Social Responsibility Among Lutherans . . . , " (unpublished Th.D. dissertation, Union Seminary, New York, 1966), p. 58. Cf. Wentz, *Lutherans in Concert,* p. 181.

39. *Ibid.,* p. 98.

40. R. H. Long, "Today and Tomorrow," in Hauge, *Lutherans Working Together,* pp. 100-102; Helen Knubel, "National Lutheran Council," *The Encyclopedia of the Lutheran Church* (3 vols.; Minneapolis: Augsburg Publishing House, 1965), III, 1705, and Wentz, *Lutherans in Concert,* pp. 105-106, 122-124, 148-151.

41. Paul C. Empie, "A Case Study in Lutheran Cooperation," (New York: unpublished manuscript, 1963), p. 5.

42. Letter: H. Conrad Hoyer-E. Clifford Nelson, 4/17/59; copy in Archives for Cooperative Lutheranism, 315 Park Ave. S., New York; Division of American Missions.

43. *The Surge of Piety in America* (New York: Association Press, 1958), p. 164. It has been suggested (Robert T. Handy) that the "surge" included three overlapping phenomena: (1) some waves of "popular piety—Graham, Peale, Pentecostalism, (2) a deepening and broadening of *church* life (buildings, membership, publications, education, etc.), and (3) a *theological* renewal in seminaries and colleges. See next chapter, section on the changing theological climate.

44. Theodore Roosevelt, *Presidential Addresses and State Papers . . .* (New York: Review of Reviews Co., 1910), III, 206-207.

45. For annual tabulations see Archives of Cooperative Lutheranism and Office of Research, etc., LC/USA, 315 Park Ave. S., New York.

46. Three churches changed their official names in the 40s: The Norwegian Lutheran Church of America became known as the Evangelical Lutheran Church in 1946; the Augustana Synod changed to the Augustana Evangelical Lutheran Church in 1948; and the Evangelical Lutheran Synod of Missouri, Ohio, and Other States became the Lu-

theran Church—Missouri Synod in 1947. The ELC became a part of The ALC (1960) and Augustana became a part of the LCA (1962). The LC-MS still remains popularly known as the "Missouri Synod."

47. LC–MS, *Proceedings . . . 1956*, p. 369.

48. Arden, *Augustana Heritage* (Rock Island: Augustana Press, 1963), pp. 333-337.

49. Dybvig's principle of "package financing" became home mission policy rather soon in other churches. See Augustana Lutheran Church, *Minutes,* 1953, p. 159.

50. P. S. Dybvig, "Operation New Church," in *Policies and Practices in Lutheran Home Mission Development* (Chicago: The National Lutheran Council, 1948), pp. 6-19. The description of the program is taken almost verbatim from E. Clifford Nelson, *The Lutheran Church Among Norwegian Americans*, II, 264-265.

51. Interview: Harms-E. Clifford Nelson, St. Louis, Mo. 8/28/68. The Missouri Synod had a notable growth. For over 20 consecutive years after 1945 the Synod had the highest numerical growth of all Lutherans. The greatest advance on a percentage basis for most of these same years was made by the ELC. See annual analysis of Lutheran statistics released by News Bureau, NLC and LC/USA, 1952-1968.

52. ULCA, *Minutes . . . 1948*, pp. 241-242.

53. ELC, *Report . . . 1953*, p. 10.

54. LC–MS, *Proceedings . . . 1956*, p. 377.

55. ULCA, *Minutes . . . 1956*, p. 1113.

56. See Gibson Winter, *The Suburban Captivity of the Churches* (New York: Doubleday and Co., Inc., 1960) for an analysis of this transformation.

57. ULCA, *Minutes . . . 1948*, pp. 300-308; *Minutes . . . 1954*, pp. 709-712; *Minutes . . . 1958*, pp. 732-766. Under the direction of the Board of Social Missions there was published a scholarly symposium in three volumes entitled *Christian Social Responsibility,* ed. by H. C. Letts (Philadelphia: Muhlenberg Press, 1957).

58. ULCA, *Minutes . . . 1948*, pp. 353-358; *ibid. . . . 1954*, pp. 912-917; ELC, *Report . . . 1948*, p. 54; *ibid. . . . 1954*, p. 69.

59. This section is largely a summary of the account found in Wentz, *Lutherans in Concert,* pp. 118-122.

60. For accounts of the service to refugees and related actions see Richard W. Solberg, *As Between Brothers. The Story of Lutheran Response to World Need* (Minneapolis: Augsburg Publishing House, 1957). Cf. also Wentz, *Lutherans in Concert;* articles in *The Encyclopedia of the Lutheran Church* (3 vols. Minneapolis: Augsburg Publishing House, 1965); Stewart W. Herman, "Lutheran Service to Refugees," *The Lutheran Quarterly,* II (February, 1950), 3-16; and "Lutheran Service to Immigrants," unpublished report of Lutheran Refugee Service, New York, October, 1957, addendum to Agenda of NLC, Division of Welfare, Sept. 19-21, 1956, Archives for Cooperative Lutheranism, 315 Park Ave. S., New York. The writer has also had access to the invaluable two-volume unpublished documentary account edited by Howard Hong, St. Olaf College, Northfield, Minn.

61. J. A. Aasgaard, president of the ELC and member of the LWC executive committee, called Hong from Detroit and insisted that he accept. Interview: Hong-ECN, 11/13/69.

62. Solberg, *As Between Brothers,* p. 144.

63. *Ibid.,* p. 138.

64. A fascinating account of this project is found in Hong, ed., "Lutheran World Federation Service to Refugees, 1947-1949," I, 273-307.

65. The original document is to be found in *ibid.,* pp. 309-316.

66. Solberg, *As Between Brothers,* p. 154.

67. *The Encyclopedia of the Lutheran Church,* I, 711-712; Wentz, *Lutherans in Concert,* pp. 139, 162; cf. E. Theodore Bachmann, *Epic of Faith* (New York: The National Lutheran Council, 1952), p. 40. Accurate statistics on retention of refugees for the Lutheran church are impossible to obtain at this time.

68. Wentz, *Lutherans in Concert,* p. 141.

CHAPTER FIVE

LUTHERANS AND CHRISTIAN UNITY

The desire to express the unity of the church was present among American Lutherans from their first years in the new world. Throughout the first two centuries this was primarily an inner Lutheran concern, the lonely exception being the ecumenical efforts of S. S. Schmucker. Incongruous as it may have been, even the theological controversy that marked so much of the Lutheran story emerged in large measure from a conscientious desire for church unity. What was debatable—and debated!—was the definition of unity. What, for example, was necessary before the churches could give expression to their unity? Moreover, if grounds for unity actually existed, was it wise to hurry the processes of union? Would it not be more prudent to allow the churches to grow together in a natural manner? It was self-evident that sociological or cultural factors simply could not be dismissed with an easy wave of the hand.

A multilingual family, such as the Lutheran church, would necessarily have to do much of its work in linguistic insularity. It was simple practical sagacity for the churches to recognize that they were cultural islands within which the faith of the fathers must be nurtured. If Swedish-Lutherans did not tend and care for Lutheranism among Swedes, one could hardly expect American Congregationalists or Presbyterians to do it. Long before modern psychology and pedagogy began to articulate a sophisticated view of the relation between language and religion, the immigrant churches knew intuitively that the language of religion was the language of the heart. The first generation Swedish-American might

156

learn English and might learn it well. To survive in the new world it was a necessity. His business was conducted in English, his school books and newspapers were printed in English, and his conversations with his American neighbors were held in English. But when he talked to God, he spoke Swedish, the language of his heart.

Consequently the question of what constituted unity in the church was complicated by the sociological question of acculturation. The doctrinal and the cultural walked side by side but not often hand in hand. Even within the national groupings, culture or ethos was not enough to assure unity. Most of the ethnic islands were sadly fragmented by theological and religious attitudes, some of which had been transplanted from Europe and often aggravated in America. What was true of the immigrant churches in general was most evident among the German, Norwegian, and Finnish Lutherans. Several streams of Lutherans whose origins were German eventually received institutional expression in America. The United Lutheran Church, itself a merger of three branches of one common stream; the Lutheran Church–Missouri Synod, an institutionalized form of the 19th century German Lutheran immigration; the Wisconsin Synod, another brand of German Lutheranism; and finally the American Lutheran Church, like the United Lutheran Church a merger of three streams, but like the Missouri Synod a sociological-ecclesiastical form of 19th century German Lutheran immigration—this was the fragmented character of the German Lutheran family in America. It was a composite of theological and cultural problems.

The Norwegians presented an even more complicated and unhappy picture. At least ten separate and independent church bodies had been formed in America by Norwegian Lutherans. One astute observer of the situation blamed their fissiparous tendencies on an unnatural alliance that some Norwegians had made with the orthodoxism of the Missouri Synod. Doctrinal rigidities spawned divisiveness rather than unity because unity always meant: "You must agree with us." On the other hand, large segments of the immigrant population were plagued with the pietistic "old Norwegian narrow-mindedness," which likewise was divisive rather than unitive.[1]

Whatever the causes, several of the Lutheran cultural islands in America were seriously divided within themselves. Doctrinal and religious attitudes rent the ethnic households asunder. The story of the coming together of the various groups is a long and confusing one, one which only the expert may be inclined to trace and in which only the truly penitent will possess spiritual power to persevere.

The movement towards Lutheran union obviously had roots going back decades and centuries. Some of these have been pointed out in previous chapters. The purpose of this chapter is to provide a comprehensible narrative of the main stages through which the drama unfolded after 1940. Before telling the story, however, note must be taken of certain forces and factors that paralleled the union movement and, in fact, wove in and out of the movement itself shaping it, conditioning it, and even changing its direction. These forces and factors should be considered separately, but not in isolation, from the movement itself.

THE MILIEU OF THE UNION MOVEMENT

The new climate during the two decades of the 40s and 50s possessed ingredients that both fostered and inhibited the union movement. Among these were influences from World War II and the changing theological atmosphere.

World War II Influences

The influence of World War II, like the Great Depression, will perhaps never be fully understood nor adequately assessed. Surely American Lutheranism, like every other segment of society, was immeasurably altered by the forces unleashed by the tragic events of the 40s. The very profundity of the effects precludes anything but a simple pointing out of the obvious results that lay on the surface for all to see.

"It takes a war to drive Lutherans together!" This cynical remark reflected what some commentators have described as unity through disaster. It is undeniable that common catastrophe tends to draw men together. Not only does misery love company, but tragedy often uncovers broad opportunities for Christian compassion and common action. Lutheran theology would maintain that one cannot neatly exclude God from any event, even war. God is always there in the world's turbulence, not as cause but as presence. He "prevents" men, going ahead of them. He is already present in the evil situation preveniently preparing men to hear the gospel. He turns death into life. This is Luther's profound theology of the cross: God's work *(opus dei)* is both "strange" or "alien" *(opus alienum)* and "proper" *(opus proprium)*. His "proper" work is to save and make alive; his "strange" work is to crush and defeat the old Adam in order that by means of death the new Adam may be born, resurrected to new life. In this manner God turns an evil, such as war, to his purposes so that in the end it becomes, in a sense, "the work of God" *(opus dei)*. Thus "the strange" work serves "the proper," the penultimate serves the ultimate, and the ultimate is the incorporation of men into Christ, the unity of all believers in him, and the consummation of his rule (the kingdom) among men.

Viewed in this light, the Lutheran cooperation that was born of the death and destruction of World War II was indeed the work of God. The marshalling of forces and resources within American Lutheranism not only brought new life to the enfeebled National Lutheran Council but helped to break down barriers between the cooperating groups within the council. Almost immediately as the churches were thrown together in raising funds for Lutheran World Action and material aid for Lutheran World Relief voices were heard urging union. Rubbing shoulders in common action with Lutherans about whom one had heard dark rumors tended to remove the suspicions and destroy the distorted images that caricatures had created. Even the Missouri Synod, which had a long and unbroken tradition of isolation from Lutherans outside the Synodical Conference, found itself drawn irresistibly into a measure of involvement. Although it hedged its cooperation with various and sundry conditions, the net result was ultimately to shatter the Synodical Conference and to bring the Missouri Synod into closer relationship with the churches of the National Lutheran Council.

Beyond improving inter-Lutheran relationships, the impact of World War II fostered Lutheran participation in the ecumenical movement. The only major National Lutheran Council church to remain outside the World Council of Churches during the latter's early years was the Evangelical Lutheran Church (Norwegian), which, by 1956, finally overcame its reluctance to join other Lutherans in the ecumenical world.

One aspect of wartime that must not be overlooked in seeking to measure the influence of those years on the union movement was the unprecedented mobility of population, both civilian and military. Wartime job opportunities drew thousands of men and women from small towns and rural areas into the industrial cities of the nation. As these people sought new church homes, they exhibited a noticeable lack of concern whether congregations were United Lutheran, American Lutheran, Augustana Lutheran, or Evangelical Lutheran. Many of the churches, they discovered, simply identified themselves as belonging to the National Lutheran Council. Missouri Synod migrants, however, were often kept for Missouri congregations by the refusal of letters of transfer to non-Missouri Lutheran congregations. Even so, many Missouri members found their way into other than Missouri congregations and vice versa.[2] What eventually happened to institutional loyalties goes without saying.

A similar pattern emerged among those who served in the armed forces. Few if any Lutherans in uniform inquired as to the church affiliation of a Lutheran chaplain before participating in the Holy Communion. As a matter of fact intercommunion was practiced among Lutherans in the military decades before the official ecclesiastical proclamation of pulpit and altar fellowship. Again it goes without saying what this did to the general attitude of Private Joe Doe who might sometimes have worn a "Lutheran" dogtag in addition to his regular Protestant identification.

The dynamics of the wartime situation simply did not permit Lutherans to live in isolation from each other or, in many cases, from non-Lutherans. The problem, which many leaders were unwilling or unprepared to admit, was not Lutheran union but rather Lutheran particularity in a religious pluralism. Lutheran union was already long overdue; one question that now clamored for an answer was how to maintain a Lutheran identity and yet participate honestly in the ecumenical movement.

The Changing Theological Climate

It has been said with justification that American Lutherans contributed little or nothing to the theological renaissance during the 30s and 40s. Many Protestants, having been thrust from the agonies of the depression into the pathos of World War II, were rediscovering the perennial relevance of Reformation theology. Dissatisfied with and disillusioned by liberalism's "ballet of bloodless categories," they were prepared to listen to European evangelical theologians who saw the contemporaneity of such Reformation themes as the theology of the cross, salvation by pure grace received through personal faith, the authority of the Word of God in sermon and sacrament, and the believer's participation in the priesthood of Christ.[3] American Lutherans, who in large measure had retained these treasures, albeit in the earthen vessels of an unhistorical confessionalism and an intellectualistic orthodoxy, had not heeded the cry of a theologically exhausted Anglo-American Protestantism to come over and help. *The Christian Century* editorialized about this in 1942:

> Its [Lutheranism's] witness to the doctrinal basis of Christianity is an emphasis which the church of Christ dare not forget or neglect. . . . All our churches are beginning to reaffirm the great truths of Christian faith to which Lutheranism especially bears witness. There is abundant evidence that the Lutheran churches have all along had elements which American Protestantism needed.

Then the editorial pointed up American Lutheran isolationism—born of the fear that cooperation and ecumenism might compromise its witness to the truth—as the inhibiting factor. The editorial continued:

> In the rediscovery by American Protestantism of the truth and the faith through which the Reformation brought new spiritual life to Western Christianity, Lutherans of America would do well to weigh the fact that they have played an almost negligible role. Their policy of isolation has debarred them from impregnating the rest of Protestantism with the very truths which it had lost and which Lutheranism possessed. . . . The gross fact is that our American churches have for two decades been moving in a general way toward the position occupied by their Lutheran brethren, but only the slightest credit can be taken by the Lutheran churches for this rapprochement.[4]

Most American Lutheran theologians were either trying to reproduce what they firmly believed was the faith of the fathers or seeking cautiously to introduce the churches to the vast field of biblical research via the historical method and thus to provide a new approach to biblical and confessional theology. Those who sought to uphold biblical inerrancy and generally to repristinate "orthodoxy," might be called "old Lutherans"; those who sought to relate contemporary theology and the Luther renaissance to American Lutheranism, "neo-Lutherans." All, however, were speaking *within* Lutheranism. It is perhaps not unfair nor an

oversimplification to say that one group sought to *preserve* true Lutheranism as it had been interpreted by the classical dogmaticians; the
other group tried to *understand* true Lutheranism by the application of
new hermeneutical principles to the study of Scripture and by a historical
approach to the Lutheran confessions. The chief questions posed by the
aggiornamento were the relations between the Word of God and the
Scriptures and between "faith" and "history."

Ever since the Reformation's repudiation of the dogmatic authority
of the pope, Protestants had found authority in *sola scriptura.* In the
polemical situation of the 17th century in which theological opponents
pitted one infallible authority (the pope) against another (the Bible),
there was developed on the Lutheran side a theory of inspiration *to assist
in carrying* "the burden of infallibility." [5]

J. A. Quenstedt (1617-1688), "the bookkeeper of Lutheran orthodoxy,"
stated the teaching of inerrancy as follows:

> The holy canonical Scriptures in their original text are the in-
> fallible truth and free from every error, that is to say, in the
> sacred canonical Scriptures there is no lie, no deceit, no error,
> even the slightest, either in content or words, but every single
> word which is handed down in the Scriptures is most true,
> whether it pertains to doctrine, ethics, history, chronology, typog-
> raphy or onomastics; and no ignorance, lack of understanding,
> forgetfulness or lapse of memory can or should be attributed to
> the amanuenses of the Holy Spirit in their writing of the Holy
> Scriptures.[6]

It was the position of "old Lutheranism" on infallibility that the
American Lutheran Conference churches in the National Lutheran Coun-
cil sought to protect in The Minneapolis Theses (1925) and which the
Missouri Synod enunciated in its Brief Statement (1932). The "neo-
Lutherans" preferred to speak of the infallibility of the theological message
("the Word of God") of the Scriptures, thus distinguishing the Word of
God and the Scriptures, but not separating them. It was primarily here
that the battle was joined in the union movement from the 40s to 1962.
Although there were "neo-Lutherans" in most of the National Lutheran
Council churches by 1940, the "old Lutherans" who formed the Ameri-
can Lutheran Conference (1930) on the basis of The Minneapolis Theses
continued to hold the upper hand in the negotiations that merged the

old American Lutheran Church, the Evangelical Lutheran Church, the United Evangelical Lutheran Church, and, later, the Lutheran Free Church in the new American Lutheran Church (1960). The remainder of the now divided council (ULCA, Augustana, Suomi, AELC) moved together into the Lutheran Church in America (1962).

Two books published under the auspices of The Conference of Lutheran Professors of Theology illustrated the theological situation. The first, *What Lutherans Are Thinking,* ed. by E. C. Fendt (Columbus: The Wartburg Press, 1947), contained "old Lutheran" and "neo-Lutheran" views, but the specific article on "The Word of God" was unmistakably "old Lutheran." The second book, *Theology in the Life of the Church,* ed. by Robert W. Bertram (Philadelphia: Fortress Press, 1963), exhibited "neo-Lutheranism" throughout.

Between the publication years of these two books numerous other books and articles appeared, most of which were oriented towards "neo-Lutheranism." Among these were Conrad Bergendoff, *Christ as Authority* (Rock Island: Augustana Book Concern, 1947); T. A. Kantonen, *Resurgence of the Gospel* (Philadelphia: The Muhlenberg Press, 1948); [7] Joseph Sittler, *The Doctrine of the Word* (Philadelphia: Muhlenberg Press, 1948); and Martin J. Heinecken, "The Authority of the Word of God," in *The Voice* (St. Paul: Luther Seminary Student Community, 1958). Dozens of articles on the same theme were published in the theological journals. Those appearing in the *Lutheran Quarterly* (representing seminaries in the National Lutheran Council) were chiefly "neo-Lutheran" in emphasis. *The Journal of Theology of the American Lutheran Conference* and its successor, *The Lutheran Outlook,* carried on a debate between the two points of view with editorial policy favoring "old Lutheranism"; and the *Concordia Theological Monthly* (Missouri Synod) predictably advocated "old Lutheranism."

Intimately associated with the theological climate of Lutheranism, of course, was the attitude of colleges and seminaries of the church. Religion departments in the colleges tended to be conservative into the 40s, largely because they were staffed by men educated in the categories of "old Lutheranism." There were individual professors in some church colleges who were "liberal," judged by prevailing ideas, but they were generally exceptions to the rule. It has been pointed out in a previous chapter that "neo-Lutheranism" began to manifest itself in United Lutheran seminaries as early as the 20s. At Augustana Seminary the break with "old Lutheranism" began in 1931. Before World War II the largest of the seminaries within the National Lutheran Council, Luther Theological Seminary (ELC), gave only occasional and individual hints of breaking out of the circle of prevailing "orthodoxy." When this occurred, it was largely the result of pietistic dissatisfaction with orthodoxism. A discernible change appeared about 1947 when some professors began to approach the Scriptures theologically and historically rather than with the a priori of inerrancy and verbal inspiration. What was a small voice in 1947 became a large sound within a decade. By 1956, when the proposed constitution of the new American Lutheran Church was voted on by the Evangelical Lutheran Church, several if not most of its professors of theology were teaching a view of Scripture at variance with the statement on the Bible in the new constitution. That is, while church administrators sought to uphold "old Lutheranism," many college and seminary professors were teaching "neo-Lutheranism."

Before concluding this survey of "para-union movement" factors, there are three additional items worthy of note. First, shortly after World War II the Missouri Synod sponsored a series of theological conferences with German Lutheran theologians at the health spa, Bad Boll, in Württemberg. The Bad Boll meetings brought Missouri theologians into face-to-face conversation with some highly respected leaders in the German theological world, such as Professors Heinrich Bornkamm and Edmund Schlink (Heidelberg), Werner Elert (Erlangen), H. Thielicke and A. Köberle (Tübingen). These men forced the Americans to look again at their teaching of verbal inspiration, and although no conversions were evident, the Missouri Lutherans were made aware of the intellectualistic, legalistic, and docetic dangers of the doctrine.[8]

Second, numerous pastors and recent seminary graduates did advanced theological study and research in the graduate schools of America, Britain, Germany, and Scandinavia after the war. Many of these men, who found their way into teaching positions in major colleges and seminaries of the Lutheran churches, including Concordia Seminary (St. Louis), had been exposed to contemporary biblical research (Dodd, Hoskyns, Wright, Albright, Bultmann, G. Bornkamm, von Rad, et al.); to contemporary theologians such as Nygren, Aulén, Barth, Brunner, Tillich, and the Niebuhrs; and to the Luther researches of Swedes, Germans,

Englishmen, and Americans (notably Wilhelm Pauck and Roland Bainton). One result was that in the course of time students were being exposed to a new brand of Lutheranism that was remarkably similar in all schools, whether in Chicago, Philadelphia, the Twin Cities, or St. Louis.

The third item to be noted flowed directly from the above changes. This was an unfortunate ecclesiastical backlash arising in part from inadequate or even careless communication of the new understanding of Lutheranism. An example of this was the all-too-well publicized "heresy trials" (1955-1956) of the Synod of the Northwest (ULCA) in which three pastors were charged with doctrinal deviations. One of the three was suspended from the ministry on nine counts, including denial of the Virgin Birth, the physical resurrection of Christ, the presence of his actual body in the communion, and the historical authenticity of the miracles. The two other pastors were similarly charged but finally acquitted. Without judging the trials, it seems nevertheless clear from the large amount of literature surrounding them that the theological issue was the meaning of "history" and "faith," the relation of "historical facts" to "the Christian faith." [9]

In due course groups of alarmed "defenders of the faith" in all churches began to form in order to protest the encroachment of "liberalism." The flinging of charges of "neo-orthodoxy," "existentialism," "heresy," "modernism," at the colleges and seminaries became the hallmark of self-styled "Confessional Lutherans" and "Lutherans Alert." It was evident that a theological ferment of some magnitude had taken the scene. Indebted in some ways to "neo-orthodoxy" or "dialectical theology," the leadership of the "liberal" movement insisted that it was unequivocally Lutheran. Although "neo-Lutheranism" drew adherents with varied and, in some cases, highly diverse backgrounds, there were certain identifiable emphases that were commonly made. For example, it was generally held that the historical-critical approach to the study of the Bible was not only helpful but a theological necessity if one was to understand the Word of God as being "in, with, and under" the Holy Scriptures.[10] This led to the realization that divine revelation was historical in character. Revelation was not the communication of sacred information about God; rather, it was the judging and redemptive action of God, his self-disclosure in history. This, in turn, made it easier to understand Luther's conception of faith as personal response to revelation, a response involving the whole personality of man, not merely his intellectual assent to certain "beliefs" or doctrines. There was, therefore, no once-for-all "revealed theology" to be accepted or rejected. Theology was dynamic and changing.

This meant an altered view of the Lutheran confessions as well. They were to be seen not as eternally binding legal documents but as historical testimonies of faith, confessions of faithful men who sought to safeguard the church's proclamation of the gospel in a given historical situation. Confessional subscription meant acceptance of the understanding of the gospel as witnessed to in the confessions. He who received the gospel as taught in the confessions was a Lutheran. This had implications *for ecclesiology:* the church is the people of God created by the Holy Spirit through the confession of Christ, the gospel of God; *for the sacraments:* as the Word is the message of God's dynamic, saving action, so the sacraments possess the character of events, for the God who acted in Israel and in Christ continues to act in baptism and communion drawing men unto his purposes; *for the ministry of Word and sacrament:* the ministry is of God, a special function (not order) of the people of God to assure the continued service of the gospel. All of this produced a new realization of the *ecumenical* character of Lutheranism rooted in Article VII of the Augsburg Confession. Finally, "neo-Lutheranism" subjected the orthodoxist-pietist distortion of Luther's "two realms" doctrine to critical re-evaluation. The secular realm ought never be understood as an absolute law unto itself separate from the spiritual realm. God's people live in both realms at once, but always under the Lordship of Christ. This had immediate implications for social action. It was no longer a question whether the church, the people of God, should be involved in society. The church was already a part of society. The question was how should the church exercise its role within its social context.

It would be asking too much of readers to plunge into the maze of Lutheran unity efforts in the 40s and 50s without some understanding of the developments described above. But with this sketchy orientation the ecclesiastical politics of these years ought to be somewhat less baffling and forbidding.

LUTHERANISM AND ECUMENISM

If one defined ecumenism as the striving for unity, the Lutheran role in it, like Gaul, was divided into three parts: (1) the Lutheran unity movement in the United States, (2) the Canadian sector, and (3) American Lutherans and international ecumenism.

The Unity Movement in the United States

Before World War II the pace of progress toward Lutheran unity was rather leisurely. As mentioned earlier (see Chapters I and III) the burst of enthusiasm that accompanied the 400th anniversary of the Reformation and the cooperative spirit forged by World War I produced the Norwegian Lutheran Church (ELC) in 1917, the United Lutheran Church in 1918, and the National Lutheran Council, likewise in 1918. There were, therefore, in 1918 two main groupings of Lutherans in America, the Synodical Conference (1872) and the newly-established National Lutheran Council. The largest body in the former was the Missouri Synod; in the latter, the United Lutheran Church in America. These two represented the polarization within confessional Lutheranism. The United Lutheran Church, moving towards a "neo-Lutheran" position, was committed to Lutheran unity on the basis of the generally received confessions of Lutheranism, resting its case largely on the Augsburg Confession: that for the true unity of the church *"it is sufficient* [italics added] that the gospel be preached in conformity with a pure understanding of it and that the sacraments be administered in accordance with the divine Word" (Article VII). Wherever Jesus Christ is there is the catholic church; the confessions merely explained how Jesus Christ is present—through the gospel and the sacraments administered according to the gospel. Theological differences might still exist, but they were not to be seen as divisive of fellowship. Among *Lutherans* differences should be ironed out *in* fellowship, not *prior* to it. The Missouri Synod, however, was not persuaded that other Lutherans reflected genuine Lutheranism despite their subscription to the Lutheran confessions. Therefore it was necessary, argued Missouri, to obtain prior agreement in extra-confessional theological statements and principles of discipline and practice. Until such "God-pleasing" unity in faith and practice was achieved, fellowship and union were *de jure* precluded.

An earlier chapter (III) has already described the unsuccessful attempts of the United Lutheran Church to further Lutheran unity by its parallel conversations in the 30s with the Missouri Synod and the first American Lutheran Church. The polarities between "neo-Lutheranism" and "old-Lutheranism," evident in those discussions were destined to continue for at least two decades. Furthermore, as noted earlier, the American Lutheran Church, while holding talks with the United Lutherans, had also been negotiating with the Missouri Synod. The Common Confession, which it worked out with Missouri, was a dressed up version of "old Lutheranism" calculated to make it attractive to the American Lutherans and acceptable to the Missourians because no substantive alteration of "old Lutheranism" was intended.[11] After the formation of the new American Lutheran Church (1960) the agreement between the former ALC and Missouri in the Common Confession was often advanced as a reason for the new ALC to seek pulpit and altar fellowship with the Missouri Synod. The constituting convention of the new ALC was informed, "The American Lutheran Church has instructed its Standing Committee on Relations to Lutheran Churches to 'continue official negotiations already established by the united Churches. . . . ' " [12]

The year 1940 had marked a definite turning point in inter-Lutheran relations (recall the fate of The Pittsburgh Agreement and the ALC overtures to Missouri), but hardly had the year slipped into 1941 when the pressures of World War II began to thrust massive responsibilities on American Lutheranism. This was the setting of the so-called "first Columbus All-Lutheran Conference" (see Chapter IV), called by the American Lutheran Conference.[13] Although general plans for coordination (not cooperation, at Missouri's insistence) in wartime services were made between the American Section of the Lutheran World Convention (NLC) and the Missouri Synod, it was stated that the desire expressed by many to move towards unity was premature: "such a movement would require agreement concerning the fundamentals of Lutheran Church unity." To this end another all-Lutheran conference was proposed.[14]

The next significant meeting, the National Lutheran Council, Pittsburgh, January 28-29, 1942, considered the proposal of the National Lutheran Editors' Association that the NLC take the leadership in bringing about an all-Lutheran federation that would be the American counterpart to the Lutheran World Convention. The council unanimously approved this, stating "such a federation may constitute a step toward that ultimate unity of American Lutheranism." [15] The special committee appointed to implement the NLC-approved editors' proposal met twice, March 13, 1942, in Chicago, and May 14, 1942, in Columbus. Between these two meetings several letters were exchanged with President Behnken, who was reluctant to accept the invitation to send representatives of the Missouri Synod. Finally, convinced that the proposed meeting at Columbus, May 15, 1942, would limit its activity to "matters involving externals," he replied,

> We accept this invitation with the understanding that we are not members of the National Lutheran Council. Hence we are not assuming responsibilities for the meeting. For obvious reasons— and I hope that this will not be misunderstood or misinterpreted —we are not taking part in the devotional worship and shall be present for only the business meeting.[16]

The meeting of May 15 began with devotional worship at 9:45 A.M. Shortly after ten o'clock the Missourians, who had been waiting in the hallway for the last "amen," walked in for the business session. Following a lengthy discussion on the proposal of the council's special committee that the American Lutheran Conference be enlarged so that its constituency might "become representative of the Lutheran Church in America" and that general conferences for consultation by all Lutherans in regard to mutual problems and opportunities for service,[17] the Missouri Synod officials said they would oppose any efforts to effect a new organization unless prior agreement in doctrine and practice had been achieved. However, although they were even "growing skeptical about 'co-operation in externals' because too many . . . confuse this with the idea of union," they were nevertheless hopeful that "co-ordinated efforts in external matters" could be arranged. But, Missouri argued, such coordination could be accomplished without a new all-Lutheran organization. When the Missourians departed, the special committee reaffirmed its earlier action to work towards achieving an all-Lutheran federation or "convention." [18]

The next autumn the American Lutheran Church passed the following interesting resolution:

> Whereas the American Lutheran Church has adopted the Pittsburgh Agreement [with the ULCA] and accepted the Brief Statement of the Missouri Synod in the light of the declaration of

commissioners of the American Lutheran Church as a basis for
pulpit and altar fellowship; and
Whereas though these documents . . . differ in wording, yet
both express the true position of the American Lutheran Church
[italics added] . . . ; Therefore, Be it Resolved, that the American Lutheran Church declare its readiness to establish pulpit and
altar fellowship with either or both of these . . . bodies. . . .[19]

This resolution was susceptible of several interpretations: (1) the American Lutheran Church was eager to be the bridge between the United
Lutherans and Missouri; (2) the ALC was ignorant of or disregarded the
basic theological difference between the ULCA and Missouri; or (3) the
ALC hoped to swing the ULCA into the "old Lutheranism" which both
the Pittsburgh Agreement and the Brief Statement enunciated. Whatever
motives or combination of motives existed, it was apparent on all sides
in 1942 that strenuous efforts were being made to advance the cause of
Lutheran unity.

In this atmosphere of heightened interest in manifesting unity, the
American Lutheran Conference met in Rock Island, Illinois (November
11-12, 1942).[20] Its Commission on Lutheran Unity, created in 1938, said,
" . . . the American Lutheran Conference must leave the door open, as
far as it is concerned, for all Lutheran bodies." It further asked that "the
Executive Committee . . . be instructed to negotiate with all other Lutheran bodies, looking toward a more inclusive organization. . . . As a
necessary step to this end this Conference urges its constituent members to
invite into pulpit and altar fellowship those Lutheran groups with whom
they are not now in fellowship." [21] This resolution, it should be observed,
was largely the work of Augustana Synod leaders, E. E. Ryden (president
of the conference), synod president P. O. Bersell, and Professor Conrad
Bergendoff. Ryden and Bersell had advanced the idea of expanding the
conference at the first and second Columbus meetings; Bergendoff was the
author of the sentence on offering pulpit and altar fellowship. What does
not appear in the minutes was the resistance of two Norwegian Lutheran
leaders to what they considered Augustana Synod pressure to include the
United Lutheran Church in the American Lutheran Conference. President
Aasgaard (NLCA) resented the "pushiness of the Swedes" (the sociological factor of Norwegian-Swedish tension is not to be underestimated in
inter-Lutheran relations); and T. F. Gullixson feared the inclusion of the

United Lutheran Church because of its "liberal" theological position. L. W. Boe, a close personal friend of both Aasgaard and Gullixson, took a broader view of the situation. His primary concern was to preserve the National Lutheran Council as the forum for Lutheran unity. Writing to Aasgaard prior to the Rock Island meeting, he said:

> I do not think that you should "oppose" any action that Ryden or Bersell may want to "impose" upon the American Lutheran Conference. [But] I would rather see the Conference dissolve and hand over its work to the National Lutheran Council than see it expanded into an organization parallel with the National Lutheran Council, and then have the Council, with its wonderful record of doing God's work these twenty-five years, sink down to be that which the Lord never permitted it to be, only an agency for cooperation in external affairs.

Showing that he appreciated Bergendoff's view, Boe continued:

> Have you [Aasgaard] and the men who will represent us at the American Lutheran Conference the courage . . . to make a declaration, based on fact if not on theory, . . . that *we are in pulpit and altar fellowship as far as we are concerned with every Lutheran body in this country?* My article, "God's Moment," is more to the point today than it was in 1934. The "crisis" is upon us.[22]

Boe's plea went unheeded and a short time later he died.

Meanwhile, the conference executive committee, which had been instructed to *negotiate* with other Lutherans and *invite* all into pulpit and altar fellowship, met in Minneapolis, January 26, 1943. The action of the committee represented a subtle shift from the intention of the 1942 Rock Island resolution. The dominating figure in the executive committee was Gullixson (Bersell was absent) and largely through his influence the committee determined that before it could carry out the instructions of the conference, it would request its Commission on Lutheran Unity to lay out necessary conditions preliminary to negotiations and the invitation to pulpit and altar fellowship. Therefore, the executive committee charged the commission "with a study of the minimum basis for pulpit and altar fellowship." In other words, the invitation to pulpit and altar fellowship with the United Lutheran Church (which would accept) and the Missouri Synod (which would reject) would be delayed. As a matter of fact, it was effectively delayed, by subsequent events, for over a quarter of a century, until 1969!

The Commission on Lutheran Unity turned to J. Michael Reu to prepare a statement of the "minimum basis," a task which his decease prevented him from completing.[23] The commission then requested Gullixson and Harold Yochum, president of the ALC's Michigan District, to draft a document. Largely the work of the former,[24] the statement was called the "Overture on Lutheran Unity." Together with a copy of The Minneapolis Theses (1925) and parts of The Chicago Theses (1919) it was sent to all Lutheran bodies in America.[25]

Although reaction within the Missouri Synod was favorable—in some instances enthusiastic—the synod itself took no notice of it. One observer said it was "sidetracked." The synod did, however, consider membership in the National Lutheran Council, but expectedly it was voted down.[26]

The United Lutheran Commission on Relations to American Lutheran Church Bodies reported at the Minneapolis convention (1944) that it had received the "Overture." Its comment was as follows: "This [document] was deemed neither forward-looking, fruitful, nor necessary as an approach to our common problem. In the Washington Declaration we already have . . . a better statement, already approved by us, of the real tests of evangelicalism." [27] From the point of view of emerging "neo-Lutheranism" this was indeed true; from the point of view of "old Lutheranism" it was grossly inadequate. An examination of the contents of the "Overture" reveals the specific reason why it was not warmly received. The document warned against doctrinal latitudinarianism, insisted on "genuine" acceptance of the confessions, and asserted the necessity of extra-confessional doctrinal theses as testimonies to unity—all of which were clear references to what some, perhaps a majority, of the American Lutheran Conference considered to be ULCA faults. However, the "Overture" continued, on the basis of The Minneapolis Theses (American Lutheran Conference), The Brief Statement (Missouri Synod), and The Pittsburgh Agreement (ULCA-ALC), pulpit and altar fellowship could be established among Lutherans.[28] The reason for such a hope, it was declared, was that these three documents were "in essential accord with one another." Here was the key phrase in the document and, as a matter of fact, in the whole carefully calculated unity strategy. The "Overture" observed correctly and forthrightly that the American Lutheran Conference could have no fellowship with the United Lutheran Church on the basis of its Washington (1920), Savannah (1934), and Baltimore (1938) declarations, all three of which addressed the problems of ecumenism, lodge membership, confessional integrity, and Scriptural authority in ways unacceptable to "old Lutheranism."

Just as the years 1919-1925 had revealed the presence of two sharply defined attitudes within the National Lutheran Council, the years 1940-1944 demonstrated the presence of precisely the same attitudes within the American Lutheran Conference. The Augustana Synod, not a partner in the original negotiations that produced the American Lutheran Conference but nevertheless drawn into its membership before the influence of its new theological professors (see Chapter III above) could be felt, wished to include all Lutherans in fellowship. Practically speaking, this meant extending fellowship to the ULCA only, because the intransigence of the Missourians eliminated any realistic hope of unity with them. Opposing this were the other members of the conference, notably the Norwegian Lutherans who feared the United Lutherans [29] and preferred the Missouri Synod. Any fellowship with this church should be balanced by fellowship with Missouri, but only on the basis of assurances, such as the "Overture" proposed, that there would be "genuine and wholehearted" acceptance of "old Lutheranism." In 1944 the Norwegian Lutheran Church surprisingly declared itself ready for fellowship with all Lutherans because it felt that the doctrinal statements of the American Lutheran Conference (Minneapolis and Chicago Theses) were in "essential agreement" with the position of the United Lutheran Church and Missouri. Therefore, it continued, "We believe no additional theses, statements, or agreements are necessary for fellowship among American Lutherans." This seemingly advanced position must be seen in light of and in response to the "Overture" and not as an evidence of "neo-Lutheranism." [30] That this was true could be seen in the attitude of its official organ, the *Lutheran Herald*. Editor O. G. Malmin commented that his church was prepared for fellowship with the Missouri Synod but not with the United Lutheran Church. The latter, he said, called into question the inspiration of Holy Writ ("as we understand it"), was soft on "unionism," and tolerant of pastors who were lodge members.[31]

The next four years saw no basic change in this pattern. Although a project for a common hymnal and service book was successfully launched (the Norwegian Lutheran Church [ELC in 1946] hesitated to participate because it feared that the spirit and theology of the United Lutheran Church would dominate the venture), the basic problems reaching back to 1919 continued to be identified as obstacles to unity.

The decade following 1947 saw the organizational crystallization of the two attitudes. In the process, three members of the American Lutheran Conference (the American Lutheran Church, the Evangelical Lutheran Church, and the United [Danish] Evangelical Lutheran Church) merged to establish The American Lutheran Church (1960). Later (1963) the latter received the Lutheran (Norwegian) Free Church into its membership. Subsequently the United Lutheran Church drew to itself three churches (Augustana, the Finnish Suomi Synod, and the American Evangelical [Danish] Lutheran Church); together they formed the Lutheran Church in America (1962).

The story of this decade revolves almost exclusively around the churches of the National Lutheran Council. The Synodical Conference was beginning to experience stress and strain that eventually led to its demise and left Missouri trying to bring itself into relationship with others. But meanwhile it stood in the wings while the drama on the National Lutheran Council stage became two separate actions. Although the chronicle of events has been recorded elsewhere, it is well to mention them briefly here in this broader frame of reference.[32]

Three National Lutheran Council member bodies met in June, 1948— The Evangelical Lutheran Church, the Augustana Lutheran Church, and the United Evangelical Lutheran Church. Two other major groups, the United Lutheran Church and the American Lutheran Church met in October. Moreover, the American Lutheran Conference convened in November. In all of these meetings Lutheran unity was a paramount issue.

The first group to meet was the Augustana Church. In response to a memorial from one of its regional conferences, the synod requested its executive council to invite all National Lutheran Council churches to discuss organic merger of the Council or federation as an intermediate step.

The Evangelical Lutheran Church, meeting the same week, anticipated an invitation from the United Evangelical Lutheran Church (meeting the following week) to begin merger conversations. Unofficial overtures from UELC leaders led T. F. Gullixson to present a "resolution of friendship" for the UELC and to ask the Evangelical Lutheran Church to name a union committee to negotiate with the UELC and "other constituent bodies of the American Lutheran Conference." It should be noted that the resolution excluded the possibility of conversations with the United Lutheran Church.[33]

The president of the UELC, N. C. Carlsen, urged merger with the ELC, but his synod feared that its small Danish-background constituency would be completely swallowed up by the much larger Norwegian church. Consequently a new proposal was adopted: that the UELC invite two or more bodies of the American Lutheran Conference to discuss organic union.

When the American Lutheran Conference met in Detroit, November 10-12, 1948, unity resolutions were passed calling for an all-Lutheran free conference under the auspices of the National Lutheran Council and commending the various efforts for unity being initiated with the conference and the council. Following the convention the five presidents— Aasgaard (ELC), Bersell (Aug.), Burntvedt (LFC), Carlsen (UELC), and Poppen (ALC)—met to consider further steps. Two decisions were reached: (1) that the NLC be petitioned to call a "free conference"; and (2) that dates be determined for meetings which Bersell and Carlsen were contemplating calling in order to implement the resolutions of their synods. It was decided that a meeting of council representatives be held at the Augustana headquarters in Minneapolis on January 4, 1949, and that the American Lutheran Conference presidents meet in the ELC headquarters, also in Minneapolis, the next day, January 5, 1949.

Considerable tension developed around the calling of these meetings. The ELC officials maintained that the Augustana proposal came as a surprise and seemed intended to undercut the meeting of January 5. President Bersell, however, said that President Carlsen had "graciously" agreed to allow the meeting of council representatives to precede the January 5 conference.[34] This was verified by Carlsen's letter to the editor of *The Lutheran Standard* (ALC) who had inquired about the matter. Carlsen reported that the Detroit meeting of American Lutheran Conference presidents decided on the dates for the discussions. "Dr. Bersell seemed to be quite concerned about getting the meeting which he was calling the day before we had ours. *No objections were made* [italics added]." [35]

The meetings of January 4 and 5, 1949, proved to be fateful for a large majority of American Lutheranism. In response to Augustana's invitation representatives of the eight National Lutheran Council bodies (henceforth known as "The Committee of Thirty-Four") convened according to schedule. The ELC representatives (Aasgaard, Gullixson, and layman S. H. Holstad) were present only as "observers," because they maintained that no mandate had been given them by their church.

The proposal before the group was two-pronged: (1) organic merger of the bodies in the National Lutheran Council, or (2) federation of the NLC as an intermediate step. After a full day of discussion, Emmanual Poppen, president of the American Lutheran Church, offered the following resolution: "Resolved, that it is the sense of this group that a closer organizational affiliation of the participating bodies in the National Lutheran Council is desirable and should be sought by all proper means." [36]

In the discussion President Franklin Clark Fry of the United Lutheran Church argued forcefully in favor of "a Church with strong federative aspects." H. F. Schuh, an ALC representative, not only pleaded for such action but insisted that a definite time should be indicated when a federation should become an organic union. "What are we waiting for?" he asked. "We are already cooperating here at home and in all parts of the world." [37] When a ballot was taken on the resolution, not a dissenting vote was cast. The group then voted to appoint a committee of 15 to prepare a structural plan and report to the full "Committee of 34" the next autumn.

Although the records show only unanimous support for the above proposals, at least two churches voiced their objections. President Carlsen of the UELC pointed out that his church would hesitate taking such steps because of the laxity in practice within the United Lutheran Church regarding dancing, drinking, and lodge membership of pastors. Gullixson, one of the ELC "observers," then objected to Schuh's intimation that the National Lutheran Council, as it now existed, had outlived its usefulness. Moreover, if there was to be union, it must be on the basis of doctrinal agreement, especially since there were evidences that ULCA seminaries were teaching views on Scripture that were contrary to what had been held in the ELC the last one hundred years.

The next day, January 5, 1949, the representatives of the American Lutheran Conference met in the ELC headquarters under the chairmanship of UELC President Carlsen. An informal approach had been made to secure Missouri Synod support and presence at this meeting by inviting Theodore Graebner, editor of the *Lutheran Witness*. Although it proved abortive, the gesture indicated the direction in which the group—with the exception of Bersell—wished to move.[38] During the meeting considerable discussion was devoted to the action of the previous day. Gullixson spoke critically and at length about the United Lutheran Church. He specifically attacked Joseph Sittler's recently published book, *The Doctrine of the Word*, which criticized the "old Lutheran" view of verbal inspiration.[39] At the conclusion of the day the group adopted a resolution that every effort should be made to bring about the plans of the previous day's meeting but that there ought to be no objection to lesser approaches to unity within the conference.

Three other conferences during 1949 crystallized the points of view evident at the January 4 and 5 conferences. The subcommittee of "The Committee of 34" met in Chicago April 26-27, 1949. President Aasgaard reminded the group that he and Gullixson were "observers" without mandate from their church. This did not deter the committee from recommending a structural plan for presentation to "The Committee of 34." The proposal suggested (1) that the parent committee request the council churches to take action on organic union, and (2) that, pending consummation of the same, a National Lutheran Federation be established. "The Committee of 34" meeting in Chicago September 27, 1949, voted to present the two resolutions to the member bodies of the National Lutheran Council.

Eleven days earlier (Sept. 16, 1949), representatives of the ELC, ALC, and UELC had met to lay their plans. The informal consensus of the group expressed the judgment that their church bodies were not in favor of organic merger of the council but preferred a federation of *all* Lutherans in America. Missouri's traditional stance made this a safe proposal and at the same time gave to what was in reality an empty gesture the appearance of even greater amplitude of concern for unity. Gullixson then presented a resolution that urged merger of the three bodies and asked that such a resolution be presented to the conventions of the ELC, ALC, and UELC.

During the first week of January, 1950, the final meeting of "The Committee of 34" was held. Of importance was the presence of representatives from the Lutheran Church–Missouri Synod, who had been invited to cooperate in the common endeavor to form an all-Lutheran federation.

President John Behnken, not unexpectedly, said that his group was present only as "observers" to obtain information. Less than a month earlier, however, Behnken had privately informed J. A. Aasgaard that he would like to have an opportunity to discuss the move being made by the ELC, ALC, and UELC to effect "a union between conservative groups in the American Lutheran Conference." [40]

The church actions of 1950 proved decisive. Both plans submitted by "The Committee of Thirty-Four" (merger of the NLC or federation as an intermediate step) were defeated. The plan for organic union had required the approval of all eight bodies, while federation required six affirmative votes out of eight.[41] This meant that the only remaining union movement was that initiated by the United Evangelical Lutheran Church with behind the scenes encouragement from the Evangelical Lutheran Church. Since the original resolution included all members of the American Lutheran Conference, invitations were extended to the Augustana Church and the Lutheran Free Church. Both accepted but with some reservations. The Augustana Church naturally preferred its own larger proposal, while the Free Church was nervous about losing its "freedom."

The stage was now set for the organic union of the American Lutheran Conference. In 1952 the Joint Union Committee of the five churches presented for action a statement on faith and life called "The United Testimony." Its curious blend—or more correctly, juxtapositioning—of "old Lutheranism" and "neo-Lutheranism" was to be explained by the theological division within the drafting committee.[42] One side presented a view such as the following: "We bear witness that the Bible is our only authentic and infallible source of God's revelation . . . and that it is the only *inerrant* [italics added] and completely adequate source and norm of Christian doctrine and life." The other side, chiefly Augustana theologians, then countered with a "neo-Lutheran" expression: "The Bible is the Word of God, given by inspiration of the Holy Spirit through human personalities in the course of human history. . . . We acknowledge with humble gratitude the condescending love of God in speaking to men through the agency of human language. *We reject all rationalizing processes which would explain away either the divine or the human factor in the Bible* [italics added]." [43] The ambivalence in The United Testimony was completely erased in the "Confession of Faith," Article IV of the constitution (1956) for the new church (1960). It defined the authority of the Scriptures in the language of The Minneapolis Theses ("[the Church] accepts all the canonical books of the Old and New Testaments as a whole and in all their parts as the divinely inspired, revealed, and inerrant Word of God. . . . "). Later, when church officials and theologians admitted the possibility of error in the Bible, they were charged by extreme biblicistic orthodoxists with departing from the constitution's "Confession of Faith," which as a matter of fact they were doing. The reply was customarily two-fold: (1) the word "inerrant" in Article IV modified "Word of God" and not Bible, and (2) The United Testimony admitted the "human" and therefore fallible nature of the Bible. The difficulty with this answer was that the history of the word "inerrant" in the debate ever since 1925 showed that it modified Bible and not Word of God. That this was also the *intent* of the Joint Union Committee was expressed by the editor of the *Lutheran Herald* in a letter replying to a UELC pastor who had submitted an article containing a "neo-Lutheran" view of Scripture and expressing dissatisfaction with the Joint Union Committee's position. The editor wrote:

> My reason for declining to publish your article is simply and singly that I am in favor of the present merger movement which includes the United Evangelical Lutheran Church of which you are a pastor. The publication of your article would do more to shake the confidence of our people in your church body than anything that I could possibly publish. . . . I have read many of your writings, and consider that you are far, far from the beaten path of our historical view of the inspiration of Scripture in The Evangelical Lutheran Church. . . . Were the views you express prevalent in the United Evangelical Lutheran Church, *I can assure you that The Evangelical Lutheran Church would be exceedingly doubtful about the wisdom of entering into merger negotiations with the United Evangelical Lutheran Church* [italics added].[44]

A second difficulty encountered by those who answered the charges of deviation by quoting The United Testimony was the fact that those portions of the document that made it possible for them conscientiously to assume a "neo-Lutheran" view in the merging new church were written by theologians of the Augustana Church which in 1952 had withdrawn from the merger negotiations. This was ironic to say the least. At best, this kind of defense was a face-saving *ex post facto* rationalization for men who were beginning to realize the profound ambiguities in the situation but were unable to admit publicly that mistakes had been made by The ALC merger-makers.[45]

The events of the decade from 1952 to 1962 had all the ingredients of a Greek drama moving irreversibly to its denouement. The Augustana Church, having withdrawn from the conference merger movement because it was "not open to all Lutheran general bodies and . . . [did] not include the consideration of the subject of ecumenical relations," [46] turned toward the United Lutheran Church. In 1954 the American Lutheran Conference was officially dissolved in *de facto* recognition of the existing circumstances in American Lutheranism. The Lutheran Free Church, as a result of congregational referendums in 1955 and 1957, found it necessary to remove itself from the projected union. In 1961, however, affirmative results of a third referendum paved the way for the Free Church to join The American Lutheran Church in 1963. Dissenters who claimed the name "Lutheran Free Church (not merged)" were denied this by the courts. They re-named themselves "The Association of Free Lutheran Congregations." [47]

In 1955 the ULCA and Augustana invited all Lutherans to "consider such an organic union as will give real evidence of our unity in the faith, and to proceed to draft a constitution and devise organizational procedures to effect union." The Missouri Synod declined on the basis of existing doctrinal differences; the Joint Union Committee declined because the three bodies (ALC, UELC, and ELC) were committed to their own union.[48]

In anticipation of the invitation from ULCA-Augustana, the Joint Union Committee had spent considerable time in discussing what ought to be done in the event an invitation would be forthcoming. The stenographic report of the discussion included the following comments:

> Gullixson: It has been very apparent that the endeavor has been to swing us all in under the auspices of the ULCA.
> Schiotz: I felt a little miffed that this had the earmarks of a squeeze play. . . . I wrote for the *Fortnightly Review* that it is not very pleasant to get invitations when we can't accept them. . . . I sent Dr. Fry and Dr. Benson a proof. To Dr. Fry I said

Augustana had had a pull toward ULC and we had a pull toward Missouri.

Schuh: When we [old ALC] met with Missouri last time, they asked me why we [JUC] didn't take the rest of the family along.

Ostermann: Dr. Schuh was exactly right when Missouri expressed the idea—why can't we [Missouri] go along to your next meeting? . . . The thing that bothers me . . . is that we are all for this [ALC-UELC-ELC] merger and we reflect that there is a possibility that sand may be thrown on the tracks [by the ULCA-Augustana invitation]. I wondered if God is permitting it to go that way to make us give thought to something we have overlooked.[49]

Numerous consciences in American Lutheranism were disturbed by the direction the union movement had taken, and echoed Ostermann's suggestion to "give thought to something we have overlooked." In 1957 the well-known and highly respected Professor Julius Bodensieck of Wartburg Seminary wrote a letter to the Joint Union Committee criticizing its proposed "Confession of Faith" as non-Lutheran, fundamentalistic, legalistic, docetic, and dishonest. It failed to exhibit the soteriological and Christ-centered character of the Scriptures. This sharp attack was rejected. Had this criticism been admitted, the chief reason for withholding fellowship and union with the United Lutheran Church would have evaporated, for Bodensieck's letter implied approval of the position of the ULCA's Baltimore Declaration (1938).[50]

The following year at the annual meeting of the National Lutheran Council, February 4-7, 1958, the council president, F. Eppling Reinartz, made a dramatic appeal calling for a halt to both merger movements before they reached "the point of no return." The proposed mergers, he said, constituted a judgment of each merging group upon the other. "Let us stop our fashioning of fresh divisions, at least long enough for us to examine our motives and purposes under the emancipating and uniting cross of Christ." F. A. Schiotz replied that the NLC's constitution did not permit it to deal with internal churchly matters such as union. The council was an agency for cooperation; therefore, Reinartz was out of order. In fact, he (Schiotz) was himself out of order for even listening to the proposal. A study committee of five (three from the ALC-UELC-

ELC group and two from the Augustana-ULCA group) brought in a resolution that the Reinartz proposal was "constitutionally outside the competence of the National Lutheran Council." It was adopted.[51]

Following failure of the Reinartz request for a moratorium, a professor from Luther Seminary (ELC) wrote a lengthy letter to the chairman of the Joint Union Committee. He had been assured that voices of protest would still be listened to by church leaders. He wrote in part:

> This letter will contain an expression of deep sorrow over the present state of inter-Lutheran relations in America and my personal reasons why I am in anguish over the proposed merger of the three bodies of whose Joint Union Committee you are the chairman. My purpose in addressing it to you is to make a respectful request that it be included in the minutes of the Joint Union Committee [no action requested] so that future church historians, whose task it will be to tell the story of these past ten years, will have the record of at least one voice in protest to the contemplated merger.[52]

The letter, which went on to analyze the situation, was never brought to the attention of the Joint Union Committee. The fear was expressed that to do so might split the church. The letter was not factually incorrect, said the president of the ELC into whose hands the letter came, but it might disturb the peace of the church. In this manner the peace, if not the integrity, of the church was preserved. The three-way negotiations continued unabated and The American Lutheran Church [53] became a reality in Minneapolis, April 22-24, 1960. The church began official operations January 1, 1961. Its first president, F. A. Schiotz, told *The Christian Century* that the new body "would not want another organic union unless it included both the Missouri Synod and the forthcoming Lutheran Church in America. . . . Failure to include the Missouri Synod . . . would create 'complications. . . .' " [54]

Meanwhile, the Lutheran Church in America was quickly taking shape. The ULCA-Augustana invitation had been accepted by the American Evangelical Lutheran Church (Danish) and the Finnish Evangelical Lutheran Church (Suomi Synod) and together these four created the Joint Commission on Lutheran Unity to prepare the necessary documents for organic union. In 1956 ULCA President Franklin Clark Fry delivered a statement on Lutheran unity that was immediately recognized as an unofficial charter for the new church and as a guide to the joint commission. Speaking of the two principles of unity and truth, he urged that those churches seeking unity should not neglect the truth and that those churches intent on upholding the truth must not neglect unity. Both principles, rooted in the biblical witness, must be viewed as centering in the Word of God that creates the church.[55]

The doctrinal statement, approved by the four churches, affirmed the Christ-centered and soteriological character of the Scriptures, which as such "are normative for the faith and life of the church." The catholic creeds were described as "true declarations of the faith of the Church." The Unaltered Augsburg Confession and Luther's Small Catechism were seen as "true witnesses to the Gospel," and the other symbols of Lutheranism were said to be "further valid interpretations of the confession of the Church." [56]

Lutheran unity efforts in the 20th century had usually foundered on three or four major problems: the relation of the Word of God to the Scriptures and confessions (addressed in the above statement), "unionism," ecumenism, and membership of pastors in lodges. The Statement of Agreement and the constitution met the latter problems. The new church would acknowledge as one with it in faith and doctrine "all churches that . . . accept the teachings of these symbols [Unaltered Augsburg Confession and Luther's Small Catechism]." Moreover, it would "strive for the unification of all Lutherans" and "participate in ecumenical Christian activities, contributing its witness and works and cooperating with other churches which confess God the Father, Son and Holy Ghost." The sensitive problem of lodge membership caused Augustana leaders to question "lax" ULCA attitudes. This led to an extended debate.[57] Finally at the insistence of the Augustana Church the Joint Commission on Lutheran Unity adopted the following statement:

> After the organization of the Lutheran Church in America no person, who belongs to any organization which claims to possess in its teachings and ceremonies that which the Lord has given solely to His Church, shall be ordained or otherwise received into the ministry of this church, nor shall any person so ordained or received by this church be retained in its ministry if he subsequently joins such an organization. Violation of this rule shall make such minister subject to discipline.[58]

Though certain phrases met sharp criticism—for example: "Any organization which claims to possess in its teachings and ceremonies that which the Lord has given solely to His Church . . . "—the paragraph was calculated to resolve the issue in the new church.

The four churches approved the union documents and voted favorably on the constitution. Having thus affirmed the merger, the constituting convention was held in Detroit, June 28-July 1, 1962. The Lutheran Church in America began its actual operation as a corporate entity on January 1, 1963.[59]

Thus by the early 60s the two points of view that had come to light in the National Lutheran Council as early as 1919 found organizational expression in these two church bodies. The forces—overt and covert— which produced them included differing theological stances as well as conflicting viewpoints of what constituted the Christian life. In addition, personality clashes, sociological factors, and unvarnished power politics were all in evidence. In the tumbling welter of circumstances a few judgments are already self-evident. It is clear, for example, that a major change had taken place in American Lutheranism since World War I. Call it "acculturation," "Americanization," "theological renaissance," or whatever, the difficulty all along had been to understand the transformation *while it was taking place.* The failure to perceive that change was occurring and inaccurate interpretation of the transformation when it occurred led to unjust accusations and serious distortions on both sides. Moreover, the description of the Lutheran Church in America as "liberal," The American Lutheran Church as "middle of the road," and Missouri as "orthodox" was a palpably egregious cliché. American Lutheranism was institutionally tri-partite, but theologically it was bi-partite. Lutheranism had not suffered the erosions of late 19th and early 20th century theological liberalism. It remained loyal to its confessional interpretation of the gospel, but theological and sociological differences had divided the denomination into two camps, "old Lutherans" and "neo-Lutherans," neither of whom had emasculated the gospel, and both of whom were to be found in varying numbers in all three church bodies, the Lutheran Church in America, The American Lutheran Church, and the Lutheran Church–Missouri Synod.

One of the major hypothetical questions of American Lutheran history remained unanswered and unanswerable in the 60s: What would have happened in the years after 1950 had the National Lutheran Council become a federation with an open door to Missouri rather than a crystal- lization of two theologically and structurally different organic mergers? Educated guesses are not the proper ingredients of historiography. How- ever much historians, like others, may have opinions, their craft limits them to the historical record. Therefore, the diagram on the opposite page attempts to summarize the union movement since World War I.

THE CANADIAN SCENE

Canadian Lutheranism developed along lines parallel to those that had emerged in the States. This was only natural because each of the major Lutheran bodies included Canadian "districts" or "synods" as integral parts of their organizational structure. With the advent of World War II Lutherans in Canada showed a growing sense of being a distinct recog- nizable Canadian entity. Like Canada itself, it was "declaring its inde- pendence" of things American.

It should be recalled that before the United States was drawn into World War II, Canada had been immediately involved (1939). This had implications for Canadian Lutherans, especially those who were associated with the National Lutheran Council. In recognition of this fact, Ralph H. Long, executive director of the National Lutheran Council, had called a conference for April 2, 1940, in Winnipeg. A commission to direct war- time services of Canadian Lutherans was created. Called the Canadian Lutheran Commission, approved by all except the Missouri Synod, the agency received some direction and financial help from the council but was self-sustaining by 1942.[60]

In 1944 representatives of the American Lutheran Church, Augustana Synod, Canada Synod of the ULCA, Lutheran Free Church, Manitoba Synod of ULCA, Norwegian Lutheran Church, and United Danish Lu- theran Church agreed that there was "unity in doctrine" and that a Canadian Lutheran Council, patterned after the National Lutheran Coun- cil, should be formed. Negotiations continued for several years. By 1947 a constitution was drafted, but the Missouri Synod, which had joined the negotiations, and the American Lutheran Church cast the deciding votes against the proposed council. The Evangelical Lutheran Church, the Augustana Church, the United Evangelical Lutheran Church, and the United Lutheran Church supported the motion. Finally in December,

Lutheran Confessionalism in the National Lutheran Council and The Synodical Conference 1918-1970

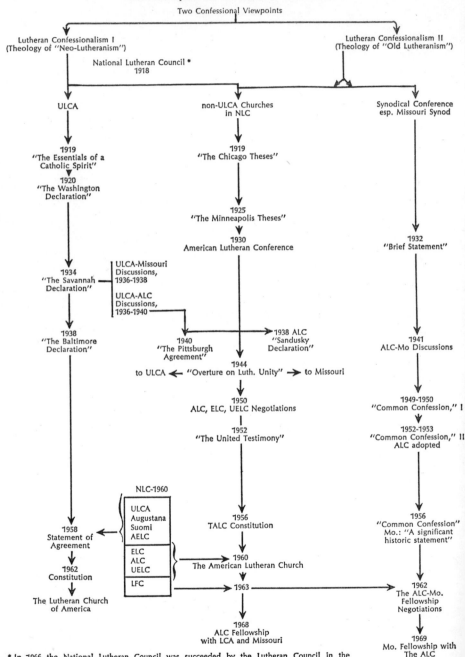

Two Confessional Viewpoints

Lutheran Confessionalism I
(Theology of "Neo-Lutheranism")

Lutheran Confessionalism II
(Theology of "Old Lutheranism")

National Lutheran Council *
1918

ULCA

non-ULCA Churches
in NLC

Synodical Conference
esp. Missouri Synod

1919
"The Essentials of a
Catholic Spirit"

1919
"The Chicago Theses"

1920
"The Washington
Declaration"

1925
"The Minneapolis Theses"

1930
American Lutheran Conference

1932
"Brief Statement"

1934
"The Savannah
Declaration"

ULCA-Missouri
Discussions,
1936-1938

ULCA-ALC
Discussions,
1936-1940

1938 ALC
"Sandusky
Declaration"

1938
"The Baltimore
Declaration"

1940
"The Pittsburgh
Agreement"

1941
ALC-Mo. Discussions

1944
to ULCA ← "Overture on Luth. Unity" → to Missouri

1950
ALC, ELC, UELC Negotiations

1949-1950
"Common Confession," I

1952
"The United Testimony"

1952-1953
"Common Confession," II
ALC adopted

NLC-1960

ULCA
Augustana
Suomi
AELC

ELC
ALC
UELC

LFC

1956
TALC Constitution

1956
"Common Confession"
Mo.: "A significant
historic statement"

1958
Statement of
Agreement

1960
The American Lutheran Church

1962
Constitution

1963

1962
The ALC-Mo.
Fellowship
Negotiations

The Lutheran Church
of America

1968
ALC Fellowship
with LCA and Missouri

1969
Mo. Fellowship with
The ALC

* In 1966 the National Lutheran Council was succeeded by the Lutheran Council in the
United States of America. It included four churches: the Lutheran Church in America,
The American Lutheran Church, the Lutheran Church—Missouri Synod, and the Synod of
Ev. Lutheran Churches (merged with the Missouri Synod in 1971).

1952, after further deliberations the Canadian Council came into being with six participating bodies: the ALC, Augustana Church, ELC, LFC, UELC, and ULCA.[61]

While the council was emerging, hopes for a united Lutheran Church in Canada were frequently expressed and discussions were occasionally held. Recognizing that Canadian Lutheranism would have to wait on developments in the States during the 50s, it was decided in 1959 that union negotiations be postponed until after the two state-side mergers were consummated. Meanwhile, attempts would be made to reach a basis for pulpit and altar fellowship among Canadian Lutherans.[62]

When The American Lutheran Church was formed, its Canada District took steps to incorporate itself as The Evangelical Lutheran Church of Canada. From the point of view of The American Lutheran Church, it remained a district of The ALC, but as far as its Canadian charter was concerned, it was a "church." The new president of The ALC, addressing the Canada District in July, 1960, suggested the possibility of an indigenous church.[63] By 1966 the necessary legal steps had been taken for the assumption of autonomy by the Canada District. A constituting convention was held in Regina, Saskatchewan (November, 1966) whereby the Canada District severed itself from The American Lutheran Church to become the first autonomous Canadian Lutheran church, effective January 1, 1967.[64] Meanwhile the three Canadian jurisdictional synods of the Lutheran Church in America were coordinated into a constitutionally approved "LCA-Canada Section," [65] and similar action in the Missouri Synod led its Canadian affiliate to be known as "The Lutheran Church—Canada." [66]

The Canadian Lutheran Council was reorganized on August 31-September 1, 1966, to include this Missouri section and the Synod of Evangelical Lutheran Churches (Slovak), thus becoming the Canadian counterpart to the new Lutheran Council in the United States of America (1966). Both the Canadian and USA councils became operative January 1, 1967.

Canadians continued to hope that a united Lutheran Church of Canada would emerge. By 1968 the Evangelical Lutheran Church of Canada (The ALC) had declared pulpit and altar fellowship with the others. The LCA-Canada Section continued the LCA tradition. The Missourians voted fellowship with the ELCC in 1969, but not with the LCA. The major roadblock was the Missourian or "old Lutheran" view of the

Bible's inspiration and inerrancy.[67] Despite this, optimistic Canadians predicted that there would be fellowship by 1971 and one Lutheran church in Canada by 1978.[68].

American Lutheran and International Ecumenism

Lutheran World Federation

Ever since 1923 the majority of American Lutherans had participated in the movement to bring world Lutheranism into closer fellowship. Two world wars and the work of the National Lutheran Council enlarged the world-consciousness of American Lutherans. World assemblies had been held in 1923 (Eisenach), 1929 (Copenhagen), and 1935 (Paris). After the Paris convention the executive committee announced that the next assembly would be held in Philadelphia in 1940. Because of World War II, the contemplated assembly in Philadelphia was cancelled. In 1946, however, the executive committee of the Lutheran World Convention, meeting in Sweden, planned an assembly for the summer of 1947. Held at Lund, Sweden, the assembly brought 44 official delegates from National Lutheran Council churches. Several Missouri Synod "observers" were also present.

Much of the leadership of the Lund assembly fell upon American Lutherans who had the financial resources and administrative know-how to cope with the massive post-war exigencies. One of the two most memorable accomplishments of the convocation was the adoption of the proposed constitution for "The Lutheran World Federation," which was defined as "a free association of Lutheran churches" to serve as an agency for autonomous member churches. Its constitutionally-stated purposes proved to be such as to lead it into activities that went beyond those of a mere agency. Regardless of protestations to the contrary, the federation often found itself engaged in definitely churchly matters. This meant that the Lutheran World Federation was involved from its beginning in a problem closely akin to the one that had plagued the National Lutheran Council: that is, how to avoid cooperation in "internals" while cooperating in "externals." The distinction was impossible to maintain. Nevertheless, the adoption of the constitution marked what has been called "a turning-point in the history of world Lutheranism. The constitution provided [Lutheranism] with more systematic and more durable integration than

[it] had ever known before." [69] The first president of the LWF was Professor Anders Nygren (Sweden) and its executive secretary was S. C. Michelfelder (USA). American members of the Executive Committee were J. A. Aasgaard, Franklin Clark Fry, Ralph H. Long, and Abdel Ross Wentz.[70]

The second major event at Lund was the decision to engage in a ministry of relief, reconstruction, resettlement of refugees and religious services for displaced persons. American involvement in the program has already been discussed and evaluated in the previous chapter.

The Second Assembly of the Lutheran World Federation, Hannover, July 25-August 3, 1952, took on the air of a religious folk festival when thousands of German and American visitors joined the delegates and official visitors in mass rallies. Once again the Missouri Synod sent official observers, 20 in number. The prominent role of Americans was in evidence at Hannover as at Lund. In order to expedite the carrying out of tasks that had fallen to the federation since 1947, its structure was modified by the creation of three departments (theology, world service, world mission). The first was intended to carry out the constitutional purposes: to cultivate unity of faith and confession, to promote fellowship and cooperation in study, and to foster ecumenical relations. In this way the truly imposing and substantial theological resources of world Lutheranism were marshalled for the benefit of the whole Christian community. The two other departments were destined to command huge sums for inter-church aid and mission cooperation and to commend the name of the federation, not as a surging power of religious imperialism, but as a faithful steward of the gospel in places of great physical and spiritual need. To fill the vacancy created by the death of S. C. Michelfelder, the federation elected Carl E. Lund-Quist, another American, to be its executive secretary. Bishop Hanns Lilje (Hannover) was elected president.[71]

The Third Assembly of the federation, upon invitation of the USA National Committee (the National Lutheran Council), was held in Minneapolis, August 15-25, 1957. Marking the tenth anniversary of the federation, the assembly struck a strong theological and ecumenical note. Under the direction of the president-elect, Franklin Clark Fry, world-renowned theologians produced a remarkable document sometimes called "The Fifty-One Minneapolis Theses" on the assembly theme, "Christ Frees and Unites." The broad ecumenical outreach was indicated by the presence of official visitors from the Lutheran Church–Missouri Synod, world confessional bodies other than Lutheran (Presbyterian, Baptist, Methodist, Congregational), the World Council of Churches, and several other international Christian associations. In retrospect, perhaps the most significant ecumenical gesture was the proposal by the German National Committee to initiate conversations with the Roman Catholic church. Without any knowledge of the up-coming Second Vatican Council, world Lutherans anticipated "the age of dialog" by appointing a Special Commission on Inter-Confessional Research, which in 1963 became the Foundation for Inter-Confessional Research. Americans who were prominently engaged in this venture were Professors George Lindbeck (Yale) and Warren Quanbeck (Luther Theological Seminary). The Minneapolis Assembly, much like the Hannover convention, became a religious festival of vast proportions. In addition to the official delegates and visitors, thousands of men, women, and children from congregations all over North America flocked to Minneapolis. Seventeen thousand were in attendance at the opening service, 30,000 participated in the "visitors" program, 60,000 in the evening public events, 25,000 in the youth rally and well over 100,000 gathered for the closing festival service on the state capitol grounds in St. Paul.[72] President-elect Franklin Clark Fry, summarized federation history by characterizing each assembly: "At Lund we learned to walk together; at Hannover we learned to pray together; at Minneapolis we learned to think together." Not long after the Minneapolis assembly, the health of the executive secretary, Carl E. Lund-Quist, began to fail. Obliged to resign in 1961, he was succeeded by Kurt Schmidt-Clausen of Germany. Lund-Quist died in 1965, an offering not unlike that of great American Lutherans before him: John A. Morehead, Lauritz Larsen, L. W. Boe, Ralph H. Long, and S. C. Michelfelder.[73]

The World Council of Churches

Guidelines for Lutheran participation in the ecumenical movement had been articulated as early as 1936. American Lutherans were present at both the Faith and Order and Life and Work conferences in Edinburgh and Oxford (1937). F. H. Knubel and R. H. Long represented American Lutherans at Utrecht (1938) when a provisional constitution for a World Council of Churches was drafted. After the war, President Fry of the United Lutheran Church called a meeting (September 6, 1945) of repre-

sentatives of American Lutheran churches to achieve a "common understanding with reference to the World Council of Churches." The meeting
decided to press for "Lutheran representation on a confessional basis,"
and sought the assistance of the executive committee of the Lutheran
World Convention. Having obtained this, the Lutheran position was presented by Abdel Ross Wentz to the Committee on Arrangements for the
First Assembly of the World Council. Meeting in England in August,
1946, the committee finally agreed to change the WCC constitution which
had called for allocation of seats on a geographic rather than confessional
basis. With "confessional representation" as one of the assured factors in
determining allocation of seats, most of American Lutheranism was prepared to consider joining the council. J. A. Aasgaard predicted enthusiastically that all but one (the Missouri Synod) church would affiliate.[74]
His remarkable gifts of leadership, however, did not make him clairvoyant;
his own church, the Evangelical Lutheran Church, made him eat crow
by refusing to join. Nevertheless, encouraged by developments spearheaded
by Wentz and Fry, five churches voted to affiliate and sent delegates to
the First Assembly at Amsterdam in 1948: the American Lutheran
Church, the American Evangelical Lutheran Church, the Augustana
Lutheran Church, the United Evangelical Lutheran Church, and the
United Lutheran Church in America.

In addition to the churches of the Synodical Conference, three National
Lutheran Council churches delayed membership: the Suomi Synod, the
Lutheran Free Church, and, as already noted, the Evangelical Lutheran
Church. The latter was to be painfully divided over the issue for a whole
decade, but in 1956 the church voted decisively—1434 to 685—to apply
for membership in the council.[75]

An incomplete but perhaps helpful explanation of the altered attitude
in the Evangelical Lutheran Church is to be found in the following factors: (1) Some of the misinformation and misrepresentation of the World
Council had, in the meantime, been corrected. The new president, F. A.
Schiotz, for example, was able to present from personal experience a complete and accurate picture of the council; this had the effect of allaying
many fears. (2) The churches with which the ELC was planning to
merge, the ALC and the UELC, were charter members of the WCC.
This fact led many to question the reasons given for continued ELC
opposition to the WCC. (3) Between 1946 and 1956 the seminary had

graduated 723 students. Many of these men were convinced of the wisdom of affiliating with the WCC and now added their voting strength to the supporters of the ecumenical movement.

The eventual presence of most American Lutheran churches in the World Council helped to make the Lutheran church the largest confessional group in the council for a time. In 1961, however, the Russian Orthodox Church was received into membership at the New Delhi Assembly, making the Orthodox communion the largest ecclesiastical family in the World Council.

In conclusion, it ought to be observed that today (1970) two-thirds of American Lutheranism (the LCA and The ALC) belong to the World Council. The Missouri Synod, having voted down membership in the Lutheran World Federation for over two decades, could hardly be expected to look favorably on the World Council. The synod's Denver convention (1969) decisively rejected a resolution to join the federation and then refused to consider WCC membership. Despite the absence of this vigorous and theologically concerned body, American Lutheranism has supplied high quality leadership to the ecumenical movement. It is difficult to exaggerate, for example, the contribution of Franklin Clark Fry (d. 1968), who for many years was the highly respected chairman of the powerful central committee of the World Council. Without immodesty the Lutheran churches of America can rejoice in leadership that has accepted ecumenical responsibility for viewing the church and her role in the world under the aspect of the gospel as witnessed to in the Holy Scriptures and explicated in the Lutheran confessions.

NOTES

1. Georg Sverdrup, "Forening mellem de norsk lutherske Samfund," *Samlede Skrifter i Udvalg,* ed. Andreas Helland, IV (Minneapolis: Frikirkens Boghandels Forlag, 1910), 101-105.

2. One irritant to NLC Lutherans seeking membership in Missouri congregations was the insistence that communicants of another Lutheran body undergo instruction and confirmation before admission to membership. This writer served as a parish pastor during the war and saw this occur frequently. One example: a lifetime Lutheran, a Lutheran college graduate, a college professor with a Ph.D., a leader in the congregation, a Bible class teacher and a veritable "pastor's assistant" moved to a distant city equipped with a letter of transfer to a Lutheran congregation. The nearest church belonged to the Missouri Synod. Its pastor, however, refused the transfer and required adult instruction and confirmation. This kind of experience occurred frequently enough to indicate a pattern.

3. For a careful statement of this rediscovery see Sydney E. Ahlstrom, "Continental

Influences on American Theology since World War I," *Church History*, XXVII (September, 1958), 256-272. Cf. also Ahlstrom's *Theology in America* (Indianapolis: The Bobbs-Merrill Co., 1967), pp. 77-84.

4. "Lutheran Isolation," *The Christian Century*, (November 4, 1942), 1342-1343.

5. The phrase is Theodore Graebner's. An essay bearing this title was privately circulated in 1948 and later published. See *Concordia Historical Institute Quarterly*, XXXVIII (July, 1965), 88-94. Graebner does not consider biblical infallibility a burden (" . . . I wholeheartedly stand by the Brief Statement in all its terms . . . , " p. 93.); he refers to the infallibility of synodical decisions.

6. Cited in Robert Preus, *The Inspiration of Scripture: A Study of the Seventeenth Century Lutheran Dogmatics* (Mankato, Minn.: Lutheran Synod Book Co., 1955), p. 77.

7. This book grew out of lectures delivered at Luther Theological Seminary, St. Paul, Minn., January 28-31, 1947, with publication rights held by the Augsburg Publishing House Lectureship Fund. The theological emphasis of the lectures so displeased the administration of the seminary and the church leadership that the publishing house relinquished its rights. See p. ix, "Foreword." It is interesting that no mention of this is made in the annual report of the Board of Publication. See ELC, *Annual Report . . . 1948*, p. 327.

8. For an account of the Bad Boll meetings, see F. E. Mayer, *The Story of Bad Boll* (St. Louis: Concordia Publishing House, 1949); M. H. Franzmann, *Bad Boll 1949* (St. Louis: The Lutheran Church-Missouri Synod, 1950); Carl Meyer, ed., *Moving Frontiers* (St. Louis: Concordia Publishing House, 1964), p. 429; and John Behnken, *This I Recall* (St. Louis: Concordia Publishing House, 1964), pp. 112-113.

9. Synod of the Northwest, *Minutes, Special Convention . . . January 36, 1956*, pp. 109-123. See also "Supplemental Report of the Examining Committee," January 29, 1957. Although the official transcripts of the trials have been placed under seal, sufficient material is available to discern the issues. Some sources: *The Lutheran*, Nov. 9, 1955, p. 45; Nov. 30, 1955, p. 43; Dec. 14, 1955, p. 44; Jan. 4, 1956, p. 45; Feb. 1, 1956, p. 43; Feb. 8, 1956, p. 9; April 15, 1956, p. 44; June 6, 1956, p. 28; Feb. 13, 1957, p. 5; Feb. 20, 1957, p. 6; May 8, 1957, p. 38; June 5, 1957, p. 4. Reinhold Niebuhr, "The Heresy Trials," *Christianity and Crisis*, XV, 171. R. P. Roth, "Heresy and the Lutheran Church," *The Lutheran Quarterly*, VIII (August, 1956), 245-252; Martin J. Heinecken, "Faith and Facts," *ibid.*, pp. 253-257; and Victor K. Wrigley, "Heresy and Christianity: A Reply to Professor Roth," *ibid.*, IX (August, 1957), 270-275. An unpublished "Statement Addressed to the Church," prepared by Professors Theo. Tappert and Martin Heinecken for the signatures of "representative theologians of all U.L.C.A. seminaries in the United States," sought to summarize the issues from an evangelical and Lutheran point of view.

10. For a short discussion of this view of Scripture see Anders Nygren, *The Significance of the Bible for the Church*, tr. by C. C. Rasmussen, Facet Books, Biblical Series; (Philadelphia: Fortress Press, 1963). Note especially chapter three.

11. E. C. Fendt, "The Theology of the 'Common Confession.' " *Lutheran Quarterly*, II (August, 1950), 308-323. Fendt declares: "The aim is not to say anything new, but to state the old faith in modern language." (p. 311).

12. The ALC, *Reports and Actions of the Constituting Convention*, April 22-24, 1960, p. 98.

13. American Lutheran Conference, "Proceedings . . . 1940," *Journal of The American Lutheran Conference*, VI (January, 1941), 85-86.

14. *Ibid.*, pp. 312-313.

15. NLC, "Minutes . . . 1942," *ibid.*, VII (1942), 388-390.

16. NLC, "Minutes. Special Committee on Cooperation, May 14, 1942," *ibid.*, pp. 457-465. It is of interest to note that Missouri had joined in prayer at the first Columbus meeting. It has been suggested that Behnken got his knuckles rapped when he reurned to St. Louis.

17. *Ibid.*, pp. 542-543.

18. "Joint Meeting with Representatives of the Missouri Synod, May 15, 1942," *ibid.*, pp. 544-554.

19. "Seventh Biennial Convention of American Lutheran Church," [October 9-15, 1942], *ibid.*, p. 860.

20. The January, 1943, issue of the *Journal of Theology* . . . *American Lutheran Conference*, VIII, is devoted to this important meeting, including reports, minutes, and addresses.

21. *Ibid.*, p. 84.

22. Letter: Boe-Aasgaard, 10-29-42; St. Olaf College Archives, Northfield, Minn.

23. Reu's obituary in *The Lutheran Outlook*, (November, 1943), 264.

24. Gullixson told the writer that Reu's statement was too heavily weighted with academic theology; therefore, in the interest of simplification, he wrote a new draft that Yochum approved with minor changes. Interview: 8-25-55. Cf. "Forgotten History in Lutheran Unity," *The Lutheran Outlook*, (January, 1944), 4-5.

25. American Lutheran Conference, *Convention Report* . . . Nov. 15-17, 1944, p. 7-8, 15-20. The entire document is found in *The Lutheran Outlook* (January, 1944), 10-12.

26. For reactions and "action" on the "Overture," see *ibid.*, pp. 69, 131-132, 163-164, 234-235.

27. ULCA, *Minutes . . . Minneapolis, Oct. 11-17, 1944*, pp. 240-242. The convention, assembled in Central Lutheran Church, a congregation of the Norwegian Lutheran Church of America, softened the unnecessarily candid language of the committee (F. H. Knubel, H. Offerman, P. H. Krauss, P. H. Roth, J. K. Jensen, E. Rinderknecht, and H. Bagger), lest the rejection of the "Overture" be a slap at NLCA hospitality.

28. The statements are readily available for comparison in Richard Wolf, *Documents of Lutheran Unity*. For a history of the "Pittsburgh Agreement," see E. Clifford Nelson, "A Case Study in Lutheran Unity Efforts" in *The Maturing of American Lutheranism*, eds. H. T. Neve and B. A. Johnson (Minneapolis: Augsburg Publishing House, 1968), pp. 207-221. Cf. *supra*, Chapter III.

29. The ULCA was regarded by many to be "liberal" not only in theology but in practice. It was judged as being too lax about lodge membership, too casual about the use of alcoholic beverages, and too permissive about certain amusements, especially social dancing. Missouri and the ALC attitudes towards drinking and dancing were not unlike those of the ULCA, but the Norwegians were strangely silent in this regard.

30. NLCA, *Report . . . 1944*, pp. 404-405.

31. *Lutheran Herald*, XXVIII (July 4, 1944), 540-541. He said that if the ULCA was sincere in its profession of the Pittsburgh Agreement, that would change the case.

32. What follows is largely based on the account in Nelson, *The Lutheran Church Among Norwegian-Americans*, II, 315-322. Full documentation is to be found in the footnotes of that volume. Therefore they are not repeated here.

33. Prominently associated with this matter was O. G. Malmin, editor of *Lutheran Herald*. See John M. Jensen, "An Old Soldier Who Will Not Fade Away," *The Lutheran Standard*, (January 10, 1967), 9.

34. Interview: Bersell-ECN, 5-20-59.

35. Letter, Carlsen-E. W. Schramm, 1-11-50, ALC Archives, Wartburg Seminary, Dubuque, Iowa.

36. See Minutes, "Conference on Lutheran Unity, Augustana Church Headquarters, Minneapolis, Minn., Jan. 4, 1949," J. K. Jensen Papers, Northwestern Lutheran Seminary Library, St. Paul, Minn.

37. "A Move Toward Unity," *The Lutheran Outlook*, XIV (Feb., 1949), 55-56.

38. See N. C. Carlsen Papers, ALC Archives, Wartburg Seminary, Dubuque, Iowa. A letter from Pastor Herbert Lindemann to President N. C. Carlsen (12-31-48) said that Graebner had requested him to attend the meeting. But because of the round-about manner of invitation, Lindemann expressed hesitation about being present. Who approached Graebner and why? Why was not Behnken asked?

39. Sittler's book was considered heretical by "old Lutherans." E. C. Fendt, dean of the ALC seminary in Columbus, noted that the ULCA did not discipline Sittler for his views. He continued: "In the ALC the president of the Church would have had him immediately charged with heresy." See Minutes, Special Commission on Relations to American Lutheran Bodies of the ULCA and the Commission on Union and Fellowship of the ALC, March 13, 1952, p. 8. Minutes are in ALC Archives, Wartburg Seminary, Dubuque, Iowa.

40. Letter: Behnken-Aasgaard, 12-10-49; Behnken Papers, Box 8, Folder 14, Concordia Historical Institute, St. Louis.

41. *The National Lutheran,* XIX (September, 1950), 12.

42. Interview: Bernhard Christensen-ECN, May 28, 1957. Cf. Arden, *Augustana Heritage,* pp. 388-394.

43. Wolf, *Documents,* p. 501.

44. Letter: O. G. Malmin-A. V. Neve, 3-18-52; files of the Joint Union Committee, Permanent Merger File, Augsburg Publishing House, Minneapolis, Minn. It is interesting to note that a committee composed of C. K. Preus, A. N. Rogness, and John R. Lavik was charged by the ELC Union Committee with the responsibility of preparing the Preamble and Confessional Statement for the Articles of Union. Article I, Section 1 of the Articles of Union reads: *"As the primary condition of union* [italics added], we declare our joint, unanimous, and unreserved acceptance of all the canonical books . . . as a whole and in all their parts, as the divinely inspired, revealed, and inerrant Word of God. . . . " See "Minutes, November 9, 1954," Minutes, Union Committee of ELC, 1953-1960, p. 16; Permanent Merger File, Augsburg Publishing House, Minneapolis.

45. The chief such *apologia* came from The ALC president, F. A. Schiotz, *The Church's Confessional Stand Relative to the Scriptures* (Minneapolis: Office of Public Relations, ALC, 1966), p. 7. The author states: "The ALC holds that the inerrancy referred to here [in the ALC constitution] does not apply to the text but to the truths revealed for our faith, doctrine and life. . . . The *United Testimony* has several long paragraphs concerning the Word . . . observe these meaningful sentences: . . . " At this point he quotes exactly the section cited above. It is interesting that in 1955 the president stated that there were two reasons which precluded fellowship or union with the ULCA: (1) its view of the Word and (2) its attitude to the lodge. One decade later, in 1966, he was affirming the ULCA position.

46. Augustana Church, *Report . . . 1953,* pp. 340-343.

47. E. L. Fevold, *The Lutheran Free Church* (Minneapolis: Augsburg Publishing House, 1969), pp. 272-302.

48. Wolf, *Documents,* pp. 543-545.

49. "Protocol of the Joint Committee on Polity and Organization of the Joint Union Committee," 1955; Minutes, May 5-6, 1955, pp. 22-27. Permanent Merger Files, Joint Union Committee, Augsburg Publishing House, Minneapolis.

50. A copy of Bodensieck's letter is in the Permanent Merger Files, Joint Union Committee, Augsburg Publishing House, Minneapolis.

51. News Bureau Releases, National Lutheran Council, 2-4-58 and 2-10-58.

52. Letter: ECN-Tillman Sogge, chairman, JUC, 2-28-58. When it was learned that this letter was considered too controversial to be placed in the permanent files of the Joint Union Committee, the author filed copies in the archives of the National Lutheran Council in New York and of the Lutheran World Federation in Geneva.

53. To distinguish itself from the American Lutheran Church of 1930, the new church capitalized the definite article "The." Objections were subsequently raised and requests were made to use the lower case. A decision was reached that "The" would have to be used in all legal documents and official designations. There would be, however, no objections to the use of the lower case in popular references and in the mass media. See The ALC, *Reports and Actions . . . 1968,* pp. 92-93, 461.

54. "A.L.C., E.L.C., U.E.L.C.—T.A.L.C.!" *The Christian Century,* (May 11, 1960), 574-576.

55. ULCA, *Minutes* . . . *1956*, pp. 29-38.

56. Wolf, *Documents*, pp. 554-556.

57. ULCA, *Minutes* . . . *1958*, pp. 696-699. Cf. President Fry's statement in *The Lutheran*, October 8, 1958; and A. D. Mattson's "Where Does the ULCA Stand?" *The Lutheran Companion*, November 12, 1958. An extensive file on the debate is to be found in the Fry Papers, Box I, Folder: JCLU, the Lodge Question, 1957-1958. The Minutes of the JCLU, volume I, contain numerous references to the discussion. Fry's papers and the JCLU minutes are in LCA Archives, Lutheran School of Theology, Chicago, Ill.

58. Wolf, *Documents* . . . , pp. 555, 567, 569, 570-571.

59. LCA, *Minutes of Constituting Convention* . . . *1962*, pp. 279-293.

60. Osborne Hauge, *Lutherans Working Together* (New York: National Lutheran Council, 1945), p. 75.

61. Wolf, *Documents*, p. 574.

62. *Ibid.*, pp. 585-586.

63. The ALC, *Reports and Actions* . . . *1964*, p. 457.

64. The ALC, *Reports and Actions* . . . *1966*, pp. 90-91. Documents relative to the new church are to be found in the 1964 *Reports and Actions*, pp. 458-482.

65. LCA, *Minutes* . . . *1964*, p. 308.

66. LC–MS, *Proceedings* . . . *1962*, p. 131.

67. N. E. Berner, "Crossroads in Canada," *The Lutheran*, (September 28, 1966), 13-15. Cf. Erich R. W. Schultz, "Tragedy and Triumph in Canadian Lutheranism," *Concordia Historical Institute Quarterly*, XXXVIII (July, 1965), 55-72.

68. "Canada: Lutheran Union . . . By 1978." *Lutheran Forum*, (February, 1969), 21. An insightful essay on Canadian Lutheranism is Walter Freitag, "Lutheran Tradition in Canada," in *The Churches and the Canadian Experience. A Faith and Order Study* . . . , ed J. W. Grant (Toronto: The Ryerson Press, 1963), pp. 94-101. "Lutherans in Canada Make Fellowship an Early Goal," News Bureau Release, Lutheran Council/USA, 12-18-69, p. 7. "Lutherans in Canada Cite Consensus for Fellowship," *ibid.*, 12-17-70, pp. 1-3; and *The Lutheran*, (Jan. 20, 1971), 25.

69. A. R. Wentz, *A Basic History*, (Revised edition 1964), p. 333.

70. LWF, *Proceedings* . . . *Lund* . . . *1947*, pp. 15-19, 29, 32-33.

71. For the account of this Assembly see LWF, *Proceedings* . . . *Hannover* . . . *1952*, pp. 11, 103, 168-198.

72. The director of the assembly reckoned that more than 2,500 persons in the metropolitan area of the Twin Cities served on various preparatory committees.

73. An inadequate account of the Third Assembly is to be found in LWF, *Proceedings* . . . *Minneapolis* . . . *1957*.

74. Dorris Flesner, "The Role of the Lutheran Churches of America in the Formation of the World Council of Churches" (unpublished Ph.D. dissertation, Hartford Seminary Foundation, 1956), p. 154. This dissertation tells the story in great detail and imposing documentation. The role of F. H. Knubel, A. R. Wentz, and Franklin Clark Fry, all of the ULCA, in the struggle for *confessional* recognition is especially noteworthy.

75. Congressman Albert Quie of Minnesota was largely instrumental in winning lay support of WCC membership.

CHAPTER SIX

AMERICAN LUTHERANISM IN THE SIXTIES

One of the most significant themes in American Lutheranism, as in Roman Catholicism, has been immigration. Using this sociological factor as at least one interpretive guide, the present attempt to tell the story of North American Lutheranism recalls that the European heritage has clung to Lutherans more tenaciously than to most Protestant Americans. Paradoxically Lutheranism, closely allied to the European scene, was also deeply rooted in the colonial American tradition. Some of the oldest American families and most typical colonial church buildings—such as Holy Trinity, Wilmington (1669) and Gloria Dei, Philadelphia (1700)— were affiliated with the Lutheran church. Thus Lutheranism faced in two directions: its life was existence in the two worlds of the Atlantic community, Europe and America. Its history could never be forced into the "frontier thesis" or other popular theories of American historiography.

This colonial ecclesiastical maverick counted 40,000 members (Roman Catholic, 25,000) at the birth of the republic, when the first wave of immigration came to an end. Between the War of Independence and 1840, immigration was little more than a trickle; contact with the European mother churches was minimal. Because of these circumstances the primary orientation of Lutherans, therefore, was to America. Lutheranism in the new nation faced the question of identity. What was the role of Lutheranism in America? Should it make common cause with other German-background (Reformed and sectarian) religious groups? Or should it give up both its "Germanism" and its Lutheranism and surrender to the Anglo-

Saxon Protestantism which was the most prestigious religious element in American society?[1] The Lutheran problem was resolved in a manner quite similar to that of the other bodies, that is, by adopting the completely new ecclesio-sociological form known as the American "denomination" that was neither "church" nor "sect" (à la Troeltsch) but had characteristics of both. Thus Lutheranism in America was a "free" voluntary association of like-minded people committed to a "churchly" confession which it held to be the true witness of Protestant Christianity. The temporary cessation of immigration provided the opportunity to discover this identity; and although influenced by the language transition and the modified and Americanized Calvinism known as "American Evangelicalism," Lutheranism emerged consciously by mid-century as a particular confessional, denominational entity in the midst of the already evident American pluralism.

The remainder of the 19th century, with the exception of the Civil War Years, was marked by a massive movement of German and Scandinavian immigrants with all the attendant problems: the continuing quest for identity, the necessity for missions and institutionalization. How could Lutherans sing the Lord's song in a strange land? By 1893 the "frontier" was gone, and the churches faced for the first time the necessity of "settling down" into the American environment, something which was to be accomplished in some measure during the 1920s.

The powerful forces unleashed by the depression and the two World Wars brought Lutheranism into the "mainstream of American life." By the 60s this communion faced another identity crisis, not unlike that in the early years of the 19th century. Numerous questions seemed to demand answers. For example: within the spectrum of American Christianity did Lutheranism have a viable future as a separate confessional church? In the face of the so-called "great issues" of the last third of the 20th century was there anything unique, and therefore worthy of preservation, about Lutheranism? Did the staggering problems of the racial crisis, the Vietnam war, poverty, the Third World, and youth's clamor demand a posture that minimized Lutheran particularity; or could Lutherans under the Lordship of Christ practice a fruitful coexistence and collaboration in the amelioration of the massive social, political, economic problems ("secular ecumenism") while remaining unabashedly and unapologetically "particular" and "confessional"? Much serious reflection and a plethora of words and activities during the decade did not provide a resolution with sharply defined contours recognizably Lutheran and ecumenical and practical. This remained unfinished business as the future rushed in upon the church, whose profile in the 60s is the subject of this chapter.

THE GENERAL WORK OF THE CHURCHES

Traditionally American Protestant denominations have carried out their "general" work under categories such as missions (home and foreign), welfare and charities, and education. All of this "general" work has required special boards, executives, and, of course, money customarily called "benevolence funds" among Lutherans. The several branches of Lutheranism have followed this pattern with remarkably little deviation and measured growth or noted failures against the criteria within each category.

Missions

By mid-60s it was clear that the "revival" of the previous decade was coming to an end. Statistics revealed that the rapid growth of the churches was ending; the statistical curve began to move downward.

American Missions

President Franklin Clark Fry saw the problem for the Lutheran Church in America in 1964 in terms of urbanization:

> The chief factor that accounts for the pitifully slow net growth . . . is the high percentage of our membership that lives in the cities. Ours is among the most urban denominations . . . ; conspicuously more so . . . than our fellow American Lutherans. . . . Here [in the urban church] . . . the summons is, Renew or die. . . . Let no one be deceived. The new-style "urban work" is going to be expensive, discouraging, slow.

Moving from this grim prophecy, Fry sought to set before his constituency the potentially rewarding aspects of urban evangelism.

> What is at stake is not merely the organization of a few flourishing congregations; it is no less than the future character of our national life. The texture and color of every culture are determined in its cities and ours will be no exception. It must not be allowed to become totally secular and pagan.[2]

Despite the urgency of Fry's message, the decline continued and the church's Board of American Missions was informed in 1969 that only 18 new home mission fields were entered in 1968. In 1967, the number had been 25; in 1964, 84. Executive Secretary Donald Houser explained that the decline was due to the "cultural crisis" that was channeling funds into specialized ministries.[3]

The executive director for American missions in The American Lutheran Church, Philip Dybvig, also noted the decline. In the biennium 1962-1964, 91 new congregations had been established in the United States and Canada. Although the National Lutheran Council's regional committees had assigned no less than 476 fields to The American Lutheran Church, he saw very little hope of occupying more than 70. The Lutheran Church in America and the Missouri Synod, by contrast, could and perhaps would each begin work in 100 fields a year. As far as the urban church was concerned, Dybvig's analysis of trends revealed that in cities of 25,000 to 50,000 gross confirmed gains showed consistent strength through 1955. The next five years showed a sharp decrease. He predicted that, if continued, this trend would mean a net loss by 1965.[4] Although the next four years showed a continuing downward movement, Dybvig's prediction was not statistically fulfilled until 1968. In that year, official figures released by the Lutheran Council in the USA showed that both The ALC and the LCA had experienced a net decrease in membership. This was repeated in 1969.[5]

The Lutheran Church—Missouri Synod, which for a quarter of a century had had the highest numerical annual increases among Lutherans, began to realize that the earlier momentum was slowing down. In 1965, the synod was still living in the statistically-created euphoria of previous years. Walter F. Wolbrecht, the energetic executive of the Board of Directors, projected Missouri membership to 1990 when it would be 8,250,000. This figure was almost equal to the whole of American Lutheranism (outside of Canada) in 1965. On the basis of Missouri's excellent record this was not an unrealistic extrapolation. If money could be raised, he said, there were good reasons for this kind of optimism.[6] In 1967, Wolbrecht's report was less enthusiastic; in fact, it was now a sober and realistic acknowledgement that the statistics, even earlier than 1965, were beginning to unfold a different story. Statistical charts showed that as early as 1960 a decline had set in. By 1966, the growth was the lowest since 1942, early in World War II. Wolbrecht predicted that, if "the decelerating trend continues unhindered at the present rate, by 1970 The Lutheran Church—Missouri Synod may be losing more members than it is gaining." [7]

Although Lutheran church bodies in North America had a combined membership in 1968 of 9,239,274, ranking third behind Baptists and Methodists, one conclusion was evident: the Lutheran churches differed only slightly from typical "mainline" Protestant churches in the experience of slow growth in mid- and late-sixties. It was small consolation that the Roman Catholic church, which like the Missouri Synod had experienced remarkable growth, was now also suffering decline. Church membership as a whole in America, though still showing slight increase, was not keeping pace with population growth.

World Missions

In preparation for the 1968 convention of The American Lutheran Church, its Board of World Missions raised several probing questions indicating that Lutherans were engaged in a latter-day "Re-thinking Missions." The questions were at once an agenda for discussion and programmatic statements for future developments:

1. Is the interest of the church in its World Mission program being diverted to the home scene by the increasing focus of attention on the American urban crisis with problems almost identical to those confronting us in our overseas program: poverty, housing, hunger, unemployment, and education?
2. Is the base of benevolence giving crumbling under the pressure of public demand for social action? If so, must the Board of World Missions anticipate a retrenchment of its overseas program?
3. Are we losing the clarity of gospel proclamation (evangelization) in this day of revolutionary theological thinking within the Christian Church?
4. Where should American Lutherans be in missions 10 years from now—operating under separate synodical boards or united under one administration of the total overseas program of the synods which comprise the Lutheran Council USA?
5. Considering the fact that The American Lutheran Church has not entered a new mission field for 10 years, is it the de-

sire of the church that the Board of World Missions explore
the possibility of undertaking an additional responsibility in a
new geographical area? [8]

Each question focused the attention of the decision-making body on
the problems that contemporary circumstances were forcing Christians
in all churches to face. Was there a basic difference between world
missions and home missions and/or social missions? Were not overseas
missions confronting almost exactly the same problem that constituted the
American urban crisis? Were theological emphases in the 60s obfuscating
the gospel? What should the future program of the churches be?

It was unquestionable that the "prototype missionary" of popular imagi-
nation was all but gone. No longer did this dominating figure reflect
the situation in which leadership was in the hands of indigenous churchmen. Rather an increasing proportion of missionaries filled specific posts
that required skills still not common in the less developed countries.

The 19th century missionary enterprise had been to a large degree
a youth crusade. The Student *Volunteer* [sic] Movement was typical of
those days. In the 60s, however, idealistic youth could turn to such organizations as the Peace Corps as well as to missionary organizations
to find expression for their concern to serve the needy. Many did. The
church too opened channels for short term service, until the "younger
churches" began to ask for people with a permanent commitment rather
than "ecclesiastical tourists." Moreover, the theological climate, like the
changing political and social situation around the world, had brought
Lutheranism as well as other churches to what the LCA missions executive Arne Sovik and the Lutheran scholar and theologian Conrad Bergendoff agreed was a crisis for Christian missions.[9] Lutherans, said Bergendoff, had no call to Lutheranize the world; their charge was to proclaim
the central doctrine of justification by grace through faith, the gospel of
the forgiveness of sins through Christ. The institutional form must follow
function lest the form become mere propaganda and not genuine mission.
In the last analysis, therefore, mission

> . . . is not a question of geography or overseas missions . . . the
> distinction we draw between overseas missions and home mis-
> sions is entirely artificial. . . . Our own [American] culture is as
> heathen as any that you can find anywhere in the world.[10]

During the triennium 1962-1965, M. L. Kretzmann, a long-time Missouri Synod missionary and theological professor in India, conducted a "Mission Self-Study and Survey." Kretzmann's report, submitted to the synodical Board of Directors, examined the theological basis, administration areas of ministry, finances, and missionary education for the mission of Christ by the whole church. The conclusions of the report—popularly known as "The Kretzmann Report"—were of such a nature that some Missouri leaders were inclined to keep it "under wraps" for a time lest the traditionalist-element in the church be frightened by the implications of its projections. When the report was unveiled (1965), it did not cause the turbulence that had been feared. This was due to a combination of circumstances. In the first place, the thorough research and careful (though not necessarily cautious) wording of the report, and its strong biblical and confessional character were the handiwork of a theologically sophisticated mind and a missionary heart sensitive to the needs of the world in the 20th century. Its obvious sincerity and earnestness were disarming. In the second place, its was evident that many of the delegates were quite unaware of the truly radical implications of the report.[11] The "conservative right," for example, was saving its fire for the anticipated battle over what had been called "the credibility of Genesis and the edibility of Jonah." At all events certain vigorous "affirmations" or resolutions, based on the report, were adopted with little opposition. As a sample of the "affirmations" the following is cited:

> *Resolved,* That we affirm as Lutheran Christians that the Evangelical Lutheran Church is chiefly a confessional movement within the total body of Christ rather than a denomination emphasizing institutional barriers of separation. The Lutheran Christian uses the Lutheran Confessions for the primary purpose for which they were framed: to confess Christ and His Gospel boldly and lovingly to all Christians. *While the Confessions seek to repel all attacks against the Gospel, they are not intended to be a kind of Berlin wall to stop communication with other Christians* . . . [italics added].[12]

One Missouri Synod editor commented that the synod would change in a radical and revolutionary manner if the Kretzmann Report could take root in the lives of the church members.[13] Actually only one result was immediately discernible. The synod took action to create a "Single

Board for Missions," combining the boards of home and world missions, missions to the deaf and blind, European affairs, and campus ministry.

An indication of the forward-looking and unity-minded attitude of the three major Lutheran world mission boards was the establishment of a joint pre-service missionary orientation program. Replacing a School of Missions operated by the Lutheran Church in America since 1957, its sessions were to be conducted successively in Chicago (1969), in St. Louis (1970), and in St. Paul (1971), providing summer courses for missionary candidates from all three churches. The director was also to supervise continuing study by first-term missionaries on the field.[14] To complement this the boards in 1969 laid plans for a "World Church Institute," a center for missiological research which would undertake to stimulate and carry on a "massive attack on the problems which face the church in its understanding of its missionary obedience," and to anticipate the "probable need for radical change in the thought patterns of the whole missionary movement." [15] After initial consideration of an independent institute closely related to a theological school, the decision was made in April, 1970, to commit this project to the Lutheran Council/USA.

On April 27, 1970, boards of the three churches agreed that in the light of increasing cooperation overseas and the apparent possibility of closer working together at home a joint committee should be formed to investigate and recommend common action in a number of areas such as recruitment, information and interpretation, policy development, and area administration. Already a common personnel policy was well on the way to acceptance.

The following day The ALC and LCA mission boards requested permission of their parent bodies to coordinate and even merge their programs. Recognizing the fact that the Missouri Synod board would not be able to consider such action, the two other boards noted that certain unusual and propitious circumstances made bilateral action desirable. The ALC executive was retiring in June, 1970, and the LCA executive, a former ALC missionary and director of the LWF department of World Missions, would be a natural selection to administer the joint work of the two boards and to enlist further cooperation by the Missouri Synod. Two weeks later The ALC board, entertaining second thoughts, rejected the proposal, fearing that the LCA/ALC action would make more difficult the cooperation of the Missouri Synod.[16]

Despite the attitude of "waiting-for-Missouri," American Lutheranism was aware of the fact that, in the face of the intricate and wide-spread unrest and profound need for missionary reorientation, the luxury of institutional disunity had to be put aside. The nature of the church as Christ's mission to the whole world, to the whole body of Christians, and to the whole of society required united efforts in planning, in implementation, and in organization.

Christian Education

The Lutheran church has traditionally laid heavy stress on education and has been actively engaged at every level: elementary, secondary, college and university, and seminary. Any profile of American Lutheranism in the 60s, therefore, must include the church's continuing role in education.

Parish Level

Parochial schools, almost exclusively to be found in churches of the former Synodical Conference,[17] were being hard-pressed financially and severely criticized educationally. Although William A. Kramer, secretary for parochial schools in the Missouri Synod, wrote in the *Lutheran Witness Reporter* that state aid to non-public schools had expanded by 1969, the economic pinch, felt even by public schools, was increasingly severe. At the same time, the effectiveness of Lutheran parochial schools was seriously challenged within the Missouri Synod itself. A study of parochial schools revealed "very few marks that differentiate the parochial school youth from the public school Lutheran youth if both come from relatively sound Lutheran families."[18] Although a sharp criticism was leveled against the study as being inadequate and even unfair, it was self-evident that the Missouri Synod, like the Roman Catholic Church, was taking a hard look at its school system.[19]

Two years earlier (1964), the Board of Parish Education of the Lutheran Church in America, having been confronted with the question of the advisability of establishing parochial schools, strongly discouraged congregations from engaging in such projects. Although a congregation had the right to conduct a parochial school, it ought to be done only when there was convincing evidence that the public schools were grossly inadequate. "Under no circumstances should . . . a school . . . provide racially or socially segregated educational facilities." [20]

Although Lutheran parochial schools were under criticism, it should be remembered that less than one third of American Lutheranism maintained a parochial system. Parish education, however—including Sunday schools, catechetical instruction, vacation schools—was common to all of Lutheranism. It was in this area that cooperation among the main churches was to develop. A cooperative program in parish education had its beginnings in the United Lutheran Church as early as 1942. The former American Lutheran Church and the Augustana Synod had expressed (prior to 1942) an interest in the joint preparation and publication of a new series of graded curricular materials. An agreement was reached whereby these three churches would produce what was to be known as *The Christian Growth Series.*[21] About 1950 the Parish and Church School Board of the United Lutheran Church began to think in terms of developing a long-range plan of parish education for the congregations. Progress was reported to the church at subsequent conventions. It was in December, 1954, however, that the major step was taken when the Board of Parish Education adopted a document setting forth the basic principles for a long-range program. The board had engaged Professor Paul Vieth of Yale Divinity School's department of Christian education to act as consultant and guide in the study. The result was the first denominational attempt in America to view parish education as a whole. It was all-embracing, moving from the graded Sunday school materials, through catechetical, vacation and week-day church school curricula to adult education, including leadership training, church camps, and family education.[22] The scope of the enterprise—both as to content and financial outlay—was larger than anything hitherto envisioned by any American church body. At the outset, both the former American Lutheran Church and the Augustana Lutheran Church (name changed in 1948) expressed an interest in cooperating in the entire plan and urged that other National Lutheran Council churches be invited. In response to this invitation, an eight-church venture was begun on the basis of a document called "A Proposal for Cooperation in a Long Range Program of Parish Education." The program was divided into four phases: Phase I—the study and development of general and age-group objectives; Phase II—the study and development of curriculum to fulfill the objectives; Phase III—the production and promotion of materials to implement the curriculum design; and Phase IV—the field testing and use of materials.[23] Phase I was to be completed by December 31, 1957; Phase II, by mid-1960; Phase III's materials should begin to appear by January, 1963, but the nature of Phase IV made it impossible to project a completion date.[24]

Although the Evangelical Lutheran Church had accepted the invitation to participate in the project and was represented at the joint meeting in Chicago, January 31, 1956, and at subsequent meetings (February 28, and March 22-23, 1956), it was reluctant to continue in the program. Furthermore, no mention of the project was made by the ELC executive director, J. C. K. Preus, in his report of 1956. Moreover, the "Proposal for a Long Range Program" was not presented to the ELC convention for consideration. Reference, however, was made in the same report to cooperative efforts under way between the ELC and the ALC parish boards.[25] In due course, representatives of the eight bodies met in Columbus, January 8-9, 1957, organizing a Joint Board Committee which would be the functioning body for all the churches. At this meeting the ELC, with support from the ALC and UELC (the partners in the tri-partite merger of 1960), pointed out certain difficulties in accepting the long-range program. It was felt that there was no freedom for participating churches to substitute or supplement the long-range program with materials of their own and that it was impossible to commit a yet-unborn church (the new ALC) to an expensive and long-range program. Later in the summer of 1957, during the Minneapolis Assembly of the Lutheran World Federation, a meeting of the Joint Staff Supervisory Committee (created at the January, 1957 meeting) was held. Once again the question was raised by the ELC whether a participating body would be permitted to publish supplementary materials if the need arose. No mutually satisfactory solution for such publication could be devised.[26] Largely because of the ELC's hesitation the Joint Union Committee (ELC, ALC, UELC) voted that it could not commit The American Lutheran Church (1960) to the project.[27]

This action was later reported to the ELC parish education board; it took action formally to withdraw "with regret" from the long range program at the end of Phase I. In a parallel action, however, it resolved to take "immediate steps" to cooperate with ALC and UELC so that the new ALC might have its *own* parish curriculum available by 1965. The UELC and ALC soon followed the ELC's example and withdrew from the program.[28]

There were at least three reasons for this action, some publicly stated, others privately spoken. There seemed to be an unresolvable structural problem in that a merger of boards or departments of parish education was required before there was a merger of church bodies. In the next place, it was charged that the expense of the program was unconscionably high (the fact that the new ALC was to embark on an equally expensive program was not reported to the church). In the third place, the "contractual arrangements . . . did not permit TALC to remain free to determine its own course. . . ." These words of the Joint Union Committee referred to the ULCA's reluctance to see supplementary materials published and to the ELC's fear of ULCA theology. When the long range program was presented to the Joint Union Committee, T. F. Gullixson, supported by R. A. Ofstedal and O. G. Malmin, felt that the proposed curriculum would be dominated by the ULCA's "liberal" view of the Bible. Gullixson subsequently said he was particularly disturbed and filled with apprehension by the fact that Professor Martin J. Heinecken of the Lutheran Seminary (ULCA) in Philadelphia, who had delivered some unsettling lectures on the inspiration of the Scriptures at Luther Seminary (ELC) in St. Paul, was an influential theologian on the Parish Education Board planning the long range program. This reaction also provided, unwittingly perhaps, another interpretive dimension to the Joint Union Committee's statement that the long range program did not "permit TALC to remain free to determine its own course." [29] Only the most defensive could fail to see that the same dynamics, present in the two merger movements within the National Lutheran Council, had been at work in the long range program for parish education.

Meanwhile, the two church mergers came about and two separate parish education curricula—LCA and ALC—were in process. To the credit of a durable good-will and an uncommon common sense that survived the tensions of 1956-1960, there were persistent efforts in the late 50s and early 60s to find ways in which the two churches could cooperate in parish education. In 1958, for example, the Eastern District of the old

ALC received a report of the Committee on the State of the Church which included these trenchant words:

> The vision [of cooperation] may not have failed but it surely faltered when the Joint Union Committee . . . withdrew its support from the Long Range Program. . . . One member of the committee [said] that the long-range program meant that "we must produce nothing else, promote nothing else, and sell nothing else." Editor Schramm . . . deplored [this] "regrettable misstatement" saying . . . "it will be a tragedy of deepest dye if TALC . . . shuns the long-range program because of the totally erroneous statements."

The report concluded by raising some sharp and even embarrassing questions:

> . . . the Joint Union Committee is committing the new Church to all manner of projects, plans and policies—why stall at this? . . . What proof do we have that our . . . material would be superior or even equal to what the LRP would produce? . . . the cost involved [is so] high in money and brains we are going to be forced to pool resources. . . . If JUC felt compelled to jug LRP they might at least have tried to find more cogent and more intelligible reasons.[30]

Some of the leaders in the parish education program of the new ALC, though obligated to proceed with the preparation of a new curriculum, were bothered by the lack of "cogent" and "intelligible reasons," and consequently sought almost immediately to prevent doors from being closed to future cooperation. In 1961 The ALC Board of Parish Education asked both the soon to-be-born LCA and the Missouri Synod if there were not some things which could be done together. The Missouri Synod responded with a polite acknowledgment but offered no participation. On the other hand, the LCA parish education staff met with The ALC staff (Detroit, 1961) and the two groups shared progress reports. In 1963 The ALC board officially approached the LCA board suggesting further conversations and cooperation. A meeting (Ann Arbor, Michigan, July 29-30, 1963) revealed that the two boards had been following remarkably parallel paths, thus providing the opportunity of using certain portions of one another's materials. A subsequent meeting (Detroit, October 31-November 2, 1963) disclosed several potentially fruitful areas of cooperative work and resolutions were prepared to implement common purposes.[31]

Although persisting problems of institutional structure and consequent relationships provided temporary obstacles, the leadership of the two churches, unlike in the 50s, was intent on removing the technicalities which previously had served as an alibi for non-cooperation. W. Kent Gilbert, who had been the guiding genius of the long range program, continued to be the leading spokesman for the LCA and exhibited both a masterful patience and a hard-nosed perseverance in bringing about a structural harmony that would facilitate cooperation. This won the support of ALC leaders such as C. Richard Evenson, executive secretary for Parish Education, Lloyd Svendsbye, the editor-in-chief of the Board of Publication, and Albert E. Anderson, manager of Augsburg Publishing House. These men together with the LCA men, Gilbert, Frank Rhody, and Donald Pichaske, soon drafted plans whereby the boards of parish education and publication of the two churches would undertake a joint program. Task forces from both church bodies would work out a central objective and organizing principle for implementation of the objectives. Phase I (the above) was completed in March of 1970. It was hoped that the first elements of a total parish education program would be ready for introduction by 1975.[32] Although attempts had been made to bring the Lutheran Church—Missouri Synod into the new enterprise and although some strong Missouri support was won, the project did not receive the synod's approval.[33]

Two areas in which the Missouri Synod was able to cooperate were the revision of the intersynodical translation of Luther's Small Catechism and the study of the theology and practice of confirmation.[34] The latter study grew out of the wide-spread interest generated by the work of the Lutheran World Federation Commission on Christian Education and its publication, *Confirmation: A Study Document.* In 1964, representatives of each of the three major churches formed the Joint Commission on the Theology and Practice of Confirmation, which after four years issued a "Report for Study" (December 28, 1967) and published a study book on confirmation and communion.[35] The report made two significant recommendations: (1) that baptized children be admitted to communion during the latter part of the fifth grade and (2) that confirmation, defined as a "pastoral and educational ministry . . . designed to help baptized children identify with the life and mission of the adult Christian community . . . , " should take place in the latter part of the tenth grade. This was a sharp reversal of traditional Lutheran practice that looked upon confirmation as an educational ministry prior to communion. The proposal, as intended, evoked immediate and sharp discussion among pastors and congregations. Pastors, having been provided guidance, were asked to conduct congregational study sessions during 1969. In November, the joint commission considered the results of the parish-level evaluations and began the preparation of a final report and recommendations to be submitted to the churches. The Lutheran Church in America and The American Lutheran Church took favorable action at their conventions in 1970. In 1971, the Missouri Synod convention voted to let each congregation do as it saw fit with the confirmation proposals.

College Education

The profile of American Lutheranism would be inadequate without a glance at its program of higher education, not least because Lutheranism in America has placed such stress on its colleges and seminaries. Despite this interest in higher education, there has been an understandable reluctance to begin new institutions. The primary reason for this is economic; the cost of higher education today boggles the minds of those who would venture anew into this realm. The most recently founded college (1961, in California), despite the support of both the LCA and The ALC, has encountered problems that illustrate the legitimate hesitation of educational leaders to ask churches to leap into fiscal waters beyond their depth. The Missouri Synod, however, authorized in 1971 the building of a 4-year college at Irvine, California, a step interpreted by some as an indication that Missouri was unwilling to entrust its youth to the nearby ALC-LCA college.

Enrollments in Lutheran colleges since World War II and especially during the 60s continued to rise. The rate of growth was not so dramatic as that in tax-supported schools, but nevertheless the church-related colleges were bursting at the seams. According to the annual statistical report of the National Lutheran Educational Conference, Washington, D.C., the academic year 1960-61 showed a total of 47,347 in Lutheran colleges and universities. The next year the figure had risen to 50,592. By 1969 the total was 53,444 full-time under-graduates. With the reckon-

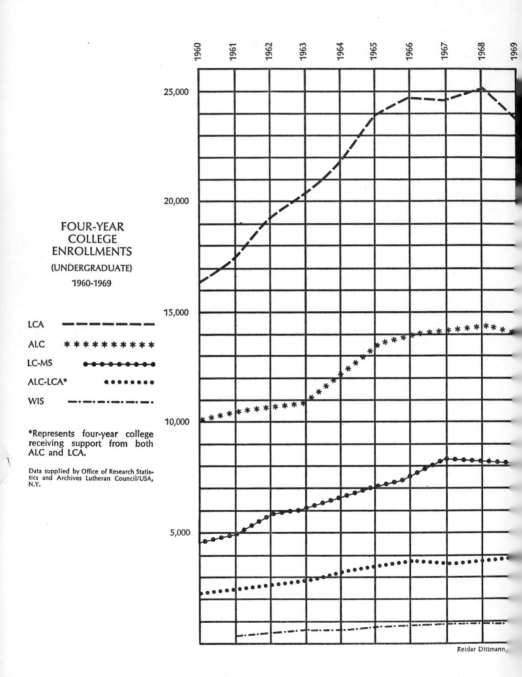

FOUR-YEAR
COLLEGE
ENROLLMENTS
(UNDERGRADUATE)
1960-1969

LCA ————————
ALC **********
LC-MS ●●●●●●●●●●
ALC-LCA* ●●●●●●●●
WIS —·—·—·—·—·

*Represents four-year college receiving support from both ALC and LCA.

Data supplied by Office of Research Statistics and Archives Lutheran Council/USA, N.Y.

1960 1961 1962 1963 1964 1965 1966 1967 1968 1969

25,000
20,000
15,000
10,000
5,000

Reidar Dittmann

ing of part-time students, graduate students, and those engaged in other programs the figure stood at 77,812.[36] The accompanying graph shows college enrollment figures by church bodies during the decade of the 1960s.

The religious affiliation of students at Lutheran colleges at the beginning of the decade was as follows:

	1960-1961	1961-1962
Lutheran	66.40%	65.25%
Methodist	6.55	7.35
Presbyterian	5.37	5.84
Roman Catholic	4.37	4.45
Baptist	3.50	3.13
Others	11.95	12.03
None	1.86	1.95
	100.00%	100.00%

College students in the Upper Midwest showed a higher than average percentage of Lutheran affiliation. The schools of the Missouri Synod, for reasons explained below, had the highest percentage. Meanwhile, during the expansion of the 60s, the proportion of students reporting Lutheran affiliation declined. College officials, not unexpectedly, disagreed as to the causes of the change. In some schools, such as those in large urban centers seeking close ties with and support from the immediate populace, there was a conscious effort to create a heterogeneous community. Where such goals were not clearly a part of institutional policy and yet changes were noted, the causes could range from rising tuitions, which middle-class Lutherans could not afford, to disenchantment of many in this same middle-class with allegedly nominal commitment of the institution to its stated religious objectives. Moreover, not a few administrators pointed to what they called "quality education" as a factor in attracting an increasing number of non-Lutheran students, thus altering the percentage of Lutheran registrants. Some educators attributed the decline to America's generally changing campus climate, especially as it reflected student rejection of "the institutional church," the religious "establishment." The diminution was most noticeable in eastern LCA colleges and least evident in Missouri Synod institutions. A partial explanation of this lay in the largely urban situation and the academic goals of the former, and the sharply church-oriented purposes of the latter. For example, most of the Missouri colleges were operated to train future teachers for Lutheran schools and to provide pre-professional education for future pastors. LCA and ALC colleges, having no responsibility to provide teachers for a parochial school system, were liberal arts colleges, a number of whose graduates did indeed go on to seminaries. But larger numbers went into teaching, business, graduate schools, military service, social work, and other fields.

Two related problems that need stating at this juncture pertain to educational philosophy and church-relatedness. The basic question of the former continued to be, What kind of educational institutions should the church be running? Ought the churches be operating schools that were primarily defenders of denominational faith? Were Lutheran colleges basically for the purpose of training teachers and leaders who would man secondary and elementary parochial schools which in turn would provide recruits for colleges and/or congregations which in turn . . . ? Was Lutheran education a Lutheran circle?

On the other hand, were Lutheran-supported colleges primarily academic institutions—religion being a part of the academic curriculum—which like other private colleges were engaged in pursuing the necessary and laudable objective of educating today's youth: that is, the church "owes" it to society to help meet the ever-escalating educational needs of men. Was the Lutheran college fundamentally no different from other liberal arts colleges seeking to help young people pick and choose among the many "value systems" with which they were confronted?

Others might be inclined to put the question differently: Was the church faced with a problem not in the philosophy of education but in the theology of education? Was it not a false dichotomy to speak of the college as being "here" and the church "over there"? Was it not "more Lutheran" to see that Lutheran college education was *basically* an ecclesiological problem? Was not the Lutheran college the church, the *ecclesia,* in higher education? If so, the mandate of the college was automatically identical with the mandate of the church—life in, with, and under the gospel. The totality of life, including the "liberating" arts and sciences was to be under God who reveals his will for righteousness in the gospel.

These viable options seemed to be the main alternatives in the 60s.

The colleges were being urged to maintain their ties with the church ("over there"?) but for varying reasons. One seemed to advocate a withdrawal from the world for the church's sake; a second urged plunging into the world for society's sake; and a third said God works with two hands, his left and right, to produce free men, liberated in a penultimate sense by education, liberated in an ultimate sense by the proclamation of forgiveness. Education and proclamation co-exist and interpenetrate each other in the church for Christ's sake, who was and is unambiguously *in* the world but not *of* it.

The legal or corporate relationships of Lutheran colleges to the institutional church vary between the churches and within the churches. In some instances, there is direct church ownership of the school. There is no separate collegiate corporation. The trustees of the ecclesiastical corporation are the trustees of the college (Example: Concordia Senior College, Fort Wayne, Missouri Synod). In other cases, ownership of the college is by a corporation whose membership is the voting membership of the church's general convention, but whose trustees (regents) are a separate legal entity from the trustees of the church (Luther and St. Olaf Colleges, ALC). In still other cases, ownership is vested in a corporation whose membership is the voting membership of one or more geographic jurisdictional units ("synods" or "districts") of the church at large or the elected representatives of these units (Wittenberg, LCA; Concordia, ALC). A fourth variation is the vesting of ownership in a corporation whose membership is identical with a church-wide "voluntary association" of congregations, (Waldorf, ALC) or of friends of the institution (Valparaiso, Missouri).[37] In these ways American Lutheranism maintains its "church-related" colleges by greater or lesser degrees of moral and financial support.

The 60s witnessed a continuing expansion of physical facilities and faculties in order to meet rising enrollments. The nation's inflationary economy meant rising costs in new buildings, increased salaries, and general education budgets. Although financial support from the church bodies with which the colleges were associated rose somewhat, the support was wholly inadequate to meet the large budgets. This usually meant two things: (1) increased tuitions and (2) broader extra-church sources of support. The former tended to limit the student bodies to youth of relatively affluent parents, despite large-scale student aid and loan programs. With the high costs and the possibility of drastic reduction in tax deductible contributions from individuals and foundations, Lutheran colleges along with other private colleges faced a crisis of the first magnitude.[38]

Seminary Education

The numerical strength of Lutheran theological schools in the 60s is illustrated by the accompanying enrollment graph. It should be noted that the LCA with eight seminaries counted some over 1,452 students; the Missouri Synod with two, some over 1,590; and the ALC with three, about 1,241.[39]

Beyond these external features Lutheran theological education exhibited some problems which were common to all divinity schools, Protestant and Roman Catholic. Granted that the task of the seminary was to prepare men for the ministry of the church in today's world, several questions were to the fore. One was the definition of terms. In the light of "today's world," which some said was writing the agenda for the church, what was meant by "ministry"? Moreover, what was the "church"? And if one could define "ministry" and "church," was the education which seminarians were receiving "relevant" to the needs of society? The specifically Lutheran aspect of the common problem brought traditional theological formulations and the concept of the functioning ministry under examination. For example, was the following still an adequate expression? Where Christ is present there is the catholic church; Christ is present through the proclamation of the Word of God and administration of the sacraments in accord with that Word; the church, the people of God, created by Word and sacrament from out of the world, is sent back into the world with the ministry of reconciliation beginning with "be *ye* reconciled to God." Is God known only through his Word in Christ, proclaimed in sermon and communicated in sacrament? Or is God present "redemptively" in the "secular world where the action is"? If so, how is "redemptive" to be defined? In an ultimate or penultimate sense? Or both? Is Christ present any place where people are engaged in the liberation of racially and economically oppressed brethren, where men and women are seeking to humanize interpersonal and social relations? If so, what does this say about the traditional concept of the church and ministry? These

SEMINARY
ENROLLMENTS

1960-1969

LCA —————————

ALC * * * * * * * * *

C-MS ●━●━●━●━●━●

VIS —·—·—·—·—·—

LC →━→━→━→━→━

MISC ————————

ata supplied by Office of Research,
atistics and Archives, Lutheran Coun-
l/USA, N.Y.

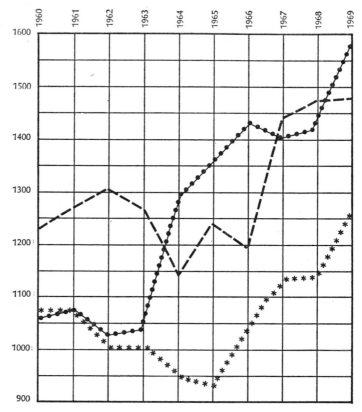

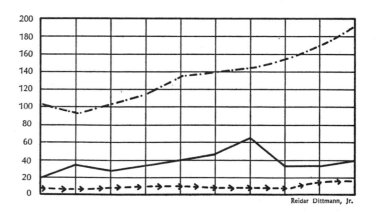

Reidar Dittmann, Jr.

were the kinds of questions with which seminary faculties were being confronted in the 60s.

All schools worked at curriculum revision. The traditional theological departments were Bible (including introduction, exegesis and theology), history (including church history and history of Christian thought), systematic theology (including introduction, dogmatics, and ethics), and practical theology (including liturgics and music, homiletics, catechetics, pastoral care, clinical or field work). Some curricula remained relatively unchanged. Others were adjusted and rearranged within the traditional framework with the purpose of better integration and the reduction of required courses and the increase of elective offerings. The system of lectures, seminars, papers, periodic examinations, and, in some cases, internships remained unaltered. Still others sought change to provide an entirely new way of theological education. It was preparation for a ministry "relevant" to the world. The most highly publicized experiment was conducted at Hamma School of Theology (LCA) in Springfield, Ohio.[40]

The major seminaries recognized the need of developing programs of continuing education for pastors in order that they might be confronted anew with the biblical and theological resources for their ministries. In the LCA the Board of Theological Education developed a program of institutes in cooperation with the seminaries and synods of the church. In The ALC each seminary provided its own program for pastors serving in adjacent regions. In the Missouri Synod the plan was to bring ten-year graduates back to the seminary for "refresher courses" during the summer.[41] In these ways, the church's concern for keeping ministers intellectually alert, theologically knowledgeable, and spiritually sensitive had moved into fruitful operation. In January, 1968, a "Consultation on the Future of Lutheran Theological Education," with representatives of the three major churches present, asked that the boards of theological education "explore ways of developing pan-Lutheran programs of continuing education." The consultation also urged a common approach to internship programs, curriculum studies, faculty development, student recruitment (studies in motivation and the problem of drop-outs), administration and financial development, and ecumenical theological education, in line with the American Association of Theological Schools' idea of "cluster schools." The proposal of "clusters" of seminaries near a university in a metropolitan area had some obvious ecumenical implications: the sharing of faculty members, the coordination of offerings to avoid duplication, the broadening of library resources, the strengthening of graduate schools, and "dialog" with the culture of the secular university. A pioneering effort occurred at Berkeley, California, where Pacific Lutheran Seminary was a vigorous partner in such a "cluster." Variations on this theme were appearing at Chicago, the Twin Cities (Minnesota), Columbus, Dubuque, Philadelphia, and Saskatoon. Although viewed as "dynamic, exhilarating, and avant-garde" by many, there was by no means unanimous support of the idea. Chief criticisms were that it was holding out false hopes of economy, that its ecumenical advantages were overstated, that a secular university was hardly the cement to hold together a Christian enterprise, that far from being avant-garde it was really rear guard. Industry, education, and medicine, rather than "clustering" their operations were decentralizing their work. In other words, the church was once again "behind the times." What seemed "new" to the church was "old hat and being abandoned by others." [42]

Efforts to coordinate and unify Lutheran theological education has had a long history reaching the present decade. Although the two Missouri Synod seminaries (St. Louis and Springfield) had begun to reflect the theological polarization in that church body, both schools participated in inter-Lutheran consultations on theological education. Nevertheless, it should be recognized that the problem of institutional unification of seminaries centered mainly in National Lutheran Council churches, especially in the former United Lutheran Church. In the judgment of some, the latter suffered from an oversupply of small and inadequately equipped schools. Two of its largest and oldest schools, Gettysburg and Philadelphia, had sought unsuccessfully for 50 years (since 1919) to merge. At the founding convention of the LCA (1962), its Board of Theological Education was given the task of preparing a "master plan" to "obtain and maintain the best theological education for our pastors." The report, largely the work of Conrad Bergendoff and hence popularly known as "The Bergendoff Report," saw the necessity of uniting and relocating schools. The church would be best served, said the report, by one seminary in the East, one seminary in the Middle West, one in the South, and one in the Far West.[43] In view of this, merger efforts were resumed between Gettysburg and Philadelphia. The two schools agreed to the appointment of a joint commission of both boards and the election of a common president (1964). After six years of negotiations and failure to agree on the location for a merged seminary, a decision was made on January 20, 1970, to drop the merger effort. The two schools, however, were urged "to continue to function with the closest kind of structured cooperation," despite the fact they would return to "separate presidencies." The Philadelphia Seminary board voted to move to the vicinity of the University of Pennsylvania, sharing the campus of the Divinity School (Episcopal) in West Philadelphia, but later (1971) found it expedient for "fiscal, academic and confessional" reasons to reverse its decision.[44]

Meanwhile in the Middle West, agreement had been reached prior to the formation of the Lutheran Church in America that four seminaries (Augustana, Chicago, Suomi, and Grand View) would merge to form the Lutheran School of Theology at Chicago. These were joined later by Central Seminary, Fremont, Nebraska. In Ohio discussions were being held between the Hamma School of Theology (Springfield) and Evangelical Lutheran Seminary (ALC) looking toward one seminary, perhaps at Columbus. In the Twin Cities, Northwestern moved to the campus of Luther (ALC) in St. Paul in 1967 with the hope that these two institutions would become one. In the Far West some ALC seminarians received a part or all of their theological education at Pacific Seminary (LCA) in Berkeley. In recognition of this The ALC had made an annual grant (since 1963) to Pacific Seminary. The first seminary in North America to be located on the campus of a state-owned university was the new Lutheran Theological Seminary at Saskatoon, Saskatchewan. Theological education in western Canada was begun by the antecedents of the ULCA and eventually also served the Augustana Church and the former ALC. The ELC had begun a separate seminary in Saskatoon in 1939, but later entered cooperative arrangements with the ULCA school. Following The ALC and LCA mergers of 1960 and 1962 serious efforts were made to unite the Saskatoon seminaries. This was accomplished on September 1, 1965, when the two schools merged under a board of regents elected by the ALC/LCA constituency.[45]

The American Lutheran Church began its life in 1960 with the concept of "one seminary" operating as four units (Columbus, Dubuque, St. Paul, Saskatoon). The idea, advanced by T. F. Gullixson, president of Luther Seminary, St. Paul, was proposed as an alternative to a merged seminary at one campus. The theological unity of the Missouri Synod and the former ELC was seen as emanating from the "oneness" of their theological education. Since the ideal of one theological campus for the new church could not be achieved, the legal device (or fiction) was adopted whereby The ALC was *declared* to have but one seminary. Dissatisfaction with the concept led to disunity rather than to the hoped for unity. The exacerbation of frustrations and irritations proved to be a hindrance rather than a help to the cause of theological education. This led ultimately to the abandonment of the concept in 1966.[46]

Among the seminary problems that remained as unfinished business at the end of the decade were the ever-present ones of adequate financing, selection of teaching personnel, confessional and academic standards, continuing education and graduate programs, student recruitment (male and occasionally female), inter-Lutheran and ecumenical (churchly and secular) relations. These and other issues confronted each of the seminaries in particular and promised to provide the working agendas for future consultations and "task forces" on theological education.[47]

Theological Scholarship

Closely related to college and seminary education was the development in the post-World War II era of an academic community of scholars. The names of earlier American Lutherans such as Charles Porterfield Krauth, C. F. W. Walther, Franz Pieper, Georg Sverdrup, Henry Eyster Jacobs, Conrad Lindberg, and J. Michael Reu were little known beyond American Lutheranism. However, the rebirth of theological interest fostered by the emergence of "neo-Lutheranism" associated with such names as C. M. Jacobs, H. C. Alleman, J. W. Richard, Henry Offermann, and A. R. Wentz was nourished in large measure between 1920 and 1925 by American translations of European Lutheran theologians, chiefly German and Scandinavian. The works of Werner Elert, Paul Althaus, Peter Brunner, Hermann Sasse, Edmund Schlink, Karl Heim, Adolph Köberle, Gustav Aulén, Anders Nygren, Olaf Moe, Sigmund Mowinckel, and others began to appear in English. Following World War II American Lutheran scholarship in its own right began to attract attention in other communions.[48] The joint publication (by Fortress Press and Concordia Publishing House) of a new American Edition of Luther's Works, the reading by non-Lutherans of scholarly journals such as *The Lutheran Quarterly, Concordia Theological Monthly, Dialog,* and *Lutheran World,* the publication of *The Encyclopedia of the Lutheran Church,* the appearance of critical histories of church bodies, and similar scholarly enterprises introduced men outside the circle of American Lutheranism to a deeper appreciation of a Lutheran theological heritage which transcended the scholastic categories of an earlier day. At first, the themes which received major attention were doctrinal and historical theology, but in the 60s the focus of interest shifted to social ethics.

FORMS OF WORSHIP AND SERVICE

Congregational Life and Piety

It was popular in the first half of the 1960s to denigrate the local congregation. It was attacked as irrelevant, outdated, and no longer an adequate instrument for Christ's mission. It was a vestigal anachronism, a "medieval" form which simply did not correspond to present reality. [49] After a period of masochistic self-flaggelation in which churchmen cried *mea culpa, mea culpa,* it was discovered that the congregation was after all both more sturdy and more malleable than the proponents of secular theology and churchmanship had judged it. This was asserted in the report of a LCA commission on the nature and mission of the congregation (appointed in 1964) which affirmed the validity of the parish "as a fit instrument for embodying Christ's mission to the world," but also called the churches to self-examination and renewal. Attached to the report was a "Manifesto" to all congregations describing the setting and plotting the direction for a program of renewal.[50] There was no Lutheran church body, "liberal" or "orthodox," that would not applaud the evangelical and evangelistic proclamation of Franklin Clark Fry, president of the LCA:

> The Spirit of God and he alone is the author of renewal. We as individuals and the structures of our churches are best compared to veins and arteries through which he flows. He moves, we receive. What we can do and must do is to pray achingly for him to come, to long for him to refresh us, and to see to it as far as lies in us that the channels in our personal characters and in our institutions are open and clean.

> We Lutherans look for the quickening Spirit to enter our lives through Word and Sacrament, which means primarily in the setting of the congregation, with the church at-large mainly in a

supportive role. . . . In spite of much empty and violent talk that has become no less than a pernicious fad lately, congregations are vital for the health of the church and its renewal. They must be vividly alive, pulsating with the Spirit, or His approach to us is impeded and at worst blocked. . . . *Veni, Creator, Spiritus.*[51]

Recognizing that the church of the Reformation, like every other church, "must always be reformed" *(ecclesia semper reformanda),* most churchmen affirmed the local congregation as the basic instrument for religious renewal.

The piety of Lutherans was exhibited in liturgy, music, arts, and architecture, as well as in "personal religion," church and communion attendance. Despite differing liturgical emphases, Lutherans were not antiliturgical. All had some "form" for public worship, even the most "informal." One of the outgrowths of the earlier liturgical renewal was a desire for a common hymnal and common liturgical form. This was realized in the publication of the *Service Book and Hymnal* in 1958.

The idea of a book for common worship in America was not new. In fact, the "patriarch" Henry Melchior Muhlenberg almost two hundred years earlier had expressed the ideal of "One Church, One Book." [52] In 1934, the American Lutheran Conference authorized a committee to explore the possibilities of a pan-Lutheran book of worship and individual church bodies engaged themselves in "studies" and "revisions." [53] The decisive year, however, was 1944, when the United Lutheran Church (which had carried on the Muhlenberg tradition), invited all Lutherans to cooperate in a common hymnal.[54] This action was implemented by the calling of a conference in June, 1945, at Pittsburgh. Persons belonging to four of the National Lutheran Council churches (ALC, Augustana, ELC, and ULCA) organized the Joint Commission on a Common Hymnal. The success of this commission led the Augustana Synod representatives to propose (September, 1945) a Joint Commission on a Common Liturgy, which first met in February, 1946, in Chicago. In this manner, the basic teams were at hand for the production of a common service book and hymnal by five churches of the National Lutheran Council (UELC joined in September, 1945). The Synodical Conference churches, having been invited to participate, declined to join the project. Missouri President J. W. Behnken said " . . . our Synod recently published a new Hymnal. Our Synod would not be interested now in effecting another change." [55]

By March, 1946, representatives of four churches (ULC, ALC, Augustana, UELC) reported overwhelming approval of the joint hymnal, but the ELC executively-selected appointee indicated that his church "would probably not co-operate in the publication of a Common Hymnal. . . . " [56] This attitude had not been reported to the ELC. Although the minutes of 1946 indicated "interest in the movement toward a common hymn-book . . . , " [57] the constituency of the church had received no progress reports through official organs and was therefore only dimly aware that conferences were being held. In July, 1946, the official journal of the American Lutheran Conference carried the first public announcement that the ELC "has indicated that it will not participate in the publication of the new book." [58] No reasons were given. This announcement, how-ever, served to trigger a minor "revolt" among pastors against what seemed to be a unilateral decision by the chief executive of the church, the management of the publishing house, and the Board of Publications, whose chairman was the president's appointee to represent ELC interests on the joint commission. When pressure was brought to bear by the organized opposition, especially at a caucus of ELC delegates to the 1946 convention of the American Lutheran Conference in Rockford, Ill., the ELC Church Council *officially* elected two representatives, one being the previous appointee. This proved to be the necessary new beginning that led the ELC into approval and use of the joint hymnal.[59]

With this accomplished, there remained a multitude of problems such as selection of tunes and texts, seeking new hymns, reworking the former "Common Service," and making it usable, not least by "the old lady with the bifocals." [60]

By the end of the decade the *Service Book and Hymnal* was being used by almost all the congregations of the Lutheran Church in America and The American Lutheran Church. Like other hymnals before it, it served the cause of unity at the congregational level in a manner which no amount of theological treatises could ever have accomplished. Containing 602 hymns of Greek, Latin, German, Scandinavian, British, and Ameri-can origin it reflected some of the richness of ecumenical hymnody. Liturgically, the commission felt under no obligation to repristinate the "Common Service." However, working from this Lutheran base and other Lutheran services, it recovered for use some pertinent forms from the early church, thus blending the liturgical tradition of the Eastern and

Western churches. Some new features were an unfamiliar (to Lutherans) text for the *Kyrie,* a series of Old Testament lessons, a new prayer for the church, the restoration of the prayer of thanksgiving (eucharistic prayer), complete musical settings for the liturgy, Matins, Vespers, and the Litany. In addition, the commission prepared forms for Occasional Services (baptism, confirmation, marriage, burial, etc.) and several offices supplementary to the Occasional Services.

With the publication and general use of the new book of worship, weaknesses—such as occasional rigid traditionalisms and theological vacuities hitherto not noted—began to be recognized and the question was inevitably raised as to the need for a completely new hymnal. Moreover, the Lutheran Church–Missouri Synod was now being drawn closer to other churches and expressed its desire in 1965 to cooperate with all American Lutheran bodies "in developing hymnological and liturgical materials." [61] At the invitation of the Missouri Synod, representatives of the LCA, ALC, the Synod of Evangelical Lutheran Churches (SELC) and the Evangelical Lutheran Church of Canada (ELCC) organized the Inter-Lutheran Commission on Worship, February 11, 1966, after hearing a series of historical and programmatic papers (published as *Liturgical Reconnaissance* [1968]). Four sub-committees, or "working committees," were subsequently established with responsibilities for hymn text, hymn tunes, liturgy, and liturgical music. Between 1966 and 1969 one and two meetings were held annually. At its second gathering, ILCW adopted a statement of purpose which stated that "the immediate goal of the commission was to produce materials which are to include (1) new liturgical forms that are contemporary in text and music; (2) new hymns that are contemporary in text and music; and (3) contemporary versions of existing worship forms that are common to the participating churches." [62] Very quickly the commission was made aware of the ecumenical significance of its work. It was reported that all denominations were "in a state of ferment" as far as the life of worship was concerned. Roman Catholics, Episcopalians, and Presbyterians were all faced with a liturgical situation which one observer described as "a mess." [63] The Consultation on Church Union (COCU), a Protestant outgrowth of the well-known Blake Proposal for a united church ("evangelical, catholic, reformed") had established a Commission on Worship whose sessions in 1967 were attended by representatives of the ILCW. It was discovered that common interests dictated a common approach to some problems. In keeping with this discovery the ILCW extended an invitation to the International Committee on English in the Liturgy of the Roman Catholic Church and to the Committee on Worship of COCU to collaborate on common wordings "for the Our Father and the Apostles' and Nicene Creeds . . . , " and that this effort be extended to include "other liturgical formularies such as the Gloria in Excelsis, Sanctus, Te Deum, etc." [64] By 1969 representatives of the Lutheran, Roman Catholic, and COCU churches had held several meetings of the "Consultation on Common Texts" (CCT) in America and participated in one overseas conference (London, April 19-21, 1969), the "International Consultation on English Texts" (ICET). As a result of the work accomplished in these conferences, CCT issued a series of proposed common texts for consideration by the churches. These included the Lord's Prayer, the Apostles' and Nicene Creeds, Gloria in Excelsis, Sanctus, Agnus Dei, Gloria Patri, Nunc Dimittis, and Te Deum. In each case the intention of the Consultation was to render the liturgical texts accurately and in a contemporary idiom.[65]

The work of the Inter-Lutheran Commission on Worship received acclaim from some observers and negative criticism from others. The editor of the *Lutheran Quarterly* (February, 1967) connected the liturgical movement which had fructified in the *Service Book and Hymnal* (1958) and the new ILCW. The former, it was said, represented "a phase of the liturgical movement"; it was a consensus-type approach to the problem. The latter marked the change from liturgical adolescence to maturity which would demonstrate the centrality of corporate worship in the structure of Lutheran devotional life.[66] The editor of the *Lutheran Forum*, however, was less enthusiastic, observing that the proposals of the ILCW were unsatisfactory theologically, liturgically, and linguistically. This weakness was traced to the neglect of the "Basic Principles for the Ordering of the Main Worship Service in the Evangelical Lutheran Church" issued by the Lutheran World Federation in 1957. Had these "Basic Principles" been considered, the Lutheran liturgical *aggiornamento* might be comparable to that in the church of Rome which began with the "Constitution on the Sacred Liturgy" of Vatican II.[67]

The liturgy commonly used in Lutheran congregations included certain invariable items (the Ordinary) and some variable (the Propers). The latter corresponded to the changing Sundays and festivals of the church year. The Service was composed of three parts: the Office of Confession, the Office of the Word, and the Office of Holy Communion. The outline follows:

Preliminary Office of Confession
> Invocation
> Confession of Sins
> > Invitation
> > Versicles
> > Confession
> > Declaration of Grace

Office of the Word
> Introit for the Day with Gloria Patri
> Kyrie
> Gloria in Excelsis
> Collect with Salutation and Oremus
> (Old Testament Lesson)
> (Hymn)
> Epistle for the Day
> Gradual for the Day (or Alleluia or Gradual for the Season)
> Gospel for the Day with Gloria Tibi and Laus Tibi
> Creed
> The Hymn
> Sermon

Office of the Holy Communion
> Offering
> Offertory
> Prayer of the Church
> (Hymn)
> (Benediction, if Holy Communion is not celebrated)
> The Thanksgiving
> > Hymn
> > Preface
> > > Sursum Corda
> > > Vere Dignum
> > > Proper Preface
> > > Sanctus
> > Prayer of Thanksgiving (or simply The Words of
> > Institution)

Pax
Agnus Dei
The Communion with Distribution and Blessing
The Post-Communion
Nunc Dimittis
Prayer with Versicle and Collect
Salutation and Benedicamus
Benediction

In addition to the officially church-sponsored cooperative efforts to aid the congregations in their life of worship, there were parallel efforts of a more informal nature. The Valparaiso Liturgical Institute (since 1959) chiefly made up of Missouri Synod Lutherans, tended towards liturgical "restoration." On the other hand, the Lutheran Society for Worship, Music and the Arts, with its journal *Response,* sought to strike the note of contemporaneity, urging cultural awareness. Whatever the mood and direction of the liturgical movement in Lutheranism, one thing had become clear at the end of the decade: renewal in worship was as much a part of the Lutheran churches as it was of the "mainline" Protestant churches and Roman Catholicism. The large question that loomed before the church was the relation between continuity and change—formal and substantive —in the desire to be contemporary, ecumenical, and Lutheran.

In a church that made so much of the Word of God in its doctrinal formulations, liturgical expressions, and pulpit declarations, there was a notable lack of highly-esteemed American Lutheran preachers. Oswald C. J. Hoffmann, who carried on the work of the late Walter Maier on the Missouri Synod's "Lutheran Hour," was well-known and commanded an appreciative audience in some Lutheran and non-Lutheran circles. Edmund A. Steimle (LCA), professor of homiletics at Union Seminary, was likewise widely known, but by an audience different from that of the "Lutheran Hour." Beyond these two, few, if any, Lutheran preachers were familiar names in the American Christian community. The cause of this paucity is almost impossible to isolate. It was no consolation to Lutherans that other Christian churches suffered from the same malaise, but it might indicate that proclamation as such had come on evil days in the action-oriented 60s. Some were wondering about the future of preaching and proposing new forms of ministry and new definitions of "proclamation." [68]

New Ministries, Evangelism, Auxiliaries

The decade also saw the continuation of trends apparent in the immediate post-World War II years. The rapidly changing social scene led the churches to set up commissions to study the nature and function of ministry in the modern world.[69] In large cities, for example, attempts were made to conduct "industrial missions" or a ministry among both management and labor. Out of this there developed, in some instances, a critical analysis of the values enshrined in the corporate systems represented by business leaders on the one hand and labor leaders and organized minority groups on the other. Alongside this there were other so-called "experimental ministries," such as that undertaken by the "jazz pastor," John B. Gensel, in New York City. "Coffee house" ministries sprang up in Washington, D.C. and near university campuses in large cities. The traditional "campus ministry" of the churches was being reexamined.[70] Furthermore, mobile ministries among vacationers in national parks and ski resorts were begun. Inter-congregational or "merged pastorates" were initiated.[71] Conferences and studies were held on the ministry to "town and country," because churchmen had become disturbed by what was happening to religious life in rural sections of Mid-America.[72] All of these areas reflected the serious efforts of the churches to fulfill their ministerial role in the midst of a turbulent world.

Closely allied with these developments was a burgeoning interest in chaplaincy services among the socially disadvantaged and spiritually crippled: the mentally ill, alcoholics and drug addicts, unwed mothers and fathers, etc. In the early 60s the Division of Welfare of the National Lutheran Council turned its attention to the upgrading of chaplaincy services. Its work took three forms. One was to let the council serve as a clearinghouse and consultation agency for the widespread Lutheran welfare societies that maintained chaplaincy services. Another function was to be a liaison with governmental agencies to insure the ministry of Lutheran chaplains in Veterans Administration hospitals and in federal prisons (the Missouri Synod coordinated its activities in this area with those of the NLC). The third sphere of involvement was clinical pastoral education (CPE). The popularity and importance of clinical experience in the preparation of pastors for specialized ministries as well as for the regular congregational ministry, led the council to appoint a staff secretary who worked closely with seminaries in setting up standards and curricula to assure some competence in what was a highly specialized service. Moreover, it provided accreditation for chaplains supervising the training of other ministries in this specialty.[73]

As these various ministries emerged, the allied question of evangelism *per se* quite naturally came under scrutiny. Did evangelism require a "new face" in the contemporary scene? Was door-to-door visitation and invitations to attend church ("churchly evangelism") much more than an institutional preoccupation with statistics? Were the mass rallies à la Billy Graham adequate for what some called "the post-Christian era"? Were Preaching-Teaching-Reaching missions—so effective in the 50s— "running out of gas"? Although these and similar questions were raised,[74] attempts to "evangelize" men continued generally to follow the patterns of earlier years. Externally these efforts seemed to meet with some success. The "revivalistic pattern" was apparent in the United States Congress on Evangelism held in Minneapolis during the second week of September, 1969. The congress drew together "neo-evangelical" representatives of several denominations (including the three major Lutheran bodies), heard Billy Graham; Oswald Hoffmann, congress-chairman and speaker on the Missouri Synod's "Lutheran Hour"; and Ralph Abernathy of the Southern Christian Leadership Conference. Described as a turning away from fundamentalistic revivalism ("soul saving") to a full-orbed emphasis on the significance of the gospel for the present age as well as the age to come, the congress was termed an evangelistic watershed.[75] Nevertheless, congregational ("churchly evangelism") and "personal evangelism" continued to receive emphasis in the official reports of evangelism commissions in most of the Lutheran church bodies [76] as the decade of the 60s drew to a close. However, a "re-thinking of evangelism" was being called for by theologians and churchmen as the new decade dawned. It was argued that social action, Christian "presence," silent service, door-to-door visitation— all of them important ministries—were not to be equated with evangelism, which, in the strict sense, "means the spoken ministry of the Christians to individuals who have had little or no prior connection with the Christian faith." But, in the new situation, evangelism must be seen as *relational* [italics added]:

> There still is a concern for the eternal welfare of the neighbor, but it is placed in relation to a concern for his temporal welfare and fulfillment. There still is a sharp consciousness of sin, but it

serves a corrective rather than a deterrent to action. There still is the call for a Christian style of life, but that style is seen as a disciplined servanthood to the neighbor. There is still an involvement in the life of the whole people of God, but it comes as a result and not as a prerequisite of the life of service.[77]

Important in all the above-mentioned ministries of the church was what was technically called "the general ministry" or "the universal priesthood" of the *laos* (*laos* = people; hence the word "laity") of God. Clergymen, strictly speaking, are a part of the "laity." Nevertheless, the church had become accustomed to think of "laymen" as the unordained ministers of God. And although much of the ministry of these laymen could be subsumed under the rubrics of "special ministries" and "evangelism," in most instances the churches provided auxiliary or ancillary organizations oriented to special lay groups. Hence there had been organized men's groups, women's societies, and youth associations, all of which altered with the times. The history of these various auxiliaries showed that men's organizations (e.g., Lutheran Brotherhood, Lutheran Laymen's League, Lutheran Church Men) functioned best when there were specific projects to be undertaken. The Lutheran Laymen's League, for example, flourished as an auxiliary of the Missouri Synod when it was challenged to provide financial support for "The Lutheran Hour." [78] It was only natural that it consequently exercised considerable influence within the synod. In the late 60s it was suggested that the league had become a powerful political force for ecclesiastical conservatism.[79] The Lutheran Laymen's Movement of the ULCA and later of the LCA filled a similar, if less spectacular, role as it made the development of the stewardship of money the major focus of its program. However, the Lutheran Church Men as a church-wide auxiliary of the LCA led a desultory existence and ended its official operations in 1966.[80] The men's auxiliary of The ALC (The American Lutheran Church Men) sought with modest success simultaneously to encourage Bible study and prayer, to foster social action by the church, and to encourage work among boys. It must be admitted, however, that the congregational men's clubs were something less than the pulse-beat of the church.[81]

It was a different story with the women's groups. In all Lutheran bodies the original purpose of the women's organizations was largely the support of foreign missions. This was reflected in their official names: The Women's Missionary Society (ULCA and Augustana), Women's

Missionary Federation (ALC and ELC), and Women's Missionary League (Missouri). The parish "ladies' aids" or "guilds" later expanded their understanding of "mission" to include support of home missions, the churches' educational and charitable institutions, and, especially in the LCA and ALC, the social action programs of the churches. The women's auxiliaries of the two latter bodies noted this broadened emphasis when they dropped the word "missionary" from their official names.[82] A decline in women's work was noted most markedly in the large cities during the 50s and 60s. The increased number of "working wives," the exodus to the suburbs, and, to some extent, the fear of attending evening meetings unescorted were contributing factors in the recession of interest especially in congregations located in heavily populated and urbanized centers.

The youth program of the churches, like that of other auxiliary enterprises, underwent considerable alteration in the post-World War II years. The Lutheran churches traditionally placed a great emphasis on parish education, culminating in a sense with catechetical instruction prior to confirmation. A major and perennial problem was the "dropout" of young people following confirmation, which ordinarily occurred between ages 13 and 15. In view of the high mortality at this point two youth-oriented instruments were used to "hold and win young people for Christ and the church." One was the carefully worked out "high school curriculum" to foster a post-confirmation religious education program. The other was the encouragement of youth organizations known as the Luther Leagues in the LCA and The ALC and the Walther League (named after C. F. W. Walther) in the Missouri Synod. All of the youth organizations had administrative offices on the national level which sought to aid the local churches in their efforts to engage the interests, loyalty, and service of the youth. Program materials, films, and youth "experts" were made available for these purposes. Summer church camps (see reference to "Bible Camp" movement in Chapter II) and large national youth conventions—largely of a devotional, inspirational nature—were part of the pattern.

Youth work was never easy, but since the war years it had become increasingly difficult. Changes of emphases seemed necessary. Up to World War II the Luther Leagues and Walther Leagues were primarily a young *adult* movement.[83] As early as 1946 the ULCA convention called for a "Comprehensive Survey of Youth Work." [84] This resulted in constitutional changes in the mid-50s which gave more autonomy to synodical units and introduced a five-fold program emphasizing evangelism, vocation, missions, recreation, and social action.[85] Following the formation of the Lutheran Church in America (1962), the youth program of the new church again came under scrutiny. Congregations and synods questioned the value of the LCA's youth program because it perpetuated parallel structures for youth work: a youth-run organization and an adult "youth" board for direction. By 1968 the Luther League, *as a youth auxiliary on the national level,* was eliminated and a Commission on Youth Ministry, combining youth and adults, was established. A major criticism of the auxiliary as such had been that it created the illusion that the church's responsibility for youth was discharged by providing a "program-centered" ministry that segregated young people as "the church of tomorrow," thus tending to keep them from present participation in the "total life of the church." The new youth ministry urged that young people be recognized as full members of the church, participants in the whole mission of the church, not in some ancillary or "auxiliary" organization.[86] The ministry of youth should be carried out locally, determined by the mission of the congregation in its community in a two-fold manner: (1) a ministry by youth to youth and (2) a joint ministry with adults in the furtherance of mutually-held goals.[87]

Youth work in The American Lutheran Church followed a somewhat similar pattern, although The ALC stress on and success with national youth conventions was more pronounced. The so-called "dual structure" of the work was developed to a high degree of sophistication by the 1960 merger. The adult side of the duality consisted of a divisional board for supervising various youth ministries including study groups, experimental programs, leadership training, camping, and focus on junior high and young adult groups. The "youth side" of the duality was the Luther League, directed by the youth themselves focusing on the high school age group.[88]

The Lutheran Church—Missouri Synod likewise found itself altering its youth program during the 60s. The synod's Board for Young People's Work was given a larger staff and budget in 1967. Recognizing that the once flourishing Walther League was no longer a young adult movement with leaders ranging from 20 to 30 years of age (leaguers were usually between 13 and 17), a way was sought to bring youth into the leadership of the stumbling Walther League. In 1968, the League was reorganized to eliminate intermediate (district, circuit) structures and to stress local and regional ministries served by volunteer full-time youth workers. Thus the synod itself assumed responsibility for youth ministry; and the Walther League, as a church-wide auxiliary, became a youth-led issue-oriented movement. Rather than being the source of structured programming, the church's Board for Young People's Work would become an agency for youth research and a resource for local Walther Leagues.[89]

In summary, one can say that youth work in all branches of American Lutheranism experienced the disappearance of the "adult" from its leadership. The inability and disinterest of high school youth to administer organizations which, in the past, adults and young adults had created and effectively managed, and the desire for local service and action ministries rather than structured programming from "above" led to a new understanding of youth work that recognized young people as an integral part of the people of God and not as an entity known as "the church of the future." This meant increased leadership and decision-making by the young people themselves.

Church and World

The religious "revival" of the 1950s was submitted to a severe critique by numerous sociologists and historians of religion in America.[90] The common charge was that religion was in danger of being too closely allied with the American ethos. To be American was to be identified with some church. The resultant "culture-religion" was generally content with the status quo.

Theoretically, Lutherans were opposed to all forms of "culture-religion," assuming in some instances a position described by H. Richard Niebuhr's phrase, "Christ against culture." They defended their attitude by pointing to the eschatological theme of the Bible and by putting divine transcendence against immanence, the latter being a hallmark of liberalism. In so doing (1) they misinterpreted, or at least gave one-sided emphasis to, a facet of Lutheran theology, and (2) they did not escape captivity to American culture by minimizing the public and prophetic role of the church. As a matter of fact, Lutheran congregations across the land in the prosperous 50s gave evidence that they were enamoured of the desire for popular approval and success. Accepting uncritically the approbation of middle class

America, Lutheranism was in danger of becoming what its theology did not allow, a "culture-religion."

In the 60s, however, the church like the rest of American society was involved in rapid and, at times, overwhelming change. Politically, American Lutherans no longer felt the need to vote against a Catholic candidate for the presidency. In fact, the official organ of the conservative Missouri Synod carried an article which, though it warned against Roman Catholic political power, insisted that John F. Kennedy should have the right to seek the presidency.[91] Some consternation occurred when a group of prominent Lutheran theologians issued a pre-election endorsement of Kennedy.[92] Nevertheless, the Kennedy candidacy, like the problems of the depression years, led the Lutherans to face the question of the political role of the churches.

In like manner, the churches found it necessary to react to profound issues raised by the problems of racial integration and civil rights in the first half of the 60s and "black power" and urban riots and violence in the remainder of the decade. Added to this was the social turmoil engendered by the war in Southeast Asia, the subsequent campus unrest, and conscientious objection to the government's Vietnam policy and war in general. The deterioration of American cities, especially in the "ghettos," the growing problem of poverty, and the increasing dismay over ecological imbalance and the population explosion—all these and more were questions which pressed themselves upon the churches, forcing churchmen to face the sober reality that continuance of life on the planet Earth could be in jeopardy.

Increasingly conscious of criticism that they were guilty of social ethical "quietism," and yet unwilling to capitulate to pressures for a "social gospel," Lutheran theologians and boards of social action began to define the public role of the church in terms of a de-scholasticized Lutheran doctrine of "the two-realms" which taught that through the presently available eschatological gospel of forgiveness and reconciliation God frees believers to cooperate with all men, Christian and non-Christian ("secular ecumenism") in God's "kingdom of the left" to establish peace and justice in the *seculum*. The ultimate character of righteousness by grace through faith does not separate a Christian from seeking penultimate righteousness on earth, but rather encourages him to cast himself with abandon into the problems of the so-called "secular" world. At the same time, the individual does not become a Christian by social action ("works"), but by grace through faith.

With this kind of theological undergirding the major branches of American Lutheranism issued position papers on social and political problems, encouraged new ministries, and channeled increasing sums of money into direct social action.[93] This did not meet with unanimous support. In fact, the churches on both the national and local levels were being polarized into "left" and "right" elements. The "left," in so far as they were theologically motivated, charged Lutheranism with being ethically listless and unable to face the radical demands of a "political theology." The "right," unable to appreciate the Lutheran dialectic that kept evangelical proclamation and social action in tension, charged that the "spiritual" character of the church was being eroded by a new "liberalism." As the 70s dawned, these polarities were compounded by decline in church attendance and financial support, all of which served to magnify the explosive nature of the unresolved problems that Lutherans in common with other Christians faced at the beginning of a new decade.

NOTES

1. The four largest and most powerful churches by 1789 were the Congregationalists, the Anglicans, the Baptists, and the Presbyterians. The Lutherans and German Reformed ranked fifth and sixth respectively. Sidney E. Mead, "Denominationalism: The Shape of Protestantism in America," *Church History*, XXIII (December, 1954), 293-294.

2. LCA, *Minutes . . . 1964*, pp. 39-40.

3. *The Lutheran*, (March 19, 1969), 26.

4. ALC, *Reports and Actions . . . 1964*, pp. 230-233.

5. "American Lutherans Report Membership . . . , " News Bureau 69-93, Lutheran Council/USA, New York, p. 2; *ibid.*, News Bureau 70-91, Aug. 24, 1970, pp. 2-3.

6. Lutheran Church–Missouri Synod, *Proceedings . . . 1965*, pp. 22-28.

7. *Ibid. . . . , 1967*, p. 75.

8. ALC, *Pre-Convention Report . . . 1968*, p. 343.

9. The installation (February 11, 1968) of Arne Sovik, former director of the World Mission Department (LWF), as executive secretary of LCA World Missions became the occasion for a consultation in depth on world missions. The entire issue of *World Encounter*, V (July, 1968), publication of the LCA Board of World Missions, was devoted to this subject.

10. *Ibid.*, p. 14 *et passim*.

11. See editorials, *American Lutheran*, XLVIII (May, 1965), 3-4; *ibid.*, August, 1965, pp. 3-6. Cf. R. J. Neuhaus, "The Song of the Three Synods: Detroit, 1965," *Una Sancta*, XXII (Trinity, 1965), 32-45.

12. Lutheran Church–Missouri Synod, *Proceedings . . . 1965*, p. 80. "The Kretzmann Report" in its entirety is printed in *Convention Workbook . . . 1965*, pp. 112-140. One should note how closely the main ideas parallel the ULCA's "Washington Declaration" (1920) and "Savannnah Declaration" (1934).

13. *American Lutheran,* XLVIII (August, 1965), 5. Progressives felt that Missouri officialdom was by-passing the Kretzmann Report as too controversial. See "Who's Killing the Kretzmann Report?" *Inner City. A Newsletter for Lutherans,* June, 1966, p. 3.

14. *Lutheran Standard,* (July 7, 1969), and News Bureau 68-75, LC/USA, New York, November 26, 1968.

15. "A Proposal for the Establishment of a World Church Institute," (published statement [Geneva: June, 1969]). No authors listed but the director of the Summer Institute informed the writer that three men collaborated: M. L. Kretzmann, Wayne Ewing, and Donald C. Flatt.

16. LCA, Board of World Missions, *Minutes . . . April, 1970.* Cf. Lutheran Council/USA, News Releases, May 7, 1970, and May 21, 1970; and *The Lutheran Standard,* (May 26, 1970), 28.

17. The word "former" refers to the fact that the Missouri Synod in 1967 saw no useful purpose being served by the conference and voted to dissolve it. LC-MS, *Proceedings . . . 1967,* p. 99.

18. Ronald L. Johnstone, *The Effectiveness of the Lutheran Elementary and Secondary Schools as Agencies of Christian Education* (St. Louis: Concordia Seminary, 1966), p. 146. For a history of Lutheran parochial education see Walter A. Beck, *Lutheran Elementary Schools in the United States* (2nd rev. ed.; St. Louis: Concordia Publishing House, 1965).

19. See William A. Kramer, "The Johnstone Study of Lutheran Schools," *Concordia Theological Monthly,* XXXVIII (January, 1967), 23-36; and Ronald L. Johnstone, "A Response to the Kramer Review," *ibid.,* pp. 37-38. Cf. criticism of Roman Catholic parochial education: Mary Perkins Ryan, *Are Parochial Schools the Answer?* (New York: Holt, Rinehart, and Winston, 1964).

20. LCA, *Minutes . . . 1964,* pp. 393-394.

21. ULCA, *Minutes . . . 1942,* pp. 395-396.

22. The published statement was called *Parish Education. A Statement of Basic Principles and a Program of Christian Education* (Philadelphia: The Board of Parish Education, ULCA, [1954-1955]). See the Board report in ULCA, *Minutes . . . 1956,* pp. 716-750.

23. *Ibid.,* pp. 731-733.

24. *A Program for Long Range Cooperation in Parish Education* (n. p.: n. d.), pp. 15-16.

25. ELC, *Annual Report . . . 1956,* pp. 118-119.

26. Interview: C. Richard Evenson-ECN, Aug. 21, 1968; and W. Kent Gilbert-ECN, April 6, 1970. The ULCA's position was partially explained by the fact that it had already invested large sums and a decade of study in the LRP. Moreover, it feared that the ELC and the new ALC would use supplementary materials to "correct" the ULCA theology.

27. Joint Union Committee, "Minutes, October 2-4, 1957," pp. 171-172; Permanent File, Minutes, Joint Union Committee, Vol. II, 1957, Augsburg Publishing House, Minneapolis.

28. ELC, *Annual Report . . . 1958,* pp. 107-108. The old ALC was reluctant to withdraw. Its convention in 1958 requested the JUC to reconsider inter-Lutheran cooperation in parish education. A similar spirit had been expressed by editor E. W. Schramm of the ALC's official organ. Cf. Joint Union Committee, "Minutes, November 13-14, 1958" and *The Lutheran Standard,* (November 30, 1957), 21.

29. Interview: C. Richard Evenson-ECN, Aug. 21, 1968. Heinecken's lectures were printed by the students of the seminary in their publication, *The Voice,* in early 1958.

30. "Report of Committee on the State of the Church," Eastern District, American Lutheran Church, June 18, 1958, pp. 5-6. This report is only referred to in the official minutes.

31. LCA, *Minutes, 1964,* pp. 394-396; *ALC, Reports and Actions . . . 1964,* pp. 328-333. Interview: W. Kent Gilbert-ECN, April 6, 1970.

32. The following documents supplied by The ALC office of Parish Education and Lloyd Svendsbye, Augsburg editor-in-chief, have been consulted: "A Plan for Developing a Comprehensive Program of Parish Education . . . ALC and LCA, April 30, 1969"; "A Central Objective for Educational Ministry . . . ALC and LCA, September 1, 1969"; "Minutes, Joint Program Coordinating Committee . . . , September 23, 1969"; and "Subcommittee on Parish Education, Joint Program Coordinating Committee, November 6-7, 1969."

33. *The Lutheran Standard,* (June 10, 1969), 23. Through the assistance of Gilbert, Evenson, and Svendsbye the writer has had access to unpublished minutes and papers which present the Joint Program of Parish Education in detail.

34. Lutheran Church-MS, *Proceedings . . . 1965,* pp. 157-158; and ALC, *Reports and Actions, 1966,* p. 376.

35. Frank W. Klos, *Confirmation and First Communion. A Study Book* (Philadelphia, Minneapolis, St. Louis: Augsburg Publishing House; Board of Publication, LCA; Concordia Publishing House, 1968). The "Report for Study" is bound as a supplement to this book.

36. See National Lutheran Educational Conference, "Lutheran Schools Experience Large Enrollment Increases," January 7, 1962; pp. 1, 3-6; and News Bureau Release, Office of Research, Statistics and Archives, Lutheran Council/USA, January 3, 1968, pp. 1, 3; and *ibid.,* January 8, 1970, pp. 1-2.

37. Another form of "voluntary association" is that reflected in Golden Valley Lutheran Junior College, Minneapolis. Its board consists of interested individuals who do not represent any church body although most, if not all, are Lutherans.

38. Hartwick College (LCA, Oneonta, N.Y.) terminated its ties with the church in 1968 in order to be eligible for New York state aid. See News Bureau Release (68-109), Lutheran Council/USA, New York, N.Y., November 12, 1968, pp. 1-2.

39. The statistical reports are from the Office of Research, Statistics and Archives, Lutheran Council/USA, New York, News Bureau Release 68-121 and 70-2.

40. Carl T. Uehling, "Fantastic!" *The Lutheran,* (June 18, 1969), 5-9; cf. *The Lutheran,* (July 16, 1969), 49: "I would like to know how it [curriculum revision] works in the areas of language, hermeneutics, and how it equips a future pastor for bringing people . . . to Christ, which is really the touchstone of the whole effort."

41. See *The Lutheran,* (March 13, 1968), 32; ALC seminary catalogs for 1968; and Lutheran Church–Missouri Synod, *Convention Workbook . . . 1969,* pp. 264-265.

42. Luther A. Gotwald, Jr., "Clustered Seminaries? No! Ecumenical School of Theology? Yes!" *Lutheran Forum,* III (January, 1969), 12-14.

43. *The Lutheran Church in America and Theological Education. A Report to the Board of Theological Education* (New York, 1963), p. 45.

44. *The Lutheran,* (March 4, 1970), 25; *ibid.,* (April 25, 1970), 50; *ibid.,* (April 21, 1971), 29; and Lutheran Council/USA News Release, May 15, 1970, p. 4. Donald Heiges became president of Gettysburg in 1962 and was elected president of both schools in May, 1964. Cf. H. F. Baughman, "The Story of Merger Negotiations," *Gettysburg Seminary Bulletin* (1962), pp. 15-21

45. For a helpful discussion of the seminary situation see E. T. Bachmann, "Historical Sketch of Lutheran Theological Education in North America" (unpublished paper presented at Inter-Lutheran Consultation on Seminary Education, Chicago, 1965); see "Minutes . . . Sept. 17-18, 1965," p. 3. Cf. article on "Theological Schools," *The Encyclopedia of the Lutheran Church,* III, 2373-2384. In addition, the reports of the two Boards of Theological Education appearing in the official minutes of the LCA and ALC between 1964 and 1968 should be consulted.

46. ALC, *Reports and Actions . . . 1964,* p. 278; and *ibid.,* 1966, pp. 308, 631.

47. ALC, *Reports and Actions . . . 1968,* pp. 413-417. Cf. "The Future of Our

Seminaries," *The Lutheran Quarterly*, XVIII (November, 1966). Cf. Release, News Bureau 70-92, Lutheran Council/USA, August 20, 1970, pp. 1-2.

48. Some of the better known names were Conrad Bergendoff, Joseph Sittler, T. A. Kantonen, T. G. Tappert, Jaroslav J. Pelikan, Edgar M. Carlson, Warren Quanbeck, Martin J. Heinecken, Jerald C. Brauer, Martin Marty, and Sydney E. Ahlstrom.

49. A spate of books and articles with titles such as "Where in the World?," "What in the World?," and "The Secular City," were directed to the problem of "relevancy."

50. LCA, *Minutes . . . 1966*, pp. 539-564.

51. LCA, *Minutes . . . 1964*, p. 39.

52. Luther D. Reed, "Introduction to the New Common Liturgy," *The Lutheran Quarterly*, II (August, 1950), 268.

53. E. E. Ryden, "The Common Hymnal," *ibid.*, pp. 269-271.

54. ULCA, *Minutes . . . 1944*, p. 436.

55. *Report of the Joint Commission on the Liturgy* (printed by the Muhlenberg Press, Philadelphia, 1948), p. 3.

56. ULCA, *Minutes . . . 1946*, p. 393.

57. NLCA, *Annual Report . . . 1946*, p. 41.

58. *The Lutheran Outlook*, XI (July, 1946), 195-196.

59. The ELC, *Annual Report . . . 1948*, pp. 16, 29, 491-492. Cf. E. E. Ryden, "The Common Hymnal," *The Lutheran Quarterly*, II (August, 1950), 277-278. The ELC president was asked what prevented ELC participation. He replied that the ULCA would dominate the commission; that meant that both ULCA theology and spirit would be reflected in the book. To illustrate this he mentioned that one of the proposed hymns was by the noted liberal, Harry Emerson Fosdick, and the mere name Fosdick would make it unacceptable to the ELC. The objectionable hymn was "God of Grace and God of Glory." E. E. Ryden, "We're Singing New Songs," *The Lutheran*, April 1, 1970, p. 12. The ELC apparently had no objections to hymns by such theological liberals as John Greenleaf Whittier (Quaker) and John Bowring (Unitarian), whose texts were included. President-emeritus C. M. Granskou (St. Olaf College), a member of the Board of Publication (ELC) at the time, has called attention to the role of a ULCA layman, J. K. Jensen, who persuaded ELC leaders (Jensen was equally at home in the ULCA and the ELC) to support the common hymnal. See C. M. Granskou Papers; letter: Granskou-ECN, 2/22/71; St. Olaf College Archives, Northfield, Minn.

60. For an account of the work of the Joint Commissions, see Edward T. Horn III, "Preparation of the Service Book and Hymnal," in *Liturgical Reconnaissance*, ed. Edgar S. Brown, Jr. (Philadelphia: Fortress Press, 1968), pp. 91-101. The "old lady in bifocals" was Horn's mother who prodded her son and through him the commission, to remember the "people."

61. A. R. Kretzmann, "The Definition of the Task Before Us," in *Liturgical Reconnaissance*, pp. 131-133.

62. "Report of the Inter-Lutheran Commission on Worship," ALC, *Reports and Actions . . . 1968*, p. 506. The full text is to be found in *ibid.*, p. 501. Minutes of the ILCW (unpublished) have been made available to the writer through the ALC office of the Commission on Worship and Church Music, 422 S. 5th Street, Minneapolis.

63. ALC, *Reports and Actions . . . 1968*, p. 503.

64. Minutes of the Third Meeting of the ILCW, November 9-10, 1967, Chicago, Ill., pp. 14-15.

65. The following have been made available to the writer by Charles Anders, a member of one of the Working Committees of ILCW: The Minutes of the Consultation on Common Texts (Feb. 13-14, 1967, June 1-2, 1969); Consultation on Common Texts. Procedures; appendix C, ILCW Minutes, 69-1, July 24-26, 1969; and the minutes of the International Consultation on English Texts, London, April 19-21, 1969.

66. "Liturgical Renewal Reconsidered," *The Lutheran Quarterly*, XIX (February, 1967), 507.

67. "A Look at the New Liturgy," *Lutheran Forum*, (July-August, 1969), 16-17. For a discussion of the common liturgy see Luther D. Reed, *Worship* (Philadelphia: Muhlenberg Press, 1959), pp. 75-115.

68. One whole issue of *The Lutheran Quarterly*, III (November, 1968), addressed this problem.

69. See William Larsen, "Specialized Ministries for Clergymen," *The Lutheran Quarterly*, XVIII (May, 1966), 136-143. This issue of the quarterly focuses on "Ministry and Ministries."

70. See *Lutheran Standard*, (March 19, 1968), 10-11; and *ibid.*, (May 27, 1969), 2-14. The whole issue of *The Lutheran Quarterly*, XXI (August, 1969) is devoted to the campus ministry.

71. See Robert E. Huldschiner, "Berkeley Lutherans Make Their Leap of Faith," *Lutheran Forum*, (August, 1967), 9-12.

72. E. W. Mueller and Giles Ekola, eds., *The Silent Struggle for Mid-America* (Minneapolis: Augsburg Publishing House, 1963).

73. Frederick K. Wentz, *Lutherans in Concert* (Minneapolis: Augsburg Publishing House, 1968), pp. 158-160. *The Lutheran Quarterly*, XIX (May, 1967) carries several articles on the subject, "A New Look at Pastoral Care."

74. Edgar R. Trexler, "The New Face of Evangelism," *The Lutheran*, (February 4, 1970), 10-13; *ibid.*, "Dr. Marshall Notes Conflict in Concepts of Evangelism," (November 5, 1969), 35.

75. Richard Ostling, "A New Evangelism," *Event*, IX (December, 1969), 26-28. Cf. Carey Moore, "Moving!" *Decision*, (December, 1969), 6, 11; and V. G. Albers, "Minneapolis: Evangelism Congress . . . ," *Lutheran Forum*, (December, 1969), 20-21.

76. See, for example, ALC, *Reports and Actions . . . 1968*, pp. 448-454.

77. H. George Anderson, "Evangelism in a New Climate," *The Lutheran Quarterly*, XXI (November, 1969), 384, 390-391.

78. Paul L. Maier, *A Man Spoke, A World Listened* (New York: McGraw-Hill Company, 1963), pp. 113 *et passim*.

79. Richard E. Koenig, "Missouri, A.D., Is Different," *Lutheran Forum*, (September, 1969), 4; cf. "Toward Renewal in Laymen's Work," *ibid.*, (December, 1967), 16-17.

80. LCA, *Minutes . . . 1968*, p. 215.

81. ALC, *Reports and Actions . . . 1968*, pp. 535-548.

82. In the 1960 (ALC) and 1962 (LCA) mergers the women's auxiliaries came to be known as the American Lutheran Church Women and the Lutheran Church Women respectively.

83. President Franklin Clark Fry pointed out that when he was elected (1944) president of the ULCA (at 44 years of age), the president of the Luther League of America was only two years his junior!

84. ULCA, *Minutes . . . 1948*, pp. 309-319.

85. ULCA, *Minutes . . . 1954*, pp. 365-372, 1028.

86. The idea of youth's full participation in the life of the church was symbolized by the election of an 18-year-old to the Executive Council of the LCA in 1970. See "Convention Report," *The Lutheran*, (August 5, 1970), 28.

87. LCA, *Minutes . . . 1968*, pp. 183-190; LCA Youth Ministry, *Foundations for Youth Ministry* (Philadelphia: [1969?]).

88. David Brown, "Youth Ministry in the Sixties: A Decade of Change" (Minneapolis: unpublished manuscript, 1968).

89. See "Young People's Work," *The Edifying Word. Convention Workbook* (St. Louis: Concordia Publishing House, 1969), pp. 368-376.

90. See Will Herberg, *Protestant, Catholic, Jew* (Magnolia, Mass.: Peter Smith, 1955). Martin Marty, *The New Shape of American Religion* (New York: Harper & Row, 1959); Peter Berger, *The Noise of Solemn Assemblies* (Garden City, N.Y.: Doubleday, 1968).

91. "Is There a Religious Issue in the Presidential Campaign?" *The Lutheran Witness,* (September 20, 1960), 5.

92. *Ibid.,* (December 13, 1960), 17.

93. The minutes and proceedings of The ALC, the LCA, and the LC-MS during the 1960s, especially the last five years, give ample documentation to the public posture of the church.

CHAPTER SEVEN

FACING A NEW DECADE

There is a certain Olympian audacity in carrying the story of American Lutheranism to the point where the writing of history gives way to journalism. Nevertheless, the events at the turn of the decade bore such a cargo of implications that a failure to report them could be judged irresponsible. The risks of journalistic history and forensic over-kill of that which is immediate are less dangerous than conscious neglect of current events that must be seen in the light of developments during the previous half century. Quite cognizant, therefore, that what is here written may be quickly out of date and even a false witness (Eusebius, "the father of church history," wrote of events up to his own day, and Robert M. Grant warns all who would follow his example with the curt judgment: "Eusebius lied!"), we take what is an unquestioned but necessary risk. The remaining material is gathered under four headings: a summary of inter-Lutheran relations, a look at the ecumenical dialog, an introduction to a scientific profile of American Lutheranism in 1970, and a postscript that seeks to identify some of the main issues in the 70s.

INTER-LUTHERAN RELATIONS

By the late 50s it was apparent that the two large associations of Lutherans in America—the National Lutheran Council and the Synodical Conference—no longer corresponded to reality. As a result of the merger movement the Council had been reduced from eight member churches to but two, The ALC and the LCA, a fact which immediately challenged the continued existence of the NLC. If the Council were to go out of existence, was there some way in which the dissolution could be graceful and fruitful? Could its death be productive of something new? Between 1958 and 1966 an affirmative answer was worked out in the formation of a successor organization, the Lutheran Council in the United States of America (LC/USA), which embraced the Lutheran Church—Missouri Synod and the Synod of Evangelical Lutheran Churches (SELC) as well as the two members of the former National Lutheran Council.

Meanwhile, the Synodical Conference was experiencing distress and internal rumblings. The difficulty was caused by the Missouri Synod's growing openness to other Lutherans. As noted earlier, World War II brought the Missouri Synod into numerous contacts with the churches of the NLC. If the Missouri Synod were to partcipate in the mainstream of church responsibilities which wartime emergencies produced, it was virtually compelled to cooperate with other Lutherans. Though reluctant to enter into official cooperation, which according to Missouri required complete doctrinal agreement, there were several areas in which boards or agencies—not the synod itself—found it expedient to work together with others. Some of these contacts evolved into formal and official synodical relationships, such as Lutheran World Relief, the Lutheran Service Commission, Lutheran Immigration Service, and Lutheran Church Productions, Inc., the latter being responsible for the highly successful film "Martin Luther." Two of Missouri's partners in the Synodical Conference —the Wisconsin Evangelical Lutheran Synod and the Evangelical Lutheran Synod (Norwegian)—repeatedly charged Missouri with "unionism." Although the latter made efforts to maintain ties with its attackers, in time fellowship was broken and the Synodical Conference existed only in name.

Against this two-faceted development within American Lutheranism the inter-Lutheran relations of the late 50s and the 60s must be placed. Before turning to an exposition of them, however, it may be helpful to note the changing theological climate in the Missouri Synod and to sketch in bare outline the break-up of the Synodical Conference.

Change in Missouri

The Missouri Synod had taken The Brief Statement (1932) as its "starting point for discussions" with the ULCA and the old ALC in the 30s. Despite the "Common Confession" worked out with the latter,

the Missouri Synod felt it had not altered its essential adherence to
The Brief Statement.[1] When, in 1944, the synod voted down membership
in the NLC, it was largely because of its fears of "liberalism," especially
in the ULCA which found the fundamentalistic orthodoxism of The Brief
Statement unacceptable.[2] The following year a challenge was issued, not
to the theology of The Brief Statement, but to a spirit of harsh, judgmental
lovelessness that had appeared in the Missouri Synod. On September 7,
1945, a group of 44 Missouri Synod clergymen meeting in Chicago adopted
what was simply called "A Statement." In it they appealed to the church
to reject the "strange and pernicious spirit . . . [which] has lifted its
ugly head in more than one area of our beloved Synod."[3] They went
on to urge the church to exhibit a greater measure of the evangelical
spirit in interpreting Scripture, in defining prayer fellowship, and in
dealing with fellow-Lutherans. Although "the signers," as they were soon
called, were careful to avoid an outright attack on Missouri's theology
(Thesis Two of the "Statement" affirmed "our faith in the great Lutheran principle of the inerrancy, certainty, and all-sufficiency of Holy
Writ"), they came to be thought of as "the liberal wing" of the synod.
As such they were summoned to meet with the synodical College of
District Presidents. The meeting resulted in an impasse and then, in the
words of Behnken, "the members of the *Praesidium* themselves took the
matter in hand by meeting with representatives of the 'Forty-Four.' As
a result the spokesmen of the signers agreed to withdraw *A Statement*
as a basis for further discussion . . . "[4] This was, in many respects,
a defeat for Missouri "progressives," a defeat partially explained by the
forthcoming celebration of the synod's centennial in 1947, when it would
be only natural to uphold "the traditions of the fathers" and affirm loyalty
to Missouri's repristrination theology.[5] Moreover, it should not be forgotten that the centennial observance was to be accompanied by a special
"thankoffering," the success of which ought not be jeopardized by a
spirit of theological permissiveness.

　　Once the centennial year was over, the progressive spirit was to surface
repeatedly. During the next two decades the influence of the "Forty-Four"
had spread into the ranks of both the clergy and the laity.[6] In addition,
several bright theological students did graduate work, especially at the
University of Chicago and in German universities. Some of these found

their way into teaching positions at Concordia Seminary, St. Louis, and in the synod's teachers' colleges. By the mid-50s the St. Louis faculty was divided into two "schools," the old-line Missourians and a growing minority of progressives. A clash in the synod was inevitable, and by 1959 the battle was joined at the San Francisco convention, when the conservatives voted through the controversial "Resolution 9," which bound all pastors, teachers, and professors to The Brief Statement and other synodically-adopted statements on doctrine and practice. Those who disagreed were not to teach contrary to these statements but were to "present their concern to their brethren. . . ." [7]

Between 1959 and 1962 one of the professors at St. Louis, Martin Scharlemann, came under attack for his teaching that the term "inerrancy" as applied to Scripture required reinterpretation. Theological "sound and fury" filled the air, and finally the synod at its 1962 Cleveland convention was faced with a resolution "to Relieve Dr. Scharlemann of His Office as Teacher." [8] Scharlemann appeared before the synod and was reduced to confessing his guilt for creating "disturbance and confusion" in the church. He assured the synod that he was "fully committed to the doctrine of the verbal inspiration of the Sacred Scriptures." He amplified this by saying, "I hold these Scriptures to be the Word of God in their totality and in all their parts and to be utterly truthful, infallible, and completely without error." He therewith withdrew the essays that had caused the uproar and asked the church to "forgive these actions of mine which have contributed to the tension in the church." Echoes of 1521 were not present as the synod, in what was a "novel form of corporate absolution," voted 653-17 to forgive him. [9]

The same convention, perhaps in remorse for the manner in which it had handled the Scharlemann affair, turned about-face and defanged the synod's action in 1959 regarding The Brief Statement. This it did by declaring "Resolution 9" unconstitutional. [10] To assure itself and others that doctrinal discipline was not now yielding to a spirit of liberalism, it resolved: "That the Synod beseech all its members by the mercies of God to honor and uphold the doctrinal content of these synodically adopted statements." [11] The point of all this paradoxical action was that the Cleveland convention refused to absolutize The Brief Statement but nevertheless reaffirmed its appreciation of and loyalty to its theology. [12]

Despite the political-theological oscillation at Cleveland, the convention took some actions that were to commit the church to a new direction. To replace the retiring president (Behnken), the synod elected Oliver Harms who was destined in the next seven years to lead Missouri into broader and deeper relationships with other Lutherans, including membership in the new Lutheran Council. Other actions that revealed a spirit of openness were approval of Missouri participation in the Lutheran-Presbyterian dialogue and permission to Missouri commissions and boards, under carefully prescribed limits, to cooperate with divisions of the National Council of Churches.[13]

Subsequent to the 1962 convention, it became common knowledge that a vigorous right-wing element in the church was organizing itself as a political force to direct future decisions of the synod. Membership on and even control of certain important boards and committees placed the conservatives in a position of strength. The effect of this tactic was evident already at the 1965 convention (Detroit) and even more so at the 1967 convention (New York). Between 1967 and 1969 this activity was to produce a serious challenge to the leadership of President Harms.

Film-Making and Lutheran Unity

As noted earlier the Missouri Synod, though reluctant to unite with other Lutherans, found it possible to cooperate "in externals." One such enterprise, which in the judgment of Paul C. Empie did more "to cement ties between Lutherans . . . than decades of theological conversations," [14] was the production of films. The National Lutheran Council entered the field of movie-making largely to promote Lutheran World Action and to develop a sense of Lutheran ecclesiastical solidarity. The award-winning (1949) film "Answer for Anne," which dealt with the post-war resettlement of refugees, was directed toward fund-raising for Lutheran World Action. Other films, "The Harvest of Years" (on Lutheran church life in America) and especially the widely-acclaimed box-office success, "Martin Luther," belonged in the category of "promoting Lutheranism." Although initiated by the National Lutheran Council, film-making drew the interest of the Missouri Synod. In order that the latter might be included as a full partner, a separate organization, known as Lutheran Church Productions, Inc., was established in 1951.[15] Later

(1957) a parallel corporation, Lutheran Film Associates, was formed and produced additional films. "Question Seven" dealt with the church-state struggle in East Germany, and "A Time for Burning," a documentary in the new genre known as *cinema verité* handled the problem of the church and racial tensions (1966). When these film organizations became a part of the Lutheran Council in the USA (1967), the Missouri Synod, as a Council member, naturally continued its support and interest in this cooperative aspect of the inter-Lutheran agency.

The Breakup of the Synodical Conference

At the 1962 Missouri Synod convention (Cleveland) President Behnken reported: "Our committee's [Committee on Doctrinal Unity] report . . . brings the sad news that the Wisconsin Synod at its last convention resolved to suspend fellowship with our Synod. I shall not belabor you with the details of this pathetic fact." [16] The "details of this pathetic fact" belong, at least in part, to an outline sketch of the last years of the Lutheran Synodical Conference.

The Synodical Conference, it should be repeated, was a federation (not an organic merger) of four church bodies: The Lutheran Church—Missouri Synod, the Wisconsin Evangelical Lutheran Synod, the Synod of Evangelical Lutheran Churches (Slovak), and the Evangelical Lutheran Synod (Norwegian). Unlike most federations, this one made complete agreement in doctrine and practice a primary requirement for fellowship. As the Missouri Synod widened its outreach in North America, Latin America, and indeed, throughout the world, it encountered increasing difficulty in preserving complete agreement in practice. It was at this point that the Wisconsin Synod and the Evangelical Lutheran Synod began their attacks on Missouri.[17] As early as 1935 the Missouri Synod had authorized a Committee on Doctrinal Unity to confer with representatives of the ULCA and the former ALC.[18] Results of this action, especially the issuance and adoption of doctrinal statements for future fellowship with the old ALC, were viewed by the Wisconsin Synod and the ELS as deviations from the aims of the Synodical Conference. Although discussions were held to allay fears, the situation did not improve. Missouri was charged with a "growing tolerance of unionistic practices." The reference was to Missouri's position on the chaplaincy in the United States Armed Services, on Boy Scouting, and "cooperation in externals" with the National Lutheran Council.

Despite Missouri's assurances that "unionism" was not present in any of these practices, the charges continued to be made.[19] One result was the withdrawal of a small number of pastors from the Missouri Synod in 1951 to organize the Orthodox Lutheran Conference. It subsequently split into three groups, guaranteeing the end of its significance. Another result was the suspension of fraternal relations with the Missouri Synod by the Evangelical Lutheran Synod in 1955 (though continuing membership in the Synodical Conference). Simultaneously the Wisconsin Synod declared itself to be in "a state of vigorously protesting fellowship with Missouri," a situation which continued until it became evident that a stalemate had been reached. Although a temporary rapproachement occurred in 1959 when Missouri reaffirmed The Brief Statement, the 1960 convention of the Synodical Conference revealed that no real progress had been made. At that time a number of pastors and teachers withdrew from the Wisconsin Synod because of its failure to break off fellowship with Missouri. This group organized itself as the Church of the Lutheran Confession. The following year the Wisconsin Synod itself voted to terminate relations with Missouri by adopting a resolution which said in part:

> We now suspend fellowship with the Lutheran Church—Missouri Synod with the hope and prayer to God that the Missouri Synod will hear this evangelical summons and will come to herself and return to the side of the sister synod of Wisconsin from whom she has estranged herself.[20]

In 1963 both the Wisconsin Synod and the ELS took formal steps to withdraw from the Synodical Conference virtually assuring its eventual demise. In 1965 the Missouri Synod voted to continue the Conference together with the SELC and to urge Wisconsin and ELS to resume discussions. This action proved fruitless and in 1967 the Missouri Synod authorized its board of directors to take the necessary steps to bring about the formal dissolution of the Synodical Conference.[21] Meanwhile, the Wisconsin Synod and the Evangelical Lutheran Synod established a new organization provisionally called the Evangelical Lutheran Confessional Forum for the purpose of preserving true Lutheranism.[22]

THE FORMATION OF THE LUTHERAN COUNCIL
IN THE UNITED STATES OF AMERICA

Two inter-Lutheran developments involving the desire to bring the Missouri Synod into closer affiliation with other Lutherans emerged about the same time in the last half of the 50s. One was the effort to establish a successor agency to the National Lutheran Council in which Missouri could be a partner. The other was The ALC-Missouri discussion to provide additional theological bases for pulpit and altar fellowship between the two bodies. These were parallel movements whose developments must be traced separately.

In view of the mergers within the National Lutheran Council and the irreconcilable attitudes within the Synodical Conference, the time seemed propitious to suggest some "reappraisal of the patterns of Lutheran cooperation." [23] Consequently, Paul C. Empie, NLC executive director, used his 1958 report to the council to propose an NLC-sponsored conference in 1959 which would implement the council's provision that: "The Council may convene general conferences of representatives of the Participating Bodies, for the study and discussion of practical problems." A key item in his proposal was the suggestion that non-council Lutherans be invited as observers. At first the Missouri Synod declined. President Behnken gave as reasons the fact that the Synodical Conference at the moment was seeking "greater Scriptural harmony in doctrine and practice" and that the doctrinal positions of the two emerging churches (The ALC and the LCA) were "in a state of flux." These words caused a flurry of unhappy reaction that led Behnken to admit that they might be "an unwarranted judgment of these bodies. . . . " To avoid further confusion he withdrew the statement. Empie informed Behnken that doctrinal discussions relating to cooperation would be a part of the agenda of any forthcoming conference. Thus assured, the Missouri Synod agreed to participate.

Three ensuing discussions, known as the Inter-Lutheran Consultations (1960-1961), indicated that sufficient doctrinal consensus existed to permit Missouri to become a member of the projected new cooperative agency.[24] Three years of planning, in which the small Synod of Evangelical Lutheran Churches (Slovak) now included itself, eventuated in the creation of a constitution committee which quickly drafted the necessary document. By June, 1966, all four bodies had approved the proposed council. The constituting convention, held November 16-18, 1966, in Cleveland, elected C. Thomas Spitz, Jr. (LC-MS) as its first general secretary. Thus the Lutheran Council in the United States of America, embracing 95 percent of Lutheranism, was prepared to begin official operation on January 1, 1967. Wentz describes it as follows:

> The new agency had a twofold purpose, namely, theological discussion and cooperation in specified areas of Christian service. All participating bodies were required to take part in the theological discussion in order "to seek to achieve theological consensus in a systematic and continuing way." Each body could elect to participate in other areas of activity or to abstain. This stress upon the theological discussion was a concession to the Missouri Synod on the part of the NLC bodies, which had avoided doctrinal discussions in connection with council cooperation since 1920. It was a turning point and a concession for the Missouri Synod, on the other hand, to agree to organized associations with other Lutherans while doctrinal differences remained. Here was a real breakthrough in approaches to Lutheran unity and union as well as a significant forward step in Lutheran cooperation.[25]

In some ways the new council was a retrogressive step, largely because of the desire to include Missouri. Missouri's belief that doctrinal agreement was still lacking prevented the new council from continuing the NLC comity arrangements in American missions. Moreover, Missouri was not prepared to cooperate in the campus ministry, a fact which necessitated the formation of a separate entity for the LCA and The ALC known as the National Lutheran Campus Ministry. In 1969, the administration of NLCM was transferred to the Lutheran Council in the USA without Missouri's objection but still without its cooperation. Moreover, the USA National Committee of the Lutheran World Federation, which earlier had been the NLC, became a separate organization because Missouri and SELC were not members of the LWF. Despite these drawbacks, it was hoped that the long-range advantages of having Missouri *within* the family of American Lutheranism would eventually make LC/USA a genuine advance over the National Lutheran Council.

The ALC-Missouri Fellowship Negotiations

It has been evident from earlier accounts that there were strong Missouri-oriented elements in the Evangelical Lutheran Church and the former American Lutheran Church. As a matter of fact, the 1949 proposal of a merger or federation of National Lutheran Council churches died a-borning because some strategists and merger-makers had in mind forming a church that Missouri would find less repelling than the former ULCA and Augustana bodies.

It was in 1957 that the first public utterance regarding an alliance between the Missouri Synod and the projected American Lutheran Church was made. President Behnken addressed the English District of the Missouri Synod and expressed the hope that his church body would begin negotiations with the new ALC shortly after its formation in 1960.[26] This was brought to the attention of the principals in The ALC merger negotiations and evidently followed up with some alacrity.[27] On August 24, 1957 (during the LWF Assembly in Minneapolis), President Schiotz (ELC) and President Henry Schuh (ALC) met with President Behnken and A. H. Grumm in the office of the Minneapolis District of the Missouri Synod. Schiotz described it later as a courtesy call to maintain brotherly feelings and to keep open communications with Missouri.[28] Behnken, however, reported to his synod's doctrinal unity committee that the meeting with Schiotz and Schuh was a conversation "with regard to the possibilities of beginning doctrinal discussions with the groups planning to merge into The American Lutheran Church. . . ." [29]

The next scene in the developing drama occurred in connection with Behnken's reply to the NLC's 1958 invitation to discuss Missouri participation in a new Lutheran council. His reply, it will be recalled, charged the doctrinal position of the NLC mergers as being "in a state of flux." In this setting, The ALC Joint Union Committee sent a telegram to Behnken asking Missouri representatives to meet with the Committee on Inter-Lutheran Relations of the Joint Union Committee in order to "interpret and clarify . . . our doctrinal position." [30] This was followed by a letter from President Schiotz, as chairman of the Inter-Lutheran Relations Committee, in which he said in part:

> . . . we stand ready to accept an invitation for a meeting . . . with your Committee on Doctrinal Unity . . . : 1. To answer questions about the United Testimony. . . . 2. To conduct doctrinal discussions looking to pulpit and altar fellowship between our respective churches.[31]

The invitation requested by Schiotz was forthcoming as a result of action taken by the 1959 San Francisco convention of the Missouri Synod and accepted at the constituting convention of The ALC in April, 1960.[32]

The stage was now set for what not a few seemed to have been eagerly anticipating for some time. Others feared that ALC-Missouri talks would serve to strain the already unhappy relations between The ALC and the new LCA. Would The ALC "be so captured by a sense of crusade in relation to Missouri that it [would] permit its 45-year-old friendship with other churches in the NLC to cool"? [33] Whether as a result of this and similar expressions of deep concern that The ALC-Missouri discussions would isolate the LCA, the executive committee of the two negotiating groups (ALC-Mo) invited (February 10, 1962) the LCA to participate in the doctrinal conversations with Missouri. This was declined for two reasons: (1) the LCA felt that action should first be taken on the projected Lutheran Council in the USA; and (2) the LCA was already officially committed to inter-Lutheran fellowship.[34] The point of the latter was that all churches that subscribed to the Lutheran confessions possessed sufficient basis for fellowship and union. To insist on agreement in extra-confessional theses or statements was to go beyond what was necessary for "the true unity of the church," according to Article VII of the Augsburg Confession.

In January, 1963, The ALC and Missouri announced that plans for doctrinal talks would be suspended temporarily because "the time was not propitious . . . in view of the scheduled meetings . . ." for the establishment of the new Lutheran Council.[35] A short time later (April), the invitation to the LCA was informally renewed, but once again, the latter declined because doctrinal discussions *among Lutherans* prior to pulpit and altar fellowship were considered redundant.[36] This was not to say that all Lutherans were in theological agreement. As a matter of fact, numerous theological issues needed discussion and clarification. But these issues were not divisive of fellowship when there was an affirmation of Article VII of the Augsburg Confession. Since American Lutherans affirmed this confession, no additional agreements were required for unity and fellowship. Thus the many unresolved theological problems among Lutherans could best be discussed in an atmosphere of trust and confessional unity as seen in pulpit and altar fellowship and even in organic union. The Missouri Synod manifestly did not agree to this Lutheran position, and The ALC, not sure what it believed, sought to be a bridgebuilder by mollifying Missouri on the one hand and by telling the LCA, on the other hand, that "we love you too." In this setting, The ALC and Missouri Synod agreed in January, 1964, to proceed with pulpit and altar fellowship discussions.

Meanwhile, the Fourth Assembly of the Lutheran World Federation, meeting in Helsinki, Finland, July 30-August 11, 1963, heard an address on the subject "The One Church and the Lutheran Churches" which called for the various Lutheran churches simply to declare themselves to be in pulpit and altar fellowship. This proposal was reinforced by the Assembly's subsequent resolution that member churches indicate to the executive committee their reasons for not being in fellowship with "other member churches of the LWF." [37] As far as the American situation was concerned, this resolution clearly asked The ALC to give its reasons why it could not declare fellowship with the LCA. Obviously it did not apply in any way to the Missouri Synod which was not a member of the LWF.[38]

In February, 1964, it was suggested that The ALC halt the conversations with Missouri and prepare a resolution asking the 1964 ALC (Columbus) convention simply to *declare* pulpit and altar fellowship with both the LCA and Missouri without further discussions. This proposal was rejected on the grounds that The ALC would have "to keep its word with Missouri" and that the Church Council would defeat such a resolution, never allowing it to get to the floor of the convention.[39]

This precipitated a series of events that resulted in the presentation of a memorial by the Minneapolis Conference to the Southeastern Minnesota District (the largest district of The ALC) requesting The ALC in 1964 to declare fellowship with all Lutherans. This was passed by a large majority despite strong objections voiced by leaders who represented The ALC president's views. The memorial was presented to the 1964 convention which accepted the Joint Council's resolution that it be referred to the Standing Committee on Relations to Lutheran Churches.[40] This had the effect of killing the resolution and supporting the president in his desire to woo Missouri.[41] In response to the "disturbed voices" in The ALC, the president set forth his views in his report to the 1964 convention. He took sharp issue with those who opposed his leadership in the matter, saying that a declaration of fellowship with the LCA "would endanger the discussions with the Lutheran Church–Missouri Synod." In fact, he continued, Missouri Synod leaders had asserted that ALC fellowship with LCA "might have disastrous effects." Moreover, the LCA ought not be offended; after all The ALC actually had "*de facto* pulpit and altar fellowship with the LCA." There remained only "the thin line of an official declaration." Meanwhile the LCA would be kept fully informed.[42] As a matter of fact, however, the LCA was already deeply offended that The ALC found it inexpedient to accept its proffered hand of fellowship and to disregard the Helsinki resolution in favor of doctrinal discussions with Missouri.[43]

In this atmosphere talks between the representatives of The ALC and the Lutheran Church–Missouri Synod were held on November 22-23, 1964; April 19-20, 1965; and January 17-18, 1966. President Schiotz had promised his church that the discussions would "eschew producing any new doctrinal statements." Theological theses, however, would be prepared to identify whatever consensus was reached.[44] Three statements were adopted by the commissioners and mailed to the pastors of the three bodies. The first was entitled "What Commitment to the Sola Gratia of the Lutheran Confessions Involves"; the second, "The Lutheran Confessions and Sola Scriptura"; [45] and the third, "The Doctrine of the Church in the Lutheran Confessions." Although the negotiators had repeatedly said that their discussions were not for the purpose of producing new and extra-confessional statements, these essays were unmistakably new and extra-confessional. The LCA looked upon these statements, whether officially adopted or not, as going beyond confessional requirements for fellowship and the true unity of the church.

On May 12, 1966, President Oliver Harms sent a letter to President Fry urging once again that the LCA join the discussions. He said: " . . . there is a strong desire to establish pulpit and altar fellowship on a *formal and clear statement of some issues which are not treated explicitly in the historic Lutheran Confessions"* [italics added].[46] This was an unequivocal expression of precisely what the LCA had feared was implicit in the fellowship discussions from the very beginning, that is, agreement in extra-confessional statements. The wording of the Harms letter made it clear that agreement on a doctrinal statement ("formal and clear") covering such a problem as, for example, the old question of the Word of God and the Scriptures, which the ULCA and Missouri had argued in the 30s, would be necessary before fellowship could be established.[47] Acceptance of Harms' invitation could mean nothing less. In other words, the basic question remained: "What is necessary for the true unity of the church?" The LCA at its 1966 convention reiterated its conviction that the Lutheran Church–Missouri Synod and The American Lutheran Church were already one with the LCA in their common Lutheran confession. Therefore, the LCA stood ready to welcome all pastors and laymen of the other two bodies to fellowship in proclamation and sacrament.[48]

In light of these circumstances and in order to offset the influence of the Harms letter that undercut the oft-repeated assurances that no "new doctrinal or extra-confessional statements" were being sought by The ALC-Missouri negotiators, President Schiotz found it necessary to prepare a personal "Addendum" to the already-drafted 1968 report of The ALC Committee on Inter-Church Relations. In this "Addendum" he recommended that The ALC in 1968 declare pulpit and altar fellowship with the LCA, the Lutheran Church–Missouri Synod, and the Synod of Evangelical Lutheran Churches. This proposal was adopted at the Omaha convention (1968) without significant debate and without general awareness, either among pastors or laymen, of the dynamics of the Lutheran ecclesiastical situation. Despite the frequent protestations regarding extra-confessional statements, the same convention *adopted* the summary theological document prepared by the commissioners of The ALC, LC-MS, and the SELC (January 23, 1967) and known as the *Joint Statement and Declaration*.[49]

Meanwhile, what was happening inside the Missouri Synod? The 1965 convention (Detroit, June 16-26) was notable for numerous actions. The "Affirmations," drawn from the Kretzmann Report, were approved; the synod voted in favor of producing a new joint hymnal and service book with the LCA and The ALC; and it gave support to professors (A. O. Fuerbringer, G. Thiele, and Martin Scharlemann) who had been charged with teaching "false doctrine." In the biggest test of administration policy, the synod overwhelmingly approved Missouri's participation in the proposed Lutheran Council. With regard to fellowship discussions with The ALC, the convention expressed its joy over the meetings which had been held and prayed that God would bring future meetings to a successful conclusion.[50] When questioned about the synod's new "progressive" stance, President Harms gave assurances that the Missouri Synod would not compromise its traditional conservative position:

> We remain on our platform that doctrinal statements come from
> Holy Scripture. We cannot deviate from historic positions, but
> we can go with them to more and more people.[51]

Furthermore, Harms had assured the synod, during the debate over membership in the proposed Lutheran Council in the USA, that there would be
no soft-pedalling of doctrinal error or unionism. "The chair has warned
against unionism. . . . Unionism will not be tolerated." [52]   Behind much
of Harms' verbalization of Missourian traditionalism was the keen consciousness of a continuing and, since 1962, an increasingly vocal and political rightist element in the church. The Harms statements were calculated
to reassure this party.

Meanwhile, the Commission on Theology and Church Relations, which
had replaced the former Committee on Doctrinal Unity in 1962, was busily
engaged in research and the preparation of position papers on the theology
of fellowship, the nature of doctrine, the Lutheran stance on contemporary
biblical studies, revelation, inspiration and inerrancy. These were printed
and distributed prior to the 1967 (New York) convention of synod. The
commission also prepared guidelines for inter-Lutheran discussions on the
local level in which it said, "Although other Lutheran churches are not
involved in [ALC-Missouri] discussions on the national level it may be
advantageous to invite all Lutherans to participate on the local level." [53]
The problem of "other Lutherans," notably the LCA, came under the
commission's concern, but no solution could be found. Looking forward
to fellowship with The ALC which would simultaneously declare fellowship with both the LCA and Missouri, the commission said, ". . . the
question of what to do when church B [ALC] is in fellowship with
church A [LCA] and C [Mo.], while the latter two are not in fellowship
with each other has not yet been fully answered." [54]

This was not a new problem. Missouri had faced it in connection with
"The Common Confession" which had been worked out following doctrinal discussions in the late 30s and the 40s (see Chapter Three above).
The problem then was that the old ALC was in fellowship with churches
in the American Lutheran Conference, some of whose members had declared they could not accept the ALC-Missouri statement on Scripture.
Missouri had concluded: "Since the American Lutheran Church is one
of the bodies composing the American Lutheran Conference, one fails to

see how under such circumstances we could establish brotherly relations with the American Lutheran Church." [55] L. W. Boe, observing from the sidelines in 1938, had also detected the illogical, if not misological, position which refused to admit that if B is in fellowship with A and C, then A and C should be in fellowship. Writing to R. H. Long, executive director of the NLC, he had said, "Just imagine the [former] American Lutheran Church being in pulpit and altar fellowship with the Missouri Synod, retaining its membership in the American Lutheran Conference and the National Lutheran Council. . . . *Things equal to the same thing are equal to each other* [italics added]." [56]

In the situation of the 60s it was not long before right-wing elements in the Missouri Synod began to criticize the proposed fellowship with The American Lutheran Church. It seemed obvious to many that, if the Missouri Synod could be in fellowship with The ALC which in turn was in fellowship with the LCA, Missouri was implicitly in fellowship with the LCA. Since this was intolerable to the right-wing and perhaps even to the majority in the whole synod, this became one of the arguments against the Missouri-ALC alliance. Consequently when the Missouri Synod convened in 1967 (New York), the hoped for consummation of fellowship with The ALC was postponed, although the synod did approve the *Joint Statement and Declaration* as revealing the existence of doctrinal agreement. Meanwhile, the synodical officials were to make clear to the entire membership the implications of fellowship and prepare "appropriate recommendations to the 1969 convention." [57]

During the next two years the forces of the right-wing continued to organize a vigorous opposition that directed its efforts to the elimination of "liberalism," the defeat of the fellowship question, and the restoration of traditional Missouri theology. Attacks were levelled against the "liberals" on the St. Louis faculty, against President Harms for tolerating "false teaching" and refusing to discipline the "guilty" professors, against The ALC, the LCA, the LWF, and the ecumenical movement.[58] The influence of the group was far-reaching and permeated much of the synod with the smell of fear. Its activity resulted in the purging of the "progressive" element in the Lutheran Laymen's League, in wounding the synod's youth program, in drying up benevolent giving to such an extent that the "Ebenezer Thankoffering" for capital needs of church extension, missions, and higher education raised less than one third of its forty million dollar goal, and in unsettling thousands of people in the congregations. Insecurity and anxiety—not unlike that in the nation itself which was caught up at the same moment in the Vietnam War, the racial crisis, and the youth revolt—spread throughout the church.

As the 1969 convention approached, the ranks of the right began to sense victory. Wrapped in the garments of "old Missouri," the attackers trained their artillery on two primary targets: President Harms and the fellowship question.

A sharply divided church met in synod at Denver, July 11-18, 1969. That the atmosphere was electric was evident when the Executive Director of the Synod, W. F. Wolbrecht, put aside his regular report on the morning of July 12 and delivered himself of an attack on unconstitutional "politicking" among the delegates. He listed various attempts to influence or bind delegates, dating back to 1962, and pointed out that for the first time in Missouri's history there had been an "open, avowed, and public candidacy" for the presidency. He referred to the campaign to replace Harms by electing J. A. O. Preus, conservative president of the Springfield seminary, and a known opponent of "liberalism," The ALC, the LCA, the LWF, and the ecumenical movement. Preus replied that he was no more a candidate than any other LC-MS pastor and that the promotion of his candidacy was done without his knowledge and consent. That afternoon Preus was elected president of the Lutheran Church–Missouri Synod.[59]

The following Monday, July 14, President Schiotz of The ALC, addressed the still-stunned convention on the subject of fellowship. He sketched briefly the history of The ALC-Missouri doctrinal discussions that culminated in "the adoption of a Joint Statement and Declaration," approved by Missouri in 1967 and The ALC in 1968, and "disclaimed allegations of hypocrisy in the American Lutheran Church in respect to the meaning of the word 'inerrant.'" He concluded: "If you accept our proffered hand, we shall regard it as a gift of God's Holy Spirit. If you do not . . . , many of our people will ask . . . whether God's Spirit may be pointing us to new directions."[60] The next day, LCA President Robert Marshall suggested several ways in which Missouri and the LCA could "enjoy unity—prayer fellowship, recognition of one baptism, allegiance to the Ecumenical Creeds and the Lutheran Confessions, and the confession of sin . . . , " especially since "each of us has been tempted on occasion to emphasize the sins of the other. . . . "[61]

Before the fellowship question came to a vote, President-elect Preus urged a delay largely because he feared there was no unity on the doctrine of the Word of God and Scripture.[62] But, he said, he would abide by the decision of the convention. A few minutes later the convention decided by the margin of 84 votes (522 to 438) to approve fellowship with The ALC.

Subsequent decisions indicated that the synod was still being pulled in two directions. On the one hand, it voted to continue talks which had begun informally in 1968 with the LCA; it approved dialog with other Christians; it opened the way to membership of women on church boards and committees; it reacted sympathetically to a presentation on behalf of the blacks; and it endorsed the principle of conscientious objection to particular wars. On the other hand, it voted down a proposal to join the LWF (a similar proposal had been rejected in 1956);[63] it declined to cooperate in a LC/USA sponsored "open-end appeal" to raise $30 million for relief and urban crises; it elected several officers who were generally known as "conservatives"; and filled 52 of the 69 vacancies on synodical boards with persons who had the endorsement of the right-wing forces.

Post-Denver developments indicated that, despite Preus' promise that there would be no "head chopping," changes were being made which were to the liking of the new administration. The synod's board of directors, meeting September 24-26, 1969, voted 8 to 6 to remove W. F. Wolbrecht as its executive director, but then reconsidered its action. Having drafted guidelines for the office which was now tightly controlled by the president and the board, the directors voted to reappoint him.[64] Late in October, the reorganized Commission on Theology and Church Relations dismissed its executive secretary, a well known and ecumenically-minded theologian, who reported that his request for a written explanation was denied.[65]

These actions, coupled with the elimination of four prominent "progressives" from important committees and the "investigation" of alleged "liberals" on the St. Louis seminary faculty,[66] led some to fear that the synod was being forced into becoming "a two party church."[67] It was clear that a major task of internal reconciliation confronted the Lutheran Church–Missouri Synod in the future.[68]

The hopes for reconciliation, however, were dimmed during the interval between the 1969 (Denver) and 1971 (Milwaukee) conventions. President Preus interpreted his election as a mandate to consolidate the position of traditional "Missourianism" in opposition to what he and others called growing "liberalism." [69] Although this present book has a cut-off date of 1970, it has been deemed necessary to carry the story of inter-Lutheran relations through the Missouri Synod convention, July 9-16, 1971.

As the convention approached, the continuing issues of biblical inerrancy and confessional subscription agitated the church and lay at the root of the mounting tensions between the conservatives and the moderates. The major agenda items for the biennial synod were thus adumbrated by issues on which Missourians generally had previously stood united against other Lutherans. Now they found their own ranks sharply polarized. Although the theme of the convention ("Sent to Reconcile") emphasized a patent need, it was quickly apparent that in itself the theme was powerless to achieve the longed-for reconciliation. The opposing parties were adamant and the positions assumed did not lend themselves to political compromise nor theological resolution in the emotionally charged atmosphere at Milwaukee.

When the convention got underway, it was manifest from President Preus' report that most of the synodical decisions would revolve around the question of the binding nature of synodically adopted resolutions and the issue of the verbal inspiration and consequent inerrancy of the Bible. Preus stated unequivocally that synodical resolutions must be considered "as the expression of the church body and must be regarded as valid and binding unless they are in conflict with the Word of God." He continued:

> A person who does not agree with the Synod's doctrinal reso-
> lutions or statements does not and cannot honor and uphold
> them. . . . In her doctrinal resolutions, the Synod is confessing
> her faith; and one either approves and accepts her confession or
> he does not. There is no middle ground.[70]

Preus implied that the issue involved not only theological truth but moral integrity:

> We are a synod of brethren linked by our common confession of
> faith. To disregard the voice of the synod is a loveless and diverse
> act and may well reflect a lack of fidelity to our confessional
> commitment.[71]

Moving on to the question of biblical authority, the president asserted that a divergence from the traditionally held view of inspiration and inerrancy would be destructive of all that the church stood for and tantamount to a redefinition of the Lutheran Church–Missouri Synod. Listing seven areas of danger, Preus said that a departure from Missouri's understanding of biblical authority would result in making the gospel "rather than the Bible . . . the norm of our theology." [72]

As the debate got under way most indicators pointed to the fact that the convention would be a conflict over doctrinal resolutions and that evangelism, missions, and other ministries of the church would receive but secondary consideration from the delegates. Preus had stated that high on the agenda would be inter-church relations because they impinged on prior questions of the Bible and the confessions. That this was indeed the case was evident in the numerous memorials urging repeal of Missouri's 1969 decision to permit the congregations to practice intercommunion and exchange of pulpits with The American Lutheran Church. These memorials indicated the temper of a sizeable segment of the delegates and echoed Preus' contention that The ALC's decision to ordain women made it necessary to reopen the fellowship question. Other memorials pointed out that rescinding fellowship with The ALC was necessary because of continuing disagreement over the doctrine of scripture, differences on the lodge question and the establishment of fellowship between the Lutheran Church in America and The American Lutheran Church.[73]

The strength of the conservative offensive was partially indicated in the vote on a resolution "To Withhold Ordination of Women to the Pastoral Office." The Division of Theological Studies of the Lutheran Council in the USA had issued a report on the ordination issue. Missouri representatives had participated in the study and had given indication of agreement on the principle that the ordination of women was within the freedom of each body in the Council and was not in itself disruptive of fellowship.[74] Both the Lutheran Church in America and The American Lutheran Church had approved ordination of women at their 1970 conventions. Moreover, each body had subsequently ordained one woman. It was in this historical context that the Missouri Synod determined by a vote of 674 to 194 that "the Word of God does not permit women to the pastoral office," resting its scriptural case on the Pauline injunction that women "keep silence in the churches" (1 Cor. 14:34) and that women were not to teach or "to have authority over men" (1 Tim. 2:12-14). The vote was no doubt an accurate reflection of Missouri's attitude. Very few of the moderates, for example, were prepared to do battle over this question.

A short time later and just prior to its vote on the issue of rescinding fellowship, the new president of The American Lutheran Church, Kent S. Knutson, addressed the convention. In a winsome and forthright manner, he sought to allay the fears of Missouri's conservatives that The ALC was something less than orthodox in its view of the Bible and in its conviction that ordination of women was not contrary to the message of the New Testament. He added that The ALC would not be offended if Missouri held to its opinion on women in the ministry, but it would be saddened if this issue became the basis for discontinuing fellowship.[75]

The following day in an emotion-packed session the convention, clearly influenced by Knutson's appeal, defeated the move to break ties with The ALC. Then, however, it went on to give conditional approval to continuing fellowship. The resolution voiced "strong regret" over the ordination of women and requested that The ALC seriously reconsider its action on this issue. Moreover, the synod advised pastors, congregations, boards and commissions to "defer implementation of fellowship" until The ALC had "opportunity to respond" to Missouri's concerns which included in addition to the ordination of women other problems such as the relation of the Word of God to the Bible.[76]

The major floor struggle at Milwaukee developed around the issue of the binding nature of synodically adopted doctrinal statements. The conservative factions sought to revive a position that had been approved at San Francisco in 1959 and then declared unconstitutional in 1962 at Cleveland. The preamble to the new resolution proposed that the "Synod once again declare its doctrinal resolutions to be of binding force until it can be demonstrated to the Synod that they are not in accord with the Word of God. . . . " After heated debate, a more moderate substitute statement (prepared in 1970 by the Council of District Presidents) was approved by a close vote (485-425). This statement, while pledging to "honor and uphold" synodically adopted doctrinal statements, differed from the original proposal by its more pastoral and evangelical tone. When the convention was reminded that it had not voted on the preamble, a member of the conservative group moved that it also be adopted. That motion was passed. This left the synod in an anomalous situation on the whole issue: the preamble reflected the position of the conservatives; the resolution proper, the position of the moderates. This paradoxical and confusing action no doubt reflected the true state of affairs in the Missouri Synod.[77]

A report on the much publicized investigation of the doctrinal views of faculty members at Concordia Seminary, St. Louis, had been expected at Milwaukee. An attempt to release the voluminous results of President Preus' Fact Finding Committee was withdrawn when two synodical vice presidents pleaded for "the sake of peace and reconciliation" that the action not be voted. The report was placed in the hands of the seminary's board of control for "appropriate action" with President Preus to announce the results to the church within one year.[78]

Several other decisions manifested the "mood of Milwaukee." One was the question of continuing membership in the Lutheran Council in the USA. The attempt of the conservatives to remove Missouri from the council was defeated but a resolution asking for a re-examination of its operations, policies, and programs was authorized. Furthermore, there was to be a re-assessment of the synod's membership in the council with a view to determining whether unity in doctrine and practice was being hindered or aided by continued affiliation.

The synod's turmoil over doctrinal problems and inter-Lutheran relations did not come to an end with this action. In fact, it faced at least two more issues. One was the recurring question of membership in the Lutheran World Federation. Having voted it down decisively in 1956 and 1969, the synod was hardly prepared in 1971 to reverse its previous decisions. For a third time the church declined to affiliate with the family of world Lutheranism.[79] The second issue was two-pronged: (1) action on "A Statement Regarding Lutheran Unity"; and (2) discussions with the Lutheran Church in America. The former had been transmitted to the convention by the Lutheran Council and looked forward to the eventual merger or federation of Lutheranism's three major bodies in America. The statement had been approved by both the Lutheran Church in America's executive committee and the convention of The American Lutheran Church in 1970. The Missouri Synod, however, declined to approve the statement but recommended that pastors and congregations study it. The second item, a result of earlier informal conversations with the Lutheran Church in America, expressed "readiness to meet officially" in order to reach doctrinal agreement for the establishment of pulpit and altar fellowship.[80]

As noted earlier, the theme of the convention had boldly, if not realistically, reminded the church that it was "Sent to Reconcile." The spirit of reconciliation was only infrequently visible in the Milwaukee deliberations, and the irony of the convention theme was not lost on either participants or observers. One commentator reported, "In general, the spirit of intimidation, control, repression, and fear still remains active in the LC-MS, perhaps even in exacerbated form. . . . " [81] The editor of *The Lutheran* (LCA) noted that President J. A. O. Preus blamed Missouri's problems on the LCA and The ALC, both of whom "acted too hastily and without consultation in ordaining women." The latter two bodies, said the editor, were moving closer together in parish education, theological education, and world missions. Moreover, by design the proposals for new structures in both churches were almost parallel.[82] Another observer, the president of The American Lutheran Church, conceded that it "would be a tragedy if our relationships with the Missouri Synod should deteriorate at this point in history," but reminded pastors and congregations that The ALC had fellowship with the LCA and had had close relationships with its people ever since World War I. Moreover, The ALC's membership in the Lutheran World Federation and its practice of intercommunion with the churches of the Lutheran world family made it imperative that nothing should be done vis-à-vis the Missouri Synod that would impair these long standing relationships.[83]

Meanwhile, President Preus, looking back on the Milwaukee convention expressed himself as being pleased and satisfied with the actions of the synod. His presidential report had set forth an uncompromising doctrinal line; moreover, at least once during the convention, he had stepped out of the chair to make an impassioned plea to give him the tool (the original resolution "To Uphold Synodical Doctrinal Resolutions") to deal with "deviations, aberrations, charges and counter-charges." [84] It was a bit strange, therefore, that he expressed in retrospect his unqualified satisfaction with the Milwaukee convention. His pastoral letter to the Missouri ministerium said among other things, "We emerged from the convention a more united and more determined church than we were before. . . . There is no question that the vote on synodically adopted doctrinal resolutions was one of the most . . . important of the convention. . . . The theme of reconciliation has prevailed. . . . " [85]

It was no secret that by midsummer 1971 the prospects for pan-Lutheran unity seemed gloomy. Ever since the 1930s attempts had been made to facilitate the movement of the Lutheran Church–Missouri Synod into closer communion with fellow Lutherans in America and overseas. The long series of meetings, the theological consultations, the behind-the-scenes maneuvers, the continuing concessions to Missouri's attitudes during more than a quarter of a century had brought on a broad sense of futility by the beginning of the 1970s. The feeling of weariness that had enveloped, by 1949, the denominations that were to become the Lutheran Church in America had now descended on The American Lutheran Church as well. Despite the latter's repeated expressions of willingness to discuss problems, it like the LCA had reached the conviction that extra-confessional positions are neither necessary nor helpful.[86]

The question that could not be answered in the atmosphere of gloom was whether the same feeling of enervation would eventually cause a break in the Missouri Synod itself. Most seasoned observers of the American Lutheran ecclesiastical scene were predicting that there would be no division in the ranks of this large and generally vigorous church body. A reporter for *The Christian Century* put the matter succinctly, if not a bit sardonically: "Hope springs eternal in the heart of a Missourian because there will always be another convention at which to search for consensus, right wrongs and win friends." [87] That this assessment may have been close to the truth came from the pen of one of the most unrelenting critics of the Preus administration, one who saw the phoenix emerging from the ashes. He wrote: "A new Missouri will rise after Milwaukee." [88]

Unofficial Talks: LCA-Missouri, 1968-1969

It will be recalled that the United Lutheran Church had official conversations with the Missouri Synod and the former American Lutheran Church in the 30s (See Chapter Three). The experiences which the United Lutheran leaders encountered in these discussions brought on a sense of dismay over this method of furthering the cause of unity. Since then the ULCA, and after 1962, the LCA, returned to the position articulated in the Washington (1920) and Savannah (1934) Declarations which asserted that all who affirm the Lutheran confessions already possess a sufficient doctrinal basis for fellowship and unity. Therefore, during the ALC-Missouri doctrinal discussions in the 60s the LCA consistently declined invitations to participate in the negotiations. As indicated above this was not to imply that there were no theological problems that needed airing; rather, it was to say that a common Lutheran confession of the gospel was reckoned as sufficient for fellowship.

Differences among Lutherans ought not be divisive of fellowship; rather they should be discussed within the context of fellowship. A few voices in Missouri agreed. For example, Martin Marty wrote " . . . in finding each other through [the Confessions], they [the Lutherans] will still be open to ecumenical Christianity because the Augsburg Confession and other early symbols were open to Catholic and Reformed parties. Grow into what we have and we shall know what we are as we face the rest of the Church and the world. Come to think of it, it is pretty hard to improve on that scenario for the future." Striking the same note was John H. Tietjen, soon to become president of Concordia Seminary: "What should be the basis for uniting the Lutherans of America? I suggest that it should be consensus in recognizing the Holy Scripture as the norm and standard of teaching and in regarding the Lutheran Confessions as the correct exposition of the Scriptures—*that and no more*" [italics added.][89] It was this position which the Missouri Synod traditionally had not been able to accept. The resulting deadlock, however, was satisfactory to neither side. The 1967 convention of the Missouri Synod had asked its president and Commission on Theology and Church Relations to invite other Lutherans to discuss the removal of "causes of misunderstanding and separation."[90] President Harms asked President Fry privately if there might be some way to resolve the problem. Fry suggested that an unofficial group from the LCA (not its Standing Committee on Approaches to Unity) would be willing to accept a Missouri invitation to be quizzed about the LCA. On the basis of this suggestion President Harms and the Missouri Commission extended an invitation to which President Fry replied:

> I understand that what you are doing—on the authority or, as you say, with the enncouragement of your Commission . . . is to invite me, together with colleagues of mine . . . whom I shall designate, to be the guests (not in the literal sense of the word!) of an official group of the . . . Missouri Synod for the purpose of informal conversation with regard to relationships, present and future, of our two churches. The specific purpose . . . is to enable your Commission . . . to have access to additional

information and to gain deepened knowledge of the Lutheran Church in America, on the basis of which it (your commission) will be able to make a more perceptive and adequate report . . . to the next convention of the Lutheran Church–Missouri Synod, in fulfillment of the instruction given it by your New York Convention.[91]

In this manner, the long-standing impasse was broken without breaching the LCA principle and yet giving the Missouri representatives the opportunity to report that they had held conversations with the LCA. Subsequently, on May 14, 1968, the two groups met at St. Louis.[92] At the request of President Harms no public release of the conversations was made. Fry reported to the LCA Standing Committee on Approaches to Unity that a highly confidential "aide memoire of the interchange" would be prepared, but meanwhile he could say that the Missouri men asked about synergism, the Scriptures, the LCA Sunday school curriculum, and unionism. This was one of the last ecumenical activities which engaged Fry's attention. Less than a month later he died of cancer.[93]

The first news of the meeting came in a speech by President Harms before the Missouri Synod's Minnesota South District in St. Paul June 4, 1969. In his address Harms reported that the Lutheran Church–Missouri Synod had "begun doctrinal discussions with the Lutheran Church in America." [94] A spokesman for the LCA immediately made a public statement that the meeting was strictly informal and not to be construed as the beginning of doctrinal discussions in the ordinary sense. The use of the ambiguous term "doctrinal discussions" appeared to produce a conflict regarding the nature and purpose of the meeting, a conflict which in actuality did not exist.[95] This was confirmed by President Harms in his personal greeting to the 1968 LCA convention (Atlanta, June 19-27) where he said in part:

> I am constrained to plead with you to find a way to pursue further the initial contact that was established between our church bodies in an *unofficial way* [italics added] on May 14.[96]

The convention responded by passing a resolution that encouraged the Standing Committee on Approaches to Unity to continue "unofficial discussions." [97] As a consequence of this a second consultation was held in St. Louis in February 20, 1969, during which the new LCA president,

Robert Marshall, and his colleagues answered questions concerning the church's constitution.[98]

The Denver convention of the Missouri Synod had heard its president-elect J. A. O. Preus say that he would "endeavor to procure consensus and fellowship with all Lutherans in America with all vigor and sincerity." But he added that he hoped doctrinal discussions could be carried on "in something beyond an informal manner." The convention then voted to continue discussions with the Lutheran Church in America for the purpose of seeking what in time-honored Missouri terminology was called "a God-pleasing fellowship."[99] As the decade of the 70s opened, this particular front on the American Lutheran sector of Christendom was relatively quiet.

ECUMENICAL DIALOG

In the judgment of some, the ecumenical movement in the 60s was in the doldrums—and it deserved to be. Ecumenism was an old man's game; the new generation was not interested in resolving theological and ecclesiastical differences. To debate ecclesiastical authority, the new hermeneutic, or Christology was a waste of precious time in the face of overwhelming social, political, and economic problems. The unity of humanity, it was argued, was more important than the unity of the church. "Secular ecumenism," *si!* Ecclesiastical ecumenism, *no!*[100]

Despite this general attitude which stretched from Geneva to Rome to Canterbury to New York with numerous intermediate stops, the 60s popularized a new word in the ecumenical vocabulary: *dialog*. Although some people were not always clear as to its nature, its forms or conditions, it became one of the "in" words of the era.[101] The term could mean "discourse" or "conversation," but it was not conversation intended to overwhelm the partner with "megatons of syllables"; it was rather conversation with a common purpose: to discover the truth. And the dialogic pathway to truth meant not merely knowing *about* one's partner, but *knowing* him. It required reciprocity and a sense of equality which did not prejudice each partner's personal conviction or opinion that his church was more authentic or closer to the truth. Dialog sought convergence; it eschewed compromise or confrontation.

It was with this understanding of dialog that the three major American Lutheran churches entered bilateral conversations with other denominations. It was most natural to begin with the Reformed or Calvinist tradition. Numerous meetings were held "to discover to what extent differences which have divided these communions in the past still constitute obstacles to mutual understanding." [102] A preparatory meeting was held February 16-17, 1962, in New York. This was followed by several theological consultations ("dialogs") between representatives of the two groups.[103] Topics discussed were naturally those which had aroused controversy, misunderstanding, and even caricature between the two traditions since the 16th century. These included the nature and role of the gospel, confessions, scripture, the Lord's Supper and Christology, justification and sanctification, law and gospel, and the "two kingdoms." [104] As an expression of the group (not of their churches), the following statement was adopted by participants at the final session:

> During these four meetings we have examined carefully the major issues which have aroused theological controversy between our traditions for generations past. At some points we have discovered that our respective views of each other have been inherited caricatures initially caused by misunderstanding or polemical zeal.
>
> In other instances it has become apparent that efforts to guard against possible distortions of truth have resulted in varying emphases in related doctrines which are not in themselves contradictory and in fact are complementary, and which are viewed in a more proper balance in our contemporary theological formulations.
>
> A number of differing views and emphases remain to be resolved, but we are encouraged to believe that further contacts will lead to further agreement between the churches here represented. We regard none of these remaining differences to be of sufficient consequence to prevent fellowship. We have recognized in each other's teachings a common understanding of the Gospel and have concluded that the issues which divided the two major branches of the Reformation can no longer be regarded as constituting obstacles to mutual understanding and fellowship.
>
> We are grateful to God that he brought us together for these discussions, acknowledging that such confrontation under the guidance of the Holy Spirit was long overdue. Although we can speak only for ourselves, we express our conviction that the

work begun in this way must not be permitted to lapse, but should be carried on to fruition by the churches we represent.

We who have had the privilege during the course of these conversations of strengthening the bonds of Christian unity and brotherly affection thank God for the evident working of his spirit in our midst and pray that what was begun in this way will be carried on to a successful conclusion with all "deliberate speed." [105]

The official report, however, was somewhat different. The original recommendation had included phrases which indicated that the churches were in sufficient theological agreement to permit fellowship. The second and final draft of the report was altered to read as follows:

> As a result of our studies and discussions we see *no insuperable obstacles* [italics added] to pulpit and altar fellowship, and therefore, we recommend to our parent bodies that they encourage their constituent churches to enter discussions looking forward to intercommunion and fuller recognition of one another's ministries.[106]

The significant words here were "no insuperable obstacles." The original draft had implied that there were actually no barriers to intercommunion, something which made the Missouri Synod representatives uncomfortable, especially with reference to the receptivity which their church might or might not accord a recommendation including these words.

Broadening the scope of dialog to include the other major 16th century antagonist, the USA National Committee of the LWF entered conversations with the Roman Catholic Bishops' Commission for Ecumenical Affairs. The first of the theological consultations (Baltimore July 6-7, 1965) dealt with the Nicene Creed. The second (Chicago, February 10-13, 1966) centered on the Sacrament of Baptism; and the third, fourth, and fifth meetings (Washington, D.C., September 23-24, 1966; New York, April 7-9, 1967; and St. Louis, September 29-October 1, 1967) concerned themselves with "The Eucharist as Sacrifice." [107]

Unlike the Lutheran-Reformed consultations, the Catholic-Lutheran dialog has continued to the present without any summary publication of the discussions. Several meetings were held between 1967 and 1970. The sixth and seventh sessions (New York, March 8-9, 1968 and Williamsburg, Virginia, September 26-29, 1968) moved in on the thorny question of "Eucharist and Ministry." This was continued at the eighth and ninth sessions (San Francisco, February 21-23, 1969; Baltimore, September 26-29, 1969) where the participants sought a "convergence" on this difficult issue. Sessions ten and eleven were held in 1970. Although misunderstandings and distortions were removed by the conversations, some basic questions involving *ministerium* and *magesterium* remain unresolved. Nevertheless, reports indicated surprising progress in mutual understanding had been achieved. *Time* magazine's religion editor commented that Roman Catholic intercommunion with Protestants might possibly be established first with Lutherans. The irony of the situation was not lost on the commentator. He observed that, while Lutheran and Roman Catholic fellowship had reached "an advanced stage," Lutherans had not yet been able to practice full intercommunion among themselves.[108]

A third theological dialog involving American Lutherans has been with representatives of the Standing Conference of Orthodox Bishops in the Americas. Two sessions were held, both in New York, November 17-18, 1967, and March 21-22, 1969. A third was scheduled for November 6-7, 1970. The first session, largely introductory, included historical papers on Lutheranism and Orthodoxy. These were followed by theological papers on the role of "Scripture and Tradition." The second session considered an Orthodox presentation on "Tradition." The subsequent discussion was guided by six questions—three prepared separately by each group—as follows:

Questions by the Orthodox:

How do you understand the concept of the self-sufficiency and the superiority of Holy Scripture? (What does *Sola Scriptura* [the Word Alone] mean today?)

How do you evaluate the Fathers of the Church as authentic interpreters of the Scriptures and as witnesses of the dogmatic and liturgical life of the Church?

By what criteria can one discern the presence and guidance of the Holy Spirit in correctly understanding and properly teaching the truths of Holy Scripture?

Questions by the Lutherans:

If tradition is viewed as the critical spirit of the Church, made acute by the Holy Spirit, and its validity is established by a consensus, how is the tradition known to be orthodox without a new Ecumenical Council?

In the light of your present understanding of Lutheran attitudes toward tradition, do you recognize any ecclesiastical reality within the Lutheran Church? If not, why not?

If the Holy Spirit sustains all Christian obedience to the bishop, what are the doctrinal implications of schism?

The 1970 consultation was to consider the subject, "The Nature of the Church" according to the Lutheran confessions and the Orthodox tradition, but at the request of the Orthodox the meeting was cancelled and talks were indefinitely suspended.[109]

Fourth and fifth bilateral discussions, under the aegis of the Division of Theological Studies of the Lutheran Council/USA, were held between American Lutherans, on the one hand, and the American Jewish Committee and the American Episcopalians, on the other hand.

The Lutheran-Jewish "academic colloquium," as it was called, convened in New York March 6, 1969. Discussion centered on the Christian and Jewish perspectives regarding "Law and Grace" and "Election and the People of God." A second meeting, May 26-27, 1970 (St. Louis), gave attention to the theme, "Promise, Land, Peoplehood" in light of the biblical record, historical tensions, and contemporary events.[110]

The Lutheran-Episcopalian theological discussion (October 14-15, 1969) dealt with "The Meaning and Authority of Scripture in the Life of the Church." A second consultation (April 7-9, 1970) considered "Our Present Understanding of the Nature of Church Unity." This colloquy emphasized the worship and sacramental life of the church. Themes for the third and fourth meetings centered on baptismal unity and apostolicity.[111]

In conclusion, it can be said that American Lutheranism in the 60s made some significant ecumenical strides through the instrument of bilateral dialogs. Chief progress was made with other churches of the western tradition, especially the Reformed and the Roman Catholic. Cultural as well as theological differences characterized the Lutheran-Orthodox conversations. Lutherans needed more time to penetrate the mystical East, and the Orthodox tended to view the Lutherans as tradition-less "Protestants." The encounters with Jews and Episcopalians, still in their infancy, provided no discernible contours as the 60s ended.

Beyond these bilateral dialogs, other ecumenical developments should be mentioned. On the international level American Lutherans, for example, were among the official LWF-appointed observers at Vatican II. Moreover, the membership of international committees for dialog included American theologians and churchmen. On the national level of ecumenical interchange the LCA was a full member of the National Council of Churches, while The ALC and the Missouri Synod found it expedient to remain outside and yet to accept the invitation to be represented in committees and commissions of their choice.[112] With regard to the Consultation on Church Union (COCU), which grew out of the well-publicized "Blake Proposal," the Lutheran churches preferred the status of "observers" to that of "participants." In 1968, the Lutheran Council/USA appointed "observer-consultants" to represent the member bodies. The Council's general secretary reported that Lutherans, Roman Catholics, the Eastern Orthodox, and other confessional communions would experience increasing difficulty with COCU in the light of its deliberate avoidance of confessional issues and its generous use of theologically ambiguous terminology.[113] The fact that Lutherans did not enter the COCU negotiations indicated that they viewed their history and confessional tradition as justifying their remaining an identifiable confessional group within the spectrum of American Christianity. Thus, as the decade of the seventies dawned the most promising ecumenical developments seemed to lie in the Lutheran attraction for those churches that reflected the classical western tradition, the Roman Catholic, the Reformed, and the Anglican communions.

PROFILE IN 1970

In 1968 and 1969 proposals were made to the Lutheran Council in the USA that it undertake a survey among the churches with the hope of determining a "profile of American Lutheranism." The first proposal failed of support largely for lack of funds.[114] The second, an attempt to revive the former on a more modest scale, encountered difficulties within the Council structures and was subsequently directed to the Lutheran Brotherhood, an insurance society in Minneapolis.[115] After careful study of the project as outlined by the Youth Research Center, Minneapolis, and after receiving the concurrence of the presidents of the three Lutheran bodies to be surveyed, the official board of the Lutheran Brotherhood agreed in July, 1969 to underwrite what was called "A Study of Generations." The study was immediately launched under the direction of a professional research team and guided by a steering committee to give counsel in matters of policy.[116]

Aware of the numerous previous sociological studies of the church, some of which had been severely criticized as inadequate in one way or another, "A Study of Generations" was carefully designed to be as scientifically accurate as possible. It was hoped that a true picture of American Lutheranism at the beginning of the decade would emerge from the data and that these data would be of maximum benefit in undergirding an authentic witness by the church. Although it was recognized that there are dimensions in the life of faith that are beyond empirical scrutiny, it was nevertheless confidently expected that the information garnered would provide significant indications of the confessional consciousness, evangelical clarity, religious beliefs and behavior of Lutherans across America. Such information was seen as potentially helpful for the church's ministry in the world, regardless of whether the results were negative or affirmative, critical or supportive. What follows is an edited version of a summary profile based on the findings of the survey.[117]

"You best can understand what Lutherans will think and do if you first know what they value and believe."

"You best can determine which Lutherans are open to a ministry of renewal and change if you know who are oriented to the gospel."

"You can assume that a constant requirement for members of a congregation today is to accept diversity and to use times of tension as times of opportunity."

These are some of the conclusions drawn from a study of Lutherans, ages 15 to 65, in the United States during 1970. A representative sample of 4,745 persons gave seven million bits of information from which a relatively detailed and reliable portrait could be drawn.

The task of assembling the information could be compared with the task of fitting together seven million pieces of a massive jig-saw puzzle with the box cover picture missing. To minimize the subjective influence of the research team in assembling the data, empirical methods were used which would allow the data to organize themselves.

Every major step in assembling the data was accomplished by procedures which, if replicated, would give essentially the same information as reported here. Most of the seven million answers organized around one of 78 descriptive dimensions and these dimensions formed 14 factors. Interpretations as to what these dimensions and factors signified were made from a study of the response patterns of all respondents.

THE VALUES AND BELIEFS OF LUTHERANS ARE THE BEST INDICATORS OF WHAT THEY WILL THINK AND DO

A common assumption is that the best predictors of a person's attitude and behavior are such factors as his age, occupation, level of education, sex, or financial status. It is true that these do account for some of the variation in beliefs, attitudes, and behavior among Lutherans. However, there is nothing as powerful in predicting a Lutheran's attitude or behavior as knowing what he values and believes.

Most Lutherans accept a transcendental view of life as their basic value orientation. Either the mind of western man has not been completely or significantly secularized, or members of Lutheran churches in 1970 are not representative samples of western man. At any rate, most Lutherans reject a secularist view which maintains that the meaning of the world lies within itself alone. They value such qualities as love, salvation, forgiveness, service to others, an ethically responsible life, and family happiness. *In general, most Lutherans choose a God-directed life over the self-directed life, the supernatural over the natural.*

In contrast to the dimension that involves an acceptance of a transcendental meaning in life is the value dimension of self-development. Persons preoccupied with values of self-development place a high priority upon pleasure, personal freedom, physical appearance, achievement, and recognition, preferring the natural over the supernatural. They adopt a world view and life style that is inimical to the purposes of the church. About one out of four reject the transcendental dimension in favor of the values of self-development.

For most Lutherans, faith in Jesus Christ is at the heart of what they value and believe. For them Christianity is to believe and know Christ; in that sense they believe and know the gospel. This life orientation emerges as one of the most distinctive characteristics of a Lutheran. Abundant evidence establishes the fact that about three in five Lutherans believe their lives are centered in the gospel.

Most Lutherans classify themselves as conservative in their theological

stance and are convinced of the historic expressions of the Christian faith.
They think in terms of a biblical world view and in frames of reference
that resemble the classical Lutheran theology of the 16th century. The
doctrines to which they hold most firmly are the biblical accounts of the
incarnation, death, and resurrection of Christ. They see the Bible as
God's word of judgment and mercy. They believe in Christ's death as
an atonement for sin. They believe in the gifts of the spirit, Baptism, the
real presence of Christ in Communion, the return of Christ, and God's
response to intercessory prayer. In short, Lutherans believe that they
hold the historic faith.

*The doctrines which are neglected by some contemporary theologians
are the most potent in the piety of Lutherans.* These are the doctrines of
providence, personal sanctification, and future life. Some Lutherans who
hold these views classify themselves as fundamentalists. Of this group a
disproportionate number tend to view their theological formulations as
the sole expression of the Christian faith. Those who classify themselves
as liberals tend to reject these doctrines. Such Lutherans view death
as an unknown but noble reality, or as simply the end of it all. A third
group, the self-labeled conservatives, by contrast, view death as the beginning of a new life.

*There is an experiential element in Lutheran piety that is related to
a sense of faith, devotion, and practice of piety.* The contribution that
it makes to personal piety, however, is not through intense special experiences, but rather through "feeling God's presence and assurance of salvation." About one out of two Lutherans report having had some type of
religious experience. A smaller group of 6% say they have had an experience of speaking in tongues; 12% say they *think* they have.

*Though Lutherans hold to a particularistic faith that makes exclusive
truth claims, most are not exclusivistic in their attitudes towards other
Christians.* Having established this basically ecumenical stance, it comes
as no surprise that the data reveal that most Lutherans accept other
Lutherans as fellow Christians. Two out of three say they are ready
for a merger into one Lutheran church. Though this proportion varies
by church body, a majority in each group (LCA—71%, ALC—70%,
LC-MS—62%) favors such action. It is fair to say that most Lutherans
yearn for a visible expression of the catholicity of the church. There is an

inchoate sense of its unity and wholeness and a search for ways to know and feel that unity.

Christologically Lutherans tend to emphasize the divinity of Jesus more than his humanity. Those who hold this view most strongly are also those who are most resistant to change, more authoritarian, and more prejudicial in their attitudes towards others. For such people, a divine Jesus is a new law giver, a second Moses, who legitimatizes their present stance.

Those who recognize Jesus' humanity, or view his two natures in balance, are generally more ready to take the initiative on the role of the church in public issues and to be more forgiving in their relationships with others. Acceptance of the humanity of Jesus is associated with a willingness to accept change and to be involved in service.

Youth accept the humanity of Jesus more readily than do adults; they also differ in their view of God. More of the young people see God as both immanent and transcendent. Older Lutherans tend to focus more exclusively upon his transcendence.

What Lutherans value and believe reflects an orientation to the dialectic of law and gospel. These two, law and gospel, are seen to be more than mere theological constructs. They emerge in the data as realities in the individual lives of church members. About three in five reflect an awareness of a personal God who cares for them in Jesus Christ, a certainty of faith, a positive attitude towards life and death, and a sense of ministry and mission. Conversely, about two in five show the effect of experiencing life as demand, exalting form over spirit. The result is a religiosity that inhibits, limits, and misdirects the understanding of the church's mission and ministry. Not strangely, therefore, about the same proportion holds to salvation by works. Of these, the greater percentage is found in the youngest and oldest age brackets. Lutherans most likely to reject salvation by works are those in the middle age group (30-49).

Contrary to some contemporary allegations that the Lutheran law-gospel dialectic is irrelevant, the data strongly indicate that Lutherans view the task of ministry and mission in terms of the relationship between: a) believing, accepting, and experiencing the gospel of grace, faith, hope, relationship, and forgiveness; and b) living under the law in the sense of structure, achievement, authority, right and wrong, and justice.

AN ORIENTATION TO THE GOSPEL IS THE BEST
INDICATOR OF LUTHERANS WHO ARE OPEN
TO RENEWAL AND CHANGE IN THE
MINISTRY OF THE CHURCH

Seven out of ten Lutherans hold that the mission of the church is to preach the gospel and to work toward improving the well-being of people. It is the conviction of the overwhelming majority that of these two emphases, the primary task of the church is to preach the gospel. The current awareness of many Lutherans and especially youth is that too little attention has been given to the second emphasis.

Most Lutherans reflect a liberal stance on social issues, and express a commitment to a just and liberalized society, but are quite evenly divided on the question of church body involvement. When interviewed as to what their ideal church would be like, the hope which Lutherans expressed most frequently was for a congregation that ministers to the range of needs in a community, including needs related to health, finances, and counseling. They showed a strong desire for a church that exemplifies and shows love to all mankind.

Though no more than one out of two Lutherans strongly identify themselves with efforts by the church to bring about social justice, most lay leaders and clergy have accepted this responsibility. If it can be assumed that the commitment of pastors and lay leaders has an effect on the members, one can look for an increased involvement of the church in social action as a part of its mission and ministry. At present about one in two are participants in some community organization. Only a minority are involved in community and political activities.

Most Lutherans look to their pastors for leadership in the struggle for justice and amelioration of suffering. They resist, however, the idea of their pastor becoming involved in some forms of activism. Most Lutherans do not want their pastor engaged in civil disobedience or in using the pulpit as a political or social rostrum. Neither do they want to be told what they must do. Rather they want the freedom of conscience to respond to situations of need as they see fit.

Within the Lutheran church there are two distinct groups of people who care about social issues. Those of one group speak out of a sense of mission, love and conscience. Theirs is a social conscience rooted in Christian commitment. Those in the other group, though using similar rhetoric, reflect a different orientation. This second group includes both advocates and enemies of social change. Both see the conflict as a power struggle. Herein are seeds of the tyranny and bigotry of both the extreme right and the extreme left.

About one out of four Lutherans view Christianity as a "social gospel." They are convinced that the church has no business in trying to change individuals religiously, but rather that it should be meeting the physical needs of people. Such persons view Christianity as a religion of good works. They reject a transcendental world view and are pessimistic in their view of life.

The primary resistance to a ministry that is open to significant changes comes from those who are oriented to the law and not the gospel. The most vehement resistance to caring about people, that is, carrying out a serving mission and ministry, is found among the two out of five Lutherans who "misbelieve." [118] Their obstacle is the need for unchanging structures. They tend to distrust others and exploit religion and society for their own advantage.

A sense of conscience, responsibility, and personal obligation to be involved in the mission of the church characterizes three out of five Lutherans. They feel quite earnest about their individual Christian responsibility and look to their church to help them become compassionate caring Christians.

Three out of five Lutherans are willing to accept responsibility in church and community activities if asked to do specific tasks. At present, only one in four volunteer to participate in church or community activities. However, an additional one in three say they would serve if asked. This greater willingness is found especially in small congregations.

Lutherans are least involved in matters which require that they take personal initiative. No more than one out of five report having been involved in some church or political issue of general concern. Of these, the primary group to spearhead action were college-educated males.

About two out of five Lutherans are actively involved in trying to share their personal faith with those around them. Such Lutherans are the most likely to support friends in crisis situations or show kindness to neighbors in times of need.

Lutherans over the age of 24 give high evaluations of the current program and ministry of their congregation. No more than one in five were sharply critical of the caring life of their congregation. Those who tended to be most negative about their congregation were also negative about their family. About two-thirds of the youth give positive evaluations of their congregation and reflected a positive stance towards their church.

The loyalty of Lutherans to their church is shown in relatively stable church memberships, and the strong tendency to marry within their own denominations.

The greatest reservoir of discontent for the church is linked with a lack of emotional certainty of faith, namely doubt. In other words, a negative evaluation of one's congregation is closely linked to an anxiety over one's faith. Such a crisis of faith is found primarily among the one out of five youth whose primary influence is their peer group.

A limiting factor in the ministry and mission of the Lutheran church centers in the fact that about two in five tend to hold prejudicial attitudes. They reject people who are different from themselves in life styles, values and beliefs. Of twenty possible groups, Lutherans express greatest rejection of communists, homosexuals, drug addicts, hippies, and members of Students for a Democratic Society. Strong feelings are also expressed toward people who will not work and those on welfare. Racial differences are less of a barrier; anti-semitic attitudes characterizing about one in five. Significantly, Lutherans in America are a racially homogeneous people, native-born Americans, most of whose forefathers claim a Scandinavian and German birthplace. Compared with the United States population, they are average in socio-economic status and above average in educational level. They are likely to have grown up in towns or small cities rather than in farm areas or large metropolitan centers.

Prejudice is mediated by the misbeliefs of Lutherans. Misbelief is most strongly the need for unchanging structure and the need for religious absolutism, reflecting the theological construct of life under the law. There is no direct relationship between prejudice and the value dimension of a transcendental view of life. Neither is there a direct relationship between prejudice and the belief dimensions which make up the heart of Lutheran piety and which do not appear as part of the misbelief factor. The indirect relationship between prejudice and belief is that misbelief appropriates and shapes the content of orthodox belief for its own purposes of legitimizing hatred and violence.

Politically the study revealed that 42% of Lutherans prefer the Republi-

*can party; 25% give a Democratic preference; and 33% give an indepen-
dent or other party preference (or a response indicating no interest in
politics).* Solid evidence of Republican preference is revealed by comparing
their voting record in the 1968 presidential election with the actual results. Whereas Nixon received 1% more votes nationally than did Humphrey, Lutherans gave Nixon 34% more votes than they gave to Humphrey.
Regional analysis shows that Nixon outdrew Humphrey among Lutherans
by 27% in Humphrey's home territory (West North Central) and by
43% in New England, where Humphrey gained 18% more votes than
Nixon. The conclusion seems inescapable.

*The highest percentage (21%) of conservatives (both Democrats and
Republicans) are found in the age group 50-65, with 11% of the 20-23
year-olds describing themselves in the same way.* Of the oldest group 44%
describe themselves as moderate conservatives, while 22% of those between
20-23 (the lowest percentage) take this stance. Interesting is the fact that
a higher percentage of moderates are found in the *youngest* age group,
those between 15 and 19 (24%). This percentage may not be sufficiently
different from that in the next age group to indicate any significant swing
to moderate conservatism among the most youthful. Although regional
variations in voting behavior can be noted, the sometimes-mentioned
swing of Lutherans during and after the Depression to the Democratic party
is not nearly as dramatic as suspected. In the East North Central and West
North Central Regions (census regions) where the Depression and
drought of the 30s were assumed to have a strong Democratic influence
on the heavy Lutheran population, the data shows a continuing strong
Republican preference. The census region showing the Republicans and
Democrats running neck and neck is the West South Central (Republican,
33%; Democrat, 32%). A major conclusion: "Lutherans share a greater
degree of homogeneity on a number of recognizable social and background
characteristics than the general population, and that this homogeneity holds
up across geographic boundaries. . . . "

ACCEPTANCE OF DIVERSITY AND TENSION IS A
CONSTANT REQUIREMENT FOR MEMBERS
IN A LUTHERAN CONGREGATION

A Lutheran congregation consists of subgroups that contrast on enough
dimensions to make tension a normal experience and acceptance of diversity

a constant requirement. The single greatest source of tension stems from differences in the values and beliefs of church members. There are wide gaps between members who accept a transcendental world view and those who are preoccupied with the values of self-development, between members who are gospel-oriented and those who are law-oriented. Tension in the area of values and beliefs was identified in the interviews of Lutherans as one of the principal obstacles to the realization of their ideal church.

Another source of difference, and presumably tension, relates to age. There is a generational conflict between youth and adults that is especially significant in certain areas. Ranking next as a source of difference in how Lutherans believe and respond is level of education. Additional sources of tension are: clergy-lay differences, inter-Lutheran differences, and sex differences. (The word tension as used here can imply times of creativity and opportunity as well as times of strained relationships.)

Generational Conflict

Lutherans differ enough by age groupings to justify speaking about four Lutheran generations in this study. The following generations emerged as distinct age groups: those born before World War I (ages 50-65); those born between World War I and the Depression (ages 40-49); those born after the Depression and before World War II (ages 30-39); and those born after World War II (ages 15-29). Smaller generational units appeared in the fourth age group which classified youth into the age groups of 15-18, 19-23, and 24-29. Lutherans in each age grouping differ enough in beliefs, values, attitudes, and behavior to be classified this way by empirical methods.

In general, the tension between youth and adults grows with increasing distance of years. However, the tension between youth and adults is not always greatest between youth (ages 15-28) and the oldest adults (50-65). When it comes to feelings of isolation and pressure, the contrasts are greatest between the youngest youth and adults of ages 29-38. In matters of life purpose, the contrast is greatest with adults ages 39-48. When it comes to prejudice, social distance, and anxiety over one's faith, the contrast is sharpest between youth ages 15-22 and the oldest Lutherans, ages 50-65. Though there is some variation, the fact remains that the contrast or tension is greatest between youth of ages 15-22 and adults of ages 50-65.

Differences between youth and adults are very little in some areas but striking in others. Dimensions where contrasts are greatest are these in descending order: personal piety, peer orientation, questionable personal activities, social distance from radical life styles, personal assistance in crisis situations, openness to change within the church, desire for a dependable world, prejudice, certainty of faith, need for religious absolutism, feelings of isolation, belief in a personal caring God, and a sense of life purpose.

Older Lutherans favor a stable and predictable world, whereas younger Lutherans place less value upon orderliness and the preservation of the past. However, there is no difference between generations in their desire for a controllable world—one that is stimulating and enjoyable. Neither is there a marked contrast in the number by age who prefer a life of detachment, a life that often is identified with the counterculture. The oldest generation, ages 50-65, rivals the youngest in their attraction to this way of life that escapes the demanding and pushing world.

The ages of 21 and 22 mark a time of flux and searching, a time when a large number of young people have suspended judgment in what they believe. With respect to belief scores, beginning at age 15, there is a drop to a low point, ages 21-22. Following that age, there is a sharp increase to about 30. Thereafter, the curve rises steadily to age 65. It is evident that fewer youth than adults know the personal aspects of the Christian faith such as certainty of faith, an awareness of a personal, caring God, and a positive attitude toward life and death. Fewer of the youth, less than half, understand or live in what constitutes the evangelical heart of Lutheran piety.

Lutheran youth's lack of certainty about their faith is matched by an inattention to practices of piety which stimulate and awaken faith. It is with respect to personal practices of a faith that the contrast between generations is especially marked. No more than one in five youth see their Christian beliefs as underlying their whole approach to life. This contrasts with one out of two adults. Also, no more than 12% of the youth read their Bibles daily or once a week. This number of Bible readers among young people is less than one-third the number of Lutheran youth (42%) who ten years ago read their Bibles daily or weekly.

Tension is high between youth and adults on matters of social issues. There is an impatience of youth mingled with strong feelings about what many see as a present lack of involvement of their church in social issues.

It is the conviction of the majority (57%) that far too little has been done. Nevertheless, youth agree with adults that it is equally important to preach the gospel and to work toward improving the wellbeing of people. The problem for more of the youth is that they feel these two emphases are out of balance.

Most youth would restyle the traditional role of the clergyman. The majority favor treating controversial topics in the Sunday morning sermon. This approach is preferred by twice as many youth as adults. Their sensitivities cry out for an action that matches words. They want the church to show it cares about the tragedies of the day. They want their pastor to become more aggressively involved in community and national issues.

Youth serve as the conscience of the church on matters dealing with people who are strongly condemned. Their openness and acceptance of oppressed people stands in sharp contrast with older adults. Only for people who embody a threatening ideology is the "open arms" attitude of youth least in evidence. For instance, no more than one in three would offer friendship or neighborliness to hippies or members of the SDS (Students for a Democratic Society).

In spite of youth's expressed concern over their feelings for people, they do less than adults in specific acts of kindness. Apparently many of the youth have not learned as yet to extend their concern to others in expressions of service. Even more significant is the fact that the majority of youth do not aspire to a life of being used to help others in some way. The values of self-development tend to overshadow the desire to seek meaning in a relationship to others and to God.

The age 19-22 marks a time when Lutherans are least willing to delay or restrain gratification. In sharp contrast to all other generations, youth of this age are the most involved in questionable personal activities. A majority admit to times when they were drunk, swore, attended x-rated movies, or read pornographic literature. About two in five admitted to sexual intercourse outside of marriage.

A few Lutherans under 22 years of age are oriented to the drug culture. This orientation is characterized by a non-establishment orientation toward religious structures, a rejection of the conventional political identity, and a rejection of the traditional religious expression of family worship. These attitudes, coupled with experimentation and use of drugs, characterize a significant group (13%) of Lutheran youth.

The institutional life of the congregation has developed in such a way that youth feel leadership and influence is in the hands of people over 30. The normal pattern of congregational life tends to isolate youth from the center of concern and decision making. About half do not feel involved or a part of the life of their congregation. Up to one half of the youth say, "Hardly anyone in the congregation would miss me if I stopped going." About half feel that the congregation is not doing a good job of involving the youth and teaching them about the Christian life.

The best predictor of which young people will be disappointed in their church is their feeling of how well they fit in with groups in their congregation. The acceptance that youth feel is a strong indicator of how they will evaluate their congregation. Over half the young people feel that they fit in well with the congregation. Those who feel that they fit in poorly (43%) may still reflect positive attitudes toward their church if the worship service is an inspiring one. Serious anti-church feelings are expressed by 14% of Lutheran youth (ages 15-22).

There is no research evidence of a generation gap between Lutheran youth and adults. The charting of scores on 78 scales by two-year levels shows no evidence of a radical break or consistent pattern of change between youth and adults. The age differences in scores between youth and adults resemble the differences found between the younger and older clergy. It should be noted, however, that contrasts between generations are not limited to differences between youth and adults. For instance, the sharpest break in attitudes of prejudice occurs between Lutherans over 50 years of age and Lutherans below that age. The sharpest contrast for all age groups in desire for detachment from the world is between youth ages 15-23 and youth ages 23-29. The older youth are less inclined to flee a demanding and pushing world than are Lutherans over 30.

Influence of Education

Misbeliefs are most likely to be found among Lutherans who have the least amount of education. More of the less educated have a need for unchanging structures, a need for religious absolutism, are prejudiced, make exaggerated truth claims, seek a Christian utopianism, and believe in salvation by works. At the same time, more of the less educated Lutherans confess their belief in a personal caring God, report religious experiences, accept a transcendental world view, and reflect a fundamentalistic stance.

College educated lay men and women are closer to the clergy (than non-college trained laity) in their rejection of misbeliefs, their attention to religious practices and their concern for social justice. College graduates, whether clergy or laity, are less likely to be threatened by change, less likely to need rigid structures or to express hostility towards people different from themselves. On the contrary, both share common concern to bring healing into the lives and structures of contemporary society.

Clergy-Lay Differences

On dimensions measuring a transcendental reference, certainty of faith, and belief in a personal caring God, the clergy-lay differences are greatest between clergy and male college graduates, and similarities are greatest between clergy and college graduate women. On basic understanding of religious doctrines, the overwhelming majority of both clergy and laity reject the fundamentalist and the liberal response. Generally, between 80% and 90% of both clergy and laity endorse intermediate choices.

The most significant difference between clergy and lay beliefs relates to their understanding of Jesus. Clergy accept the dual nature of Jesus. Though the overwhelming majority of the Lutheran laity accept the divinity of Jesus, they find it difficult to endorse his humanity.

The widest differences occur between clergy and laity on practices of personal piety and involvement in church and community affairs. The vast majority of lay Lutherans take little or no initiative in making their views known to responsible leaders and here clergy and laity differ the most. As may be expected, the next greatest difference relates to sharing one's faith and being diligent in the practices of a personal piety.

The clergy-lay disparity on salvation by works indicates that the ancient heresy is still found in the Lutheran church. Grace through faith in Jesus Christ is yet to be understood by two in five Lutherans. To extrapolate this means that over 3½ million crypto-Pelagians are scattered among American Lutheran congregations.

One attitude that is found more frequently among clergy than laity is an emphasis on the exclusive truth claims of Christianity. Laity may be prone to soft-pedal or deny that Christianity makes a radical truth claim about the finality of Christ as the mediator of salvation. Conversely, some clergy make excessive claims that would narrow the instruments of God's grace to one visible earthly institution. Clergy for whom this is true tend to be older in age, prone to fundamentalism, resistant to change, and likely to over-divinize Jesus. Such clergy are, however, a small minority. For both clergy and laity, such a view is more typical of persons over age 50.

DIFFERENCES AMONG LUTHERANS DUE TO REGION, SEX, AND CHURCH BODY ARE RELATIVELY SMALL

There are differences among Lutherans that have been exaggerated beyond their true significance. Three commonly observed sources of such differences are region, sex, and church body. Though discernible and measurable differences among Lutherans can be attributed to these sources, it is noteworthy that the differences are relatively small.

Region and Size of Church

Slight differences do exist among Lutherans when divided by region. When an analysis for regional differences controls for the possible effects of church body and congregational size, slight regional effects are noted on beliefs, practice of the faith, and concern for social justice. Eastern Lutherans score slightly lower on major belief dimensions and practices associated with their faith. However, they score slightly higher than other regions on scale dimensions involving concern for social justice.

Size of congregation, by itself, has relatively little overall effect on variations in beliefs, attitudes and life styles. The one area where size of congregation has unmistakable effects is practice of the faith. There is a direct relationship between congregational size and involvement in church affairs. Persons in congregations under 250 persons are more likely to report being active than persons in large congregations. A higher proportion of relatively inactive members are found in the large congregations.

Male-Female Differences

More Lutheran women than men reflect a gospel orientation. This difference between men and women is even greater among those with college educations. A higher proportion of the college educated women accept a transcendental view of life, believe in a personal caring God, reflect an emotional certainty of faith, and consider matters of faith to be "very important."

Lutheran women, whether college trained or not, are stronger practitioners of their faith. They are more diligent in practices of a personal piety, and more willing to share their faith verbally with others. Interestingly, they do not differ from men on levels of congregational activity and church and community involvement.

Church Body Differences

Contrasts between members of the three major Lutheran church bodies is one of degree, not of kind. All three bodies are generally conservative, stress the Christocentric nature of the faith, define the faith in confessional terms, and express loyalty and support for church programs.

A higher proportion of Missouri members consistently show greater willingness to set out clearly the limits of the Christian faith, saying in effect that a person must believe thus or he is not a Christian. There is a stronger emphasis upon the Christocentric nature of the Christian faith among members of the Missouri Synod. They are also more insistent upon the exclusive truth of the Christian faith, to the point of embodying that truth in a particular ecclesiastical form. Quite expectedly they are more strongly insistent upon the verbal inspiration of Scripture, the denial of evolutionary theory, the acceptance of charismatic gifts (this may be a surprise), maintenance of the pastoral "office of the keys" and spiritual discipline, and the depravity of man. Consistently members of this church choose responses that limit the Christian faith to a single theological stance more frequently than members of the Lutheran Church in America or The American Lutheran Church.

Members of the LCA and The ALC are the most highly oriented toward church involvement in social issues while members of the LC-MS are more inclined to resist involvement. Members of LCA more frequently value service to others and ethical life more than the other church bodies. There are no significant differences on general orientation to change but rather on the question as to how and where change is to be brought about. Members of the LCA and ALC are more inclined to openness to change in practices within the church than members of the Missouri Synod. There are no significant differences in degree of hostility to the church.

Members of the LCA are more inclined to see works as contributing to salvation while Missourians show more recognition of the doctrine of salvation by grace. Members of LCA are more inclined to endorse statements reflecting American "religion-in-general" than members of the Missouri Synod. There are no significant differences in level of prejudice nor on general orientation to change. There is a tendency for the latter to show a higher degree of religious absolutism. The LCA tends to show a slightly higher level of pessimism, alienation, and isolation among its members.

There are no significant differences between church bodies on involvement in congregational activities. Members of the Missouri Synod are more highly involved in personal practices of piety than LCA or ALC. They are also more highly involved in personal and congregational evangelism activities. Likewise they show a higher degree of biblical information than LCA or ALC members. There are no significant differences in level of questionable personal activities.

THE ISSUES IN 1970

In 1968 the Lutheran Church in America received three published reports from its "Task Group for Long Range Planning." [119] Recognizing that the 60s had been marked by rapid and sometimes radical change, the church had determined that "an assessment of current trends" was needful as the 70s approached. This was done in full knowledge of the historical insight and consequent caveat of Elson Ruff, the editor of *The Lutheran:* "We'll have to wait for the church historians of the 22nd century to figure out the dominant trends in church life in the 1970s." [120]

One of the reports made the judgment that contemporary thought gave little emphasis to such traditional Lutheran concerns as the significance of Word and sacrament as means of grace, the nature (not mission) of the church itself, and the concept of the church as the custodian and proclaimer of the gospel.[121] That this observation could be applied to all Lutherans or even to all members of the Lutheran Church in America would be highly problematical. Nevertheless, it raised the interesting question: what were the major issues that seemed to be surfacing as the churches entered the decade of the 70s?

This "concluding unscientific postscript" (with apologies to Søren Kierkegaard and with an eye cocked on the *scientific* survey reported in the previous section) will single out the obvious questions facing Lutherans.

First and foremost is the nature of the gospel. Lutherans have long prided themselves on their evangelical rectitude and precision. Few Lutheran theologians would disagree with Kent S. Knutson, president of The

American Lutheran Church,[122] that "the Lutheran confessions define and preserve the gospel in a way which is unparalleled in Christian history." [123] As true as this is, unexpectedly high numbers of Lutherans in all age groups and all social, economic, and educational strata have difficulty in articulating the central thrust of Christianity. The gospel is often confused with law; "being a Christian" is often described as "obeying the Ten Commandments," or "living by the Golden Rule," or "loving your neighbor" or "being relevant to social needs." Despite carefully designed curricula in parish education, serious catechetical instruction, and generally evangelical preaching, the central confession that man is saved by grace through faith in Jesus Christ is blurred and indistinct.

Mesmerized by an enchantingly "modern" Pelagianism (i.e., man saves himself, or contributes to his salvation, by his good activities), not a few Lutherans in all walks of life have substituted an unevangelical moralism, social and individual, for the gospel. Luther's teaching that the gospel is really identical with "justification by faith" (the gift of forgiveness of sin and new life) and that this same gift is bestowed in the sacraments (Luther said of the Lord's Supper, "Where there is the forgiveness of sins there is also life and salvation") is often only vaguely understood. If it is true that justification is "the article of a standing and falling church," and if "God's Word and Gospel are interchangeable terms" (Edmund Schlink's phrase),[124] the Lutheran churches in America could be in spiritual danger. Clarity regarding the gospel appears, therefore, to be high on the working agenda in the 1970s, not least when one considers the ecumenical dimension of the Lutheran confession: "For the true unity of the church it is enough *to agree concerning the teaching of the gospel* [italics added] and the administration of the sacraments" in accordance with the gospel (Augsburg Confession, Article VII).

Second, and closely related to the above, is the question of confessional integrity in an ecumenical age. Lutheran convictions regarding the content of the gospel are not without the attendant dangers of institutional pride and "morphological fundamentalism." That such attitudes have been present in the past and are an ever-present possibility cannot be denied. A basic misreading of the confessions has too often led to confessional legalism and Lutheran sectarianism. There is no guarantee that such things will not happen again. Nowhere in the confessions, however, is there a "Great Commission" to go into all the world and make Lutherans of all nations.

The confessions are not self-conscious; they are evangel-conscious. The confessions are not concerned with denominational survival but with confessional integrity vis-à-vis the catholic and apostolic faith. Their chief concern is to safeguard the proclamation of the gospel by the church.

This conviction has led several Lutheran theologians to ask pointedly what the role of American Lutheranism is in an ecumenical age. Jaroslav Pelikan put the question: "American Lutheranism: Denomination or Confession?" [125] Warren A. Quanbeck described the problem in an essay, "Confessional Integrity and Ecumenical Dialogue," in which he urged consideration of the historical context and doxological character of the Lutheran confession. He argued that it [the Lutheran confession] "is confession in the primary biblical sense of the word, the praise of God in the heralding forth of his mighty saving deeds. It . . . calls attention to the way God has acted for human salvation in Christ, and how he continues to act in the life and witness of his church." [126] James A. Scherer called it "The Identity Crisis in Contemporary Lutheranism," and commented:

> It is an unpleasant but undeniable fact that Lutheran identity today consists mostly of the cultivation of Lutheran *adiaphora* [hymnal, liturgical practice, model constitutions, education materials, centralized boards, etc.]. So pervasive is our sense of Lutheran . . . identity at this level that we are apt to think that it is the main thing about our churchmanship. We are, in short, most identifiably Lutheran precisely at the point where the reformers said there should be the greatest liberty.

In light of this huge irony, Scherer charges that the issue of Lutheran identity has been left largely in the hands of administrators who have tended to make it a pragmatic rather than a theological problem. And insofar as this has happened, "Lutheranism today has either lost or temporarily misplaced the central concerns of the Reformation." [127]

These kinds of searching questions and criticisms led the recently-elected president of The American Lutheran Church to say, "This is the decade [1970s] in which Lutherans must reach some decisions about themselves." [128]

What these decisions will be remain unknown, but it is fairly certain that they will have implications for understanding the church's nature and mission, its unity, and its structure.

This leads to a third issue: the church and its purposes. A theological answer to questions about the nature of the church and its function is a necessity if the church is to meet the challenges growing out of the historical situation. There is nothing novel about this affirmation; it has always been true that the church's self-understanding has shaped its mission. The question of ministry and mission cannot be separated from the question of the church's being. Hence what the church is and what it does have a reciprocal relationship.

The recent discussion about "secularity" has caused some to assert that the "world writes the agenda for the church," that the world is the chief locus of God's action. Therefore, it is argued, one must seek and find God in the world. In the light of this, it is asked, is the definition of the church as the assembly of believers "among whom the gospel is preached in its purity and the holy sacraments are administered according to the gospel" (Augsburg Confession, VII) adequate for our day? Rather than being "the people of God" to whom has been entrusted the kerygmatic Word, it is said that the church is a "Christian presence" in the world. This "presence" affirms that all efforts seeking the liberation of men, equality and justice for all, eradication of hunger, disease, pain, and oppression are tokens of the "redemptive" activity of the cosmic Christ. The church consists, according to this view, of all those who recognize and cooperate with this "Christic" action in the world and celebrate this presence by means of table fellowship and eucharistic offering.

Against this view is that which asserts that the church is indeed "the people of God" serving the world, but under the mandate "to bring men the word of the living God in judgment and mercy, to call them to repentance, to assure them of forgiveness, to free them for their work in the world. . . . " The church is not "to exhaust itself in . . . activities in which . . . it has no special competence and for which it has no monopoly of compassion. Its task must center on what others have no competence in doing nor any mandate. . . . "[129] It is here that the emerging struggle between two views of the church and its mission is joined. It is here, too, that the adequacy or inadequacy of Luther's teaching concerning "the two realms" of God's action (the realm of civil righteousness and the realm of righteousness by faith) comes under scrutiny.

Closely related to this is the fourth issue: the question of the church's unity. If Christ is present in all men of goodwill who have concern for humanity, it naturally follows that "secular ecumenism" is the expression of the church's unity. If Christ's presence, however, is marked by the ministry of the church-creating Word and sacraments, then the unity of "the people of God" is confessional. Lutherans have seen both their identity and their unity in the confession of Christ's presence in Word and sacrament. It is this conviction that has made the divisions in Lutheranism so painful and needless. One of the main questions confronting confessional Lutherans currently is not their unity—the Missouri Synod to the contrary notwithstanding—but their particularity in the ecumenical scene. American Lutheran unity, fifty years overdue, will come eventually because Missouri cannot forever escape the implications of its own confession. Meanwhile a burden of concern rests upon those who see the ecumenical heart of the Lutheran confession of the gospel as God's Word to the whole world.

The fifth and final item in this random selection of issues is the question of structure. Lutheran ecclesiology has always taught that structure is not constitutive of the church. This is not to say that polity is a matter of complete indifference. Central to Lutheran ecclesiology is the conviction that structure must always assume the form of a servant; any other form would be inappropriate to the gospel. Though structure is of God, it is not in itself divine. It is a creature, and as a creature it is subject to the temptation of becoming an end in itself. Having reminded themselves of this danger, Lutherans nevertheless believe that God uses visible and tangible means to carry forward his work in the world. Hence the church is constantly seeking a proper institutional embodiment.

In 1970 over ninety-five percent of American Lutherans were members of three institutional groupings: the Lutheran Church in America, The American Lutheran Church, and the Lutheran Church–Missouri Synod. Moreover, these three had created an additional structure, the Lutheran Council in the United States of America, to serve as an agency for cooperative ventures. The question that requires the attention of the churches as they prepare for full pulpit and altar fellowship is: what form should the united Lutheran church of the future assume? Is a national merger of the three—patterned after one of them or on some combination of elements from all three to produce a structural mishmash in an attempt to please everyone—a genuine solution? It has been suggested that the long range planning commissions of all three bodies work together to produce a new model that would provide regional churches uniting all Lutheran congregations in a given geographic area.[130] Whether the present

Lutheran Council in the USA can become the structure to embody the church at a national level is a moot question. The council was created as an "agency" in the hopes of *furthering* cooperation and fellowship rather than as *the national form* of the church. Established primarily in order to facilitate the participation of the Missouri Synod in some pan-Lutheran enterprises, the council was a "cart-before-the-horse" arrangement that evoked criticism even before it got wheels. Current comment recognizes the necessity of "a checkup, and possible overhaul." [131] Some would insist that Lutheran unity at the national level must be ecclesial; the visible form of confessional fellowship should be "church" and not "agency."

Although the issue of structure does not lie at the heart of Lutheran theology, it is patent that the "body and soul" of the church are inextricably conjoined. The congregation of God's people seeks expression at all levels—parochial, regional, national, and global. The structure will be ministerial, not magisterial; confessional, not triumphal, affirming its confidence that "one holy church is to continue forever" (Augsburg Confession).

*   *   *   *   *

The historian of Christianity or the historian of anything, for that matter, knows both the temptation and the folly of forsaking his role *qua* historian and assuming the mantle of seer. Moreover, the Christian historian, no more than the historian of Christianity, is privy to no special revelation about the future. Like all believers he is limited to affirmations of faith when he speaks about tomorrow's church. He rests content in saying that believers cannot know *what* is in the future; they can only say *who* is in the future. In the 1970s American Lutherans continue to confess that Christ is present now and in the future through Word and sacrament. At the same time they are learning to see the catholic dimension of their confession: "Where Christ is there is the catholic church" (Ignatius).

NOTES

1. J. W. Behnken, *This I Recall* (St. Louis: Concordia Publishing House, 1964), pp. 167-174. Cf. Behnken's essay, "The Way We Have Come," *Concordia Historical Institute Quarterly,* XXXIX (July, 1966), 51-63.

2. *Lutheran Witness,* (August 1, 1944), 248-249.

3. "A Statement" was published in *The American Lutheran* (November, 1945) and in *The Lutheran Outlook* (December, 1945). It has been included in C. S. Meyer, ed., *Moving Frontiers* (St. Louis: Concordia Publishing House, 1964), pp. 422-424. Behnken describes his distress over the "Statement" in *This I Recall,* pp. 190-193. Behnken's

official report and the Synod's official action are recorded in Missouri Synod, *Proceedings* . . . *1947*, pp. 15-16, 523.

4. *This I Recall*, p. 192.

5. It is strange that the episode surrounding "A Statement" is not mentioned in A. C. Repp, "Changes in the Missouri Synod," *Concordia Theological Monthly*, XXXVIII (July-August, 1967), 458-478. A survey of articles in the *Concordia Theological Monthly* for the Centennial Year 1947 provides evidence to the Missouri Synod's preoccupation with The Brief Statement's declarations on Scriptural inspiration and inerrancy. See W. Arndt, "Foreword," January, 1947, pp. 2-3; "Theological Observer," *ibid.*, pp. 48-51; J. W. Behnken, "Fellowship Among Lutherans," February, 1947, pp. 120-127; W. Arndt, "Missouri's Insistence on Acceptance of the Word of God and the Confessions of the Lutheran Church as a Condition of Church Fellowship," March, 1947, pp. 171-177; "A New Heresy in the Christian Church," April, 1947, pp. 298-299; Th. Engelder, *"Haec Dixit Dominus,"* July, 1947, pp. 484-499; and August, 1947, pp. 561-571.

6. Behnken admits that over 200 additional signatures had been obtained for the "Manifesto," as it came to be known. *This I Recall*, p. 192.

7. LC-MS, *Proceedings* . . . *1959*, p. 191.

8. LC-MS, *Proceedings* . . . *1962*, pp. 106-107. The reader is reminded of the case of Prof. Ralph H. Elliot, who was dismissed from Midwestern Baptist Theological Seminary, Kansas City, Mo. He, like Scharlemann, was charged with "liberal" views of the Bible, but refused to yield and consequently was relieved of his position. See *The Christian Century*, (November 14, 1962), 1375-1376.

9. This example of synodical "forgiveness" was repeated in 1967 when Harms asked the synod to rehabilitate Dr. A. Brux who had been disciplined in the thirties because he had prayed with non-Lutherans in India. When the convention approved Harms' request, there was no indication that the synod itself might have incurred guilt in its original disposition of the Brux affair. LC-MS, *Proceedings* . . . *1967*, pp. 44, 163. Cf. F. Dean Lueking, *Mission in the Making* (St. Louis: Concordia Publishing House, 1964), pp. 270-276.

10. The controversial resolution actually required subscription to statements additional to those specified in the synod's constitution (Scriptures and the Confessions), and therefore had the effect of amending the constitution by simple resolution. See LC-MS, *Proceedings* . . . *1962*, pp. 122-123.

11. *Ibid.*, pp. 105-106.

12. See H. T. Mayer, "The Triangle of Tension," *Concordia Theological Monthly*, XXXIV (July, 1963), 389.

13. Martin Marty, "Head First but Not Headlong," *The Lutheran Standard*, (August 14, 1962), 2-5, 112.

14. F. K. Wentz, *Lutherans in Concert* (Minneapolis: Augsburg Publishing House, 1968), p. 153.

15. Empie felt that "Martin Luther" (1953) and the Lutheran Service Commission (cooperation in services to military personnel) were two ventures which were most instrumental in opening the Missouri Synod to other Lutherans. *Ibid.*, p. 153.

16. LC-MS, *Proceedings* . . . *1962*, p. 10.

17. An objective historical account of the inner-Synodical Conference developments is to be found in *The Lutheran Witness*, (March 7, 1961), 11-17. The documentary data are to be found in R. C. Wolf, *Documents of Lutheran Unity* (Philadelphia: Fortress Press, 1966), pp. 429-455.

18. For details see Chapter 3.

19. See "Report of the Standing Committee on Church Union," prepared for the 1951 convention of the Wisconsin Synod. Behnken Papers, Box 9, Folder 2, Concordia Historical Institute, St. Louis, Mo.

20. News Bureau Release, NLC, New York, August 21, 1961.

21. LC-MS, *Proceedings* . . . *1965*, pp. 104-105; *ibid.*, 1967, p. 99.

22. *The Lutheran Standard,* (December 26, 1967), 21.

23. This account of the steps leading up to the establishment of LC/USA is based largely on Wolf, *Documents* . . . , pp. 614-637 and F. K. Wentz, *Lutherans in Concert,* pp. 171-174.

24. Doctrinal essays, reports, and decisions were published jointly by the Lutheran Church–Missouri Synod and the NLC under the titles *Essays on the Lutheran Confessions Basic to Lutheran Cooperation* and *Toward Cooperation Among American Lutherans* (St. Louis and New York: 1961). The first collection dealt with "The Doctrine of the Gospel" and "The Significance of Confessional Subscription"; the second, "What Kind of Cooperation Is Possible in View of the Discussions to Date?" The essayists were Professors Conrad Bergendoff, Martin Franzmann, Theodore Tappert, Herbert Bouman, and Alvin Rogness.

25. *Lutherans in Concert,* pp. 172-173.

26. "4th Lutheran Church Plans Merger Study," *Chicago Tribune,* June 13, 1957. Behnken later charged that the report was a distortion of what he had said. Then he continued: "I cannot commit our Synod to any merger or negotiations for merger. . . . However, I should gladly recommend such negotiations. . . . " *Lutheran Witness,* (July 16, 1957), 5. Cf. *Lutheran Standard,* (July 13, 1957), 5.

27. On June 25, 1957, the writer, returning to Minneapolis from a speaking engagement in Iowa, was seated on the airplane next to a highly-placed member of the Joint Union Committee who produced the above-cited (note 26) article from the *Chicago Tribune,* and commented: "Why wait till 1960? We are ready to unite with Missouri now. As soon as this plane reaches Minneapolis, I am going to Fred's [ELC President F. A. Schiotz] office and tell him to get on the next plane for St. Louis to talk to Behnken. If we can persuade Missouri to join its strength with ours, we'll show Mr. [*sic*] Fry who is king!"

28. Interview: Schiotz-ECN, October 26, 1969.

29. Minutes, Meeting of the Committee on Doctrinal Unity, October 6, 1957, Chicago, Ill., p. 1. See Behnken Papers, Box 8, Folder 13, Concordia Historical Institute, St. Louis, Mo.

30. Telegram: Young-Behnken, March 3, 1959. Behnken Papers, Box 9, Folder 3, Concordia Historical Institute, St. Louis, Mo.

31. Wolf, *Documents* . . . , pp. 622-623.

32. LC-MS, *Proceedings* . . . *1959,* pp. 196-197; ALC, *Reports and Actions* . . . *1960,* p. 98.

33. Editorial, *Lutheran World,* (May, 1962), 168.

34. ALC, *Reports and Actions* . . . *1962,* pp. 375-376.

35. ALC, *Reports and Actions* . . . *1964,* p. 484.

36. This same view was expressed, not only by an increasing number of persons in The ALC, but also by some in the Missouri Synod. See "We Have a Basis," *American Lutheran,* (March, 1964), 5.

37. LWF, *Proceedings* . . . *1963* (Berlin: Lutherisches Verlagshaus, 1965), p. 390.

38. President F. A. Schiotz offered an amendment at Helsinki suggesting that member churches "give serious consideration to entering into discussions that might remove the barriers to fellowship." It was clear that this was a reference to ALC-Missouri discussions. When the vote was taken, the Schiotz amendment was overwhelmingly defeated, leaving the burden of proof on The ALC for its refusal to declare fellowship with the LCA. *Ibid.,* pp. 392-393. Seven years later, with the Missouri Synod still debating membership in the LWF, the Fifth Assembly of the LWF meeting in Evian, France (July, 1970) voted unanimously that the Helsinki proposal for a declaration of fellowship by member churches be implemented. LWF, *Sent Into the World* . . . *Proceedings* . . . *1970,* p. 82.

39. Interview: F. A. Schiotz-ECN, February, 1964.

40. ALC, *Reports and Actions* . . . *1964,* p. 658.

41. Schiotz accused those opposed to his policies as "self-appointed counselors" whose

organized activities would dash his hopes for ALC-Missouri fellowship indefinitely—at least for another decade. He resented especially an essay by associate editor Kent S. Knutson, "Article VII and the Fellowship Question among Lutherans," *Dialog*, III (Summer, 1964), 223-225.

42. ALC, *Reports . . . 1964*, pp. 80-81. On Jan. 20, 1964, The ALC had issued a news release in which it affirmed that LCA representatives *had encouraged* The ALC-Missouri talks. *The Christian Century* printed a story based on this erroneous information in its issue of February 12, 1964, p. 221. As a result of a conversation between Fry and Schiotz, the news release was corrected to say that the LCA would not interfere or put any obstacles in the way. This was quite different from "encouraging" the talks. Interview: Fry-ECN, March 4, 1964. A letter from an LCA pastor printed in *The Lutheran Standard* (Dec. 29, 1964) commented: "While Dr. Schiotz found numerous persons in the LCA who understood the delicate position in which The ALC found itself, let me assure you that there are other numerous persons in the LCA who are disappointed, hurt, and perplexed. Our mutual relationships now assume something of the color of an illicit love affair—existing out of necessity, but not legitimatized until something more satisfying can be worked out with a more desirable suitor."

43. After almost two years had passed, Schiotz sent a communication (April 14, 1965) to the Executive Committee of the LWF in which he replied to the Helsinki Assembly request for the reasons which made it impossible for The ALC to declare fellowship with member churches of the LWF. He said: "The American Lutheran Church cannot limit its concern . . . to member churches . . . but is committed to seeking such fellowship with all Lutheran Churches." As a matter of fact, the Helsinki resolution had not been addressed to The ALC's concern for fellowship with the Missouri Synod but to the question of fellowship within the LWF of which Missouri was not a member. As far as The ALC was concerned, this meant giving the reasons why it rejected the LCA hand of fellowship. See ALC, *Reports and Actions . . . 1966*, pp. 187-188.

44. ALC, *Reports and Actions . . . 1964*, p. 485. The Synod of Evangelical Lutheran Churches (Slovak) joined the discussions in April, 1965.

45. This document possessed a quite different tone from "The Brief Statement."

46. LCA, *Minutes . . . 1966*, p. 711. Fry commented on the Harms invitation in a letter to the LCA Standing Committee on Approaches to Unity: "Dr. Schiotz has affirmed to me again and again that no 'statements' will need to be drafted for the achievement of pulpit and altar fellowship; all that will be needed, he has said, will be a statement. In this context I appreciate Dr. Harms' candor all the more . . . , " Letter, May 19, 1966, F. C. Fry Papers, LCA Archives, Lutheran School of Theology, Chicago.

47. That this was the intention was underscored by President Harms' highly significant statement in *The Lutheran Witness Reporter*, an official organ of the Missouri Synod, on July 3, 1966 (note the proximity of this date to the date of his letter to President Fry). In the article he came out for the literal interpretation of the Genesis account of Creation, the historicity of Adam, and the illegitimacy of evolution: " . . . the Genesis account tells us historical truth. God created the world and everything in it in six days, according to Genesis 1. . . . Our synodical fathers shared this conviction. So do we." ("Dr. Harms Speaking," p. 3.)

48. LCA, *Minutes . . . 1966*, p. 712.

49. For the "Addendum" and the 1966 and 1968 convention actions see ALC, *Reports and Actions . . . 1966*, pp. 92-93, 573; and *Reports and Actions . . . 1968*, pp. 636-638.

50. LC-MS, *Proceedings . . . 1965*, pp. 105-106.

51. Cited in *The Christian Century*, (July 21, 1965), 922.

52. Cited in *The Cresset*, (September, 1965), 4.

53. "Guidelines for Inter-Lutheran Discussions . . . , " June 2, 1967; Papers and Minutes of the Commission on Theology and Church Relations, Box 2, Concordia Historical Institute, St. Louis.

54 Minutes . . . CTCR, January 17-19, 1967, St. Louis, CTCR Papers and Minutes, Box 2, Concordia Historical Institute, St. Louis.

55. "Report of the Committee on Doctrinal Unity . . . , " January 23, 1947, pp. 6-7. Behnken Papers, Box 9, Folder 4, Concordia Historical Institute, St. Louis.

56. Letter: Boe-Long, August 6, 1938, R. H. Long Papers, Box 6, NLC, Archives for Cooperative Lutheranism, Lutheran Council/USA, New York.

57. LC-MS, *Proceedings . . . 1967*, pp. 102-103.

58. The official organs of the Missouri Synod were not open to the attacks from the right, so the latter used the columns of an ecclesiastically independent paper, *The Lutheran News* (later, *The Christian News*). Widely-circulated, this theologically Birchite paper unquestionably served to widen the rift in the Missouri Synod.

59. News Releases, Department of Public Relations, LC-MS, July 12, 14, 1969. Cf. LC-MS, *Proceedings . . . 1969*, p. 20, 22.

60. News Release, LC-MS, Dept. of Public Relations, July 14, 1969. Cf. LC-MS, *Proceedings . . . 1969*, p. 25.

61. News Release, LC-MS, Dept. of Public Relations, July 15, 1969.

62. Preus quoted "an ALC theologian" to the effect that the problem of Scripture had not been faced head-on.

63. The constitution of the LWF was amended at Helsinki (1963) in a vain attempt to make membership more palatable to the Missouri Synod. LWF, *Proceedings . . . 1963*, pp. 296-297, 325, 402.

64. *Lutheran Witness Reporter*, (October 5, 1969), 2. Cf. *The Christian News*, (September 29, 1969), 3. Wolbrecht finally lost his position as a result of action by the 1971 convention. LC-MS *Proceedings . . . 1971*, pp. 147-148.

65. News Bureau Release, October 30, 1969, LC/USA, New York, pp. 1-2. Cf. *Minneapolis Star*, November 22, 1969. Preus later blocked the theologian's appointment to the St. Louis faculty. Cf. *The Christian Century*, February 25, 1970, p. 230. He subsequently became provost of Pacific Lutheran University, an institution supported by The ALC and the LCA in Tacoma, Wash. See News Bureau Release, June 1, 1970, LC/USA, New York, p. 5.

66. See President Preus' desk letter, "Brother to Brother," Pentecost, 1970, and the *Lutheran Witness Reporter*, (Nov. 1, 1970). Cf. "Hunting Lutheran Heretics," *Newsweek*, August 3, 1970, p. 47; "Missouri Lutheran Leader Eyes Liberal Clergy, Teachers," Washington *Post*, July 27, 1970; "Investigation Stirs Tempest," *The Lutheran Standard*, (August 18, 1970), 22; St. Louis *Globe Democrat* and St. Louis *Post-Dispatch*, July 13, 1970.

67. David Runge, "Progressives Raise Flurry about Synod," *The Milwaukee Journal*, November 15, 1969.

68. Herbert T. Mayer, "The Task Ahead," *Concordia Theological Monthly*, XL (September, 1969). Cf. "Unsettled Missouri," *Lutheran Forum*, (December, 1969), 13-14.

69. Lutheran Church–Missouri Synod, *Proceedings of the Forty-ninth Regular Convention of the Lutheran Church–Missouri Synod . . . July 9-16, 1971* (St. Louis: Concordia Publishing House, 1971), p. 55.

70. *Ibid.*, pp. 52-53.

71. *Ibid.*, p. 54.

72. *Ibid.*, p. 55.

73. See "Missouri in Milwaukee," *The Lutheran Standard*, (June 15, 1971), 63.

74. The ALC, *Commentator*, (September, 1971), 9.

75. Knutson's address appears in LC-MS, *Proceedings . . . 1971*, pp. 101-103.

76. The resolution appears in *ibid.*, pp. 136-137.

77. *Ibid.*, pp. 117-120.

78. *Ibid.*, p. 123. Cf. Lutheran Council/USA, *Interchange*, August, 1971. See also "Lutheran board studies inquiry of seminary faculty," *The Minneapolis Star*, September 25, 1971, p. 14A.

79. LC-MS, *Proceedings . . . 1971*, p. 131.

80. *Ibid.*, pp. 133, 135-136, 138-139.

81. Glenn C. Stone, *Forum Letter,* American Lutheran Publicity Bureau, New York, August 10, 1971, p. 5.

82. Lutheran Council/USA, News Bureau 71-111, September 24, 1971, p. 2.

83. The ALC, *Commentator,* (September, 1971), 9.

84. Stone, *Forum Letter,* p. 4.

85. *From the Desk of the President. Brother to Brother,* July 27, 1971, pp. 1-2.

86. The ALC, *Commentator,* (September, 1971), 9.

87. James E. Adams, "Lutheran Church–Missouri Synod: Dynamic Tensions of Sect and Church," *The Christian Century,* (September 8, 1971), 1062.

88. Richard Koenig, "Missouri—Free, United, Evangelical," Letter # 19, July 20, 1971, p. 3.

89. *Lutheran Forum,* (December, 1967), 9; *ibid.,* (March, 1967), 11.

90. LC-MS, *Proceedings . . . 1967,* p. 98.

91. Letter: Fry-Harms, March 15, 1968; F. C. Fry Papers, LCA Archives, Lutheran School of Theology, Chicago.

92. LCA: President Fry, Robert Marshall, Martin J. Heinecken, and Thomas Basich. Missouri: President Harms, Vice-president Theo. Nickel, H. J. A. Bouman, and C. A. Gaertner.

93. Letter: Fry-Standing Committee on Approaches to Unity, May 16, 1968; F. C. Fry Papers, LCA Archives, Lutheran School of Theology, Chicago. Fry's death, June 6, 1968, occurred before the *aide memoire* was prepared. This document, the contents of which are confidential, is in the LCA files, 231 Madison, New York.

94. "Missouri Synod Discusses Doctrine with LCA," *Minneapolis Star,* June 6, 1968.

95. News Bureau, Lutheran Council/USA, New York, June 13, 1968, and June 17, 1968.

96. LCA, *Yearbook 1969* (Philadelphia: Board of Publication, LCA, 1968), p. 21.

97. LCA, *Minutes . . . 1968,* p. 671.

98. News Bureau, Lutheran Council/USA, New York, February 27, 1969.

99. News Releases, LC-MS, Dept. of Public Relations, July 14, 1969; July 17, 1969; News Bureau, Lutheran Council/USA, New York, July 23, 1969. Cf. LC-MS, *Proceedings . . . 1969,* p. 36.

100. For a careful critique see Richard T. Koenig, "Ecumenism: secular and churchly," *Lutheran Forum,* (April, 1967), 4-5.

101. Patrick Cardinal O'Boyle put it expressively: "Dialogue, dialogue. I've dialogued so much in the last few years that I can't even spell the word any more." *The Christian Century,* (July 2, 1969), 898.

102. Originally the invitation of the North American Area of the World Alliance of Reformed Churches Holding the Presbyterian Order was addressed to its counterpart, the USA National Committee (NLC) of the LWF. The latter expressed the desire that the Missouri Synod, though not a member of the NLC-LWF, participate in the conversations. The Missouri Synod agreed to do this. ALC, *Reports and Actions . . . 1962,* pp. 442-443.

103. The Lutheran participants were Conrad Bergendoff, H. J. A. Bouman, George Forell, Martin Franzmann, Martin Heinecken, William Narum, Warren Quanbeck, Theodore Tappert; alternates: Paul Bretscher, Harold Ditmanson, William Lazareth, Fred Meuser; consultants: Paul C. Empie, Virgil Westlund. See *Marburg Revisited,* eds. Paul C. Empie and James I. McCord (Minneapolis: Augsburg Publishing House, 1966).

104. *Ibid.* Most of the volume consists of the papers read and discussed on these subjects.

105. *Ibid.,* Preface.

106. *Ibid.,* p. 191.

107. Reports of the Lutheran-Roman Catholic dialog have been published: USA National Committee of the LWF and the Bishops' Commission for Ecumenical Affairs,

The Status of the Nicene Creed as Dogma of the Church (Washington: National Catholic Welfare Conference, 1965); *One Baptism for the Remission of Sins* (New York and Washington: USA National Committee of the LWF and NCWC, 1966); and *The Eucharist as Sacrifice* (New York and Washington: USA Committee of LWF and United States Catholic Conference, 1967); and *Lutherans and Catholics in Dialogue IV: Eucharist and Ministry* (New York and Washington: USA Committee of LWF and the Committee on Ecumenical and Interreligious Affairs, National Conference of Catholic Bishops, 1970. Cf. Lutheran Council/USA, News Releases 70-109 and 112, Oct. 30, 1970. Lutheran participants, alternates, and consultants included Arnold Carlson, Paul C. Empie, Bertil Gärtner, Kent Knutson, Fred Kramer, George Lindbeck, Paul Opsahl, Arthur Piepkorn, Warren Quanbeck, John Reumann, Joseph Sittler, Krister Stendahl, and Virgil Westlund. The full name of the R. C. ecumenical arm in the USA is The Bishops' Committee for Ecumenical and Interreligious Affairs.

108. *Time,* (May 25, 1970), 76.

109. News Bureau, Lutheran Council/USA, New York, March 24, 1969, pp. 1-3; and *ibid.,* Nov. 4, 1970, p. 6. Lutheran participants in these two meetings were: Richard Baepler, Arnold Carlson, Paul C. Empie, Egil Grislis, Merlin Hoops, Toivo Harjunpaa, Jacob Heikkinen, E. Clifford Nelson, Nels L. Norquist, Paul D. Opsahl, and Warren G. Rubel.

110. News Bureau, Lutheran Council/USA, New York, 69-32, March 10, 1969, and 70-61, June 1, 1970.

111. News Bureau, Lutheran Council/USA, New York, 70-46, April 10, 1970, pp. 1-4; and *ibid.,* Nov. 23, 1970, pp. 1-4.

112. Both the LCA and The ALC published statements on the NCCC. LCA, *The Lutheran Church in America and the National Council of the Church of Christ in the United States of America* (Philadelphia: Board of Publication, LCA, 1964); ALC, *The American Lutheran Church and Inter-Church Relations* (Minneapolis: Memorandum from the President, n.d. [1969?].

113. "COCU Too Vague about Creeds . . . , " *The Lutheran,* (March 5, 1969), 29.

114. The first proposal was made by Ronald L. Johnstone, director of the Office of Research, Statistics and Archives, LC/USA, New York. The second proposal was made by this writer.

115. Letter: ECN-Kenneth Severud, Secretary, Lutheran Brotherhood, January 28, 1969.

116. Research team: Merton P. Strommen, Ralph C. Underwager, Milo L. Brekke, and Arthur L. Johnson. Other experts joined the team as the study progressed. Steering committee: Norman D. Fintel, Board of College Education, ALC; Luther O. Forde, Lutheran Brotherhood; Arthur L. Johnson, professor, University of Minnesota; Kent S. Knutson, president, ALC; Adalbert R. Kretzmann, pastor St. Luke's (LC-MS), Chicago; Malvin H. Lundeen, assistant to the president, Minnesota Synod, LCA; and E. Clifford Nelson, professor, St. Olaf College.

117. Through the courtesy of the Youth Research Center, Minneapolis, Minn. Cf. Merton P. Strommen, ed., *A Study of Generations* (Minneapolis: Augsburg Publishing House, 1972).

118. The term is used in the study to indicate a legalistic rather than an evangelical attitude.

119. The reports were entitled: *Significant Issues for the 1970s, Theology* and *Social Change* (Philadelphia: Fortress Press, 1968).

120. *The Lutheran,* (July 15, 1970), 50.

121. *Significant Issues . . . ,* pp. 8-9

122. Knutson was elected by The ALC during its convention at San Antonio, Texas, October 21-27, 1970. He succeeded F. A. Schiotz. The other two major Lutheran bodies likewise had recently elected presidents: the LCA chose Robert J. Marshall to succeed Franklin Clark Fry (d. 1968); the LC-MS in 1969 elected J. A. O. Preus Jr. over incumbent Oliver Harms.

123. Kent S. Knutson, "The State of the Church: Hope and Anxiety," *Report of the President* (Minneapolis: The American Lutheran Church, 1971), p. 2.

124. *The Theology of the Lutheran Confessions,* tr. by P. F. Koehneke and H. J. A. Bouman (Philadelphia: Muhlenberg Press, 1961), p. 139. An especially lucid discussion of the terms "Word" and "gospel" is to be found in Theodore G. Tappert, "The Word of God According to the Lutheran Confessions," in *The Maturing of American Lutheranism,* eds. H. T. Neve and B. A. Johnson (Minneapolis: Augsburg Publishing House, 1968), pp. 60-67.

125. *The Christian Century,* (December 25, 1963), 1608-1610.

126. *A Reexamination of Lutheran and Reformed Traditions—IV,* ed. by Paul C. Empie and James I. McCord (New York: North American Area, World Alliance of Reformed Churches and USA National Committee, LWF, 1966), pp. 41-47.

127. *Context. Journal of the Lutheran School of Theology at Chicago* (Autumn, 1967), 34-41, and 55-56.

128. Kent S. Knutson quoted in News Release, Lutheran Council/USA News Bureau, 9/17/70, p. 8.

129. Martin J. Heinecken, "The 'Hidden' Church and How the 'Hidden Life of Love Must Be Known by Its Fruits,' " *The Lutheran Quarterly,* (November, 1969), 325.

130. Such a proposal was published in the early part of the 60s in the *Lutheran World,* IX (May, 1962), 169; it was elaborated in "Does American Lutheranism Need a New Form?" *Dialog,* IV (Winter, 1965), 47-53. Cf. Kent S. Knutson, "Musings on the Future of American Lutheranism," *The Lutheran Quarterly,* XXI (February, 1969), 46-48.

131. "Time for a checkup," *The Lutheran Standard,* (March 2, 1971), 15-16.

BIBLIOGRAPHICAL NOTE

Although the footnotes of this book include bibliographical data on primary and secondary research materials, the reader may find it helpful to know the categories and the locations of main sources cited.

One group of printed materials extensively consulted was the official proceedings (minutes) and official organs and periodicals, yearbooks, and other reports of church bodies and their subdivisions (synods/districts). In addition, reports of federations and agencies, e.g. the National Lutheran Council, were used. These materials are to be found in the libraries of most Lutheran colleges and seminaries. This writer has used the colllections in the libraries of the following institutions: St. Olaf College, Northfield, Minn.; Luther Theological Seminary and Northwestern Lutheran Seminary, St. Paul, Minn.; Concordia Seminary and Concordia Historical Institute, St. Louis, Mo.; Wartburg Theological Seminary, Dubuque, Iowa; Lutheran School of Theology, Chicago, Ill.; Lutheran Theological Seminary, Philadelphia, Pa.; the University of Minnesota, Minneapolis, Minn.; and the Lutheran Council in the USA (formerly National Lutheran Council), New York, N.Y.

A second group of printed materials has been statements and pamphlets issued by departments and divisions, standing commissions and committees, and ad hoc committees and "task forces" of church bodies; and presidential and other official reports and memoranda. These are also to be found in several of the libraries mentioned above.

Other printed materials that have been invaluable are collections of official statements issued by church bodies. Examples are:

The Union Documents of the Evangelical Lutheran Church. Minneapolis: Augsburg Publishing House, 1948.

Doctrinal Declarations. St. Louis: Concordia Publishing House, 1957.

Richard C. Wolf, *Documents of Lutheran Unity in America.* Philadelphia: Fortress Press, 1966.

Carl S. Meyer, ed., *Moving Frontiers.* St. Louis: Concordia Publishing House, 1964.

A fourth category consisted of published histories and biographies. Chief among these is the pioneer general history of Abdel Ross Wentz, *A Basic History of American Lutheranism,* revised edition. Philadelphia: Fortress Press, 1964. Scholarly histories of most of the individual church bodies were also available. Included in this general category should be the two histories of the National Lutheran Council:

Osborne Hauge, *Lutherans Working Together.* New York: n.p., 1945.

F. K. Wentz, *Lutherans in Concert.* Minneapolis: Augsburg Publishing House, 1968.

Helpful historical and biographical articles are to be found in *The Encyclopedia of the Lutheran Church,* 3 vols. Minneapolis: Augsburg Publishing House, 1965.

Unpublished materials most frequently used were doctoral dissertations and personal papers of prominent leaders. A list of "Doctoral Dissertations in the Field of American Lutheranism," compiled by Robert C. Wiederaenders for the Lutheran Historical Conference (New York, 1963) was helpful. Of the personal papers consulted the following were most extensively used:

The Papers of L. W. Boe in the Archives, St. Olaf College, Northfield, Minn., and the Archives, The American Lutheran Church, Luther Theological Seminary, St. Paul, Minn.

The Papers of Franklin Clark Fry in the Archives, Lutheran Church in America, Lutheran School of Theology, Chicago, Ill.; and the offices of the Lutheran Church in America, 231 Madison, New York.

The F. H. Knubel-H. G. Stub Correspondence, Library, Lutheran Theological Seminary, Philadelphia, Pa. (Microfilm copy, Library, Luther Theological Seminary, St. Paul, Minn.)

The Papers of John L. Behnken, Concordia Historical Institute, St. Louis, Mo.

The Papers of N. C. Carlsen, Archives, The American Lutheran Church, Wartburg Theological Seminary, Dubuque, Iowa.

The Papers of Ralph H. Long, Archives for Cooperative Lutheranism, Lutheran Council/USA, New York, N.Y.

The Papers of J. K. Jensen, The Library, Northwestern Lutheran Seminary, St. Paul, Minn.

The Papers of the Joint Union Committee, The Archives, The American Lutheran Church, Wartburg Seminary, Dubuque, Iowa (the writer used the bound papers temporarily on deposit at Augsburg Publishing House, Minneapolis, Minn.)

The Papers of the Joint Commission on Lutheran Unity, Archives, the Lutheran Church in America, Lutheran School of Theology, Chicago, Ill.

The Papers of the Committee on Theology and Church Relations, Concordia Historical Institute, St. Louis, Mo.

These collections include addresses, essays, minutes, correspondence, and miscellaneous items. The letters are especially rewarding for they include correspondence with many of the well-known Lutherans of the era under study: John A. Morehead, Frederick H. Knubel, T. E. Schmauk, H. E. and C. M. Jacobs, A. R. Wentz, S. C. Michelfelder, Paul C. Empie, J. A. Aasgaard, P. O. Bersell, F. A. Schiotz, Carl E. Lund-Quist, J. Michael Reu, C. C. Hein, H. F. Schuh, E. Poppen, T. F. Gullixson, Theodore Graebner, Oliver Harms, and numerous others who played roles in the public life of American Lutheranism.

Beyond the titles mentioned here, no attempt has been made to provide a bibliographical listing of individual works cited. Such a list, even a selective one, would become too unwieldy. The reader who is interested in pursuing items further is referred to the documentation in the footnotes.

INDEX

Aasgaard, J. A.
  President, Norwegian Lutheran Church
    of America, 30
  funds for armed services ministry, 127
  postwar rehabilitation work, 144
  and American Lutheran Conference,
    170
  member Executive Committee, Luther-
    and World Federation, 189
Abrams, Ray H., 117
Academy movement, 52, 65 n.42
Ahlstrom, Sydney, 68, 108 n.7
All-Lutheran federation, proposed, 177
Alleman, H. C., 84, 98, 114 n.101; 115
  n.118
American Evangelical [Danish] Lutheran
  Church, 3, 76, 174
American Evangelicalism, 10-11, 198
American Lutheran Church (1930)
  formation of, 28-29
  in American Lutheran Conference, 30
  finances during depression, 53
  major issues of the 30s, 74
  and social ethics, 89-90
  discussions with ULCA, 95-106
  Common Confession with Missouri
    Synod, 107, 168
  and world missions, 149
  fellowship negotiations with Missouri
    Synod, 168-170
  statement on fellowship with ULCA,
    169-170
  in merger of The American Lutheran
    Church (1960), 178-179
The American Lutheran Church (1960),
  30, 107
  formation of, 174, 182
  legal name of, 195 n.53
  Canadian district becomes indepen-
    dent, 187
  and American missions, 200
  and world missions, 201-202
  and parish education, 209
  fellowship negotiations with Missouri
    Synod, 250-265
American Lutheran Conference (1930)
  formation of, 29-32
  groups in, 77
  role in 30s and 40s, 78-83
  attitudes toward ULCA and Missouri,
    80

effect on National Lutheran Council,
  81
Commission on Social Relations, 89
and "old Lutheranism," 162
Rock Island meeting (1942), 170
differing views within, 82, 173-176
and merger of The American Luther-
  an Church, 178
dissolution of, 180
"American Lutheranism," 11, 13
American missions, 130-132, 199-201
American Missions, Commission on, 131
American Missions
  See also
  Home missions
Americanization, 3-4, 8-10, 12, 51
Anderson, Albert E., 59
Anderson, C. A., 85
Apostolic Lutheran Church of America
  (1962), 77
Arden, G. Everett, 85
Armed services, ministry to, 18, 126, 127,
  185
Arndt, William, 94
Ashram, 59
Augsburg Confession (Article VII), 15,
  72, 166, 167
Augustana College, Rock Island, Ill., 50
Augustana Lutheran Church (Augustana
  Synod to 1948)
  Augustana Synod, 3
    and ULCA, 16
    and American Lutheran Confer-
      ence, 30
    and The Minneapolis Theses, 31
    issues of the 30s, 74-75
    new theological climate, 84-85
    and social ethics, 89-91
    attitudes toward war, 123-124
  Augustana Lutheran Church
    home missions, 136
    pulpit and altar fellowship, 170
    view of unity, 173-174
    question of organic merger of
      National Lutheran Council
      churches, 174
    withdrawal from American Lu-
      theran Conference merger
      movement, 180
    in Lutheran Church in America
      merger, 182-184
Augustana Lutheran Seminary, 50, 75, 164

305

LUTHERAN FAMILY IN NORTH AMERICA

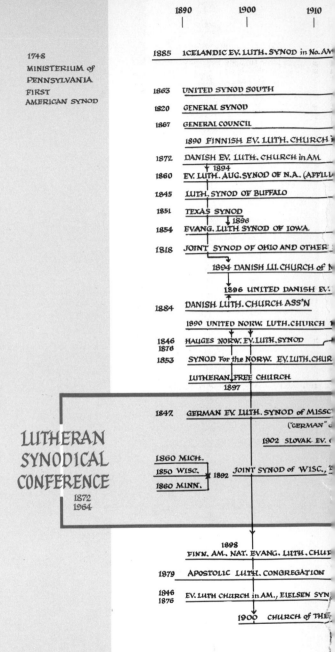

1748
MINISTERIUM of PENNSYLVANIA
FIRST AMERICAN SYNOD

| | 1890 | 1900 | 1910 |

1885 ICELANDIC EV. LUTH. SYNOD in No. AM

1863 UNITED SYNOD SOUTH

1820 GENERAL SYNOD

1867 GENERAL COUNCIL

1890 FINNISH EV. LUTH. CHURCH

1872 DANISH EV. LUTH. CHURCH in AM.

† 1894
1860 EV. LUTH. AUG. SYNOD OF N.A. (AFFILI

1845 LUTH. SYNOD OF BUFFALO

1851 TEXAS SYNOD
↓ 1896
1854 EVANG. LUTH SYNOD OF IOWA

1818 JOINT SYNOD OF OHIO AND OTHER

1894 DANISH LU. CHURCH of N

1896 UNITED DANISH EV.

1884 DANISH LUTH. CHURCH ASS'N

1890 UNITED NORW. LUTH. CHURCH

1846
1876 HAUGES NORW. EV. LUTH. SYNOD

1853 SYNOD For the NORW. EV. LUTH. CHUR

LUTHERAN FREE CHURCH
1897

1847 GERMAN EV. LUTH. SYNOD of MISSO

("GERMAN"

1902 SLOVAK EV.

1860 MICH.
1850 WISC.   ✳ 1892   JOINT SYNOD of WISC.,
1860 MINN.

LUTHERAN SYNODICAL CONFERENCE
1872
1964

1898
FINN. AM. NAT. EVANG. LUTH. CHUR

1879 APOSTOLIC LUTH. CONGREGATION

1846
1876 EV. LUTH CHURCH in AM., EIELSEN SYN

1900   CHURCH of THE